MODERN FRENCH CRITICISM

MODERN FRENCH CRITICISM

From Proust and Valéry to Structuralism

EDITED BY *John K. Simon*

THE
UNIVERSITY OF CHICAGO PRESS
CHICAGO AND LONDON

ISBN: 0–226–75854–0 (*clothbound*); 0–226–75855–9 (*paperbound*)
Library of Congress Catalog Card Number: 79–160840
THE UNIVERSITY OF CHICAGO PRESS, CHICAGO 60637
THE UNIVERSITY OF CHICAGO PRESS, LTD., LONDON

Published 1972. Second Impression 1974
Printed in the United States of America

Contents

John K. Simon
Prefatory Note

"One must then never conclude from the work to a man—but from the work to a mask—and from the mask to the machine."[1] The fundamental unity of the critical tradition treated in this volume can be measured by the appropriateness, in the current context, of these words of Paul Valéry, originating in symbolism and a late nineteenth-century inquiry into artistic creation. The "machine" referred to here may be at its origin a Renaissance one, but it differs little from the *schéma*, structure, or code sought by the critics of today. Indeed it is quite apparent from the number of cross-references that, finally, we are presenting and charting for further study here a body of critical work that has the same coherent validity, and in some cases the same proponents, as "modern literature."

The most obvious common ground among this diversity of authors is a series of rejections, an attempt to put an end to personalist and positivist critical beliefs of the nineteenth century as well as the spread of loose impressionistic forms of appreciation. The names are familiar. Marcel Proust's title *Contre Sainte-Beuve* is self-explanatory enough as it cites the most influential (and, as a connoisseur, wrong-headed) of the preceding generation. Beyond exonerating and avenging Baudelaire

---

In the editorial and bibliographical work for this volume, the editor received the support of the Graduate School Research Board of the University of Illinois, Urbana. He wishes to express his appreciation also to the courteous and efficient staff of the University of Illinois Library.

1. "Il ne faut donc jamais conclure de l'oeuvre à un homme—mais de l'oeuvre à un masque—et du masque à la machine." Valéry, *Tel Quel*, 1, Cahier B, 1910.

and Flaubert, modern critics have in mind following through on the basic aesthetic tenets of their precursors, acknowledging the existence of the work as an entity apart from personal and circumstantial factors of its creation, repudiating the establishment of a hierarchy whereby certain elements in the fabric of literary history take precedence over others. Thus Hippolyte Taine's subordination of the artist and the work to matters of biography, social history, and the like are put to rest. But the opposite tendency is not reinvoked to replace it: the writer and his creation seen as some sort of self-generative spirit looming above an abyss capable of provoking only vague expressions of wonder or empathy. Rather, a balanced view is sought from within the work as a dynamic organism where relationships can be plotted and analyzed and the mechanism discovered as an internal system.

Among the older critics, most of all, the nemesis is Ferdinand Brunetière, who codified, scholasticized, and edified the ideological bias of nineteenth-century positivism and gave it the appearance of a science. Since Taine and Brunetière there have been, to be sure, professors of literature in French academia who have not fully participated in the premises of this ideology—Gustave Lanson and some of his students whose literary sense has allowed for eclecticism, a more flexible application of the academic training. But it is evident that most of the significant literary criticism in France—apart from the useful but limited work involved in the study of sources, the establishment of texts, the documentation of historical background—has appeared outside the academy, toward which it has maintained an attitude of ignorance, ridicule, contempt, or spite. Even Thibaudet, who looks, at a distance, the part of a genial and learned academician, was in this sense a victim of the university (although the greater victims are of course those who, within, suffered and still suffer from the built-in forms and prejudices of academic training).

Only recently, as with other official institutions—the national theater, for example—has the conflict come clearly out in the open. The occasion, the Picard-Barthes controversy described elsewhere in this volume, results from a conjunction of factors: the academy feels threatened, since it sees its assumptions doubted by its own students and even by society, most of whom are attracted to less specialized theories of behavior, ones which make use of or seem to make use of the models of the social sciences applicable to "problem-solving" in a larger sphere. Furthermore, increasing numbers of its own students have established themselves in research institutes outside the academy (and often the country), where the resentment which has always been felt against the oligarchic basis for exclusion is now voiced with greater prestige and response.

In fact, the current situation carries with it a danger of co-optation, the threat of a *new* academy with its own ideological bias, its own Molièresque accouterments, its own laws of exclusion. Indeed, that this danger is imminent if not already upon us seems quite clear from the tone of recent debate. For one recurrent thread in the development of criticism from Valéry and Proust on has been its confidence in regarding the enemy as one it holds in common with creative writers. Most often this has plainly been society, with the official academy a minor social manifestation among others. As it would be for the artist, the danger of co-optation here is much more far-reaching, since the new academy could become estranged from its life blood. The shift in stance and new demands could create an atmosphere of technological specialization and mask off or obscure the greater questions.

The positive side of the unity characterizing the French critics discussed in this volume resides in the consistency of their ultimate goal. "A novelistic technique," writes Jean-Paul Sartre, "always refers back to the metaphysics of the novelist. The task of the critic is to draw out the latter before going on to evaluate the former."[2] It is hard to be more ex-

2. "Une technique romanesque renvoie toujours à la métaphysique du romancier. La tâche du critique est de dégager celle-ci avant d'apprécier celle-là." Sartre, "A propos de *Le Bruit et la fureur*: La Temporalité chez Faulkner," *Situations I* (Paris: Gallimard, 1947), p. 71.

plicit in describing an inductive method applied to an epistemological quest. One man's "machine" is another's "métaphysique," to go back to Valéry's admonition. No coincidence then that authors as dissimilar as Charles Du Bos and Sartre ask *Qu'est-ce que la littérature?*—a question implicitly formulated in almost all significant French critical writing of this century.

It must be admitted that this tendency toward abstraction, the seemingly relentless display of ontological muscle in every critical pronouncement, has alienated many readers of the so-called Anglo-Saxon world. There have been no real exchanges between new criticism, American style, and the *nouvelle critique*, which should not surprise us. (Leo Spitzer's stylistics at Johns Hopkins with its influence upon Georges Poulet, Jean Starobinski, and others does not seem especially relevant here.) French criticism, in the definition of structures it draws from the work as it pertains to the human psyche and the depiction of social exchange, always mediates its findings through some firmly based philosophical methodology. This has little to do with the American method which is said to have its origin in experimental psychology following I. A. Richards. The nearest analogy that could be offered would be Kenneth Burke. (Northrop Frye's system of classification, however elaborate and sophisticated, is more concerned with historical mythology and anthropology than their psychic or societal function today.) Only recently has there been any success at all in transatlantic communication.[3]

The French follow Baudelaire's famous dictum: "To be right, that is, to have its *raison d'être*, criticism must be partial, passionate, political, that is to say, written from an exclusive

3. One example of unprofitable exchange on this subject dates back to right after the Second World War when Henri Peyre took up the defense of French critics attacked by H. A. Mason (see *Scrutiny* 15 [1948]: 19–23, 137–47, and 16 [1949]: 54–60). Another occurred more recently when Alan M. Boase took umbrage at some remarks of Yves Bonnefoy in *Encounter* (July 1958), and a discussion ensued at the 1963 meeting of the Association Internationale des Etudes Françaises at the Collège de France in Paris (see *Visages de la critique depuis 1920* in the Selected General Bibliography). The present volume is intended of course as part of a new constructive effort in the direction of real exchange.

point of view, but from the point of view that opens up the widest horizon."[4] Critics are impatient with viewpoints which might seem to isolate the world of the imaginary; they seek to bring it into focus with other domains: natural sciences, the spiritual, epiphanies of the banal, the world of dreams, the psychology of perception, anthropology, etc. Reciprocally, it is not surprising to note more and more the phenomenon of men whose formation has been elsewhere—in philosophy, archaeology, psychoanalysis, linguistics—finding in literature an ideal field for the elaboration of their theories.

Like modern literature itself, the goal of twentieth-century criticism transcends "literature" or else transforms the original sense of this word into "writing" (*écriture*, in Roland Barthes's terminology). It then sees the act of writing as one particularly significant means of apprehending and communicating the world and our experience of it. Or rather of experiencing it at first hand, since, for the modern critic, transitively, we write and read the world, and we can grasp its totality and understand its system only by constant and repeated manipulation of its contents as they are given us.

But this too is not a recent iconoclasm. Contemporary critics invoke the same literary figures as Valéry—Baudelaire, Rimbaud, Mallarmé, Poe—to describe an apocalyptic situation in poetry, and the intransigence and silences of Valéry himself speak eloquently in support. Dissatisfaction with the novel—which makes such strange bedfellows as Valéry, André Breton, and E. M. Cioran—is widespread and even universal, if we think of "fiction" or "romance" in the American sense. *Monsieur Teste* and *La Nausée* are not really far apart, nor are the narratives of the surrealists, Maurice Blanchot and Philippe Sollers's group. They all display a similar refusal of "events," part of a process where nothing preexists the words on the page, since any prior experience would be replaced by them

4. ". . . pour être juste, c'est-à-dire pour avoir sa raison d'être, la critique doit être partiale, passionnée, politique, c'est-à-dire faite à un point de vue exclusif, mais au point de vue qui ouvre le plus d'horizons." Baudelaire, "Salon de 1846," *L'Oeuvre de Charles Baudelaire* (Paris: Le Club Français du Livre, 1955), pp. 600–601.

and they are now signifiers projecting toward meanings which our reading experience may discover.

It is obvious that no special status can then qualify one type of "literature" in comparison with another. And long before that there has been a blurring of boundaries separating the conventional literary genres. In their stead, and deliberately undefinable as parts of a traditional taxonomy, we are offered pages, logbooks, diagrams—a fragmentary world. "Tel Quel," Valéry's title, after all, was easily adopted by Sollers for his periodical.

While this disintegration began with symbolism, paradoxically, it was carried out, perhaps with less awareness than we have now of its ultimate consequences, under the aegis of the *Nouvelle Revue Française*, that workshop of the novel. From our present perspective the most typical product of André Gide and the group around him was, from the beginning, not an ordinary piece of fiction with external referents but "une prose," an example of style, a piano exercise exhibiting the mood or style of the performer. In many ways the word "prétextes" is essential to Gide, but "incidences," "feuillets," "dictées," "pages de cahier" are used and taken up by others so that, as with certain of Gide's *récits*, the "creative" mode of *NRF* writing takes a form close to fragmentation and is marked by the same "anti-literary" intrusion of criticism.

The fragmentary aspect of this *esprit critique* is characterized by a dialogue tradition carried to the extreme. In Gide all efforts at thought and description, indeed behavior, are seen in a diptych, and this explains many of the typical elements of his career: the debates at Pontigny, his relationship with diverse correspondents, the "imaginary interview," his view of the literary influences he underwent and those he developed, but most of all perhaps the elaborate trick with mirrors that the diary form became for him and that he further confounded in narrative form.

It is time, however, to recognize that all is not so easily unified in the critics we are introducing. We have glossed over an important variance in attitude and emphasis. As would be apparent from any discussion of the *NRF*, inherent in this group there is a basic classicism, a quest to restore the equivalent of old values, a maintenance of some form of order, in sum a defense of literature against incursions which would seem to threaten total destruction of its special place. As Jean Paulhan once confided:

> After all, Montaigne lived in a more troubled time than ours, and more difficult. That did not prevent him from being Montaigne. Don't you think that the *NRF* has the goal precisely of helping someone (or several) to be Montaigne?
>
> *Europe*, of course, is something else again.[5]

The *NRF* established itself like a Hôtel des Grands Hommes outside some figurative Panthéon and tried to maintain its doors open from the relatively contemplative time of late symbolism to the terrorism of our modern era. They may have succeeded but they did so by remaining uncommitted with an outward appearance of complete *disponibilité*, and thus at the expense of becoming anachronistic.

An early key to the anachronism is the rejection of Proust's manuscript. Although they quickly redeemed themselves, Gide and a number of the others including Ramón Fernández never fully understood the fundamental modernity of certain aspects of *A la Recherche du temps perdu*. In Fernández, just as elsewhere in Gide and Jacques Rivière, Montaigne and other standard-bearing shibboleths crop up at most crucial moments in the form of a judgment. The seriousness of Rivière, the traditional morality of Fernández, turn the gratuity of Gide's title *incidences* into classical *études* or ethical *messages*. It is as

5. "Après tout, Montaigne vivait dans une époque bien plus troublée que la nôtre, et plus difficile. Ça ne l'a pas empêché d'être Montaigne. Ne pensez-vous pas que la *NRF* a précisément pour but d'aider quelqu'un (ou quelques-uns) à être Montaigne?

"*Europe*, bien entendu, c'est tout autre chose." From a letter to Roger Martin du Gard, quoted in his and Gide's *Correspondance* 1 (Paris: Gallimard, 1968): 532. Gide, in reply to Paulhan's letter, objects, quoting his own *Paludes* contemptuously, "as for me, it's all the same, because I'm writing *Paludes*," and adding, "Peace and tranquillity is the lot only of the dead." But this was 1932 and a rather atypical period for Gide. Paulhan maintained a more characteristic identity for the review, one which Gide would soon readopt, in any event with the coming of World War II and *Thésée*.

though in the creative domain one were free to experiment and thus participated in the process, but with the donning of the robe of criticism, the consciousness of one's role as maintainer of the patrimony makes one fall back upon the application of some sort of classical model like the representational.

Indeed the debate over *moralisme et littérature* which occurred between Fernández and Rivière, significantly enough on Swiss soil, epitomizes the paradoxical image of the *NRF*, because its subject, the wrongdoing of romanticism, the split between the reprehensible undercurrents of passion and the parts of man capable of imposing wisdom is a vestige of nineteenth-century origin, and because the very nature of debate suggests the other side of the apparent uncertainty of Gide's dialogue tradition, the final standstill which the *NRF* comes to represent through a refusal to commit itself. Rivière, like Gide, only toys with the "unfathomable" in Dostoevsky, as with Freud. Abstractions for him must maintain a moral construction; words, an existence as ideas; there is no taste for the uncomposed or nostalgia for the precomposed state of being; the comic does not become absurd, and the search for a new way to see and analyze should not "disturb the rhythm of seeing," in Rivière's phrase (from his part of *Moralisme et littérature*). The pure sensitivity and intelligence remain somehow virginal in patience, attention, and love, in admiration, uncontaminated by the lower appetites as the findings are tested and verified. The ideal artist is a "classical modern," one who creates through a careful process of assimilation, perfecting his instrument and leaving nothing to chance. Such a stance could not be further removed from surrealism; there could be no real meeting ground with Dada or André Breton.[6]

There is thus a continuation of a certain humanistic tradition in the *NRF*, originally propelled by and appropriating many of the motivations behind the *Action Française* and the *Revue Critique* movements—distaste for the excesses of romanticism and nineteenth-century values, quest for a renewal of classical

6. See René Lourau, "André Breton et la *N.R.F.*," *Nouvelle Revue Française* 15 (1967): 909–17.

traditions (discipline, tempered style, a respect for classical authors), a certain nationalism, etc.—but without the dogma and cant and most of the infamous political ideology.

The result is, together with a rejection of positivism, an accent on the humanistic. Thibaudet, Paulhan (and to a certain extent Georges Poulet) may be seen here in this volume to represent this point of view—though less weakly than might be provided by depending upon Gide, Rivière, Fernández, and the secondary writers of the *NRF*. The former stand stoutly by themselves as defenders of humanism staving off the inevitable death of man. That their effort too has been a somewhat passive (not really reactionary) one, a temporary consolidation giving way in the end, is apparent from more recent developments. The *NRF*, that Hôtel des Grands Hommes, without a real program or critical commitment, would seem to have lodged the last of the men of letters.

It will be apparent that there are other omissions in our table of contents. Most of these are deliberate, the result of necessary choices. There are critics whose work at this time does not seem to justify a chapter apart for one reason or another—often not because it is unsuccessful in its project, but rather because it does not represent a tendency and congeals around something other than an identifiable theoretical viewpoint. Some critics have been subsumed under other headings and cited at one point or another in the text or the bibliographies. Similarly, there seemed little reason for including a discussion of academic criticism as such; the Lansonian method is a fully developed tool which can be applied well or poorly, and the best *recensement* would be a simple annotated bibliography.[7]

Also, there are no separate chapters on certain methods like psychoanalysis and linguistics because the center of activity in these areas does not seem to be French. Attempting to provide information about psychoanalytical or linguistic criticism per

7. An excellent brief description of Lanson's method is given by Wallace Fowlie, *The French Critic*, pp. 14–15. See also Henri Peyre's edition of Lanson's essays and the Baldensperger and Rudler items, all listed in the Selected General Bibliography.

se can be more appropriately fulfilled at this point as a bibliography or encyclopedia, which is not our intent. In any event, these are methods applied within a broader field such as is treated under the heading of structuralism, and they have often been most successfully assimilated by critics such as Bachelard, Sartre, Merleau-Ponty, or Barthes, each of whom has formulated his own critical point of view.

And this is precisely the point: In the face of a radically new context for literature, the art object no longer enjoys a special privileged status. As a machine it is in direct correspondence with a totality that we must probe and apprehend through a variety of means—language, studies of behavior, the psychoanalysis of the imaginary—without opting, as with positivism, for placing a new precedence and source for creation in one or another of these different modes of knowledge.

Ralph Freedman

1

Paul Valéry: Protean Critic

In an age of "theory," of multiple philosophies of literature, the critic Paul Valéry, much like the poet, stands out as a lonely and Protean figure. He appears isolated because of the depth and the multiplicity of his critical writings—from poetics to studies of meter, to music, architecture, and the dance—and because he faced with courage the task of being theorist without losing touch with the reality of poetry which he so consummately practiced himself. But he was also a Protean figure—as critic as he was as poet—because he summed up an entire development in nineteenth- and twentieth-century poetic thought. For Valéry was also a most coherent philosopher of criticism. To be sure, his prose writings, spanning many decades and having been too often inspired by particular commissions or assigned tasks, appear diverse and scattered. They come to us in seemingly disconnected collections in the five volumes of the *Variétés*, as well as in other individual books. But actually the ideas expressed in the 1890s are still carried to maturity in the 1930s and beyond.[1] In fact, the profound unity of Paul Valéry's work may be comparable in scope, and even in intent, to the Critical Philosophy of Immanuel Kant. It is a *summa* of the modern position. More profoundly, perhaps, than T. S. Eliot, who made the term famous, Valéry developed a "philosophy" of the "objective correlative," exploring the relationship between the poet's private sensibility and the concrete or autonomous poem as its equivalent in art.

1. See Jean Hytier, *The Poetics of Paul Valéry*, trans. Richard Howard (New York: Doubleday, Anchor Books, 1966), p. 8.

In assessing the importance of Paul Valéry as a philosopher or theorist of criticism, we might focus on this particular aspect of his work. The base from which he set out had been the "impasse" of Mallarmé, who could solve the duality between the sense content of poetry and the "pure" idea only by negation. By replacing this "negation" with his emphasis on intellectuality, yet retaining Mallarmé's stress on the poet's creative act, Valéry opened up fresh approaches to the perennial problem of literary criticism: the disjunction between sensibility and idea, between self and work. Our task will be to show how Valéry reformulated this ancient problem in the context of recent intellectual history and how he built it into his own poetics. Hence the poetics itself will not form the focal point of our inquiry. Like his aesthetic, Valéry's poetic theories have received detailed attention elsewhere, most notably, of course, in Jean Hytier's classic, *The Poetics of Paul Valéry*. Our endeavor will be to trace a particular relationship between experience and form, which has been most influential in his poetics, and to view it within the wider perspective of his philosophical position as a whole.

The perennial problem to which we have referred epitomizes the course of nineteenth-century thought, because it still focuses on the age-old "reconciliation of opposites." The impulse toward "inspiration" (involving a psychologizing of the artistic process) is countered by, and to be squared with, the impulse toward formal coherence (involving, for Valéry, the mechanical elaboration of artistic form). Or, to put it in a different way, the problem as it formulates itself for Valéry is how consciousness can relate itself to, and impose itself upon, the formal properties of the work of art which consciousness creates and perceives.

From the point of view of intellectual history, then, we encounter a modern version of an eighteenth- and nineteenth-century problem, to which many romantic theories from Coleridge's and the Schlegels' to Poe's and Baudelaire's had been addressed. Whether the term was "imagination" or "romantic irony" or the orchestrating quality of "beauty," the disjunction between the self's act of creation and the formal order of the work was erased as both were telescoped in a single paradoxical unit. Valéry's critical theory stands at the end of this romantic development, pointing toward new solutions and foreshadowing a very different approach to poetry and the creative act. In this respect he may close a cycle opened by Kant, who had approached the identical problem with a parallel set of theories at the beginning of this development. It is one of the purposes of this essay to show that, between them, Kant and Valéry suggest two opposite yet complementary points in the history of modern criticism.

The critical situation during the second half of the eighteenth century, which gave rise to romantic ideology, was indeed very similar, in many important ways, to the critical situation at the turn of the twentieth century when Valéry made his debut as poet and critic. A mere enumeration of well-known trends and theories in the eighteenth century, developing psychological or inspirationist doctrines against the still widespread belief in superimposed formal "rules," shows the gravity of the disjunction. Various psychological theories had been developed from empiricist thought, such as the "associationism" of Condillac and the linguistic reductions of the French encyclopedists. The growth and change in the concept of the imagination in England further suggests the deep concern of these generations with the power of private experience straining to meet the formal requirements of art. Similarly, in Germany the debate between Lessing's essential formalism and Herder's psychologizing is evidence of this conflict, which Herder sought to solve with his notions of organicity and of the reconciling energy or *Kraft* (a binding power akin to the imagination). Clearly the confrontation of these ideas with the prevailing doctrines of an increasingly ambivalent neoclassicism —from Dryden and Voltaire to Dr. Johnson—dramatizes this dichotomy with particular vividness. For the variety of these theories, and the growing distances between them, suggest the very tension which Kant reflected, and at least partially solved, in a larger philosophical spectrum.

In the late nineteenth and early twentieth centuries, these tensions seem to re-emerge in an amazingly analogous development. In England, we encounter T. E. Hulme's and Ezra Pound's rejection of the sentimentalism of their elders, and their proclamation of a new "formal" classicism: the "hard" external object, as opposed to the "soft" general emotion, to become the proper material of poetry. The duality of Rilke's *New Poems* of the early 1900s would be yet another example of the revival of the tension which ultimately romanticism could not solve: now experienced as a discrepancy between the poet's attempt to infuse objects with consciousness and his attempt to represent objects as they are, formally, without the infusion of consciousness. But, of course, the tension was most clearly felt during the late flowering and decline of the French symbolist movement. Externally, the symbolists faced Sainte-Beuve and Anatole France, their adherents and successors: an "establishment" that asserted a combination of realism, classicism, and, perhaps, sentimentalism, and that excluded the elevation of consciousness as such to a poetic mode. But internally, too, symbolist theory had always reflected the tension of the age in its confusion between the vague, suggestive image, its dissolution of linguistic into musical form on the one hand, and on the other, the symbol as artifact, as pure "jewel," from which sense content is withdrawn—in other words, the tension between its romantic and Parnassian ingredients. Valéry confronted this situation at the turn of the present century as, in a different context, Kant had confronted his own situation earlier.

This analogous development which Kant and Valéry shared at different moments in intellectual history accounts for many of their similarities, even if the center of their attention did not coincide. Although both had hoped for a fusion of science and art in a comprehensive system, Valéry, unlike Kant, remained in the end primarily a poet whose philosophical views were ultimately conditioned by his concerns as a poet. But it is possible to say that Kant (however marginally related to poetry his intentions may have been) accomplished for poetic theorists of his age what Valéry accomplished for our own time. Kant created a complete system of knowledge (in which art and poetry were but an afterthought to be made crucial by later generations). He designed a coherent scheme in which the

Our comparison of Kant and Valéry is based on the fact that both thinkers focused on the crucial disjunction between consciousness (of self and of objects) and the formal shape of things, and that both solved this disjunction—one from within the Age of Reason and the other in a deliberate return to it—by discerning coherent mental structures within which these contradictions could be resolved.

The obvious point of departure for an exposition of Valéry's view of consciousness is provided by two youthful works, his "Introduction à la méthode de Léonard de Vinci" (1895) and "La Soirée avec Monsieur Teste" (1896). The "Méthode," written in 1894 and published in 1895, is an amazingly coherent yet abstract blueprint of the "universal mind." Leonardo da Vinci was a particularly suitable subject, because he was able to express himself in such a variety of forms—painting, architecture, battle plans, inventions, etc.—without losing a sense of unity or organization. Although Valéry allows in his later "Note et digression" that his essay had been based on relatively sparse knowledge of Leonardo's actual work, he felt he could use Leonardo's *mind* as a prototype for a universal mental structure.

The term *structure* is crucial to our purpose, and crucial as well to Valéry's thought. But how is this structure seen? Valéry makes it quite clear to us:

> This symbolic spirit encompasses the most expansive collection of forms, a treasure, forever clear, of the aspects and attitudes of nature, an ever imminent power which grows with the extension of its domain. It is composed of a crowd of beings, a crowd of possible memories, the ability to recognize in the extension of the world extraordinary numbers of distinct objects and to arrange them in a thousand ways.[4]

4. My translation, as elsewhere when not otherwise identified. (See also *Variety*, trans. Malcolm Cowley [New York: Harcourt, Brace, 1927], pp. 252–53.) "Il garde, cet esprit symbolique, la plus vaste collection de formes, un trésor toujours clair des attitudes de la nature, une puissance toujours imminente et qui grandit selon l'extension de son domaine. Une foule d'êtres, une foule de souvenirs possibles, la force de reconnaître dans l'étendue du monde un nombre extraordinaire de choses distinctes et de les arranger de mille manières, le constituent." *Variété*, pp. 240–41.

And again, viewing Leonardo as an impersonal genius, detached from time, place, and tradition: "The number and the communication of his acts produce a symmetrical object, a kind of *system complete in itself* or which makes itself such continually."[5] This organizing principle, that discerns the system, is "intelligence."[6]

What Valéry suggests, then, in a spirit not wholly alien to Kant, is that by means of his intelligence (as exemplified by the "universal mind" of Leonardo), consciousness reconstructs the order of a diverse world, mirrors its intricacies, and imposes harmony upon its many and often contradictory manifestations. It is the kind of mind that can give reality a Euclidian shape. Actually, of course, this "shape" derives its rationale not from Kant, or Euclid, but from René Descartes, whom Valéry admired and to whom he devoted several cogent essays.[7] Moreover, the title of the first Leonardo essay, "Introduction à la Méthode de . . . ," suggests not too subtly that something similar to the Cartesian "method" may be attempted, and that whatever "structure" of the mind is to emerge from its pages may exhibit a Cartesian quality.

Valéry's method reflects Descartes's in a number of ways. First of all, he repeats, in his own terms, the idea of the *displacement of feeling* by the rational intellect which is implied in the Cartesian method of doubt. For Descartes all elements of "feeling" and external perception—"primary qualities" like extension and "secondary qualities" like color—are subject to doubt. The residue that remains is the *Cogito ergo sum*, the fact of self-consciousness, the capacity for rational thought

5. (See also *Variety*, p. 258.) "Le nombre et la communication de ses actes en font un objet symétrique, une sorte de *système complet en lui-même*, ou qui se rend tel incessamment." *Variété*, p. 245.

6. Moreover: "The greatest possible poet is the nervous system—the inventor of everything—but the only poet." "Le plus grand poète possible c'est le système nerveux. L'inventeur de tout—mais plutôt le seul poète." *Mélange* (Paris: Gallimard, 1941), p. 87.

7. "Descartes," "A View of Descartes," "Second View of Descartes," etc. Cf. *Variété*, V (Paris: Gallimard, 1945), 209–60. (*Masters and Friends*, trans. Martin Turnell, *The Collected Works of Paul Valéry*, ed. Jackson Matthews, Bollingen Series, IX [Princeton: Princeton University Press, 1969], 13–71.)

through which the universe can be reconstructed. Second, Valéry, like Descartes, assumes the *isolation* of the self. In Descartes's system, the thinking, self-conscious *ego* is isolated as the only certainty and—because its capacity for rational thought permits reconstruction—as the only guarantor of knowledge. Similarly, Valéry's exposition of the universal structure of Leonardo's mind inversely mirrors Descartes's method of doubt, which traces capillaries of questioning as it pursues all possible avenues of knowledge down to their final point of self-consciousness. Leonardo's intelligence, Valéry writes, is confounded with the invention of a unique order, a likely form, or system, which it imposes. The clearest example of this achievement is the mysterious creation of the famous smile of the *Mona Lisa*, which is produced by a precise arrangement of objective relationships that make up the composition.[8]

The function of the Cartesian method in Valéry's philosophical (and poetic) scheme can be seen at work in his description of the work of art. The following passage, combining the notions of *abstraction* and *construction* in a single statement, may serve to clarify the Cartesian parallel as well as Valéry's method as a whole:

> Thus it is through abstraction that the work of art can be constructed, and this abstraction is more or less energetic, more or less easy to define, to the degree that those of its elements which are taken from reality exist in more or less complex constellations. Inversely, it is through a kind of induction, through the production of mental images that the entire work of art is judged; and this production of imagery must also be more or less energetic, more or less tiring, whether it is attracted by a simple ornament on a vase or a fragmented sentence from Pascal.[9]

8. *Variété*, p. 254. (*Variety*, pp. 267–68.)

9. (See also *Variety*, p. 266.) "C'est donc par une abstraction que l'oeuvre d'art peut se construire, et cette abstraction est plus ou moins énergique, plus ou moins facile à définir, selon que les éléments empruntés à la réalité en sont des portions plus ou moins complexes. Inversement c'est par une sorte d'induction, par la production d'images mentales que toute oeuvre d'art s'apprécie; et cette production doit être également plus ou moins énergique, plus ou moins

And at a later point, speaking of Leonardo as a scientist, Valéry refers to all natural experience as an abstraction. But what does this mean? In our terms, it suggests that all experience must be understood in its essential meaning, the "elements borrowed from reality" being seen in particular constellations imposed by the discerning, comprehending mind. Abstraction also involves the invocation of an idea and the direction in which the relationships of "elements" can be defined; it involves distilling the intellectually accessible meaning from an otherwise chaotic assemblage: a drive, if consistently pursued, toward the *cogito*. For "pure" relationships are conceived only by the isolated, comprehending consciousness.[10] Abstraction from reality, thus, represents Valéry's inverse way of imitating the Cartesian method of doubt. Similarly, the "construction" or "reconstruction" of the work of art parallels, even more clearly, Descartes's reconstruction of the world by the conscious intellect. Hence, Valéry's definition of the nature and process of art, in its creation (by the poet) and in the reverse course of its perception (by reader or viewer), represents a paradigm of the two elements of the Cartesian method—abstracting analysis and reconstruction.

Despite its overt philosophizing, all this reasoning had profoundly personal and even dramatic implications for Valéry. The paradoxical notion that the most universal mind (Leonardo) must also be the most isolated one suggests a latter-day romantic revival not only of the isolated poet-hero but also of all intellectual activity as presupposing the detached and insulated pose of the perennial soliloquist. As we shall see, Valéry does not exclude the irrational element of the mind, and its creative drive, but like all other "elements borrowed from reality" he abstracts it and confines it to isolated moments. On the whole, the Cartesian reduction of all activity to the self-conscious "I" reinforced that deep sense of essen-

---

fatigante selon qu'un simple entrelacs sur un vase ou une phrase brisée de Pascal la sollicite." *Variété*, pp. 252–53.

10. See Franz Rauhut, *Paul Valéry* (Munich: Max Hueber, 1950), pp. 145–46.

tial egotism which Valéry ascribed to the thinking mind in general and to the artist's lonely task in particular. It accurately reflects the paradoxical vision of a mind so universal that it can hold together the most disparate aspects of reality on which it imposes its order, and so singular that it is isolated, abstract, a pure mental act divorced from both body and other selves.[11] But as Descartes led reconstruction from such a point on, so Valéry, too, uses the creative act as the irreducible point from which to develop a whole by logical, geometrical, or aesthetic variations of all the elements the self-conscious intelligence had discerned. To return to Kant, the creative structure of Leonardo's mind, his ability to tie analogies and contiguities together, provides the matrix within which the act of creation and the formal projection are contained. This formal act, as we noted, arises from the precise source of the *mind* which determined it.

A similar view of consciousness and its Cartesian analogies is also present in the "novel" *Monsieur Teste*. This character of allegorical fiction, representing pure thought or *tête*, is endowed with the same characteristics as the supposedly nonfictional internal physiognomy of Leonardo. He is capable of ordering, hence desensualizing, the chaotic reality around him through the power of his thought. He is also pure self-conscious "I"—a rather wooden incarnation, however witty, of the Cartesian *cogito* as a character of fiction. But since the outward form of this work, which is essentially a treatise, permits conversation, some action, a demonstration of behavior toward others, we have a clearer idea both of Valéry's concept of the nature of the pure self and of his manner of relating to objects and other selves in "reality." Edmond Teste is almost entirely devoid of nonrational, even external characteristics, in his appearance, his habits, even, almost, in his life and marriage. He does not read any longer, but contemplates all he knows and retains it with his remarkable memory. Significantly, his livelihood is derived from manipu-

11. See W. N. Ince, *The Poetic Theory of Paul Valéry* (Leicester: Leicester University Press, 1961), pp. 38–51. Cf. *Variété*, pp. 200–201. (*Variety*, pp. 212–13.)

lations at the stock exchange. The description of him, early in the book, makes the point:

M. Teste was perhaps forty years old. His speech was extraordinarily rapid, and his voice quiet. Everything about him was fading, his eyes, his hands. His shoulders, however, were military, and his step had a regularity that was amazing. When he spoke he never raised an arm or a finger: *he had killed his puppet.*[12]

And the author, Valéry, setting up an effective dialogue between himself and his extraordinary double, wonders about his subject's memory and imagines "unequaled intellectual gymnastics."

Both elements are combined in this description: the first is that of self-consciousness, the isolation from all elements outside the self. Hence the colorlessness of M. Teste's appearance. Regularity of movements and their extreme constraint (the "primary qualities")—"he had killed his puppet"—and pigment of eyes and face ("secondary qualities") equally retreat and evaporate before this pure thinker. In a touching note in a later letter by Mme. Emilie Teste his wife describes him in the park as essentially alone—in the "monologue condition" of pure intelligence. But the second "constructive" element of ordering is present, too. It is punctuated by the *regularity* of M. Teste's movements. "This man had early known the importance of what might be called human *plasticity*. He had tried to find out its limits and its laws."[13] A brilliantly developed scene at the opera shows how M. Teste possesses the same orchestrating qualities of mind—bringing order into the chaos

12. "An Evening with M. Teste," *Monsieur Teste*, trans. Jackson Matthews (New York: Alfred A. Knopf, 1948), p. 12. "M. Teste avait peut-être quarante ans. Sa parole était extra-ordinairement rapide, et sa voix sourde. Tout s'effaçait en lui, les yeux, les mains. Il avait pourtant les épaules militaires, et le pas d'une régularité qui étonnait. Quand il parlait, il ne levait jamais un bras ni un doigt: *il avait tué la marionnette.*" *Monsieur Teste* (Paris: Sagittaire, 1931), p. 27.

13. *Monsieur Teste*, p. 13. "Cet homme avait connu de bonne heure l'importance de ce qu'on pourrait nommer la *plasticité* humaine. Il en avait cherché les limites et le mécanisme." *M. Teste*, p. 29.

of the multitude—that are to be shown by the music, and the performance, on the stage. M. Teste, then, like Leonardo, is an isolating intelligence, yet capable of organizing or constructing a coherent form from the disparate elements furnished by reality.

It is easy to see that we confront a version of the duality between self, or pure consciousness, and form. It is not quite the Kantian duality, in which the internally formed material of the sensibility is rationally "placed" by the intelligence and transformed into the transcendental schema, nor is it the only duality we discover in Valéry. But it sets up the paradigm, the pattern into which the varying roles of consciousness fall. More important, the *Léonard* and *M. Teste* cycles introduce configurations of ideas about self, reality, and the "structure" of the mind which accompany Valéry throughout most of his life. The *Léonard* "structure" occupies his interest for nearly thirty years, commented upon and somewhat revised in "Note et digression" in 1919, to be discussed again in "Léonard et les philosophes" in 1929. Similarly, "La Soirée avec M. Teste," written, like "Léonard," in 1894 (though not published, in *Le Centaure*, until 1896), was followed by several later additions, including a "Journal" in 1910 and the interesting "Log-book de M. Teste" in 1925.[14] Both cycles develop, without crucial change, the relationship between consciousness and the world it constructs.

In "Note et digression," for example, Valéry refines and develops the relationship between consciousness as a pure activity and its empirical manifestations. Since cognition knows no boundaries, and since no idea exhausts the task of consciousness (which is limitless), cognition must perish in an incomprehensible event which is not rationally accessible. Intelligence must now apply itself to its task of ordering process. But by sifting its objects and relating them to one another, it discovers no changes or gradations. In an extraordinary statement, extending over several pages, Valéry

14. The "Log-book" portrays from within, so it seems, the hero's consciousness, also rendered elsewhere from the perspective of his wife ("Letter from Mme. Emilie Teste") and his double, the author-narrator (Paul Valéry or his mask).

argued that while man obtains his identity through consciousness, he is forced to expel, by virtue of his consciousness, all appearances from his mind, and, by extension, from himself.

The characteristic of man is consciousness; and that of consciousness a perpetual emptying, a detachment, without rest and without exception, from all that appears there, whatever appears. Inexhaustible act, independent of the quality as of the quantity of appearances, through which the man of intellectual sensibility should finally be reduced, knowingly, to an indefinite refusal to be anything at all.[15]

Since all appearances are equally dispelled by the mind, interior feelings as well as images "borrowed from reality" come to exist on an identical plane, without gradations or change, and can be substituted for one another. Variety in the universe, then, is resisted by the self as a conscious intelligence. It imposes "unity" which becomes sameness. It is abstract consciousness.

It is no coincidence that at this point we introduce apparently Kantian terminology, for, indeed, Valéry's passages on the role of consciousness and its relationship to experience take on more and more of a Kantian hue. In fact, it has been shown that parts of the "Note et digression" suggest, beyond Kant, German romantic terminology and thought, notably that of Fichte. The definition of personality as a phenomenon (physical and psychological) as opposed to a noumenal "naked ego" or *moi*, suggests romantic distinctions.[16] But it is especially the relationship between unlimited "pure" consciousness and the attempt by the empirical consciousness to limit it in cognition, as in the determination of value, that harks back to a Fichtean dialectic. At the same time, this assertion of "pure" consciousness, as a defining characteristic

15. (See also *Variety*, p. 212.) "Le caractère de l'homme est la conscience; et celui de la conscience, une perpétuelle exhaustion, un détachement sans repos et sans exception de tout ce qu'y paraît, quoi qui paraisse [*sic*]. Acte inépuisable, indépendant de la qualité comme de la quantité des choses apparues, et par lequel l'*homme de l'esprit* doit enfin se réduire sciemment à un refus indéfini d'être quoi que ce soit." *Variété*, p. 200.

16. See Rauhut, *Paul Valéry*, pp. 72–76.

of man, *eo ipso* involved a rejection of unconscious experience as a main motivating force. Hence Valéry did not travel the romantic way to surrealism. He remained "classical" in the Kantian sense, and that of Descartes, in which a strong sense of cognition as a defining characteristic of man is accompanied by the conviction that the mental activity cognition presupposes is conscious and rational.

These discussions are carried on with particular cogency in "Léonard et les philosophes" where they are turned into a special plea asserting the predominance of the artist over the philosopher as the principal purveyor of knowledge and ethics alike. The essay sets out with a definition of the self as pure thought, with which we are familiar, reasserts that it must therefore reject the presence of others, but then asks what the philosopher can do about the situation. The artist, through his persona, may be able to absorb all realities into himself, but the philosopher, who usually wants to do more, has to endow them with understanding. This leads to an ethic and an aesthetic:

> He [the philosopher] wants to understand; he wants to understand them [the realities] in the strongest sense of the word. He then proceeds to meditate constructing a science of the values of action and a science of the values of the expression or of the creation of emotions—an ETHIC and an AESTHETIC—as if the Palace of his Thought must seem to him imperfect without these two symmetrical wings in which his all-powerful and abstract Ego could hold passion, action, emotion and invention captive.[17]

17. "Leonardo and the Philosophers," *Selected Writings of Paul Valéry*, trans. Anthony Bower (New York: New Directions, 1950), p. 110 (somewhat revised). "Il [le philosophe] veut *comprendre*; il veut les comprendre [ces réalités] dans toute la force du mot. Il va donc méditer de se construire une science des valeurs d'action et une science des valeurs de l'expression ou de la création des émotions,—une ETHIQUE et une ESTHÉTIQUE—comme si le Palais de sa Pensée lui dût paraître imparfait sans ces deux ailes symétriques dans lesquelles son Moi tout-puissant et abstrait pût tenir la passion, l'action, l'émotion et l'invention captives." *Variété*, III (Paris: Gallimard, 1936), 143.

The philosopher, however, cannot really succeed, for, by definition, he must look for general concepts. At the same time those classical forms of art which may be said to follow a prescribed pattern set by the general concept of beauty are no longer relevant. Instead, models "attendus par l'esprit" have been replaced by impulses of the unconscious, the irrational, the instantaneous. Beauty is a "corpse." Yet the artist returns us to a sense of beauty by his built-in objective standard which allows him to combine, and coordinate, at each instant, the arbitrary and the necessary, the expected and the unexpected. The artist's work, like the mental structure, consists of a *system*, a "universe." Cognition, in this later essay, then, involves its equivalents in the world of value. Without abandoning the focus on the rational mind, indeed by enhancing it, Valéry places the artist's consciousness above the philosopher's. The creative mind, which can first reflect phenomena and then reorder them, produces a fresh and coherent universe that cannot be further explained. And Valéry concludes this passage with the assertion that such a universe can also be found in the philosopher's system, in Kant's, for example, whose ethic and aesthetic are founded on a "myth of universality," a total universe capable of being projected by the mind. The artist, then, by creating and developing a new order, overcomes the hazards of the empirical world, yet, by imposing this order, he reconciles the need to "abstract" (to find order among phenomena) with the need to "construct" (to develop the coherent structure). Like the pure thinker, he has varied himself, but with a difference. He has invented, created, established a world.

These notions extend the original concepts of the isolated self as *cogito* and the world which must be reduced to form by the abstract consciousness and lead to a fuller conception of the artist as creator. Similar changes may also be discerned in the "Log-book of M. Teste," which deals more specifically with the relationship between feeling and affect, on the one hand, and rational self-knowledge on the other.[18] But actually

18. See, for example, M. Teste's prayer at the opening of the "Log-book": "*A prayer*: Lord, I was in the void, infinitely nothing

all of these notions were somehow present in the original statements. Throughout Valéry's work, they suggest a duality between the impulse of the mind to refine its cognitions and the attendant impulse of the mind to vary and reconstruct them. In both the *Léonard* and *M. Teste* cycles, these two impulses are made to cohere. They show how the duality of self and form successfully held together by the romantic "paradox"—whether it be called "irony" or "imagination"—could be reinterpreted by a devout rationalist. It is now my purpose to show how these structural properties of the mind are applied to particular aspects of Valéry's poetics.

Paul Valéry's description of consciousness and its function may provide an understanding of his numerous pronouncements on the nature of poetry. Unlike that of his antipode Kant, whose systems of epistemology, ethics, and teleology are the primary focus of most readers' interests, the essential character of Valéry's theory is described by his definitions of poetry and art. Whatever his involvement with Descartes, with pure thought, or with the nature of cognition may have been, it is no coincidence that in "Léonard et les philosophes,"

---

and tranquil. I was disturbed from that state, to be thrown into this strange carnival . . . and you took care that I should be endowed with all I needed in order to suffer, enjoy, understand, and be wrong; but incompatible, these gifts.

"I consider you the master of that darkness I look into when I think, and upon which the last thought will be inscribed.

"Give me, O Darkness, that supreme thought. . . .

"But in general any commonplace thought may be the 'supreme thought.'" *Monsieur Teste*, p. 39.

"UNE PRIÈRE DE M. TESTE: Seigneur, j'étais, dans le néant, infiniment nul et tranquille. J'ai été dérangé de cet état pour être jeté dans le carnaval étrange . . . et fus par vos soins doué de tout ce qu'il faut pour pâtir, jouir, comprendre et me tromper; mais ces dons inégaux.

"Je vous considère comme le maître de ce noir que je regarde quand je pense, et sur lequel s'inscrira la dernière pensée.

"Donnez, ô Noir,—donnez la suprême pensée. . . .

"Mais toute pensée généralement quelconque peut être 'suprême pensée.'" *M. Teste*, p. 69.

it is the *artist* who displaces abstract self-consciousness with his concrete organization.

The "structure of consciousness"—the awareness of intricate relationships between cognition, self-knowledge, and the organization of knowledge—reveals itself, for Valéry, through the creation and function of poems by which poetry can define itself as a form of art. We have already seen how for Valéry the act through which the self relates itself to reality and the act through which it constructs or organizes the universe are analogous to the composition of the work of art. Indeed, comprehending the poem through the creative process (as an analogue of the process of consciousness) and seeing it simultaneously as activity and object, by means of consciousness, is his significant contribution.

The starting point in Valéry's poetics, then, is the assumption that the poem is a "mental" act. It is, of course, as he reassures us, something we can listen to or read, a constellation produced by words, by language, but at the same time it is also something that can be understood only in relation to what its words "do" as they are created by poets and formed by them to be received by readers in whom analogous states are evoked. Two elements discussed with particular frequency in his various essays are clearly prominent, describing simultaneously the creation of the poem and its nature. These are the "poetic state" (*l'état poétique*) and the construction or, as he calls it in his later essays, the "fabrication" of poems. Clearly, his exposition shows that Valéry views the poem as a reproduction of consciousness, in miniature, through the medium of words. But it remains one of the most interesting features of his poetics that the very activity of creation that develops the poem is also the latter's definition. True, one may deduce from this fact Valéry's romantic lineage, but it also suggests a rationalistic variation of Rimbaud's *voyant* whose total vision of himself is also his most objective vision—the poem.

Upon closer scrutiny, then, it appears that the two elements engaged in the *creation* of poetry reflect the two elements which generally compose the work of art as Valéry describes it. For the *état poétique* obviously resembles abstraction. It is what the mind does when it is confronted with sudden awareness and fresh recognitions. Similarly *fabrication* suggests the process of geometrical and musical elaborations through which the initial poetic state is made meaningful. But before we concern ourselves with these two elements and their place in the definition of the poem, we might view them more specifically in Valéry's context of thought. As in Gide's various pronouncements of the 1890s, so in the early and indeed even in the later Valéry, these terms are seen in relation to states of the self—the sincere self, the poet, as Gide termed him—and the artificing quality required by the work of art—the prevaricator, the artist. For like Gide and others of his time, Valéry defined the psychological and philosophical relationships involved in art by means of the opposition between the natural impulse of the self and its formal restriction—the inspiration and formal elaboration, the emotion and the mask.

These tendencies are made clear in Valéry's controversial stand on the nature of the novel and his concomitant praise of poetry as the superior (i.e., more formal) genre. Similarly, it is revealed in Valéry's well-known preference for "classicism" over "romanticism." And both prejudices are deeply concerned with the way he viewed the nature and function of the *moi*, the "lyrical self." For it is indicative of Valéry's point of view that most of his essays on poets begin with their lives and, more pertinently, their psyches, despite the deep commitment to a "classical" formalism in his critical thinking. We may only recall the parallel between Villon and Verlaine, as persons, the discussion of Voltaire, the personal "situation" of Baudelaire, the death of Mallarmé, or the concepts and egotisms of Stendhal. In each case the relationship between consciousness and its rational elaboration is reflected in an analogous contrast between a personal life and its formal projection.

Valéry's essay on Stendhal is a case in point. Throughout this lengthy appraisal of a novelist, he paradoxically denigrates his subject's novels. For he holds the position, which leads to his rejection of the novel as a form, that "truth" and "life" represent disorder, suggesting the inchoate content of consciousness that mirrors the world. Raised against it is "fabrication"—the "order" of comedy, of form, which is accompanied by a "zest for precision."[19] Again in terms reminiscent of his contemporary, Gide, Valéry speaks of the specific "literary egotism" of Stendhal, who links the inchoate world with that of the inchoate "sincere" self. In this way, the natural ego must be refashioned by convention before it can become acceptable as art. Clearly this is a commonplace, but beneath the apparent banality of his statement, Valéry reveals a more pertinent, deeper intention. The "world" to be put in shape is identified with the self. Beyle's consciousness, Valéry wrote of Stendhal, became a stage. Stendhal came to know himself by "foreseeing" himself and playing a role. And as the *moi* purifies itself (through vanity and pride), it turns from a realm of feeling to one of precise thought. It is this role, this "comedy," which to Valéry was far more significant in Stendhal's writing than the fictions he created.[20] The plots, the incidents did not matter to him: he was looking, as he tells us, for the "inner plot"—the "living system"—which, in turn, is revealed only as the disorder of life is *re-created* as mask, as form.

Clearly, by rejecting Stendhal as a novelist, Valéry reaffirmed his famous stand on the novel. Reflecting the controversies between Mallarmé and Zola, his identification of "naturalism" with the "novel" suggested precisely the kind of critique of experience, and of the *moi*, which was developed

19. "But truth and life add up to disorder; connections and relationships which are not surprising are not real." "Stendhal," *Masters and Friends*, pp. 178 ff. An earlier rendering in English of this essay can be found in *Variety: Second Series*, trans. William A. Bradley (New York: Harcourt Brace, 1938), pp. 101–56. "Mais la vérité et la vie sont désordre; les filiations et les parentés qui ne sont pas surprenantes ne sont pas réelles." *Variété*, II (Paris: Gallimard, 1930), 79.

20. "To know yourself is simply to predict yourself; to predict yourself ends in playing a part. Beyle's consciousness is a theater, and there is a good deal of the actor in the author." *Masters and Friends*, p. 182; see also pp. 182–86 passim. "Se connaître n'est que se prévoir; se prévoir aboutit à jouer un rôle. La conscience de Beyle est un théâtre, et il y a beaucoup de l'acteur dans cet auteur." *Variété*, II, 85–86. See also pp. 85–94 passim.

in his essay on Stendhal. The novel was inchoate, whether it was projected outward onto a stage of "reality" to simulate history or whether it was part of a writer's or hero's inner vision. The lack of intelligence which Valéry believed he perceived in Flaubert, his critique of Stendhal's fiction (and his preference for the latter's "comedy") all suggest this stringent point of view.[21] Fabrication, i.e., the creation of a rational order, became the chief means whereby the impulse of poetry as an act of the "natural self," could be tamed and civilized as art.

This distinction between unformed experience and formed art is also present in Valéry's view of romanticism and classicism. In fact, this distinction, which he develops forcefully among others in his essay on Baudelaire, parallels his statement about Stendhal and the novel. Here he holds that classicism implies a concerted voluntary act modifying natural production "in conformity with a clear and rational conception of man."[22] Suggesting that man's "natural" self must be seen in the mirror not of a general system of values but of a universally acceptable concept of man's state, Valéry speaks like a denizen of the Age of Reason. Man can be rational and orderly only through an acceptance of conventions which, in turn, are derived from a predefined view of the human condition. A second, concomitant point is equally significant. A classic, Valéry writes in the same essay, "is a writer who carries a critic within him and who associates him internally with his own work." (Racine thus carried Boileau within him.) The impulse toward the expression of self, like that of Gide's and Valéry's dancers, must therefore be continuously checked. This statement, as Valéry saw clearly, also reflected a peculiarly French view of poetry, of art, and indeed of the world—the insistence on continuing, or returning to, the premises of the seventeenth and eighteenth centuries. At the same time it also expresses a consistent position which Valéry's theories of poetry entail.

21. See the fine summary of the subject in Joseph Frank's introduction to *Masters and Friends*, pp. xiii–xv.

22. "The Position of Baudelaire," *Variety: Second Series*, pp. 82–84. "La Situation de Baudelaire," *Variété*, II, 155–56.

The essay on Baudelaire is particularly interesting because it fashions these ideas within a context which is both historically and critically conditioned. The poetic act, as we trace Valéry's view of it, appears more and more as a reflection of the history of poetry and poets, and especially the French poets who are unusually beset by the need to find rigorously formal equivalents for the sensibilities and inchoate expressions of the self. Although, as Valéry allowed, Baudelaire was originally a romantic and "even a romantic by taste," he *appeared* as a classic. Indeed, Baudelaire did not have the largesse, the vulgarity, the great power over his subject and language which are attributed to Victor Hugo. He had to overcome all of them (as it is the classic's fate to overcome the romantic effusion) before he could define himself. And he did so by creating a new type of poetry unique in its history.

An interesting turn is evident in this appraisal of Baudelaire as a historical figure and as an exemplar of a new kind of poetry. For Valéry arrived at a fresh definition of poetry by viewing the familiar dichotomy between impulse and convention in the peculiar light of the Baudelairean achievement. *Les Fleurs du mal* was different from other poems of its time because, as a collection, it was neither romantic in the usual sense nor classical nor Parnassian. The methods used in its poems were not narrative, the subjects neither historical nor legendary nor political. Rather, the poems were *music*—a "powerful and abstract sensuality," rendering a combination of flesh and spirit. This achievement, Valéry recognized, was linguistic. Poetry so conceived modified the rendering and elaboration of the *état poétique* by using a special kind of language to re-create a world which could be romantic and classical alike. Moreover, this musical language determined both the process of creation and the manner in which the object of creation, the poem, would communicate itself to the reader. The catalyst who, according to Valéry, presented us, as he presented Baudelaire, with a totally new set of terms, was Edgar Allan Poe.

Valéry followed Baudelaire in an intense and illuminating reappraisal of the American poet and saw contained in Poe's "personal metaphysical system" the substance and the terms of a new kind of poetic language. For Poe's concern with the psychological requirements of a poem led to a telescoping of the processes of language and the processes of creation. Valéry welcomed this and evidently saw here a fresh departure in Baudelaire's practice for which Poe's "poetic principle" had been responsible. It rendered in the act of language simultaneously an intensely passionate experience and a purely formal statement. Moreover, Poe's bias in favor of the small self-contained poetic unit (expressed in his antididacticism, his rejection of long poems, etc.) had already presupposed the poetic form as a "pure" state—inspiration distilled by formality. "Absolute poetry," wrote Valéry, returning to our familiar terminology, is defined by "exhaustion" —a "sort of mathematics united with a sort of mysticism." Clearly parallel to Ezra Pound's famous anticipation of the "objective correlative," Valéry thus uses Poe as a key to that special kind of "subjective objectivity" which Baudelaire had bequeathed to subsequent French poets.[23] In Valéry's terms, the simultaneous rendering of the *état poétique* and its formal or purified elaboration become a principal characteristic of a new poetic language which, being subjective and objective alike, parallels most closely that fusion of mathematics and mysticism which he had perceived in his three great models beyond Leonardo: Poe, Baudelaire, and Mallarmé.

The self in its natural state and the form in which it is fashioned as art represent, in modern and "classical" terms, the two sides of the opposition between self and other, impulse and control. The scheme in which they function exists not only in the aesthetic of Valéry's specific time but actually in the romantic and post-romantic world as a whole. For if we go beyond the trivial statement that every work of art is composed of a content or inchoate feeling and an organization of form, we arrive at a general notion which describes a post-

23. *Variety: Second Series*, p. 92. *Variété*, II, 166. Cf. Ezra Pound: "Poetry is a sort of inspired mathematics which gives us equations not for abstract figures, triangles, spheres but for human emotions." *Spirit of Romance* (New York: E. P. Dutton, 1910), p. 7.

Aristotelian, post-neoclassical poetics in terms nonetheless rational. Despite all his "classicism," Valéry accurately reflected the post-neoclassical concern of the critic: now familiar questions about the possibility of poetic knowledge and about the relationship between the ontological fact of a poem and its creation.

In response to these questions Valéry developed a most coherent theory (even though it appeared scattered among many essays), which led to his complete formulation of the *état poétique*. For if one were to proceed not by the synthetic process of creation, which Valéry described in "Mémoires d'un poème" and elsewhere, but by the more circuitous path of analytic reconstruction (as a critic would have to do in following Valéry's path), the *état poétique* would emerge as the core of the poetic process. Valéry explained its meaning for the poet in his famous essay "Poésie et pensée abstraite" (1939): "A poet's function—do not be startled by this remark—is not to experience the poetic state: that is his private affair. His function is to create it in others."[24]

The poetic state, then, is an "inspiration" which the successful poem induces in a reader. But, as Valéry showed in the same passage, such an effect of poetry and the "artificial synthesis of this state in a work" are two different matters. The latter is a reasoned construction of a body of language, one of whose purposes is to create the poetic state. Still, it is one of the implications of the statement as a whole that the poem, too, is basically a mental activity. Since both poet and reader participate in the poetic state by means of their consciousness, the poem as an "artificial synthesis of this state" is also defined by consciousness.

In this analysis, then, the relationship between the poetic state and the poem's construction appears to involve primarily the poet's effect on the reader (he *creates* the *état poétique*). But it is the poem that is at issue. And the poem, too, elaborating the state of mind that gave rise to it, partakes of the poetic

24. "Un poète . . . n'a pas pour fonction de ressentir l'état poétique: ceci est une affaire privée. Il a pour fonction de le créer chez les autres," "Poésie et pensée abstraite," *Variété*, V, 138. "Poetry and Abstract Thought," *The Art of Poetry*, p. 60.

state. Consequently, as the activities of poet, reader, and poem are all viewed in the same light—that of the *état poétique*—the latter becomes an irreducible point for both the poetic process and its result. Whatever other functions it may perform (for it may also occur elsewhere), the poetic state becomes that criterion of difference through which poetry and nonpoetry can be distinguished.

We have compared the poetic state with the mind's capacity to abstract as Valéry explained it in the Leonardo essay. Although these terms are very closely related, we can now see that this comparison was only partially correct. The two concepts share the intent—the organization of perceptions into a whole—and both involve an awareness of the self's isolation (the poet's or artist's or that of any discerning intelligence). Moreover, the *état poétique* implies passivity: inspiration, as it were, comes to the poet who receives it, then uses it to develop the poem. But unlike "abstraction"—and unlike the Cartesian *cogito*—the poetic state, as an isolated moment, is deeply nonrational. It represents the single point which Valéry allows the "affective" side of the self. In *Le Calepin d'un poète* he described the poet's work as an "expectation—for the unexpected word—through hearing."[25] Once more we seem to confront the traditional posture of the romantic poet as percipient who remolds his sensations as he transforms them into art, inspired by their hidden analogies or buried effects. Noteworthy is the emphasis on *ear*, to supplement and, in this case, to replace the *eye* as the visionary's principal organ, since the *ear* conforms well to Valéry's general poetic stance in favor of musical numbers and dispositions. Yet, as in all of Valéry's work, while it starts out with the romantic premise—the isolation of the self, its tenuous relationship to other selves and all "elements borrowed from reality," the idea of the poet as passive percipient—it turns in a different direction. Being pre-romantic in tone, it sees the forming inspiration, though irrational and unexpected and communicated by the senses, as *ultimately* rational. In various "auto-

25. "A Poet's Notebook," *The Art of Poetry*, pp. 174–75. "Calepin d'un poète," *Oeuvres*, I, Pléiade (Paris: Gallimard, 1957), 1448.

biographical" sketches Valéry sounds the identical theme: how he was seized by sudden unexplained rhythms which made him view all disparate experience as a unity, evoking a "poetic state," or how "Le Cimetière marin" began with a brief rhythmical unit (like a musical theme) which was expanded and varied during the subsequent "construction."[26] In each case, the unexpected, irrational element is present. But in each case we also encounter M. Teste's impressive feat of consciousness in reassembling multiplicity as unity through the power of his mind. All acts of perception, Valéry wrote in *Léonard*, of necessity involve abstraction. This statement defines the poet's state of mind at the moment of creation most succinctly.

In following Valéry's theory of creation to the point where it merges with his conception of the poem, we realize not only the role played by the *état poétique* as a source of creation but also the burden it must assume for criticism. For whatever else henceforth happens in and to the poem, as the poet endlessly works and reworks its phrases, expands its images, and constructs its rhythms, the poetic element, the criterion that defines it as poetry, remains the *état poétique*. It is therefore not only a signal or symptom of the self at its moment of inspiration, but a *junction* of the poet's "involved self" and the progressively more and more impersonal poem detaching itself from the original moment in its musical and geometrical variations.

The "subjective objectivity" which we noted in Valéry's concept of poetic language is also reflected in his manner of telescoping instantaneous inspiration and the task of construction in the poetic process as a whole. And by analyzing the process of creation, as Valéry views it, we arrive at results similar to those he notes in his critiques of poets like Poe, Baudelaire, and Mallarmé, or of novelists like Flaubert and Stendhal. In this way, he approaches a solution to the perennial problem of distinguishing between the experiences of "life" and the formal properties of the poem as a work of "art." In

26. The same anecdote is told in "Mémoires d'un poème" and in "Poésie et pensée abstraite."

fact, Valéry's view of the problem recalls an almost Kantian sleight-of-hand: the poetic state, as a general response to an inner impulse that orders seemingly fortuitous perceptions, corresponds to the Kantian internalization of experience and its organization by means of categories—also a kind of "subjective objectivity." And as for Kant the general theory of perception is made to correspond to its appropriate analogues in art—the *Analytic* of the first critique paralleling the *Analytic of the Beautiful* in the third—so for Valéry the poet's "structure of consciousness" becomes the starting point, as well as an essential ingredient, in the poem's construction.

As Valéry shows us in discussing the language of Baudelaire, the *état poétique* and its *fabrication* both become part of the poetic act. They correspond to the isolation of the self in its act of cognition, its awareness, and its subsequent attempt to sift accidents and to form concepts. Valéry showed how this can be done in the most varied ways, bringing Poe's "Philosophy of Composition" to bear on essays like "Mémoires d'un poème" and on descriptions of the construction of "Le Cimetière marin." Modifying, amplifying the particular philosophical relationships Valéry perceived in Poe, he followed a basic pattern. With Poe, he showed again and again how the poet begins with a single line or word and how, in trying to communicate the intended effect from the poem to the reader, he fabricates a lyrical structure through the medium and rhythm of language. Poems, for Valéry, are not dreams or confessions (i.e., not part of life inchoate and impure from which the poetic state takes its rise) but are words produced by variations of consciousness within musical or rhythmical patterns that could not be found in the unstructured vagaries of the mind. Instead, musical harmonies are created through the medium of language. And language is the material the mind uses in poetry as pigments and canvas in painting, or the observations and calculations the mind combines in the different, yet creatively similar, realms of science and invention.

In following Valéry's descriptions of the creative process, as in following his appraisals of other writers, we find that the poetic act reaches its linguistic, formally accessible manifestation in the concrete work of art—the object that can be read and listened to. Mind here is viewed as condensed into the publicly "visible" medium of words. As in the case of Wagner, so in Valéry, such a view stretches the utility of words beyond their original function and approaches dimensions that point to the nonverbal. Indeed, such a use of words, as he suggests in "Mémoires d'un poème," would be preferable. Yet here, too, we arrive at that paradoxical "subjective objectivity." To the extent that a poem is literature, mind of necessity is related to it through language, and the initial impulse is realized in linguistic form. Language thus extends its function from being the formal matter of poetry to being poetry itself—the way in which sense experience is reshaped to achieve greater precision, to be given fresh meaning and form. As for poets like Ezra Pound and Wallace Stevens, so for Valéry, literature is an extension and application of the properties of language (as literary history is actually the history of the language as well). But the language used in poetry—being neither denotative nor connotative in our sense —exists only for itself. Valéry cites the anecdote of Degas's colloquy with Mallarmé. When Degas, trying his hand at poetry, complained that he had all the ideas but could not fit them into words, Mallarmé answered that ideas have no place in poetry, that poetry is exclusively composed of words.[27] This, of course, is the crux of the distinction between poetry and prose which forms the substance of "Poésie et pensée abstraite."

Poetry, then, is a mental act which finds its distillation in language: the linguistic presence gives the poem a shape of solidity and makes it appear as if it were a thing. Figures formed by poetic language (used like symbols in mathematics) are inseparable from the words which describe them. On the one hand, the poet is required to sift the words he uses, to employ them in their precise and pure original value; on the other hand, he must use them for what they are in themselves, not for any ideas they may stand for. Although much poetry

27. "Poésie et pensée abstraite," *Variété*, V, 141. "Poetry and Abstract Thought," *The Art of Poetry*, p. 63.

may contain elements of "prose" (the use of words to state or express ideas or actions), its essential characteristic, as a configuration of words, is to develop its own mode of being, its own "universe." Needless to say, this universe, being a creation of *mind* through language, retains the outlines and characteristics of the "structure of consciousness."

The distinction between poetry and prose (or abstract thought), which Valéry developed in his famous essay, is useful not only as a new description of these two different ways of using words but also as a statement about the nature of poetry and its place in Valéry's scheme. We are again faced with the duality between the poem as object (the linguistic unit) and the poem as activity (the act of consciousness). As in his discussions of Baudelaire and other writers, Valéry shows that poetry is superior to prose (as the lyric is superior to the novel) because it can exist as a verbal world sufficient unto itself. To clarify this point Valéry employed various metaphors: the poem is likened to a machine inducing the poetic state in the reader; the poem is seen as dance (opposed to prose as purposive walk); the poem is a self-sufficient world whereas the prose statement is nothing in itself, because it derives all its meaning from the ideas or objects it designates. Each of these metaphors suggests that basically the poem is an act or a state of mind utilizing language.

The view of the poem as a replica of the "structure of consciousness," then, explains many of the well-known dicta of Valéry's poetics. Form and content are indistinguishable, for the meaning of words (i.e., their paraphrasable content) is not significant to the poem as a formal unit using words as self-contained symbols for a mental state (the *état poétique*). Poems, being actually forms of mental activity, are therefore never finished. In his essay on "Le Cimetière marin," Valéry contrasts an academic analysis with the poem's actual state. The academician's clever explication, Valéry felt, did not really meet the substance or meaning of the poem, because he lacked a clear comprehension of the distinction between poetry and prose, because he saw the poem as a finished unit (i.e., exclusively as a thing) rather than as the open-ended activity it actually was. Valéry contrasted this mistaken treatment of his poem with the description of how it had actually found its way into print. He had varied the initial theme, and changed and reworked the poem, endlessly until one day Jacques Rivière, reading and liking it, carried it off to be printed. There are several assumptions behind this story, but the most important one, of course, is that the poem, if it is an "object" at all, is a *jeu d'esprit*, a playing with words and images for their own sake, adumbrating the "poetic" state of mind. And it also shows that the poem as such is seen as the equivalent of the process of creation which went into its making.

The poem as "universe," as "machine," as both architectonic structure and open activity of consciousness, is most clearly seen through the analogy of the dance. In his essay "Au Sujet du 'Cimetière marin,'" Valéry writes, after discussing the great difference between the composition of prose and that of poetry:

> In the same way, in the art of the Dance, the state of the dancer . . . being the object of that art, the movements and displacements of the bodies have no limit in *space*—no visible aim, no *thing* which, being reached, annuls them; and it never occurs to anyone to impose on choreographic actions the law of *nonpoetic* but *useful* acts, which is: to be accomplished *with the greatest economy of effort* and in the *shortest possible way*.[28]

This idea is most fully developed in the dialogue "L'Âme et la danse" (1923), in which the reciprocal displacement of space by "number" (music in time) is seen equally as a mutual displacement of body by mind.[29] It is this kind of interchange that

28. "Concerning *Le Cimetière marin*," *The Art of Poetry*, pp. 146–47. "Ainsi, dans l'art de la Danse, l'état du danseur (ou celui de l'amateur de ballets), étant l'objet de cet art, les mouvements et les déplacements des corps n'ont point de terme dans *l'espace*,—point de but visible; point de *chose*, qui jointe les annule; et il ne vient à l'esprit de personne d'imposer à des actions chorégraphiques la loi des actes *non-poétiques*, mais *utiles*, qui est de s'effectuer *avec la plus grande économie de forces*, et *selon les plus courts chemins*." "Au Sujet du 'Cimetière marin,'" *Variété*, III, 62.

29. "L'Âme et la danse," *Oeuvres*, II, Pléiade (Paris: Gallimard, 1960), 171–72. ("Dance and the Soul," *Dialogues*, trans. William McCausland Stewart, *Collected Works of Paul Valery*, ed. Jackson

distinguishes Valéry's notion of the poem as both a linguistic whole and an activity of consciousness, a *jeu d'esprit* with words and a verbal "universe." And it is just this kind of relationship which repeats in the realm of artistic creation the processes of abstraction from the "given" phenomena of experience and of their reconstruction in freshly formed wholes. One need not press the Kantian analogy too far to see that Valéry managed to find his own terms for an analogous solution to the disjunction between the (creative) activity of the self and the formal world of the poetic work of art. By becoming someone other than himself (the embodiment of himself in the poem through the creative act), yet by resolutely remaining himself, the poet has composed an analogue of his own acts of consciousness yet has set them apart from himself through the formal elaborations. The figure of the dance as an activity that exists through space but displaces space, and that has no "reality" (i.e., no purposive function) outside itself, is the most profound metaphor for Valéry's response to the perennial disjunction between the artist's self and the form which he has made yet which must ultimately exist by itself.

The foregoing exposition of Valéry's views was designed not so much as a general introduction to his poetics as an illustration of his central position in the development of modern critical thought. By interpreting the poem as the creative act that gave rise to it, yet by viewing it also as separate and distinct, he brought the romantic "paradox" up to date. He sought to reconcile the private and the public aspects of the poem—to perform that arduous transition from the feelings of "life" to the "emotions" of art. In this sense he achieved for modern poetics that Copernican revolution in criticism which Kant had attempted for all knowledge. The self-sustained "harmony" of the poem's "world" is also equivalent to a state of mind.

Valéry's contribution to criticism, then, has been his use of the structure of consciousness to solve the paradoxical simul-

---

Matthews, Bollingen Series, IV [New York: Pantheon Books, 1956], 56–58.)

taneity, yet discrepancy, in the function of the poem as a mental act and in its existence as artifact. This, as we have noted, is what the romantic ''paradox'' was about, and this is also the problem T. S. Eliot attempted to solve when he formulated the theory of the ''objective correlative.'' To be sure, Valéry did not address himself to questions about the legitimacy of ''ethical'' or any other kind of programmatic relevance of the poem to the external world. In fact, he said specifically that all thought, all ''ideas,'' must remain in the realm of prose. And although he felt that there probably remain ''prose'' elements in most poetry, he clearly did not admit didactic or programmatic functions of language into the temple of pure poetry. Yet his analysis of the poetic act as a combination of the *état poétique* and the elaboration of form suggests the point at which he began to deal with the problem. He saw a clear line from poet to poem to reader, all three partaking of the ''poetic state.'' He maintained the notion of the poem as an autonomous work of art; yet by including both the creation and the effect of the poem within a comprehensive universe of consciousness (the poet as creator; the poem as ''machine'' causing effects in the reader), he maintained the connection between the work and its human context. This is particularly true of his analysis of the relationship between poet and poem, which rests on the analogy between the harmony of the poet's state of consciousness and the harmonious and rhythmic ''world'' he creates. To comprehend the poem through the creative process, to see it simultaneously as process and object, was the enduring achievement of Paul Valéry.

BIBLIOGRAPHY

WORKS BY PAUL VALÉRY

Oeuvres. Edition established and annotated by Jean Hytier. 2 vols. Bibliothèque de la Pléiade. Paris: Gallimard, 1957–60 (as specified below).

I. *Poésies*, *Mélange*, *Variété* (1957).

II. *Monsieur Teste*, *Dialogues* (incl. ''Eupalinos ou l'Architecte,'' ''L'Âme et la danse,'' ''Dialogue de l'arbre,'' ''L'Idée fixe, ou Deux hommes à la mer,'' ''Mon Faust''), *Histoires brisées, Tel quel, Mauvaises pensées, Regards sur le monde actuel et autres essais, Pièces sur l'art* (1960).

These volumes contain all of Valéry's writings except the following: *Vues* (see below), his correspondence, and the complete *Cahiers* (see below). Jean Hytier's notes are most complete, listing variants, sources, reprintings, minor writings, and including essays, letters, poems, fragments, and notes, some of which had not been previously published. Extensive, if not highly selective, bibliography lists translations and presents a large segment of the corpus of writing on Valéry (grouped by publication dates).

Oeuvres. 12 vols. Paris: Le Sagittaire (Vols. A and B) and Gallimard (all other volumes), 1931–50 (as specified below). Special edition in quarto volumes.

A. "L'Âme et la danse"; "Eupalinos ou l'architecte" (1931).
B. *Monsieur Teste* (1931).
C. *Album de vers anciens, La Jeune Parque, Charmes* (1933).
D. *Variété* (1934).
E. *Discours* (1935).
F. *L'Idée fixe* (1936).
G. *Variété* II (1937).
H. *Pièces sur l'art* (1938).
I. *Léonard de Vinci* (1938).
J. *Regards sur le monde actuel* (1938).
K. *Conférences* (1939).
L. *Ecrits sur Mallarmé* (1950).

(*The Collected Works of Paul Valéry.* 15 vols., published and projected. Edited by Jackson Matthews. The Bollingen Series. New York: Pantheon Books, 1956–67. Princeton: Princeton University Press, 1968–. Specific information is listed below. [It should be noted that in any future edition of the *Collected Works*, all volumes will bear the imprint of Princeton University Press regardless of the original publisher.]

I. *Poems* [not yet published].
II. *Poems in the Rough.* Translated by Hilary Corke. Introduction by Octave Nadal. Princeton: Princeton University Press, 1968.
III. *Plays.* Translated by David Paul and Robert Fitzgerald. Introduction by Francis Fergusson. New York: Pantheon Books, 1960.
IV. *Dialogues.* Translated by William M. Stewart. Two prefaces by Wallace Stevens. New York: Pantheon Books, 1956.

V. *Idée fixe*. Translated by David Paul. Introduction by Philip Wheelwright. New York: Pantheon Books, 1965.

VI. *Mr. Teste* [not yet published].

VII. *The Art of Poetry*. Translated by Denise Folliot. Introduction by T. S. Eliot. New York: Pantheon Books, 1958. [See also the paperback edition of this volume. New York: Random House, Vintage Books, 1961.]

VIII. *Leonardo, Poe, and Mallarmé* [not yet published].

IX. *Masters and Friends*. Translated by Martin Turnell. Introduction by Joseph Frank. Princeton: Princeton University Press, 1968.

X. *History and Politics*. Translated by Denise Folliot and Jackson Matthews. Introduction by Salvador de Madariaga. New York: Pantheon Books, 1962.

XI. *Occasions*. Translated by Roger Shattuck and Frederick Brown. Introduction by Roger Shattuck. Princeton: Princeton University Press, 1970.

XII. *Degas, Manet, Morisot*. Translated by David Paul. Introduction by Douglas Cooper. New York: Pantheon Books, 1960.

XIII. *Aesthetics*. Translated by Ralph Manheim. Introduction by Herbert Read. New York: Pantheon Books, 1964.

XIV. *Analects*. Translated by Stuart Gilbert. Introduction by W. H. Auden. Princeton: Princeton University Press, 1970.

XV. *Moi* and Bibliography [not yet published].

Cahiers. 29 vols. Paris: Centre Nouvelle de la Recherche Scientifique, 1957–61. Published serially, complete in these 29 volumes. See also, below, Edmée de la Rochefoucauld's and Judith Robinson's guide to and analyses of Valéry's notebooks.

Discours sur Emile Verhaeren. Brussels: Stols, 1928. See *Oeuvres*, Pléiade, I, 756–62.

Ecrits divers sur Stéphane Mallarmé. Paris: Gallimard, 1950. See *Oeuvres*, Pléiade, I, 619–79, 706–9.

Introduction à la méthode de Léonard de Vinci. Recent edition. Paris: Gallimard, 1964. See *Oeuvres*, Pléiade, I, 1153–1268.

Introduction à la poétique. Paris: Gallimard, 1938.

L'Idée fixe. Paris: Gallimard, 1934. See *Oeuvres*, Pléiade, II, 195–275.

Mélange. Paris: Gallimard, 1941. See *Oeuvres*, Pléiade, I, 285–425.

Monsieur Teste. Paris: Editions du Sagittaire, 1931. See *Oeuvres*, Pléiade, II, 11–75. (Translated by Jackson Matthews. New York: Alfred A. Knopf, 1948.)

"Propos me concernant." In: André Berne-Joffroy. *Présence de Valéry*, pp. 9–61. Témoignages. Brussels: Raoul Henry. Présences. Paris: Plon, 1944.

Souvenirs poétiques. Taken down by a listener in the course of a lecture at Brussels, 9 January 1942. Paris: Guy le Prat, 1947.

Tel quel. 2 vols. Paris: Gallimard, 1941. See *Oeuvres*, Pléiade, II, 473–784.

Variété. I. Paris: NRF, 1924. II. Paris: Gallimard, 1930. III. Paris: Gallimard, 1936. IV. Paris: Gallimard, 1938. V. Paris: Gallimard, 1945. Miscellaneous collections of Valéry's critical, aesthetic, and philosophical writings, including the Leonardo essays and other material cited in the essay. Most of these essays are reprinted —and regrouped according to subject matter—in the section labeled *Variété* of the *Oeuvres*, Pléiade, I, 427–1510. However, this edition also includes many additional essays gathered from periodicals, lectures, etc. To locate any particular essay in the *Oeuvres*, consult the detailed tables of contents at the back of each volume of the Pléiade edition.

(*Variety* I. Translated by Malcolm Cowley. New York: Harcourt, Brace, 1927. *Variety* II. Translated by William Bradley. New York: Harcourt, Brace, 1938. Both volumes contain translations of various essays collected in the *Variété* volumes, including the Leonardo essays and other writings [although they do not fully correspond to the French *Variété* I and II]. They are being rapidly superseded by the translation of the Bollingen edition of the *Works*. However, since some of the most important essays, such as the Leonardo articles, have not yet appeared in the Bollingen translation, the reader is directed to these volumes in lieu of the improved versions. Reference is made to the *Variety* volume only where more up-to-date translations are not yet available. One piece from *Variété* I: "I Sometimes Said to Stéphane Mallarmé." Translated by Malcolm Cowley. *Kenyon Review* 27 [1965]: 94–112.)

Vues. Paris: La Table Ronde, 1948.

(*Selected Writings*. Edited by Anthony Bower and J. Laughlin. New York: New Directions, 1950. A rather haphazard collection of Valéry's poetry, essays, and various selections from some of his major critical texts, being rapidly displaced by the Bollingen translation of the *Works*.)

SELECTED WORKS ON PAUL VALÉRY'S CRITICISM AND THOUGHT

Books

Aigrisse, Gilberte. *Psychanalyse de Paul Valéry*. Paris: Editions Universitaires, 1964.

Bémol, Maurice. *La Méthode critique de Paul Valéry*. Paris: Nizet, 1950, 1961. A fairly complete work on Valéry's practical and theoretical criticism, covering critical method, relationship of method to theory, etc.

———. *Variations sur Valéry*. Vol. 1. Sarrebruck: Université de la Sarre, 1952. Vol. 2. Paris: Nizet, 1959. Contains chapters on theory of language, Valéry's theory of literature, method (including Leonardo da Vinci), aesthetic theories, etc.

Benoist, Pierre F. *Les Essais de Paul Valéry, vers et prose, expliqués et commentés*. With a portrait of Valéry by Picasso. Paris: Editions de la Pensée Moderne, 1964. This volume takes the word "essay" in its widest sense, including (as the title indicates) poems, some of the dialogues, etc. This flexible use of the term leads to a rather general tone and to somewhat idiosyncratic conceptions. Interesting but not overly useful for a study of Valéry's criticism.

Berne-Joffroy, André. *Présence de Valéry*. Témoignages. Brussels: Raoul Henry. Présences. Paris: Plon, 1944.

Bolle, Louis. *Les Lettres et l'absolu*. Geneva: Perret-Gentil, 1959. The first part of this study is devoted to Valéry's thought, method, and aesthetic.

———. *Paul Valéry*. Fribourg: Egloff, 1944. A rather pervasive study of Valéry's views, particularly of the relationship among art, artist, and criticism. Pertinent to and useful for the study of Valéry's critical theory.

Bosanquet, Theodora. *Paul Valéry*. London: Hogarth Press, 1933. An appraisal of Valéry as a thinker and critic, stressing his personal relationship with Mallarmé, his literary indebtedness to Poe, etc. One chapter is specifically devoted to the Leonardo cycle, another to Valéry's essays, etc. A good, if dated, summary for readers in English.

Bowra, C. M. *The Heritage of Symbolism*. London: Macmillan, 1933. This famous book defining the reconstitution of the symbolist idea in twentieth-century poetry and poetics begins its main argument with a chapter on Valéry (chap. 2).

Cain, Lucienne. *Trois Essais sur Paul Valéry*. Paris: Gallimard, 1958. Each of the three essays seeks to elucidate another aspect of Valéry's work. The first essay, entitled "L'Utilisation du monde sensible," deals essentially with the development of Valéry's sensibility—his "thought shaping itself"—and includes a comparison with and comment upon the criticism of Mallarmé. The second essay, "Poe et Valéry," is essentially concerned with critical method. The third essay, "L'Etre vivant selon Valéry," stresses the Leonardo cycle and concludes with comments upon the renewed simplicity of Valéry's thought.

Chauvet, Louis. *La Poétique de Paul Valéry*. Liège: Dynamo, 1966.

Cioran, E. M. *Valéry face à ses idoles*. Gloses. Paris: L'Herne, 1970.

Doisy, Marcel. *Paul Valéry: intelligence et poésie*. Paris: Le Cercle du Livre, 1952. A pertinent study of the relationship between Valéry's thought and his art. Includes a full chapter on Leonardo da Vinci (chap. 6).

Eigeldinger, Marc, ed. *Paul Valéry. Essais et témoignages inédits*. Neuchâtel: La Baconnière, 1945. Essays by several hands on Valéry's poetry, criticism, and philosophy. Contributors include Marcel Raymond, Louis Bolle, Jean Starobinski, Théophil Spoerri, and others.

Eliot, T. S. *From Poe to Valéry*. New York: Harcourt, Brace, 1948. See also "From Poe to Valéry," *To Criticize the Critic* (New York: Farrar Straus, 1965), pp. 27–42. This well-known essay by T. S. Eliot traces, in effect, the evolution of modern poetry and poetic language from its beginnings in Poe to its apex (and at least partial *dénouement*) in Valéry.

Gaede, Edouard. *Nietzsche et Valéry*. Paris: Gallimard, 1962. This study of the relationship between Valéry's and Nietzsche's thought is useful for a study of Valéry's poetics.

Genet, Louis. *Autour de Paul Valéry*. Preface by Paul Valéry. 2d ed. Grenoble: Arthaud, 1944. A complete, if somewhat dated, study of Valéry's ideas, including ideas on method, poetics, and aesthetic. Includes a good discussion of Leonardo.

Grubbs, Henry A. *Paul Valéry*. New York: Twayne Publishers, 1968. A well-organized account of Valéry's work in the Twayne World Authors Series, constituting a fine introduction in English for the interested reader. Specifically germane is chapter 5, "The Poetic Theory of Paul Valéry." Good selected bibliography of primary and secondary texts, including bibliographical notes and comments.

Guiraud, Pierre. *Langage et versification*. Paris: Klincksieck, 1953. Although this book is mostly devoted to metrics, it contains a pertinent chapter on poetics and Valéry's theory of "fabrication" (chap. 9).

Hytier, Jean. *La Poétique de Paul Valéry*. Paris: Colin, 1953. (*The Poetics of Paul Valéry*. Translated by Richard Howard. New York: Doubleday, Anchor Books, 1966. See also current imprint: Magnolia, Mass.: Peter Smith, n.d.) A full study of Valéry's poetics, "classical" in its proportion, volume, and relative completeness.

Ince, W. N. *The Poetic Theory of Paul Valéry: Inspiration and Technique.* Leicester: Leicester University Press, 1961. A useful and perceptive introduction to Valéry's poetics for readers in English.

Lanfranchi, Geneviève. *Paul Valéry et l'expérience du moi pur*. Lausanne: Mermod, 1958.

La Rochefoucauld, Edmée de. *En lisant les Cahiers de Paul Valéry*. 3 vols. Paris: Editions Universitaires, 1964–67 (as specified below).

I. *Cahiers*, I–X (1894–1925). (1964)

II. *Cahiers*, XI–XX (1925–38). (1966)

III. *Cahiers*, XXI–XXIX (1938–45). (1967)

Most helpful guide to and analysis of Valéry's notebooks. (See also entry *Cahiers*, above.)

———. *Images de Paul Valéry*. Strasbourg: Le Roux, 1949. Includes a chapter, "La Poétique selon Valéry," which contains a discussion of Leonardo.

———. *Paul Valéry*. Paris: Editions Universitaires, 1954. Includes chapters on *Charmes* and poetic theories as well as on Valéry as essayist.

Latour, Jean de. *Examen de Valéry*. Paris: Gallimard, 1935.

Lefèvre, Frédéric. *Entretiens avec Paul Valéry*. Preface by Henri Bremond. Paris: Le Livre, 1926.

Mackay, Agnes Ethel. *The Universal Self: A Study of Paul Valéry*. Toronto: University of Toronto Press, 1961. A useful, scholarly study especially appropriate for the serious student seeking an exposition in English of Valéry's poetics (and of his concept of the objectified *moi*).

Mondor, Henri. *La Précocité de Valéry*. Paris: Gallimard, 1957.

Noulet, Emile, ed. *Suites: Mallarmé, Rimbaud, Valéry*. Paris: Nizet, 1964. Contains valuable contributions of criticism on Valéry's major writings (poetry and poetics), including Bémol, Hytier, and others. Especially pertinent is Noulet's own discussion of *Variété*, III.

———. *Paul Valéry. Etudes*. Brussels: La Renaissance du Livre, 1950. Pertinent are sections discussing the *Teste* and *Léonard* cycles. See especially the chapter "Paul Valéry et la philosophie" and its references to Bergson and Leonardo.

Parisier-Plottel, Jeanine. *Les Dialogues de Paul Valéry*. Paris: Presses Universitaires, 1960.

Parize, Jean H. *Essai sur la pensée et l'art de Paul Valéry*. Paris: Richard, 1946.

Pelmont, Raoul André. *Paul Valéry et les beaux arts*. Cambridge, Mass.: Harvard University Press, 1949.

Perche, Louis. *Valéry: Les Limites de l'humain*. Paris: Editions du Centurion, 1966. A fine study that seeks to elucidate Valéry's mysticism and his equal devotion to the "lucid" function of mind and words. The result is a general and reasonably complete treatise on Valéry's thought and work, including his critical and aesthetic writings. His *method*, involving both Descartes and Leonardo, receives particular attention.

Pire, François. *La Tentation du sensible chez Paul Valéry*. Paris: Renaissance du Livre, 1964.

Pommier, Jean-Joseph Marie. *Paul Valéry et la création littéraire*. Paris: Editions de l'Encyclopédie Française, 1945. Useful particularly from the point of view of the relationship between the poem and its process of creation.

Prévost, Jean. *La Pensée de Paul Valéry*. Nîmes: Fabre, 1926.

Rauhut. Franz. *Paul Valéry, Geist und Mythos*. Munich: Hueber, 1930. An excellent if somewhat dated ideological study of Valéry. This book is especially remarkable for the parallels it draws between Valéry's theory of poetry and its Cartesian and its German idealistic elements. A useful book.

Raymond, Marcel. *Paul Valéry et la tentation de l'esprit*. Neuchâtel: La Baconnière, 1946. A standard work of criticism, noteworthy for its chapters on the *Teste* and *Léonard* cycles and the discussion of the relationship between thought and Valéry's critique of language.

Rideau, Emile. *Introduction à la pensée de Paul Valéry*. Paris: Desclée de Brouwer, 1944.

Robinson, Judith. *L'Analyse de l'esprit dans les cahiers de Valéry*. Paris: J. Corti, 1963. A useful analysis of the notebooks and Valéry's thought in connection with them.

Scarfe, Francis. *The Art of Paul Valéry*. London: Heinemann, 1954.

Sewell, Elizabeth. *Paul Valéry: The Mind in the Mirror*. Studies in Modern European Literature and Thought. Cambridge: Bowes and Bowes, 1952. A brief, interesting essay on the relationship between Valéry's concept of the self as it is developed both in his poetry and in his critical and philosophical prose. The essay is necessarily limited by its brevity, but it is most useful and suggestive.

Shaw, Priscilla Washburn. *Rilke, Valéry, Yeats: The Domain of the Self*. New Brunswick: Rutgers University Press, 1964. Although this book (including its chapter on Valéry) is devoted exclusively to a reading of poetry from a specific point of view, it is also most useful for a study of criticism. The chapter on Valéry demonstrates many of the theses about the relationship between poetry and the self which Valéry discusses in his critical writings.

Soulairol, Jean. *Paul Valéry*. Paris: La Colombe, 1952.

Thibaudet, Albert. *Paul Valéry*. Paris: B. Grasset, 1923.

Essays and Articles

Bémol, Maurice. "La Représentation de l'esprit et l'expression de l'exprimable." *Revue d'Esthétique* 15 (1962): 139–65.

Boudot, Pierre. "Nietzsche et Valéry." *La Revue des Lettres Modernes*, nos. 76–77 (1962–63), pp. 57–63.

Brombert, Victor. "Valéry: The Dance of Words." *Hudson Review* 21 (1968): 675–80.

Burne, Glenn S. "An Approach to Valéry's *Leonardo*." *French Review* 34 (1959): 26–34.

Decker, Henry. "Baudelaire and the Valéry Concept of Pure Poetry." *Symposium* 19 (1965): 155–61.

Diéguez, Manuel de. "Critique et méthode." *Critique* 20 (1964): 955–62.

Frank, Joseph. "Paul Valéry: *Masters and Friends*." *Sewanee Review* 75 (1968): 393–414. See also entry in *Collected Works*, IX, above.

Genette, Gérard. "La Littérature comme tel." In *Figures*, pp. 253–74. Tel Quel. Paris: Seuil, 1966.

Gerlötel, Eugène. "Méditations valéryennes: Principes de recherches conformes à la poésie classique." *Revue d'Esthétique* 10 (1957): 65–76.

Green, René. "Valéry's Criticism of Rousseau." *Modern Language Journal* 49 (1965): 41–47.

Hytier, Jean. "The Refusals of Valéry." *Yale French Studies* 2, no. 1 (Spring–Summer 1949): 105–36. ("Les Refus de Valéry." In *Questions de littérature: Etudes valéryennes et autres,* pp. 56–81. Geneva: Droz, 1967.)

Matthews, Jackson. "The Poetics of Paul Valéry." *Romanic Review* 46 (1955): 203–17.

Richthofen, E. von. "Quelques observations fondamentales de Valéry sur le problème de la forme, contenues dans ces *Cahiers*." *L'Esprit Créateur*, no. 4 (1964), pp. 28–33.

Robinson, Judith. "The Place of Literary and Artistic Creation in Valéry's Thought." *Modern Language Review* 56 (1959): 497–514.

———. "Language, Physics, and Mathematics in Valéry's *Cahiers*." *Modern Language Review* 55 (1960): 519–36.

———. "Valéry critique de Bergson." *Cahiers de l'Association Internationale des Etudes Françaises*, no. 17 (1965), pp. 203–15.

———. "New Light on Paul Valéry." *French Studies* 22 (1968): 40–50.

Saisselin, Rémy G. "Paul Valéry: The Aesthetics of the Grand Seigneur." *Journal of Aesthetics and Art Criticism* 19 (1959): 47–52.

John Porter Houston

2

Proust, Gourmont, and the Symbolist Heritage

By the end of the nineteenth century French criticism had, on the whole, become indifferent to contemporary literature and its aesthetic preoccupations. Journalistic criticism had little patience with the convoluted *symboliste* manner, while academic criticism concerned itself primarily with problems in the evolution and social background of earlier literature. In other words, there was a lack of critics capable of reading books, both recent and older, from a serious and distinctly modern point of view. This void was finally filled in France, as in the English-speaking world, by a number of writer-critics who established their reputations between 1900 and 1920. Of these Proust and Remy de Gourmont were among the earliest and were perhaps the closest to late nineteenth-century writers in their conceptions of style.

Marcel Proust is not usually thought of as a critic, but in his occasional comments on literature he revealed himself as one of the most subtle French aesthetic theorists and one of the first modern French analysts of style. Proust's criticism represents, on the one hand, a break with typical nineteenth-century approaches to literature (exemplified by Sainte-Beuve); on the other, it is a great coherent summation of aesthetic ideas emanating from the symbolists. First of all, the general tone of Proust's criticism recalls *symboliste* attitudes: art is exalted at the expense of life, the real and the ideal are contrasted in a vaguely Platonic way, and a theological-liturgical vocabulary emphasizes the replacement of Christianity by aestheticism. Furthermore, Proust would have endorsed Mallarmé's famous comment on the intangible but real character of the world of language: "I say 'a flower,' and . . . musically there arises the very Idea of it, and delicate, the one absent from all bouquets."[1] This paradoxical playing with the notion of reality—in which aesthetic perception seems more "real" than ordinary apprehension—is joined, for both Proust and the symbolists, with an admiration for analogy and metaphor as the great sources of art.

However, what is so often vague rhapsodizing in the critical writings of Baudelaire, Mallarmé, and others becomes a harmonious philosophy of art in Proust. No small credit for this is due to the fact that Proust had a "culture of ideas" far superior to that of most French writers. His aesthetics are, in fact, merely one facet of a coherent and cogent system of thought.

The philosophy that Proust studied at the *lycée* was a Gallic version of German idealism, a "spiritualist" reaction against scientific materialism. Throughout his life Proust was to refer occasionally to such basic doctrines as Kant's categories, and the whole tenor of his thought reflects the idealist emphasis on subjectivity, on the distinction between phenomena and the "true" realm of the noumenal, and on the importance of intuition. The personal element which Proust introduced into the idealist philosophy of the two realms, the phenomenal and the noumenal, has to do with habit and perception; he considers the intuition of noumena as possible but as generally suppressed by habit. Proust also makes a connection between the memory of events and the reality which lies beneath appearances. Obviously Proust is striving to depreciate our ordinary experience of the outer world in order to enhance the value of stylized impressions of it—memory, dream, literary narration. The mental character of the external world is proved by the example of dreams as well as by the survival of the past as an active influence upon us.[2] In fact, the point of

1. "Je dis: une fleur! et . . . musicalement se lève, idée même et suave, l'absente de tous bouquets." *Oeuvres complètes*, Pléiade (Paris: Gallimard, 1951), p. 857.

2. See *A la Recherche du temps perdu*, Pléiade (Paris: Gallimard, 1954), 3:914 and 2:418. All translations from *A la Recherche* are my own.

departure of Proust's idealism might be characterized as "the contradiction between memory and nothingness." Other aspects of Proust's thought are more obviously derived from German philosophy; the unknowable thing-in-itself becomes another person's subjectivity, while aesthetic pleasure, assimilated to the irrationality of dream or of memory, provides the sole means of escaping from the frustrating world of time and appearances. The peculiar value of art is that it allows us to participate in another person's vision, to achieve knowledge of someone else. Proust places great emphasis upon this; the individual subjectivity in all its discreteness is the object of aesthetic contemplation. Though Proust speaks occasionally of "essences," he does not mean anything like Platonic ideas; for him there are no abstractions more true and harmonious than aesthetic impressions. The reality of art (Proust uses "reality" in both an idealist philosophical sense and in an antithetical ordinary one) is concrete.

The creative process and the relation of the finished book to the reader receive, for obvious reasons, far more attention from Proust than from most critics. He conceives of the impulse toward creativity as residing in the irrational psychological states mentioned above; involuntary memory, dreams, the sudden vision of enchanting landscapes, and moments of awakening call upon the writer to preserve them. The artist "translates" the emotive burden of these moments into his chosen medium, taking care that the totality of the experience be preserved, for Proust anticipates Eliot's "objective correlative" when he insists that disparate, seemingly unrelated impressions all contribute to a whole. Proust does not try to explain how music, the highest art for him, springs from the composer's emotion, but in regard to literature he gives a specific example. The narrator of *A la Recherche* sees the steeples of Martinville, does not understand that their beauty lies in his subjectivity rather than in these banal spires themselves, but writes a prose poem which "rids" him of the steeples and their secret. This is not a process of description and notation, the vulgar pseudo-art of the realist, but of transposing emotion into language. Later on, the narrator will realize that art is a redemption of the artist's otherwise wasted life and that each writer merely writes one book, of which individual volumes are but fragments and which he does not "invent" but finds within himself.[3]

As for the reader, his "own wisdom begins just where that of the author's finishes."[4] A novel is like a dream, more vivid than those we experience while sleeping, a dream in which we come to know "all possible fortunes and misfortunes that we might take years, in life, to know but a part of."[5] We understand others through a series of images we make them conform to, and "the ingeniousness of the first novelist consisted in understanding that, in the apparatus of our emotions, the image being the only essential element, the simplification which consists merely in suppressing real people would be an absolute stroke of perfection."[6] Thus art tells us about life without in the least attempting to imitate it. We have only Kant's categories of time, space, causality, and so forth by which to order our commonplace impressions; art provides a further and higher kind of perception in which we do not confuse the object and our impression of it, for art is pure impression, freed from bondage to phenomena and the external world.

We must finally consider among Proust's theoretical reflections on art one which concerns only literary style. Consistent with his distinction between the world of phenomena, subject to the tyranny of time, and the noumenal realm of art

3. For the appropriate passages in *A la Recherche* alluded to in the last paragraphs, see, in order, 2:769; 3:890; 3:870; 3:374–75; 3:890; 3:375–76; 3:890.

4. ". . . notre sagesse commence où celle de l'auteur finit." *Pastiches et mélanges* (Paris: Gallimard, 1919), p. 248. *Marcel Proust: A Selection from His Miscellaneous Writings*, trans. Gerard Hopkins (London: Allan Wingate, 1948), p. 125.

5. ". . . tous les bonheurs et tous les malheurs possibles dont nous mettrions dans la vie des années à connaître quelques-uns." *A la Recherche* 1:85.

6. "L'ingéniosité du premier romancier consista à comprendre que dans l'appareil de nos émotions, l'image étant le seul élément essentiel, la simplification qui consisterait à supprimer purement et simplement les personnages réels serait un perfectionnement décisif." Ibid.

and eternity, is Proust's philosophy of metaphor. For him a good metaphor snatches two objects out of the domain of contingency and confers an "eternity to style."[7] What makes a good metaphor Proust cannot say, but he observes that, just as water boils only at 212° F, a metaphor which fails to achieve perfection has failed utterly.[8] Gautier's prose is singled out as an example of the use of comparisons which do not spring from any "stirring impression."[9] The use of image and analogy is strongly contrasted with the false, mendacious practice of observation and description from life, which records only the phenomenal world. Beauty is apprehended only by the imagination, a faculty which cannot exert itself on present things, and thus the theory of realism stands condemned.[10]

Because of certain coincidences of vocabulary—words such as duration, matter, memory—it has been customary to posit an influence of Bergson on Proust. Properly short shrift has been made of this facile idea, and we shall not bother to refute it here.[11] The really deep influence on Proust's thought came, oddly enough, from Ruskin; the rather unmetaphysical English aesthetician contributed to the French novelist's theories in numerous ways.[12]

Proust's translations and studies of Ruskin (*The Bible of Amiens*, *Sesame and Lilies*, and his prefaces to them) occupy a significant place in his development as a writer and thinker; they stand midway between his derivative early work (*Les*

7. *Chroniques* (Paris: Gallimard, 1927), p. 193. *Marcel Proust: A Selection*, p. 224.

8. Preface by Marcel Proust to Paul Morand's *Tendres Stocks* (Paris: Gallimard, 1922), p. 25. See *Marcel Proust: A Selection*, pp. 223–24.

9. Preface to John Ruskin, *Sésame et les lys*, trans. Marcel Proust (Paris: Mercure de France, 1906), p. 48. See *Marcel Proust: A Selection*, p. 138.

10. See *A la Recherche* 3:865, 889; 3:872; 3:881.

11. See Robert Champigny, "Temps et reconnaissance chez Proust et quelques philosophes," *PMLA* 73 (1958): 129–35, translated as "Proust, Bergson and Other Philosophers," in *Proust: A Collection of Critical Essays*, ed. René Girard (Englewood Cliffs, N.J.: Prentice-Hall, 1962), pp. 122–27.

12. See Jean Autret, *L'Influence de Ruskin sur la vie, les idées, et l'oeuvre de Marcel Proust* (Geneva: E. Droz, 1955), passim.

Plaisirs et les jours, *Jean Santeuil*) and *Contre Sainte-Beuve*, in which already parts of *A la Recherche* are adumbrated. Although Ruskin's thought is riddled with contradictions, we can define certain of his characteristic preoccupations which reveal why he, and not any *French* writer, so deeply fascinated Proust. To begin with, Ruskin was an aesthete but of a kind rare in France. The typical French believer in *l'art pour l'art* disdained moral questions and tended to have a rather selective, "decadent" sense of the beautiful. He admired the ancient, the exotic, and the immoral with distinct partiality. Ruskin, on the other hand, despite his annoying broadsides against wicked Renaissance culture, had exceptionally rich and varied taste, and could perceive beauty of form in stones and trees as well as in medieval Venetian architecture. He was, above all, free from the constant urge to be antibourgeois which vitiated so much French aesthetic thought. As a result Ruskin's books strike one as more untrammeled, more inquiring, than those of any French writer on art—with the exception perhaps of Viollet-Le-Duc and Emile Mâle, both of whom Proust also admired. Ruskin's deep concern with all kinds of beauty in both nature and art forms seems especially to have charmed Proust, whose work was to show a similar concern for aesthetic values of all kinds—in landscapes, fashions, names, and customs, as well as in painting, music, or other recognized art forms. Specifically, Proust seems to have derived his notion of the artist's individuality from Ruskin. Since the latter dealt most frequently with the visual arts, he was greatly concerned with the varying ways in which artists render the same object. Ruskin ascribes these variations to an idiosyncratic vision which exists in the individual artist. This conception of art tends to minimize the role of convention and tradition in order to stress the unity of each artist's *oeuvre*. (Such an approach is the exact opposite, for example, of Malraux's in *Les Voix du silence*, where every artist's work is seen as an outgrowth of previous artistic stylizations, rather than as a direct vision of nature.) The advantage of Ruskin's method is that it emphasizes recurrent characteristic features of the individual imagination.[13] Thus

13. See ibid., p. 116.

he was concerned with elements of repetition in art just as Proust was later to point out *phrases-types* in analyzing literary styles. Such an approach is basically antihistorical, though valid in its own way, and we shall discover, as we continue to examine Proust's critical principles, that historicism seemed to him a shallow way of looking at art.

The second great influence on Proust's aesthetics exerted itself by contrast: the exasperating example of Sainte-Beuve's practice first led Proust to write literary criticism as such. Sainte-Beuve's criticism is inseparable from the characteristic nineteenth-century view of literature; like the romantic writers themselves, he conceived of literature as springing exclusively from the writer's personality, and therefore he chose to write of books and their authors on the same plane, judging both by the same standards and without distinction. Stendhal, to take only one famous example, was merely M. Beyle, who was a likable enough fellow but of course wrote only "makeshifts";[14] dining with M. Beyle would have been far more amusing than reading *Le Rouge et le noir*. The dangers of this method in dealing with one's literary contemporaries are obvious, and in the polemical sections of *Contre Sainte-Beuve* Proust is particularly concerned with the critic's obtuseness in regard to Balzac, Flaubert, and Baudelaire.

Commenting, in a letter to George Sand, on the state of literary criticism in his age, Flaubert once wrote:

> You spoke of criticism in your last letter, saying that it will soon disappear. I think the contrary, that its dawn has barely begun. It's simply that its trend is the reverse of what it once was. In the time of La Harpe critics were grammarians; in the time of Sainte-Beuve and Taine they are historians. When will they be artists, nothing but artists, real artists? Where have you seen a criticism that is concerned, intensely concerned, with the work *in itself*? The milieu in which it was produced and the circumstances which occasioned it are very closely ana-

14. *Contre Sainte-Beuve, suivi de Nouveaux Mélanges* (Paris: Gallimard, 1954), p. 139. *Marcel Proust on Art and Literature, 1896–1919*, translated by Sylvia Townsend Warner, New York: Meridian, 1958), p. 101.

lyzed; but the unconscious poetics which are its source? Its composition? Its style? The author's point of view? Never!

Such criticism would require great imagination and great generosity. I mean an ever ready faculty of enthusiasm, and then *taste*, a rare quality even among the best—rare to such a point that it is no longer even mentioned.[15]

Flaubert's "artistic" criticism was finally provided by Proust, and it is therefore not unreasonable to consider him one of the originators of modern literary studies.

Proust seems to have written his best criticism not in a methodical, detached fashion, but under the stimulus of some timely question or through irritation at "professional" criticism: his annoyance with Sainte-Beuve, a public argument over Flaubert's style, or the Lemoine trial, which inspired his great series of pastiches. Although he wrote notes of some interest about writers as different as Stendhal, Nerval, and Dostoevsky, his greatest pieces of critical writing deal with the masters of French realism, Balzac and Flaubert.

The lesson of Balzac was evidently a decisive one for Proust. From Balzac he learned both how ambitious in scope fiction could be—no less than a total account of society—and, at the same time, how the novel risked falling short of other literary forms if a complete mastery of stylistic resources was not achieved. The great aspects of Balzac's work that he insists on,

15. "Vous me parlez de la critique dans votre dernière lettre, en me disant qu'elle disparaîtra prochainement. Je crois, au contraire, qu'elle est tout au plus à son aurore. On a pris le contrepied de la précédente, mais rien de plus. Du temps de La Harpe, on était grammairien; du temps de Sainte-Beuve et de Taine, on est historien. Quand sera-t-on artiste, rien qu'artiste, mais bien artiste? Où connaissez-vous une critique qui s'inquiète de l'oeuvre *en soi*, d'une façon intense? On analyse très finement le milieu où elle s'est produite et les causes qui l'ont amenée; mais la poétique *insciente*? d'où elle résulte? sa composition, son style? le point de vue de l'auteur? Jamais! Il faudrait pour cette critique-là une grande imagination et une grande bonté, je veux dire une faculté d'enthousiasme toujours prête, et puis du *goût*, qualité rare, même dans les meilleurs,—si bien qu'on n'en parle plus du tout." Gustave Flaubert, *Extraits de la correspondance ou Préface à la vie d'écrivain*, ed. Geneviève Bollème (Paris: Editions du Seuil, 1963), pp. 246–47. Gustave Flaubert, *Selected Letters*, trans. Francis Steegmuller (New York: Vintage, 1957), p. 216.

in the course of refuting Sainte-Beuve's hazy appreciation of the novelist, are several: characterization through speech, plots which begin slowly but, like a tightening noose, end in a stranglehold, and, above all, the recurrence of characters from one novel to another.[16] Proust's example of the latter is the masterly concluding scene of *Illusions perdues*, in which the reader must guess, from his knowledge of *Le Père Goriot*, that the Spanish priest is Vautrin in disguise and about to embark on another homosexual attachment.

At the same time Proust recognized that there is a peculiar quality in Balzac that makes him only partly a literary figure: "Because of this half-baked realism, too fabulous for life, too prosaic for literature, we often get very much the same kind of pleasure from Balzac's books that we get from life."[17] Proust goes on to speak of Balzac's interest for us as the "historian of the unhistoried."[18] The reasons, however, for Balzac's failure to achieve completely an effect of fictional reality are linguistic ones, and here Proust analyzes with great brilliance exactly what creates or destroys the illusionism of the novel.

Balzac's style, properly speaking, does not exist.[19] By this Proust does not mean that certain linguistic mannerisms cannot be identified as Balzac's but that "all the elements of a style which is still to come exist together, undigested and untransformed."[20] Proust's conception is that a true style represents a selective vision of the world, far from an all-inclusive one, but sufficiently integrated and harmonious to hold the reader in its illusion. Underlying Proust's theory is the distinction between language as practical communication and as an aesthetic instrument. The practical nature of Balzac's

16. See *Contre Sainte-Beuve*, pp. 194–226. *Proust on Art*, pp. 157–89.

17. "Cette réalité à mi-hauteur, trop chimérique pour la vie, trop terre à terre pour la littérature, fait que nous goûtons souvent dans sa littérature des plaisirs à peine différents de ceux que nous donne la vie." *Contre Sainte-Beuve*, pp. 202–3. *Proust on Art*, p. 165.

18. *Contre Sainte-Beuve*, p. 204. *Proust on Art*, p. 167.

19. See *Contre Sainte-Beuve*, p. 207. *Proust on Art*, p. 170.

20. "Dans Balzac . . . coexistent, non digérés, non encore transformés, tous les éléments d'un style à venir qui n'existe pas." *Contre Sainte-Beuve*, p. 207. *Proust on Art*, p. 171.

"style" is what Proust stresses; Balzac explains and qualifies rather than suggests. Here is Proust's example: "His expression was appalling. At that moment, his glance was sublime."[21] Similarly, Balzac's images are those of a great conversationalist, which are striking but "do not fuse with the rest":[22] "Her complexion had taken on the tone of a porcelain vase with a light inside it."[23] Balzac's famous digressions are a further example of undigested material; he states every idea that comes to mind. Finally, Balzac does not hesitate to tell one that a character's words are "well-chosen" or that he is incredibly witty, but without the slightest substantiation. In short, Balzac's language keeps slipping from the plane of novelistic illusion to that of mere storytelling or *reportage*.

The case of Flaubert is precisely the opposite of Balzac's. In Flaubert's style

> all the elements of reality are rendered down into one unanimous substance, into vast, unvarying polished surfaces. No flaw remains in it. It has been rubbed to looking-glass smoothness. Everything is shown there, but only in reflection, and without affecting its uniform substance.[24]

In contrast to Balzac, what counted for Flaubert, rather than an account of actions, was the "rendering of his vision,"[25] one of a tranquil sequence of impressions. Things loom large in Flaubert. To convey this, he devised a peculiar rhythm which would assure a "narrow and closed continuity of style."[26] Proust notes that Flaubert used long adverbs and prepositions

21. "Il eut une affreuse expression. Il eut alors un regard sublime." *Contre Sainte-Beuve*, pp. 208–9. *Proust on Art*, p. 170.

22. *Contre Sainte-Beuve*, p. 207. *Proust on Art*, p. 170.

23. "Son teint avait pris le ton chaud d'une porcelaine dans laquelle est enfermée une lumière." *Contre Sainte-Beuve*, p. 208. *Proust on Art*, p. 170.

24. ". . . toutes les parties de la réalité sont converties en une même substance, aux vastes surfaces, d'un miroitement monotone. Aucune impureté n'est restée. Les choses sont devenues réfléchissantes. Toutes les choses s'y peignent, mais par reflet, sans en altérer la substance homogène." *Contre Sainte-Beuve*, p. 207. *Proust on Art*, p. 170.

25. *Chroniques*, p. 196. *Marcel Proust: A Selection*, p. 226.

26. *Chroniques*, p. 195. *Marcel Proust: A Selection*, p. 226.

primarily for rhythmic effect. For example, "immense prospectuses, where the name of Jacques Arnoux unfolded magisterially."[27] Flaubert also preferred to use "and" at the beginning of sentences for purely aural effect and to omit it elsewhere, creating asyndeton: "When he entered the living-room, everyone got up, they kissed him; and, with the chairs, they made a half-circle around the hearth." The complex interplay of paragraph structure and blanks also attracts Proust's attention, as does Flaubert's abundant use of the vague, "eternal" imperfect tense. But for all the minute analysis he makes of Flaubert's style, Proust claims not to like it especially. The reason for this would principally seem to be Flaubert's inadequate command of figurative language, for "there is, probably, in the whole of Flaubert, no single instance of a really beautiful metaphor."[28]

Given the enormous importance he ascribes to metaphor, it is curious that Proust's comments on poetry are not more extensive or more satisfactory. He contents himself with remarks here or there about mystery in verse or the color of the moon in nineteenth-century French literature.[29] Neither of his essays on Baudelaire attains the level of anything more than good impressionistic criticism. One cannot even comment on these essays, since hardly a single well-expressed idea can be found in them.

Prose, however, is another matter, and here Proust worked out some fine observations on style. We have seen how in the cases of Balzac and Flaubert he succeeded in analyzing characteristic ways of communication and patterns of rhythm. In much briefer comments on Chateaubriand, Stendhal, Dostoevsky, and Hardy,[30] Proust suggests recurrent images or themes which characterize these writers. With Chateaubriand he notes, as we might note ourselves about Proust's novel,

27. This and the later quotations from *L'Education sentimentale* were chosen and translated by me.

28. *Chroniques*, pp. 193–94. *Marcel Proust: A Selection*, p. 224.

29. See *A la Recherche* 3:408.

30. See, respectively, *Contre Sainte-Beuve*, pp. 407–8, *Proust on Art*, pp. 367–68; *Contre Sainte-Beuve*, pp. 414–15, *Proust on Art*, pp. 374–75; *A la Recherche* 3:378–79, and 3:377.

that there is a constant and typical contrast between the author's insistence on the transitory character of all things and the seeming permanence of his record of their beauty. To describe a flower magnificently and to declare that that very flower shall wither emphasizes the tension between things and language, art and its subject, to a poignant degree. Proust has hit here upon a remarkable definition of how the elegiac and nostalgic tone is produced in literature. His remarks on Stendhal, Dostoevsky, and Hardy are similarly acute but narrower in scope; he points out the coincidence of physical and spiritual altitude in *Le Rouge et le noir* and *La Chartreuse de Parme*, the labyrinthine architecture of sinister houses in the Russian novelist, and Hardy's geometry of the stonecutter.

Taking all in all we must admit that while Proust was a remarkable critic—his thought flawed by no cliché—he was a fragmentary one. Criticism for him was not a true genre—indeed, most of his literary essays are quite erratically composed—but a function of reading and part of his apprenticeship. We must remember that as soon as *A la Recherche* was well underway, he ceased to write criticism (and that even in *Contre Sainte-Beuve* fiction obtrudes continually) until the day when, as a famous novelist, he felt obliged to make some public remarks on Flaubert and Baudelaire. And even the very acute critical remarks which are to be found in *A la Recherche* have their origins in the Ruskin prefaces and in *Contre Sainte-Beuve*.

One final word should be said about Proust's pastiches. Although they cannot be easily described without an intricate discussion of French stylistics,[31] one must mention them, for they remain, in many ways, his most penetrating piece of literary analysis. If Proust constructed his critical essays in a haphazard manner, the *Pastiches* are impeccable examples of writing. They owe their origin to a then-famous trial of a certain Lemoine who swindled financiers with his claims to have invented a way to manufacture diamonds. Proust tells aspects of the case in the style of Balzac (a society scene), that of

31. See J. Milly, "Les Pastiches de Proust: Structure et correspondances," *Le Français Moderne* 35 (1967): 33–52, 125–41.

Flaubert (the courtroom), that of Sainte-Beuve reviewing Flaubert's book, as well as in the manners of Henri de Régnier, Edmond de Goncourt, Michelet, Faguet, Renan, and Saint-Simon. Although pastiche is a favorite genre in France, nothing is comparable to Proust's exercises in the style of others. And nothing like it exists in English except perhaps for the hospital episode in *Ulysses*. To study Proust's pastiches is to know exactly what constitutes the style of the writers he is imitating. There is no greater example of *practical* criticism.

While Proust's theory of style is metaphysical, Remy de Gourmont (1853–1915) worked out a psycho-physiological conception of it. Gourmont was also concerned with imagery but, far more than Proust, he tried to explore the relations between sensitivity to experience and verbal expression. Where Proust spoke merely of "translating" impressions into art, Gourmont attempted a thorough investigation of why some people can convey experience through words and why others are incapable of anything but hollow clichés. This insistence on *sensibilité* was to have great repercussions on Anglo-American criticism of about 1920; Murry, Hulme, Pound, and, most of all, T. S. Eliot underwent the influence of Gourmont.[32] If the French critic is somewhat forgotten today, it is nonetheless impossible, without reference to him, to study the intellectual ambit of younger Anglo-American writers of the period. His place in French letters is also of some historical importance: Gourmont is the critic most associated with *symbolisme*, and his inquiries into language as an aesthetic instrument must have been prompted by the stylistic complexity of recent literature.

Gourmont has what may be thought a necessary tool for any analyst of style: a grounding in the essentials of philology. Indeed, many of his essays are of a purely linguistic nature and deal with etymology, orthography, semantic fields, and neologism. *Esthétique de la langue française*, for example, discusses

32. See Glenn S. Burne, *Remy de Gourmont: His Ideas and Influence in England and America* (Carbondale, Ill.: Southern Illinois University Press, 1963), pp. 111–53.

the tremendous increase in nineteenth-century France of new words formed from Greek roots and the phonological consequences of this phenomenon. The general problem of French vocabulary and syntax greatly preoccupied him, and he was quick to see what aesthetic effects any new tendency in the language might have. Gourmont sensed accurately that French, with its limited capacities for derivation and word-formation, would undergo a crisis as modern technology and thought continuously demanded the creation of new terms, and that the pleasing homogeneity of the language would be threatened. With equal concern for the past and future artistic resources of French, he also commented on the archaic character of French prosody, the expressive value of the mute *E*,[33] and the possibilities of popular versification. All in all, Gourmont was an extraordinary combination of philologist and aesthetician.

The most important classification of styles which Gourmont devised is based on image and description as opposed to abstraction. Gourmont divides writers into *visuels* and *émotifs* according to the degree of originality they display in conveying sensory impressions.[34] Visual personalities remember through clear images; emotive ones can reconstruct only the emotional content of a situation, not the physical circumstances of it. Naturally this distinction is not absolute, and Gourmont mentions Flaubert, always his ideal of the perfect writer, as one in whom both kinds of memory are balanced. But by and large Gourmont tends to identify visual memory with good style—even if, as in the case of Chateaubriand, style, apart from content, exists in almost superabundance. The emotive mind, on the other hand, has substituted linguistic signs for things; it tends toward abstract language and derives as much impact from clichés as from fine sentences. An expression like "a beautiful spring day" is as evocative for an emotive personality as the most gorgeous description in Chateaubriand or Proust. The emotive mind is more advanced intellectually insofar as it replaces the confusion of reality with a closed

33. See *Le Problème du style* (Paris: Mercure de France, 1902). Other allusions are to *Esthétique de la langue française* (Paris: Mercure de France, 1899).

34. For all the following see *Le Problème du style*.

system of semantic shorthand, but it is incapable of true aesthetic feeling: style for Gourmont is a "specialization" of perception, not emotion.

Akin to the emotive personality's incapacity for visualizing language is the problem of mixed metaphor. One philological question that especially interested Gourmont was the way in which concrete words become abstract in the course of semantic evolution (to take a simple example, Hebrew *gehenna*, "hell," has become French *gêne*, "discomfort," "embarrassment"). But if one juxtaposes semi-dead metaphors they have a way of springing bizarrely to life for the visual personality ("the project ran into a bunch of snags" might serve as an example from familiar English). The more vocabulary increases through metaphoric extension, the greater the danger for the stylist, the greater the difficulty in maintaining a proper sense of words. Gourmont was aware that many once concrete words were becoming increasingly abstract in his own day, such as the political expression "sphere of influence," which rarely designates anything round. He thus foresaw the menacing character which jargon more and more assumes in our civilization.

Gourmont's theory of the visual and the emotive is useful not only in regard to everyday clichés but also in analyzing the style of certain writers, such as Rousseau. The emotive content of the *Confessions* or the *Nouvelle Héloïse* is considerable, yet the Alpine background of many episodes lacks vividness and imaginative closeness. Rousseau, for all his love of nature, is not a *visuel*; he speaks of the emotion the object calls forth, not of the object. Another problem arises with French neoclassical poetry: there, mixed metaphors are tolerated as forms of metonymy, although they may jar the modern reader (the same phenomenon occurs in Shakespeare). Thus Gourmont was insensitive to Corneille and Racine because he could not accept a convention of traditional rhetoric. Keeping in mind this historical objection to his idea of style we can now turn to Gourmont's general conception of literary history.

One of Gourmont's rare accounts of the development of style adds a refinement to his theory of the visual memory. Although he values description, he prefers figurative language, and metaphor strikes him as more civilized than simile. He claims to find no metaphors in Homer (it seems that he read him more in Leconte de Lisle's translation than in Greek) and contrasts the *Iliad* with the Vedic hymns in which metaphor is highly developed. On the whole, one feels that while Gourmont can praise the *Chanson de Roland* and other pieces of early literature, his taste lies far more within the domain of contemporary work (his excursuses into "mystic Latin" or folkloric verse seem primarily intended as denigrations of the official classics). Gourmont speaks with conviction of synesthesia as necessary to modern sensibility and dismisses the abstract, common style of the eighteenth century with ambivalence and regret. Part of his uncertain feelings about past literature seems to come from his obsessive concern with stylistic innovation; he claims that earlier writers, although original, have become cliché-ridden for us because of their imitators. (Fénelon's *Télémaque* is his favorite example.) It is therefore difficult to read them with complete appreciation. On the other hand, Mallarmé's verse, with its absence of set expressions, approaches purity of style—although at the risk of obscurity.[35] Here Gourmont's contrast between cliché and live language leads him into one of those impasses which are not rare in his thought: the commonplace does have some worth as a form of immediate communication. In the meanders of his essays he always avoids the consequences of confronting his more radical notions, such as contrasting Homer's primitiveness with Mallarmé's sophistication. One senses that Gourmont's view of the history of literature was not systematic and that his own preoccupations as a symbolist poet and novelist somewhat distorted his taste as a critic. But to recall the negative example of Sainte-Beuve, which Proust was so fond of, it is probably less relevant to pontificate on the literature of the ages than to read and understand that of one's own day. In respect to problems of style in the early twentieth century, Gourmont could not have been more perceptive.

The question of hackneyed language so preoccupied Gourmont that he tried, in *La Culture des idées* (1901), to approach

35. See *Esthétique*, p. 326.

the problem without reference to his theory of "visual" and "emotive" personalities. This later work goes beyond the perhaps dubious hypothesis that there are two kinds of memory, and explores the problem of associations of meaning among words. The basic premise is that cliché-ridden style is a function of poor thought, or of "stock responses" in I. A. Richards's terminology. Thus one idea—say, death—brings on another, for example, necessity or cemetery. Even worse are the pairing of virtue and reward, crime and remorse, the future and progress, etc. These combinations help to avoid facing unpleasant thoughts, but the only way to think clearly is to practice a "dissociation of ideas," a form of semantic analysis. Gourmont's most elaborate example is a dissociation of the ideas of decadence and modern literature, which were closely joined for many of his educated contemporaries. He points out that the "decadent" period of classical literature is one of imitation, not innovation, and that therefore the present-day literary scene must be the opposite of decadent.

A useful application of Gourmont's theory bears on poetic style. The worn-out language of the minor *petrarchisti* or the lesser authors of neoclassical tragedies obviously derives from indissoluble associations of ideas, feelings, and expressions. We see here the filiation between "la dissociation des idées" and T. S. Eliot's "dissociation of sensibility." The famous passage in "The Metaphysical Poets" tries to suggest a process of reassociation when Eliot speaks of the unity of the sound of the typewriter, Spinoza, and falling in love. And the fact that Eliot quotes the *symbolistes* as an example of fine modern sensibility shows how closely his ideas are related to Gourmont's. But it was Eliot who best applied the notion to literature, probably because Gourmont, always a better theorist than practical critic, was basically not interested in the whole sweep of European poetry and preferred to examine "dissociation" in regard to everyday language. We can certainly apply Gourmont's ideas to a prevailing ideology which has ceased to correspond to the realities of life, and the sentimental strain present in much nineteenth-century literature can be considered as just such a fixed association of ideas. Also, the patriotism and nationalism of Gourmont's day can be analyzed in these terms. Thus "dissociation of ideas" is a linguistic concept which, while useful in literary analysis, has an even broader scope.

Proust and Gourmont were not the only critics of their period interested in style. Thibaudet had a public controversy with Proust over Flaubert's prose, and an occasional academic book of the period is devoted to imagery or versification in nineteenth-century poets. (The best is Emmanuel Barat's *Le Style poétique et la révolution romantique* [Paris, 1904].) It is not unexpected, of course, that style should have commanded such attention; since the mid-nineteenth century most French writers had been experimenting with language, not just the symbolists, but also the naturalists with their arty prose styles and the "classicists" like Gide and Valéry, who were given to archaisms. It is impossible to read French authors of that period without realizing that there was indeed a "problem of style" such as had never existed in English prose or late Victorian verse. Yet this early work in stylistics did not create a real tradition in France. Certainly Spitzer, Eliot, and Richards, better than any French critic, represent in the twenties and early thirties what we can call style criticism. Proust's idea of *phrases-types* especially reminds one of Spitzer's search for recurrent elements of style, while Gourmont's theory of visual personalities leads directly to I. A. Richards's "practical criticism." On the other hand, both Proust's and Gourmont's conceptions of style suggest present-day ontological criticism, which tries to define the peculiar character of the individual imagination. Thus, even though we can establish no clear filiation of influences on contemporary critics, Proust's and Gourmont's work must still stand at the beginning of truly twentieth-century French criticism.

BIBLIOGRAPHY

WORKS BY PROUST

A la Recherche du temps perdu. Edited by Pierre Clarac and André Ferré. 3 vols. Pléiade. Paris: Gallimard, 1954. A résumé of topics and an index are included. There are a number of English and American editions. Aesthetic theory and critical comments are scattered throughout the novel.

Chroniques. Paris: Gallimard, 1927. (The important pieces of literary criticism in *Chroniques* have been translated by Gerard Hopkins in *Marcel Proust: A Selection from His Miscellaneous Writings* [London: Allan Wingate, 1948]. This volume also includes selections from *Pastiches et mélanges* [Paris: Gallimard, 1919], and a translation of Proust's preface to Paul Morand's *Tendres Stocks* [Paris: Gallimard, 1922]. *Pastiches et mélanges* includes versions of the studies on Ruskin.)

Contre Sainte-Beuve, suivi de Nouveaux Mélanges. Paris: Gallimard, 1954. (The translation, by Sylvia Townsend Warner, is entitled *Marcel Proust on Art and Literature, 1896–1919.* New York: Meridian, 1958. With this translation, all of Proust's important critical essays have become available in English.)

Les Pastiches de Proust. Critical edition with commentary by Jean Milly. Paris: Armand Colin, 1970. Hitherto unpublished material is included.

SELECTED WORKS ON PROUST'S CRITICISM AND AESTHETICS

Autret, Jean. *L'Influence de Ruskin sur la vie, les idées, et l'oeuvre de Marcel Proust.* Geneva: E. Droz, 1955. A useful summary.

Bonnet, Henri. *Le Progrès spirituel dans l'oeuvre de Marcel Proust.* Vol. 2. *L'Eudémonisme esthétique de Proust.* Paris: Vrin, 1949. A thematic dictionary of aesthetic and philosophical ideas in *A la Recherche.*

Butor, Michel. *Les Oeuvres d'art imaginaires chez Proust.* Cassal Bequest Lectures. London: Athlone, 1964.

Chantal, René de. *Marcel Proust, critique littéraire.* 2 vols. Introduction by Georges Poulet. Montreal: Les Presses de l'Université de Montréal, 1967. An immensely detailed and thorough study of the subject which manages, surprisingly, to be quite readable. There is much comparison with other writers' aesthetic theories but little strict philosophical analysis.

Fiser, Emeric. *L'Esthétique de Marcel Proust.* Paris: Redier, 1933. A discussion of subjective idealism.

Genette, Gérard. "Proust palimpseste." In *Figures,* pp. 39–67. Tel Quel. Paris: Seuil, 1966.

———. "La Littérature et l'espace." In *Figures II,* pp. 43–48. Tel Quel. Paris: Seuil, 1969.

McLendon, Will L. "Ruskin, Morris et la première esthétique de Marcel Proust." *Le Bayou* 21 (1957): 402–14.

Nathan, Jacques. *Citations, références et allusions de Proust dans "A la Recherche du temps perdu."* Paris: Nizet, 1952.

Strauss, Walter A. *Proust and Literature: The Novelist as Critic.* Cambridge, Mass.: Harvard University Press, 1957. A compendium of Proust's literary opinions. Little aesthetic theory.

Vial, André. *Proust: Structure profonde et naissance d'une esthétique.* Dossier des Lettres Nouvelles. Paris: Julliard, 1963. A perceptive example of the kind of "existential psychoanalysis" that Sartre made fashionable.

CRITICAL WORKS BY GOURMONT

Of Gourmont's many volumes, the theoretical ones on language are perhaps the most significant. All of these are collections of essays on various topics:

Esthétique de la langue française. Paris: Mercure de France, 1899.

La Culture des idées. Paris: Mercure de France, 1901.

Le Problème du style. Paris: Mercure de France, 1902.

In translation there are:

A selection from *Le Problème du style.* In Ludwig Lewisohn's *A Modern Book of Criticism.* New York: Modern Library, 1919.

Decadence and Other Essays on the Culture of Ideas. Translated by William Aspenwall Bradley. New York: Harcourt, Brace, 1921. A version of *La Culture des idées.*

The Book of Masks. Translated by Jack Lewis. Introduction by Ludwig Lewisohn. Boston: J. W. Luce & Co., 1921. Freeport, N.Y.: Books for Libraries Press, 1967.

Selected Writings. Translated and edited with an introduction by Glenn S. Burne. Ann Arbor: University of Michigan Press, 1966.

SELECTED WORKS ON GOURMONT'S CRITICISM AND AESTHETICS

Bencze, Eugène. *La Doctrine esthétique de Remy de Gourmont.* Toulouse: Editions du Bon Plaisir, 1928. A good résumé.

Burne, Glenn S. *Remy de Gourmont: His Ideas and Influence in England and America.* Carbondale, Ill.: Southern Illinois University Press, 1963. A very useful, well-researched work, with abundant literary-historical details.

Jacob, Paul-Emile. *Remy de Gourmont.* University of Illinois Studies in Language and Literature. Urbana: University of Illinois Press, 1933. Some discussion of Gourmont's literary criticism.

Uitti, Karl-D. *La Passion littéraire de Remy de Gourmont.* Paris: Presses Universitaires de France, 1962. Contains interesting information on Gourmont's theories of language and their sources in contemporary linguistics.

Angelo P. Bertocci

3 Charles Du Bos and the Critique of Genius

With the title of his first book, *Approximations* (1922), Charles Du Bos succeeded in imposing his own peculiar inflection upon a word signifying an approach to literature. The special meaning of the term was to become clearer by 1933 as the number of volumes grew to six. The author's method was revealed in essays largely on major nineteenth-century figures in English and German as well as French literature. Significantly, Du Bos's first important articles had been in English for readers of *The Athenaeum*. Strains of Anglo-American and Polish blood in the French critic might explain some of his foreign affinities. Also, the France of Descartes, where only grudging recognition was granted to Henri Bergson, made Du Bos uncomfortable. In French writing he missed that richness of inspiration and that inevitability which he found conjoined with a Keatsian ease and charm in English poetry. He felt French literature to be relatively lacking in the *spirituel* and in the *Stimmung* of Stefan George or a Novalis. Though he could appreciate a certain French reticence, he found more authenticity in the voices of Chekhov and Tolstoy. Yet, his *approximations* we shall discover to be motivated, after all, by the characteristically French idea of pushing one's own comprehension to the limit.

What Charles Dédéyan studied under the rubric of literary cosmopolitanism[1] by following the youthful Du Bos to Oxford,

1. Charles Dédéyan, *Le Cosmopolitisme littéraire de Charles Du Bos*, vol. 1 (Paris: Société d'Edition d'Enseignement Supérieur, 1965). See bibliography for further details.

Italy, and Berlin was in fact, seen from the inside, an exploration of the possibility of a comprehensive modern humanism. And Du Bos became convinced that such a humanism, in the logic of its momentum, must be a return to Christianity. The critic had gradually withdrawn from an earlier belief, though remaining in a state of nostalgic disaffection. The *Extraits d'un journal, 1908–1928* (1929), plotted the high points in a spiritual itinerary that led him back to Roman Catholicism. A reading of the *Extraits* gives plain evidence of a hidden dimension in *Approximations*.

Contemporary criticism sees a motive of literary creation in the discovery of what one has to say. In relation to *Approximations*, Charles Du Bos's *Journal* presents his most spontaneous "secretions" in response to a work of literature. For the French introspective, the *Journal* is both a priming of the pump and the receptacle for a geyser-like inspiration more given than solicited. Here, too, strategies are planned for a brief *approximation*, or perhaps a volume, never written, on Pater, Browning, or Keats. While André Gide will accompany *Les Faux-monnayeurs* with a journal on the novel, Du Bos writes an *approximation* and a journal looking forward—and sometimes looking back—to the essay.

Thanks to the *Journal* we can sometimes see a given *approximation* in its total context. In addition to offering a distillation of the intellectual and artistic life of Paris and, in a sense, of Europe between the two world wars, the *Journal* presents the figure of Charles Du Bos himself, with his ever present problems of finance and ill-health, his various devices to accelerate and give order to a spasmodic literary yield, his moments of meditation and self-exhortation or of aesthetic and religious exaltation. Montaigne, the Rousseau of the *Confessions*, and Amiel fuse in the *Journal* with the dominant image of Saint Augustine. For, if the earlier volumes present a deep religious response—in the most general sense of the word—to secular literature seen as an intimation of man's fundamental predicament, the later volumes, with their meditations on sacred texts, take on—in the narrower sense—the character of spiritual autobiography.

Approximations and the *Journal* thus form an indissoluble union. Du Bos always maintained that art offered its finest fruit, both for the creator and for the creative critic and reader, in the implicit injunction, as in Rilke's archaic Apollo, "Du musst dein Leben ändern," a variation of Rimbaud's "changer la vie." Most of Du Bos's other writings also demonstrate how the response to literature becomes a way to explore the self and discover its relation to other selves, the world, and God. Thus *Le Dialogue avec André Gide*, published in 1929, is intimately connected with his conversion, but at a level not plumbed by critics who reject its judgments, find something too aggressive in its tone, or question the appropriateness of its publication (since Gide and Du Bos had been friends for a decade). Four years later, writing on *François Mauriac et le problème du romancier catholique*, the French critic was to reject any moral curb on literature except sincerity and a genuine examination of motives. He hated that exploitation of life by literature of which he accused Gide all the more because he thought literature and life could render to each other indispensable services.

The criticism of Du Bos, then, is characterized by its *engagement*, the discovery of a common poetic experience in both the creative genius and the reader or critic. To such experience the young man turns when in 1902, abandoning the study of philosophy, he determines to live by "ethics alone" and certain "individual truths." (The latter will become his guidelines especially between 1918 and his return to the Catholic faith in July 1927.) Du Bos, lacking, like his Baudelaire and Shelley, *la vie végétative*—that anonymous state in which we go on living when we do not feel really alive—experienced existence either as the "plenitude gorgeous" (*sic*) of Keats and his favorite poetry[2] or a vision of ashes as in his Benjamin Constant.[3] The critic will make much of Tolstoy's refusal to live until he has come to terms with the problem of death.[4] Du Bos's response to life and even more

2. *Journal, 1924–25* (Paris: Corrêa, 1948), 2 May 1924.
3. *Grandeur et misère de Benjamin Constant* (Paris: Corrêa, 1946), pp. 172, 177.
4. "Vues sur Tolstoï," *Approximations* (Paris: Fayard, 1965), pp. 771–828.

to art was characterized by complete listlessness—as with Hugo, Balzac, Descartes, Voltaire—or ascension to the "top of sovereignty," a reaction ideally in the Keatsian mode.

The latter experience he joyfully hailed in the episodes of the steeples of Martinville and the *madeleine* in *Du Côté de chez Swann*, which he reviewed in 1921.[5] Proust's name for the state had been "adoration perpétuelle," the original idea for a title of *A la Recherche du temps perdu*. Du Bos will call it "exaltation," experienced *mutatis mutandis* by both poet and critic, the link between poetic creation and criticism, between literature and life. Exaltation is an invulnerable protection for all emerging truths seemingly disconnected or even diametrically opposed, but in reality exempt from the law of contradiction. Du Bos is carrying farther an experience which the older criticism referred to as *discordia concors* and which Coleridge attributed to imagination. This state Du Bos considers to be the second reality, that level where the fact of life itself ceases to be a problem. "Le moi profond," as Abbé Bremond will call it, is not self-centered, but is characterized by a sense of unity with mankind.[6]

The diary entry of 2 June 1925 describes an instance of such an experience in which Du Bos, visiting a sick friend and feeling almost incapable of uttering a word, suddenly comes alive in a surge of felicitous thought and language. He finds in such sustained impulses to expression an antidote to sterility and attributes them to what he calls the "moi du Deus," an aspect of the self subject to something divine. He pictures it as a passage beyond in a gyration of concentric circles. This experience he connects with the insight he had attributed to Novalis in a lecture of 14 December 1923, namely, that "spiritual and artistic creation continuously pursued, projecting antennae everywhere, was, everything considered, the surest instrument of truth."[7] On 27 March 1926 he commits

5. *Approximations*, pp. 81–132, esp. pp. 89–95.

6. *Journal, 1921–23* (Paris: Corrêa, 1946), 14 Sept. 1923.

7. ". . . la création spirituelle et analytique indéfiniment poursuivie, projetant partout ses antennes, était en fin de compte le plus sûr instrument de vérité." *Cahiers Charles Du Bos*, no. 7 (July 1962), pp. 16–17.

himself to a program of experiment. He will seek truth, not in the direct process of introspection but indirectly and through meditation upon exaltation in response to literature or in the act of artistic creation.[8] Du Bos's return to Catholicism is, on one level, the logic of such experimentation pushed to its conclusion. He overcomes his hesitations by the indignant reflection: "To think that what I have done spontaneously all my life for Keats, I bargain over with God and Christ!"[9] Du Bos finally requires of himself an act which he feels is in keeping with his constant sense of the metaphysical beyond in the poetry of Keats: he renders unto the words of Christ what he has been willing to render unto the language of Keats.

Yet as early as 1921 Du Bos, reflecting upon exaltation in connection with Proust's Marcel and Pater's Marius and a famous text in the latter's *Renaissance*, had recognized that "to maintain, to perpetuate this ecstasy would be to live even now in a second reality."[10] The great problem for the man of genius would be precisely to establish an ideal relation between his art and the self that artistic creation shapes. Nor will artists respond alike to the challenge. One artist will keep the passage for the afflux open, sustaining himself courageously in its current.[11] A Goethe, anti-introspective by nature, will allow exaltation to spiritualize him, finding life itself a satisfactory goal, maintaining even in the authentic Orphic poetry of his "Urworte" an "equilibrium in the very midst of a glimpse of the beyond." Du Bos, inclined to view Goethe as "le plus beau de mes étrangers," will warmly concede in a study of Goethe for the centennial of 1932 that the Marienbad

8. See the essay on Amiel of 1921, *Approximations*, pp. 133–56.

9. ". . . ce que spontanément j'ai fait toute ma vie pour Keats, je le marchande à Dieu et au Christ!" *Journal III, 1926–27* (Paris: Corrêa, 1949), 27 July 1927.

10. "Maintenir, perpétuer cette exaltation, ce serait vivre dès à présent dans la réalité seconde." *Approximations*, p. 91.

11. Something he thought he perceived in Mme. de Noailles's lyrics. See *Journal VIII, Janvier 1933–Décembre 1933* (Paris: La Colombe, Editions du Vieux Colombier, 1959), 1 May 1933. Du Bos considered contemporaries like La Comtesse de Noailles and Maurice Barrès the "two greatest French romantics," the earlier French romanticism generally being vitiated by an excess of eloquence.

elegy marks the poet's greatest conquest. The suffering of love working in conjunction with the alchemy of music and memory bestows on the poet a spiritual quality not native to his endowment.[12]

But the options of poetic genius could be a source of disappointment and even of mental fight for the critic. Proust disappointed by yielding to the pressures of critics as well as of his special nature and turning from the spiritual element toward moral analysis and a subject matter which, however defensible in a novelist of stature, tended to juxtapose indiscriminately all levels of life and value.[13] A Valéry, intent on the purely artistic elaboration of the *vers donné*, refused to inquire into its source.[14] Finally André Gide allowed his art to become the self-indulgent means of moral subversion.[15] Since Du Bos considered Gide's act a betrayal of the *spiritualité* he assumed authentic in the original Gide, he felt it his duty in this single instance to bear witness against an artist.

To welcome exaltation as a spiritual exercise would seem to require an implicit trust in the intimations of our high moments. But what if one should encounter, as Du Bos did early in life, a writer who could create a state of exaltation by a heroic distrust of the illusory promise of exaltation itself? No wonder that Friedrich Nietzsche was for Du Bos the dearest enemy, the only enemy who counted. For Nietzsche's mode of thought, which Du Bos called "la pensée contre soi," systematically distrusted—or attributed to the purely natural in man—those experiences which gave the French critic an intimation within of something not the self and transcending the self. For some years the Nietzschean heroism of doubt served Du Bos as a major spiritual resource. Eventually he came to feel that the *pensée contre soi* was itself the product of a will-to-power and self-deification which had resulted in driving

12. *Goethe* (Paris: Corrêa, 1949), pp. 71–79, 162–63, 202, 231, 375. See also my "Charles Du Bos and Goethe," *Romanic Review* 50 (1959): 41–54.

13. *Journal, 1921–23*, 7 Sept. 1923.

14. Ibid., 10 June 1922.

15. *Journal III, 1926–27*, 7 Sept. 1927.

Nietzsche to abandon the value he had placed on the quest for truth.[16]

In struggling against the influence of Nietzsche, Du Bos drew on another intellectual resource whose importance he never sought to minimize. Opening the *Essai sur les données immédiates de la conscience*, he had felt "the birth of what in me is the real self."[17] For a while he entered not so much into philosophy as into Bergson. Later, when Keats won over the young philosophy major in 1902, the poet and philosopher formed a mutually supporting pair.[18] Bergson delivered Du Bos first from the Nietzschean naturalism and secondly from the chains of determinism. In *What Is Literature?* Du Bos's last work, though the road leads back to Plato and Plotinus, it is via Bergson. As Romeo Arbour points out, Bergson's influence worked especially in the area of psychological observation and introspection.[19] In *l'intuition* Du Bos found his experience of exaltation theorized. *Approximations* will present the critic's efforts to coincide with the *durée* of the author or of the work. *Durée* will be the basis of memory idolized by Du Bos; but, perhaps most important, it will be interpreted as justifying the use of the word *âme* in the Augustinian sense. Bergson thus serves Augustine, whose role increases steadily. At the end of Du Bos's life two figures loom on his horizon, and to the mysticism of each he plans to devote a book: Keats as an instance of the profane and Augustine as an instance of the sacred.

Meanwhile the meaning of the passage on Proustian exaltation and the *Deus in nobis* has expanded. In the post-conversion *Journal* (2 June 1931) where Bergson's intuition is seen in relation to the doctrine of the Soul, the sense of a transcendence by which the poet's imagination creates its ideal forms

16. Ibid., 12 Aug. 1926; *Journal IV, 1928* (Paris: Corrêa, 1950), 24 Aug. 1928.

17. *Cahiers Charles Du Bos*, no. 1 (December 1956), p. 22.

18. *Journal VI, Janvier 1930–Juillet 1931* (Paris: La Colombe, Editions du Vieux Colombier, 1955), 20 Oct. 1930.

19. *Henri Bergson et les lettres françaises* (Paris: Corti, 1955), pp. 393–415.

is identified with Claudel's *Quelqu'un*, that "someone in me more myself than I can be."[20]

All great literature, then, for Du Bos can be interpreted as contact with the immanent God. Even as a convert he will refuse to accept the sharp distinction made in Maritain's *Art et scolastique* between poetic mysticism and religious mysticism. He is closer to Bremond's *Prière et poésie*, for he has come to religion himself, he reflects, from poetry and especially from music.[21]

What is an *approximation*? In contrast to Sainte-Beuve's method, incomparable in dealing with surfaces but which "never starts from beneath," an *approximation* is a critique deriving from "that central image which hovers before the mind like a luminous mist, and in its dealings with which the mind is thrown entirely on its own resources."[22] Such an image is the result of the spiritual interpreter's penetration into the self-sufficient world of the artist, a world with which he has previously made himself thoroughly familiar. To interpret an artist's work is to penetrate to "that vegetative life which circulates without his knowing it through all that he does and there to surprise the formation and the rising of its vapors."[23] Such "vegetative life" is what Du Bos will call the "milieu intérieur" in his well-known essay on Flaubert. Like a diver skilled in underwater tasks—how Du Bos loves these images of water: he once calls Bergson "an underwater swimmer"![24]—the interpreter must draw up and expose the flora without raising it to the surface above the level where its

20. "Quelqu'un qui en moi-même est plus moi-même que moi." "Vers d'exil," *Théâtre* (première série), 4 (Paris: Mercure de France, 1931): 226.

21. *Journal IV, 1928*, 27 Oct. 1928.

22. *Athenaeum*, no. 4703 (18 June 1920), p. 813.

23. "C'est encore descendre chez l'artiste jusqu'à cette vie végétative qui circule à son insu à travers tout ce qu'il fait, surprendre la formation et la montée de ses vapeurs." *Approximations*, p. 582.

24. "Il est essentiellement le nageur sous-marin." *Journal, 1921–23*, February 1922.

virtue is most effective. An *approximation* then is a penetration and a *subtraction* without abstraction.

Encouraged by Bergson's theory and practice, the critic installs himself at the core of the text and conveys intimations of what Pater would call the quality to be appreciated. To Pater, always his master, Du Bos is glad to concede the triumph of the brief, magical metaphor of criticism, grasped only by his equals in sensibility. He is content himself to serve the less gifted; his characteristic emphasis is on describing "not exactly the work he has under his eyes, but the spiritual state it engenders in the spectator."[25] While Du Bos as interpreter seeks to add his own intonation, that meditative murmur must be not only a melody but an aid to reflection.

There is a polarity in a Du Bos *approximation*. He seeks not merely to identify with the cause, the source in the writer, and thus Du Bos becomes, according to Georges Poulet, the model for many modern critics. His intuition emerges from such identification with the particular possessing generality or universality. Du Bos's subtitles here acquire significance: "Walter Pater, ou l'ascète de la beauté," "Jacques Rivière et de la perfection abstraite," "Benjamin Constant, ou la grandeur de la sévérité envers soi-même," "Joubert, ou de la perfection." His writers become eminent instances of a moral quality or predicament or of an aesthetic problem, but the instance is sought among the nicer discriminations of morals or aesthetics. One may question whether the Bergsonian Du Bos does not slip into the typology of his other admiration, Dilthey. Yet in the world of Du Bos's criticism the types do not so much stand on their own feet as determine a coexistence of differences. The young Goethe with his "vulgarity" or the Lydgate of *Middlemarch*[26] are played off against a Benjamin Constant who, for all his weaknesses, remains loyal to memory, sensitive to the possible suffering of the beloved. In the background hover Robert Browning and Elizabeth

25. *Journal III, 1926–27*, 20 Mar. 1926. In Georges Poulet, "La Pensée critique de Charles Du Bos," *Critique* 21 (1965): 491–516, one of the few indispensable writings on the critic, we miss only this stress.

26. *Goethe*, pp. 84–88.

Barrett Browning, to whom Du Bos hopes some day to devote a book with the subtitle, "la plénitude de la vie humaine."[27]

But frequently the analytic impetus in Du Bos, no doubt stimulated by Proust, carries him beyond even the criticism metaphor accessible to the faithful schooled in Pater. Spiritual families challenge intuition of what is presented in sensation. The quality of "mineral beauty" is said to distinguish figures obviously as different in other respects as Piero della Francesca, Vermeer, Jan Van Eyck, Gide, and Emerson.[28] "Crystal spirits" include Leopardi, Vaughan, Novalis in one aspect, Scarlatti.[29] There are poets who "are situated" and those who "situate" through the power of "negative capability." The latter category includes Keats, Shelley, Hofmannsthal, Verlaine, Rilke, and Baudelaire. It is a pedantic game, as Du Bos recognizes, yet significant in its attempt to find the locus for the concept that classifies in sense and feeling.

The more extreme of Du Bos's critical metaphors, like poetry since Baudelaire, create meaning through violent juxtaposition. "Profundity at full speed" is the quality he finds in Mauriac, "abandoned brevity" in Hofmannsthal, "singing opacity" for Ingres.[30] In Keats what fascinates him is the fusion of the sensuously replete and the immaterial, of vigor and joy. Joy, ever for Du Bos the sign of creative emotion reaching its objective, in Keats, as in Giorgione and the best Coleridge, unites the dynamic with the static like "a dithyramb in the open sky," "the calm of a Bacchanale immobilized in eternity."[31] The characteristic *adagio* of Keats comes of a language so saturated in associations that even Baudelaire's compares with it only as an "incense-burner" to a "peach." In every supreme masterpiece of Keats there is an indefinable superposition of trajectories produced by the ordering of words, and the highest of these, the most unique,

27. *Approximations*, p. 208.

28. *Journal IV, 1928*, 2 June 1928.

29. *Le Dialogue avec André Gide* (Paris: Au Sans Pareil, 1929; Paris: Corrêa, 1946), p. 72 n.

30. *Journal, 1924–25*, 4 Apr. 1925; *Approximations*, p. 947 n.; *Journal, 1924–25*, 3 Dec. 1924.

31. *Journal, 1924–25*, 10 Oct. 1924.

seems to be born of the touch of a fruit upon a star."[32] We seem to be *en plein Chagall*!

Any critical approach assumes a theory of the elements entering into a work of art. For Du Bos, literature happens "through creative emotion" which, when incarnated into form, manifests at its highest and at its most complete the personality of the artist. Yet he is always impressed by the objective, "sidereal" quality in the music of Bach, preferring it to the kind of emotion transposed one finds in Mozart. Art can be the expression of emotion or emotion contemplated, but these are distinctions of quality, not of value.

The strategy of organization is musical, the "condition of music" assuring a metaphysical quality. Tone and tempo count more than a writer's ideas or even his feelings in revealing the substructure of his being. The "monotony of genius" in great writers expresses itself not only in recurrent themes or images but also in a single tempo: an *adagio*, an *allegro moderato*, a *presto*, a primitive pulsation around which gather all the harmonics of the fundamental. According to Du Bos, a critic, like a figure in a Giorgione landscape, should be "always listening."

Ideally also, an *approximation* is written in the tone and tempo of the writer approached: the projected book on Pater, in the register of Bach's Suite in D, something slow and intimate which depends essentially on the pedal, with a tone like the music of memory itself, the themes being mysteriously echoed and surviving in each other. A Thibaudet, that other Bergsonian, will try the same kind of thing more broadly; the perfectionist Du Bos simply did not have world enough and time.

It is disconcerting, in following Du Bos's thoughts on language, to meet Longinus as well as Bergson. Du Bos will have

32. "Chez Keats, il y a dans toute pièce suprême je ne sais quelle superposition de trajets suivis par l'agencement des mots, et le plus haut situé de tous, le plus unique c'est celui qui semble naître de l'attouchement d'une étoile par un fruit." *Journal, 1921–23*, 1 Dec. 1922.

it both ways: he finds words beautiful in their essence, and also beautiful if rightly chosen and placed. The "light" of a beautiful word as the "sign of the true birth of thought" can reveal the fullness but also the void of thought. As a result he will praise Chateaubriand's artistry though his content be less than null. Yet he entertains Bergson's conviction that great art is simply the notation of the to-and-fro of thought. Comparing the first paragraphs of Bergson's *Essai sur les données immédiates de la conscience* and Corot's "Castel Sainte-Elie," he marvels that, without even a hint of deformation legitimized by art, style is everywhere.[33]

Du Bos's romantic view of literature is thus closer to Baudelaire's *symbolisme* than to that of either Mallarmé or Valéry. Exaltation creates for Du Bos those moments of revelation wherein the Baudelairean symbol emerges. He praises Novalis both for the universality and the depth of feeling he gave the symbol[34] but he uses the term almost nowhere else. Yet he loves to quote from John Middleton Murry's *Keats and Shakespeare* the passage on a "truth so mysterious it cannot be made current or passed from lips to lips save in that living flesh of speech with which it was clothed."[35] Du Bos calls Coleridge on one occasion "the greatest of critics," and, though he never discusses his theory of literature, one may think that Coleridge's turning from discussion of the "poem" to definition of the "poet" is the strategy of Du Bos's own work. The French writer's objection to classicism has its center in such ideas. The "false classical synthesis," he thinks, trisected human unity in the man, the writer, and the Christian; the achievement of Rousseau—for all his faults—and of the romantics was to restore literature as the expression of the total man.

33. *Extraits d'un journal, 1908–28* (Paris: J. Schiffrin, 1929; Paris: Corrêa, 1931), 22 June 1915; *Journal, 1921–23*, 16 Feb. 1922.

34. *Cahiers Charles Du Bos*, no. 7 (July 1962), pp. 23–24; from a course on Novalis given 14 December 1923.

35. John Middleton Murry, *Keats and Shakespeare* (London: Oxford University Press, 1925), pp. 2–3; quoted in *What Is Literature?* (New York: Sheed and Ward, 1940), p. 26.

For this Bergsonian, what made the difference between romanticism and classicism was not discipline but *what* was subjected to such control and *how*. "The magic mountain of German aesthetics"—Novalis, and among contemporaries Wilhelm Dilthey and the poet Hofmannsthal with his *Unterhaltung über Gedichte*—still cast their spell upon an "impenitent romantic" who would acknowledge only "the classicism of faith."[36] Romanticism could never be for Charles Du Bos, in T. E. Hulme's phrase, merely "spilt religion"; for what had spilled in his case had nurtured his religious belief.

Du Bos's view of literature seems to fit the lyrical and even the meditative poem better than it does the novel or the play. "Whatever else it may be beyond that, Literature is first of all Life becoming conscious of itself when, in the soul of a man of genius, it joins its plenitude of expression."[37] His admiration for a certain quality of stoical and muted pessimism which he found in various forms in George Eliot, Hardy, Keats, Tolstoy, and the Russians and especially Chekhov's "tender mezzo voice,"[38] is perhaps best expressed in a paradox resolved only in his own experience: "The greatness of life is to turn out a failure; the greatness of life is its open wound."[39] Du Bos ends significantly by finding in Henry James, whom he considers on the aesthetic plane "the greatest of modern artists," no more than a "parallelism" to life.[40] Late in life Du Bos shifts increasingly toward works which engage him profoundly on a more comprehensive level.

As a matter of fact, Du Bos finds it increasingly difficult to lose himself in the novel which, like Valéry, he finds arbitrary as a form. "Sur le 'milieu intérieur' chez Flaubert," which Jean Rousset calls one of the charters of modern

36. *Approximations*, pp. 155–57, 672; *Journal, 1921–23*, 2 Feb. 1923; *Journal VIII, Janvier 1933–Décembre 1933*, 9 Apr. 1933.

37. *What Is Literature?*, p. 14.

38. *Journal, 1921–23*, 24 May 1923.

39. "La grandeur de la vie, c'est d'être un échec; la grandeur de la vie, c'est d'être une blessure." Jean Mouton, *Charles Du Bos* (Paris: Desclée de Brouwer, 1954), p. 137.

40. *Journal, 1924–25*, 23 Sept. 1924.

criticism,[41] was undoubtedly written in an effort to resolve the resistance he naturally felt toward any form of fictional transposition, novelistic or theatrical.

The *milieu intérieur* in Flaubert is for Du Bos's intuition a heavy, sluggish, undifferentiated psychic mass swirling with particles each of them related to the whole. Its core resists even revery and turns everything, including feeling, into sensation. Such a state Du Bos infers from a kind of vulgarity in the novelist's feeling for language: Flaubert at his best will lack a certain atmosphere and *legato* of style. Yet, with a discipline which fulfilled a religious need, the artist undertook to "work out through the Beautiful the living and the true just the same" and to create a book with "something eternal like a principle" in it. Now Dante, Milton, Keats achieved just this effect; in them the maximum of beauty brings a maximum of *justesse*. Through beauty they acquit themselves of what they owe to truth, and they let the "living" take care of itself. But Flaubert's ambition was to attain to *le beau*, *le vrai*, *le vivant* separately, and through a hybrid form like the novel! The result is *Madame Bovary*, the only novel that is a work of art in the strictest sense of the word. But, as in the case of Henry James's novels, Du Bos turns from the beautiful *sans plus* to other values and prefers *L'Education sentimentale* for its effect of immersion in time and for that dull tonality which is the voice of life itself.

Although the *milieu intérieur* is Du Bos's main field of exploration, he is most at home when it is the locus for visitations of the *spirituel*. The novelist at best is midstream in life; the *spirituel* is Keats's poet, with no "character" of his own, only the "word" and the "universe." *Byron et le besoin de la fatalité*, and the posthumous *Grandeur et misère de Benjamin Constant* are sallies in partial biography of men who exercised a certain fascination over Du Bos. But, *Du Spirituel dans l'ordre littéraire* is the critic's most systematic study in the psychology of genius. It was intended as a study of *le spirituel* in its modes and

41. *Approximations*, pp. 165–82; Jean Rousset, *Forme et signification* (Paris: Corti, 1961), p. xvii.

gradations from a natural to a religious mysticism—a kind of "Varieties of Spiritual Experience." An unfinished series of essays, it is at once a kind of psychology, aesthetics, and even implicit theology of artistic inspiration. It is far more characteristic of Du Bos than *What Is Literature?* This last volume—through which, unfortunately, the English reader is likely to approach Du Bos—in contrast with *Du Spirituel*, displays something of which Du Bos had always been keenly aware: the difference between a philosophical mode of expression with its abstract conclusions and the kind of thought which adheres to the concrete literary *approximation*.

In his essays on the "spirituel," using symbols of an old-fashioned psychology—"innateness," "the heart," or even the "heart of the mind," the "soul"—Du Bos illuminates the quality of various poets: in Milton, the distinction between the sublime as a kind of transport sustaining its own climate and the *spirituel* as an opening; in Shelley, "poetry at its upper limits" when man is at last freed from life and the illusion that his social message will be heeded, and the spirit becomes all the more itself in love and adoration of the Veiled Spirit;[42] in Maurice de Guérin, one of the few French writers in whom Du Bos discerns the *spirituel* as an inborn quality, a strange displacement producing "psychic hedonism," the soul, the organ of delectation, becoming at the same time the horizon or the cosmos—a state of incest and self-deification.[43]

Elsewhere, modifying an unfavorable first impression, as he did also with Goethe, Du Bos presents Wordsworth's creative silhouette in terms of the poem "The Thorn"—a "mass of mottled joints," standing erect like a "stone with lichens . . . overgrown." When the tough bark is deserted by the sap of spiritual power, it is held rigid with a strange majesty like a dolmen. Wordsworth was a man of sensation by birth; yet the very love of nature engendered the *spirituel*, a quality Du Bos attributes to the "staying power" of contemplation, the im-

42. "Poésie des confins," *Vigile*, Cahier no. 1 (1930), pp. 235–80.

43. *Vigile*, Cahier no. 4 (1930), pp. 133–222.

portance given to "second impressions," and an introspection that gravitated around universals.[44]

In *Les Fleurs du mal* the poet's soul becomes incarnate even when he thinks he is describing a passing state and writing an "occasional poem." As early as 1921, in "Méditation sur la vie de Baudelaire,"[45] Du Bos described how the poet, considering life mere "mud" which somehow he must turn into "gold," had created a supra-lyricism by means of a soul distraught and out of tune, integrated only by the poetic voice. In the process the man destroyed himself. On the other hand, in a Stefan George, a Keats, a Dante—poets better able to master their moral dualisms—the entire soul, being in tune, enjoys "monumental intimacy" as a natural element. They have developed "psychic space"—a condition best described in terms of the first two quatrains of Baudelaire's "Les Correspondances." It seems to be a kind of sacred inner dimension where the sensuous and the religious mysteriously interfuse beyond the law of contradiction, such synesthesia happening in an atmosphere of the strangely familiar.

The state where the "voice" and the "soul" become one and the same can be variously interpreted. George achieves a supra-lyrical harmony in contrast to the melody of a Heine and a Verlaine, and sees in it an attribute of human dignity. Pater's Marius will ascribe this increased and heightened dimension of being to an "elder Brother" and "Companion." Finally, in Claudel, the "Quelqu'un" becomes nothing less than a personal God. Having held himself back from Claudel since 1911 because of certain unattractive qualities in the man and in the form of his poetry, Du Bos turns toward the poet in 1925 and comes to see him increasingly after 1927 as, even beyond Pascal, "la plus haute réponse humaine" France has to offer in the face of Shakespeare. For, Du Bos writes in his last journal, Shakespeare accepts man as *donné*, Claudel sees him as *créé*. His poetry with its quality of "sacred familiarity" is the result

44. *Vigile*, Cahier no. 4 (1931), pp. 142–217. See also *Journal VII, Août 1931–Octobre 1932* (Paris: La Colombe, Les Editions du Vieux Colombier, 1957), 3 and 5 Mar. 1931.

45. *Approximations*, pp. 183–237.

of the "evangelization" of the entire being.[46] Thus Du Bos celebrates in a modern French poet what he had found in greater measure in English and German poetry and what he believes Keats might have achieved had he lived longer—the restitution to its source of the profane mystery of beauty.

Few in France will agree with his friend Jacques Maritain that Du Bos is the "greatest of French critics,"[47] though many in France and England might agree that he was so for the period between the two world wars. To what extent was Du Bos, innovative in criticism like Proust in the novel, nevertheless a critic in the old sense? He was satisfied to be called an "interpreter," as a pianist or violinist interprets. He liked to think of Oscar Wilde's definition: "Criticism is a creation within a creation."

Within criticism in this sense Du Bos specializes in the psychology of genius. Yet, an André Suarès, if he fails to attain objectivity in his dramatic portraits, can be satisfied to have contributed a self-portrait to literature. But Du Bos's self-reproach implies a straining toward objectivity. His *Journal* is an arsenal for hostile critics. He knows that he trusts his intuition too much sometimes, without the safeguards of a historical scholarship which he respects when it is not deterministic and too external in its biographical approach.[48] An extraordinary development of "psychic space" in Du Bos himself will tempt him in the case of his contemporaries to supply the harmony to slight, though usually interesting tunes. Had not Keats said, "When Man has arrived at a certain ripeness in intellect any one grand and spiritual passage serves him as a starting-post towards all 'the two-and-thirty Palaces'"? Du Bos is the safest guide among figures of established scope,

46. *Journal IX, Avril 1934–Février 1939* (Paris: La Colombe, Editions du Vieux Colombier, 1961), 16 Feb. 1939.

47. Jacques Maritain, *Creative Intuition in Art and Poetry* (New York: Pantheon Books, 1953), p. 325.

48. *Grandeur et misère de Benjamin Constant*, pp. 69–70; also *Approximations*, p. 870. See also Du Bos's remarks on his error in the "portrait of virtue" of Lady Byron. *Journal VI, Janvier 1930–Juillet 1931*, 11 Mar. 1931.

not only with writers he calls "his" but with those not "his" who present a characteristic human pathos with force and beauty.

Du Bos represents, then—to speak broadly—the ancient tradition of art as revelation, a Neoplatonism he contrives to circle back to from Bergson. The psychological approach marks him as a child of the eighteenth century and after, though its complexity is Proustian. But the effort, under certain conditions, to arrive at the objective from within, through an interfusion of subject and object, is a post-Baudelairean continuation of the romantic experiment, and it also illustrates the romantic tendency toward a view of literature with metaphysical attachments.

Du Bos would not easily fit into a Catholic criticism as diverse in its specimens as Bergsonian criticism.[49] Among Catholic critics, Albert Béguin, treated elsewhere in this volume, comes closest to him. Du Bos stands nearer to Abbé Bremond than to his other friend Jacques Maritain, though the latter's *Creative Intuition in Art and Poetry* may be seen as an effort to bridge the gap between the author's Thomism and a position like that of Du Bos.

Du Bos can be listed among the leaders of the Catholic literary "Renaissance," but he wears his rue with a difference. More than one of the critics contributing to that Renaissance severely tried his Christian charity. In comparing him with Péguy, for instance, who also owed so much to Bergson and who, after an estrangement, also returned to Catholicism, we find him drawing his inferences less from the poet's words than from the poetic experience as such. Unlike Péguy he is not inclined to find in literature what amounts to a sacred text announcing a specific dogma. Du Bos, though searching for the deepest meaning of what the spiritual interpreter overhears in the voice of genius, still remains within the limits of criticism.

49. See on this subject Gonzague Truc, *Histoire de la littérature catholique contemporaine* (Paris: Casterman, 1961), pp. 230–47, 288–90; also H. A. Hatzfeld, "The Growth of the French Revival," *Renascence* 1 (1948): 7–28.

BIBLIOGRAPHY

WORKS BY DU BOS

Extraits d'un journal, 1908–28. Paris: J. Schiffrin, 1929. 2d edition enlarged: Paris: Corrêa, 1931. Up to 1921 this volume contains materials not to be found in the later journals.

Journal 1921–23. Paris: Corrêa, 1946. As with each successive volume, there is an index of names.

Journal 1924–25. Paris: Corrêa, 1948.

Journal III, 1926–27. [This volume is the first numbered.] Paris: Corrêa, 1949.

Journal IV, 1938. Paris: Corrêa, 1950.

Journal V, 1929. Paris: La Colombe, Editions du Vieux Colombier, 1952.

Journal VI, Janvier 1930–Juillet 1931. Paris: La Colombe, Editions du Vieux Colombier, 1955.

Journal VII, Août 1931–Octobre 1932. Paris: La Colombe, Editions du Vieux Colombier, 1957.

Journal VIII, Janvier 1933–Décembre 1933. Paris: La Colombe, Editions du Vieux Colombier, 1959.

Journal IX, Avril 1934–Février 1939. Paris: La Colombe, Editions du Vieux Colombier, 1961.

Approximations. Prefaces by André Maurois and François Mauriac. Paris: Fayard, 1965. ("Meditations on the Life of Baudelaire." Translated by A. Hyatt Major. *Hound and Horn* 4 (1931): 461–97. "Points of View on Proust." Translated by Angelo P. Bertocci. In *From the N.R.F.*, pp. 103–7. Edited by Justin O'Brien. New York: Farrar, Straus and Cudahy, 1958. Reprinted as "The Profundity of Proust." In *Proust: A Collection of Critical Essays*, pp. 132–135. Edited by René Girard. Twentieth Century Views. Englewood Cliffs, N.J.: Prentice-Hall, 1962. "On the 'Inner Environment' in the Work of Flaubert." Translated by Paul de Man with "some very minor deletions." In *Madame Bovary*, pp. 360–71. Edited by Paul de Man. Norton Critical Editions. New York: Norton, 1965.

Le Dialogue avec André Gide. Paris: Au Sans Pareil, 1929; Paris: Corrêa, 1946.

Byron et le besoin de la fatalité. Note by Juliette Charles Du Bos. Paris: Corrêa, 1929, 1946, 1957. (*Byron and the Need of Fatality.* Translated by Ethel Colburn Mayne, with a preface by the author. London and New York: Putnam, 1932.)

Du Spirituel dans l'ordre littéraire. Preface by Georges Poulet. Introduction by Madame Charles Du Bos. Paris: Corti, 1967. First appeared in *Vigile*, Cahier no. 1 (Paris: Grasset, 1930), pp. 235–274; Cahier no. 4 (Paris: Grasset, 1930), pp. 133–222; Cahier no. 4 (Paris: Desclée de Brouwer, 1931), pp. 139–217.

Goethe, Paris: Corrêa, 1949. Contains material from as early as 1932.

François Mauriac et le problème du romancier catholique. Paris: Corrêa, 1933.

What Is Literature? New York: Sheed and Ward, 1940. Four lectures delivered in English at Saint Mary's College, Notre Dame, Ind. in 1938. *Qu'est-ce que la littérature?* Translated into French from the original English by Juliette Charles Du Bos; with a "Dernier Journal Intime." An important part of this book is devoted to a "Hommage à Charles Du Bos." Présences. Paris: Plon, 1945. This is a convenient collection of most of the best writing on Du Bos; it should be added that its tone is uniformly favorable.

Grandeur et misère de Benjamin Constant. Paris: Corrêa, 1946.

Choix de textes de Charles Du Bos. Edited by Juliette Charles Du Bos. Preface by Etienne Gilson. Paris: La Colombe, 1959.

There are also a series of articles written as "Letters from Paris" for the periodical, *The Athenaeum* (*Nation and Athenaeum*):

"The Prix Goncourt." *The Athenaeum*, no. 4693 (9 April 1920), pp. 491–92. Apropos of awarding a prize to Proust for *A l'Ombre des jeunes filles en fleurs*.

"The Centenary of Lamartine's *Méditations poétiques*." *The Athenaeum*, no. 4697 (7 May 1920), pp. 618–19.

"A Few Belated Reflections on the Commemoration of Sainte-Beuve's Death." *The Athenaeum*, no. 4703 (18 June 1920), pp. 813–14.

"The Symbolist Movement in French Poetry." *The Athenaeum*, no. 4708 (23 July 1920). pp. 126–27; no. 4709 (30 July 1920), pp. 158–9.

"Poe and the French Mind." *The Athenaeum*, no. 4732 (7 Jan. 1921), pp. 26–27; no. 4733 (14 Jan. 1921), pp. 54–55.

"A Battlefield of the Study." *Nation and Athenaeum* 29, no. 6 (7 May 1921): 214.

"The Third Centenary of La Fontaine's Birth." *Nation and Athenaeum* 29, no. 23 (3 Sept. 1921): 798.

SELECTED WORKS ON DU BOS

Books

Bertocci, Angelo P. *Charles Du Bos and English Literature: A Critic and His Orientation*. New York: King's Crown Press, 1949. Bibliography and Index. Contains a more detailed discussion of Charles Du Bos's criticism in general and especially his views on English novelists, poets, and critics.

Dédéyan, Charles. *Le Cosmopolitisme littéraire de Charles Du Bos.*

I. *La Jeunesse de Charles Du Bos (1882–1914).* Paris: Société d'Edition d'Enseignement Supérieur, 1965.

II. *La Maturité de Charles Du Bos (1914–1927).* 2 vols. Paris: C.D.U. et S.E.D.E.S. réunis, 1966.

III. *Le Critique catholique ou l'humanisme chrétien (1927–1939).* 2 vols. Paris: C.D.U. et S.E.D.E.S. réunis, 1967.

Gouhier, Marie-Anne. *Charles Du Bos.* Preface by François Mauriac. Essais d'Art et de Philosophie. Paris: Vrin, 1951. The author states that the book was written in the last four years of Du Bos's life and was "lu à mesure par lui." Contains biographical material but deals largely with the critic's method and thought. Makes a start toward the study of Du Bos's style. Indispensable bibliography, going up to 1946.

Mouton, Jean. *Charles Du Bos. Sa relation avec la vie et la mort.* Followed by writings by Charles Du Bos on "Le Bonheur," "Les Iles." Paris: Desclée de Brouwer, 1954. This volume counteracts views of Du Bos as withdrawn from life. It offers more than the title promises.

Savouret, Marie. *Nietzsche et Du Bos.* With three unpublished fragments by Du Bos on Nietzsche. Confrontations. Paris: Minard, 1960.

Articles and Sections of Books

Archambault, Paul. "Charles Du Bos." In *Témoins du spirituel,* pp. 103–36. Paris: Bloud et Gay, 1932.

Barrière, Jean-Bertrand. "Hommage à Charles Du Bos: le journal d'un critique." In *Critique de chambre,* pp. 1–17. Paris: La Palatine, 1964.

Béguin, Albert. "Charles Du Bos et les textes." In *Qu'est-ce que la littérature?* pp. 210–16. Deals with Du Bos's whole work as an intimate journal.

Bertocci, Angelo P. "Tensions in the Criticism of Charles Du Bos." *Yale French Studies* 2, no. 1 (Spring–Summer 1949): 79–85.

———. "Charles Du Bos and Goethe." *Romanic Review* 50 (1959): 41–54.

Cahiers Charles Du Bos. 1956–. Published by the Société des Amis de Charles Du Bos. Includes *inédits,* letters to and by Du Bos, articles, bibliography.

Curtius, Ernst-Robert. "Charles Du Bos." *La Revue Nouvelle* 20–21 (15 July–15 Aug. 1926): 31–43.

———. "Charles Du Bos." *Die Neue Rundschau* 4 (1952): 500–524. Translated into French in *Cahiers Charles Du Bos* no. 2 (December 1957), pp. 18–41. One of the severer criticisms of Du Bos, part of the aftermath of the *Dialogue avec Gide*.

Daniélou, Jean, S. J., "L'Oeuvre de Charles Du Bos." In *Qu'est-ce que la littérature?* pp. 259–64. The relation of art and morality in Du Bos's criticism.

Daniel-Rops. "La Compréhension de Charles Du Bos." In *Qu'est-ce que la littérature?* pp. 189–93.

Dieckmann, Herbert. "Charles Du Bos." *Symposium* 1, no. 3 (November 1947): 31–45.

———. "André Gide and the Conversion of Charles Du Bos." *Yale French Studies*, no. 12 (Fall–Winter 1953), pp. 62–73. An impartial treatment of a delicate subject by a friend of Du Bos.

Fernández, Ramón. "Approximations II." *Nouvelle Revue Française* 28 (1927): 827–31. This and the following reviews, also by Fernández, contain some of the most searching criticism of Du Bos:

"Approximations IV." "Extraits d'un Journal." *Nouvelle Revue Française* 38 (1932): pp. 1100–4.

"*Vigile*." ("Du spirituel dans l'ordre littéraire.") *Nouvelle Revue Française* 34 (1930): 778–80.

Heurgon, Jacques. "Les Dons de Charles Du Bos." In *Qu'est-ce que la littérature?* pp. 241–48. Du Bos as a metaphysical critic.

Jones, P. Mansell. In *French Introspectives: From Montaigne to André Gide*, pp. 95–96, 108–11. London: Cambridge University Press, 1937.

Leleu, Michèle. "Une 'météorologie intime,' le Journal de Charles Du Bos." *Cahiers de l'Association Internationale des Etudes Françaises*, no. 17 (1965), pp. 133–50.

Magny, Claude-Edmonde. "Les Impasses de la critique: A propos de Charles Du Bos." *Poésie 47*, no. 38 (March 1947): 117–26.

———. "Plaidoyer pour la Critique." *Esprit* 9 (1941): 635–46.

Madaule, Jacques. "La Fidélité de Charles Du Bos." In *Qu'est-ce que la littérature?* pp. 198–209. Emphasis on a profound consistency in Du Bos.

Marcel, Gabriel. "In Memoriam." In *Qu'est-ce que la littérature?* pp. 165–71. Du Bos and philosophy.

Maurois, André. In *De Gide à Sartre*, pp. 49–91. Paris: Perrin, 1965.

Moeller, Abbé Charles. "Charles Du Bos et le pélerinage vers l'espérance." In *Littérature du XX*e *siècle et Christianisme* 4. Paris: Casterman, 1960. Study of Du Bos's religious growth after conversion.

Poulet, Georges. "La Pensée critique de Charles Du Bos." *Critique* 21 (1965): 491–516.

Richard, Jean-Pierre. "La Méthode critique de Charles Du Bos." *Modern Language Review* 62 (1967): 420–29.

Rousseaux, André. "Charles Du Bos ou la béatitude littéraire." In *Littérature du vingtième siècle* 2:79–86. Paris: Albin Michel, 1939.

Sencourt, Robert (pseudonym for Robert E. G. George). "Byron et le besoin de la fatalité." "Le Dialogue avec André Gide." *Criterion* 9, no. 34 (October 1929): 122–27.

Seznec, Jean. *On Two Definitions for Literature.* Oxford: Clarendon Press, 1952. Comparison of Du Bos and Sartre.

Thibaudet, Albert. "Le Quartier des philosophes." *Nouvelle Revue Française* 28 (1927): 797–804.

Truc, Gonzague. In *Histoire de la littérature catholique contemporaine,* pp. 240–41, 311. Paris: Casterman, 1961.

Vaudoyer, Jean-Louis. "Souvenirs." In *Qu'est-ce que la littérature?* pp. 152–60. Du Bos and painting.

René Wellek

4

Albert Thibaudet

In the twenties and early thirties of this century Albert Thibaudet (1874–1936) seems to have assumed a position similar to that of Sainte-Beuve in the fifties and sixties of the nineteenth century. His regular articles in the *Nouvelle Revue Française*, his books on Maurras, Barrès, Flaubert, on Bergsonism, on Valéry, and particularly in 1926 the expanded version of *La Poésie de Stéphane Mallarmé*, which had gone almost unnoticed in the original 1912 edition, established a great reputation. After his death the *Histoire de la littérature française de 1789 à nos jours* attracted much respectful attention, and his "Réflexions," collections of his articles from the *NRF* kept his memory bright right up to World War II. The comparison with Sainte-Beuve seems not inappropriate if one thinks of the range of Thibaudet's work and of the unmistakable similarity of temperament, the tone of detachment, fair-minded justice, and toleration extended to the most diverse kinds of writing. Thibaudet, in frequent asides, speaks himself of his "literary pantheism," his "pluralism," his "multilateralism," his "anti-cyclopism"[1]—meaning his disapproval of a one-eyed view of the world—and one can speak of Thibaudet's frank Epicureanism and skepticism as one can speak of Sainte-Beuve's. It is not by chance that Montaigne was a revered model for both. (Thibaudet had been preparing a book on Montaigne for many years.)

A stillness has, however, settled around Thibaudet. There was a number of the *NRF* devoted to his memory and there have been two books on him, one by an American pupil,

1. *Cluny*, Portrait de la France (Paris: Editions Emile-Paul Frères, 1928), p. 30; *Réflexions sur la littérature II* (Paris: Gallimard, 1941), pp. 137, 16, 172.

Alfred Glauser, the other by an Australian scholar. There is a brilliant article by Leo Spitzer, which, oddly enough, remained unknown to the two writers of the books on Thibaudet. While the silence of the French since the war is ominous, the almost total disappearance of Thibaudet from the horizon can, in part, be accounted for easily enough. Much of his writing for the *NRF* concerns ephemeral publications of the time. Some of his main topics, Maurras, Barrès, Amiel, do not today excite much critical interest. Many of his writings are studded with allusions to people, books, and characters in books which today need commentary almost as much as Dante's allusions in the *Divine Comedy* or Pope's in the *Dunciad*. Some of his stylistic mannerisms may seem merely tiresome: the *calembours* and obvious rhetorical figures and particularly the extraordinarily luxuriant undergrowth of his metaphors. Many of these are pleasant and witty but others seem merely fanciful and ultimately pointless. Spitzer and Glauser describe and analyze them admiringly as examples of "creative" criticism. But there is little illumination in comparing Hugo's work with a triumphal arch or the Iberian peninsula, or Lamartine's with the Greek archipelagos, or the prose of Chateaubriand with the contours of the gulf of Naples. We may smile at hearing Sainte-Beuve compared, punningly, with the meandering river Doubs, but what is achieved in comparing Amiel's journal with Lake Geneva, Gide's with the Arve, and Valéry's with the Rhône?[2]

One could also argue that much that Thibaudet has written has been superseded. The book on Mallarmé is overshadowed by the massive efforts of the last decades, from Kurt Wais's stout volume to Jean-Pierre Richard's *Univers imaginaire de Stéphane Mallarmé*. The little book on Valéry is outdated merely by the fact that Valéry wrote so much after its publication. Thibaudet shares the fate of many pioneers.

Still, all this cannot be decisive. A critic is not forgotten because of the exuberances of his style or even the inevitable

2. *French Literature from 1795 to Our Era* (New York: Funk & Wagnalls, 1967), pp. 137–38, 134, 46; *Histoire de la littérature française de 1789 à nos jours* (Paris: Stock, 1947), pp. 155–56, 151, 53; also "André Gide," *Revue de Paris* 34, part IV (1927): 757.

obsoleteness of some of his themes and concerns. He is neglected or condemned because of the perversities of his theories, the obtuseness of his taste, the mistakes of his rankings, the narrowness of his information, the falsity of his outlook. And here Thibaudet cannot be found wanting. The present near-oblivion seems simply mistaken. Thibaudet needs rehabilitation by a restatement of his principles and ideas which, in substance, are sane and true.

Thibaudet holds a sound and flexible theory of criticism. Contrary to frequent assertions that he was an "impressionist" —or as he quotes Julien Benda about himself, "un debussyiste intellectuel"[3]—Thibaudet upholds an intellectual ideal of criticism. It should, he repeats over and over again, translate what is conceived in poetic terms into intellectual terms. Criticism, he says, can be understood as "a kind of comparative philology which establishes the roots and changes common to the two languages and techniques" of poetry and philosophy. Criticism changes the concrete into the abstract, obeying "the inevitable necessity of its vocation: like Faguet, to hold up the poet somewhere in the woods, and ask him for his 'ideas.'"[4] Thibaudet chides André Barre, the author of a thesis on symbolism, for abdicating his task. He quotes him as saying that Verlaine's poetry is music—"it can be felt but cannot be analyzed." "Excuse me," Thibaudet interrupts, "but this is your job as a critic. What you feel strongly you must analyze profoundly."[5] All poetry, Thibaudet insists, is finally intelligible; even Mallarmé's and Valéry's always make sense. He attempts to understand them, read their poems as he would

3. *French Literature from 1795 to Our Era*, p. 464; *Histoire de la littérature française de 1789 à nos jours*, p. 528.

4. "Une sorte de philologie comparée, qui établit les racines et les mouvements communs de deux langues et de deux techniques." *Paul Valéry*, Les Cahiers Verts (Paris: Grasset, 1924), p. 135. ". . . cette inévitable nécessité du métier: attendre, comme Faguet, le poète au coin d'un bois pour lui demander ses 'idées.'" Ibid., p. 153.

5. ". . . elle se sent, elle ne s'analyse pas." "Pardon! c'est pourtant votre métier de critique. Ce que vous sentez fortement, vous devez l'analyser profondément." *Réflexions sur la littérature* (Paris: Gallimard, 1938), p. 16.

read any other poems. Valéry's *La Jeune Parque* has its logic "which criticism and its technique are allowed to put into the form of an argument." Still, while insisting on this task of analysis and translation, Thibaudet knows its perils. He is afraid "to substitute for the profound clarity of an image the semi-obscurity or the shadow of an idea."[6] Art and thought, literature and philosophy, are and will remain distinct.

Analysis, close reading, interpretation, and translation into intellectual terms are, however, only some of the procedures of criticism. It requires two others: pure criticism and historical criticism. Pure criticism is Thibaudet's term for what we would call theory of literature. "Not a study of works but of essences: of genius, of genre, of the Book." A theory of genres is the main problem of this higher criticism. It is the problem of universals, the problem of the Platonic ideas which, he decides, must today be seen rather in the Kantian terms of a regulative idea. Genres are obviously nothing fixed or stable. "To create in a genre, means to add to a genre: to change its form, to surpass it. . . . The genre is behind the artist; it is not in front of him."[7]

In practice, Thibaudet's concern was mainly with the novel as a genre. The drama is mostly used only as a contrast to it. He wanted to write a book on the novel which would culminate in a metaphysics of the novel for which he devised an ingenious classification by themes based on empirical psychology. He would begin with the novels of pleasure and pain and then consider types of novels according to the psychological motives they use: the impressionism of sensation, the world of sentiments and passions, the problem of conscience

6. ". . . qu'il est permis au critique et à sa technique propre de mettre en discours." *Paul Valéry*, p. 126. ". . . substituer à la clarté profonde d'une image la demi-obscurité ou l'ombre d'une idée." Ibid., p. 160.

7. ". . . non sur des oeuvres, mais sur des essences. . . . Le génie, le genre, le Livre." *Physiologie de la critique*, Les Essais Critiques (Paris: Editions de la Nouvelle Revue Critique, 1930), p. 139. "Créer dans un genre, c'est ajouter à ce genre. . . . c'est le déformer, le dépasser. . . . Le genre, il est derrière l'artiste; il n'est pas devant lui." Ibid., p. 188.

(here also of analysis), the problem of memory (the autobiographical novel and the different *Recherches du temps perdu*), the play of association of ideas and the imagination (Giraudoux), the world of intelligence and of genius (the intellectual novel), chapters on the will and on free will (the novel of destiny and the novel of action), then the moral problems, with the rich world of *romans à thèse*. Only part of this project is carried out in the essays collected in *Réflexions sur le roman*, which study also, with great subtlety and perception, the technique of the novel, the role of the narrator, the use of tenses, the sense of time. Thibaudet always takes an undogmatic view of different theories. Thus he considers the objective novel, with the narrator absent or concealed (Flaubert, Maupassant) as aesthetically superior to the older type, but still he warns sensibly that "the essential thing is not to have one or the other theory but to have genius, with either one or the other."[8] He contrasts the well-composed French novel with the loose works of Tolstoy and the English novelists, recognizing that these are simply two different aesthetic ideals for which he finds an explanation in a different feeling for time.

Thibaudet has read and studied Bergson and constantly uses his concepts. *Durée* is a key word in his writings. It is used in many different contexts which allow considerable freedom and ambiguity. It is the individual's sense of time; it is the time of a work of art; it is the stream of history; it is the survival of the past in the present. Thibaudet believes that no two people live the same kind of time and suggests that a more advanced psychology would find the formula for each person's time, an idea which must have been the starting point for the speculations of Georges Poulet. Thibaudet merely indicates that every man puts a different accent on his present, past, and future, and gives examples which seem also to make historical distinctions. Chateaubriand and Bossuet lived in the past, Stendhal in the present, and Nietzsche and Mallarmé in the future.

8. "L'essentiel n'est pas d'avoir l'une ou l'autre des deux théories, il est d'avoir, dans l'une ou dans l'autre, du génie." *Réflexions sur le roman* (Paris: Gallimard, 1938), p. 24.

But usually Thibaudet employs the concept of *durée* for the sense of time implied in a novel. He contrasts, on this point, the French and the English novel. The French novel tends to imitate French tragedy, to eliminate or at least to foreshorten time, while in the English novel (and in the French exception, Stendhal's *Chartreuse de Parme*), there is a seemingly perfect isochrony between the unfolding of the novel and the normal unfolding of life. "The time of the English novel," he asserts, "does not undo or destroy, it constructs." Thus the English are supposedly incapable of writing short stories, while Americans have succeeded in that form. One wonders about the truth of such generalizations on national characteristics. Thibaudet's own example—the contrast between a novel by Bourget constructed in theatrical terms and novels such as *The Mill on the Floss* (his particular favorite among the highly admired novels of George Eliot) and *Anna Karenina*—recognizes that the majority of great European novels are not "rhetorical or dramatic compositions, but life creating itself through a series of episodes."[9] Thibaudet himself ends the essay by speaking of the new French *roman-fleuve*, *Jean-Christophe* and *Les Thibault*. He hints at art here dissolving into life. "At the theoretical limit of the novel is a pure scheme of life just as at the limit of the theater there is a pure scheme of movement."[10]

Thibaudet also tries another classification of the novel allowing him to rank novels according to their artistic value, which at the same time is an approach to the true sense of life. He draws distinctions between hazard, chance, and destiny shaping a novel, with novels of hazard as the lowest kind, novels of chance as those by Dumas and Dickens second, and those of destiny ranked highest. In *Wilhelm Meister* and *Madame*

9. "La durée du roman anglais ne défait pas, ne détruit pas, elle construit." Ibid., pp. 95–96. "'Compositions' oratoires ou dramatiques, mais de la vie qui se crée elle-même à travers une succession d'épisodes." Ibid., p. 184.

10. "A la limite théorique du roman, il y aurait un pur schème de vie, comme, à la limite théorique du théâtre, il y aurait un pur schème de mouvement." *Gustave Flaubert, 1821–1880: Sa vie, ses romans, son style* (Paris: Gallimard, 1935), p. 89.

Bovary "the events are modeled on the feelings, the external modeled on the internal, the line of chance modeled on the line of destiny."[11]

The other kind of criticism is historical criticism which must be nourished by a knowledge of literary history without which no critic can become part of literary history. The main task of historical criticism is to "establish sequences of writers, to compose families of the mind, to make out the diverse groups situating and balancing each other in a literature. A work can be classified in a series, considered within a literary order, in a family, with its antecedents and descendants."[12] The echoes of Sainte-Beuve's article on Chateaubriand and of Brunetière's defense of the order of literature are obvious, but we must not identify Thibaudet's outlook with either Sainte-Beuve's or Brunetière's on this point. Thibaudet is not interested in the psychological typology which Sainte-Beuve demanded, nor does he approve of Brunetière's evolutionary theories. Rather he conceives of the past of literature in two complementary ways: either as geography or as genealogy.

The critic contemplates the map of literature which Thibaudet assumes to be something seen, something out there somehow. He has a rather surprising attitude toward the rankings and situations of a past time. For instance, he would not want to assign Benjamin Constant a higher place than Madame de Staël though he recognizes that *Adolphe* is a better book than any one of hers. One must, he says, "preserve in literature the character of an order, respect the places attained, refuse to abandon literature without ranks to the anarchy of personal tastes."[13] Thus Thibaudet disapproves of Léon Daudet's indig-

11. "Les événements modelés sur les sentiments, l'extérieur modelé sur l'intérieur, la ligne de chance modelée sur la ligne de la destinée." *Réflexions sur la littérature*, p. 239.

12. ". . . à établir des 'suites' d'écrivains, à composer des familles d'esprits, à repérer les divers groupes qui se distribuent et s'équilibrent dans une littérature. . . . L'oeuvre peut être classée dans une série, être pensée dans un ordre littéraire, dans une famille, avec des ascendants et des descendants." *Paul Valéry*, p. 1.

13. *French Literature from 1795 to Our Era*, p. 50. ". . . garder tout de même à une littérature le caractère d'un ordre, respecter des situations justement acquises, refuser de la livrer sans cadres à

nation at the overpowering conceit of Hugo. "*Le Satyre* is there as Versailles is there. Cheops probably lacked humility. But with a grain of humility he would not have built his pyramid."[14] Hugo is looked at as a fact of nature like a mountain which we have to climb.

Criticism becomes literary geography not only in this metaphorical sense but also literally, as Thibaudet has a strong sense of the locality from which French writers came or where they lived and wrote. There is "un massif breton" in French literature consisting of Chateaubriand, Lamennais, and Renan. There are two Burgundies, one northern and one southern. Northern Burgundy produced "the powerful, eloquent and virile Saint-Bernard group, the Bossuets and Rudes," while the southern part is the country of Lamartine, Quinet, Prudhon, and Greuze, whose temperaments are more feminine.[15] Thibaudet's belief in the stability of regional characteristics goes so far that he explains Renan's skepticism by his maternal ancestors from Bordeaux, the country of Montaigne. In drawing a parallel between the art of Lamartine and that of Prudhon he thinks it worthwhile to tell us that Lamartine's ancestors came from Cluny, the birthplace of Prudhon. Benjamin Constant, who wrote the first novel of the battle of the sexes, is mysteriously linked with his compatriot from Lausanne, the general Jomini. One sometimes does not know whether this is merely fancy, wit, and display of farfetched information or whether it has to be taken seriously as a kind of *Blut und Boden* theory. Certainly the fact that Montaigne, Proust, and Bergson—all greatly admired authors—were half Jewish seems to Thibaudet very important. They all three exemplify the mobility, the restlessness of Israel—the tents which Bossuet took to be the symbol of the chosen people as opposed to the house on the Roman rock.

---

l'anarchie des goûts." *Histoire de la littérature française de 1789 à nos jours*, p. 56.

14. "*Le Satyre* est là comme Versailles est là. Chéops manquait probablement d'humilité. Mais avec un grain d'humilité, il n'eût pas bâti sa pyramide." *Réflexions sur la critique* (Paris: Gallimard, 1939), p. 124.

15. *Cluny*, p. 10.

On occasion Thibaudet recognizes the tenuousness of such ideas. The sunny South, the succession Greece-Rome-Provence is "un mythe oratoire."[16] Neither can one say that southerners are frivolous; rather, the Marseillais strikes him as sad. Thibaudet is not duped by such a notion as "French and German truths" which may be "a principle either of tolerance or of fanaticism."[17] Though Thibaudet served in the First World War at the front and admired Barrès and Maurras extravagantly, he always tries to preserve a sense of equity toward the Germans. He defends, for instance, their classical scholarship and corrects obvious misinterpretations of Kant and German philosophy. Still, the "explanation of man by the earth, . . . the realism of a gardener"[18] appeals to him strongly. He dislikes an abstract rationalism such as that of Julien Benda, who, he complains, has a positive hatred for the peasant. Thibaudet self-consciously played the role of a provincial with deep roots in his native Burgundy.

Thibaudet's spatial and racial view of the history of literature (which may remind one of the Austrian Josef Nadler's parallel effort to write a history of German literature according to regions and tribes)[19] is outweighed in practice by his sense of time and flux, by his Bergsonism. But he is misunderstood if he is interpreted as a worshiper of an irrational Bergsonian flux. He always holds firmly to a space-time scheme of history. Bergsonism equals for him historicism. He expressly endorsed an identification of the two but refused to consider historicism merely as relativism, suspension of judgment, anticriticism.

Rather, Thibaudet recognizes the necessity of judgment in regard to the past and of a criticism of defense and prosecution for the present. He is by no means averse to making judgments himself: sometimes superlative praise or strong disparagement. To call Hugo "the greatest phenomenon in French literature" may be considered an objective statement, but to call him "the greatest of personal lyrics" and to speak of his love letters "as

16. *Réflexions sur la littérature*, p. 118.

17. *Réflexions sur la littérature II*, p. 285.

18. Ibid., p. 286.

19. *Literaturgeschichte der deutschen Stämme und Landschaften*, 1st ed., 4 vols. (Regensburg: J. Habbel, 1912–18).

the most beautiful . . . in the world" seems extravagant.[20] Lamartine represents to Thibaudet "the high point of Christian poetry."[21] *Suzanne et le Pacifique* is "one of the most beautiful books ever written."[22] But he can also say that Béranger is a bad, unreadable poet, that Quinet writes fourth-rate prose, and that Catulle Mendès's poetry is "a museum of specimens from the whole production of the Parnasse, where everything soon dissolves into refuse and rubbish."[23] A wickedly witty article condemns Henry Bordeaux as a facile and feeble writer. Throughout the *History* there is a constant ranking, grouping, and weighing. Implicitly, the way Thibaudet exalted Mallarmé and Valéry and drew the line of descent of French poetry through them was an act of judgment which merely by silence implied a refusal to acknowledge the claims of rival traditions and tastes.

Thibaudet says rightly, "There is no criticism without a criticism of criticism."[24] Many articles, chapters in the *History*, and the short somewhat rambling *Physiologie de la critique* (1930) provide a fairly complete survey of the history of French criticism: unsystematic, often disproportionate, and on occasion unjust (as I think in the case of Hennequin and Zola), but far superior to anything that had been produced in France before. Thibaudet admires Sainte-Beuve, but criticizes Taine as a "methodical orator" with a "pseudoscientific imagination."[25] His opposition to Brunetière and Faguet is pronounced, as they must seem to him doctrinaire, and he keeps up a running polemic against the *certitudiens* of his time: Maurras, Lasserre, Massis, and the very different Benda. Thibaudet admired Maurras excessively and devoted a whole

20. *French Literature from 1795 to Our Era*, pp. 155, 134, 255; *Histoire de la littérature française de 1789 à nos jours*, pp. 176, 151, 253.

21. *French Literature from 1795 to Our Era*, p. 114; *Histoire de la littérature française de 1789 à nos jours*, p. 128.

22. *Réflexions sur le roman*, p. 147; cf. ibid., p. 149.

23. "Un musée d'échantillons de toute la production parnassienne, où bientôt tout fond en déblais et en platras." *Revue de Paris* 40, part IV (1933): 119; quoted by Glauser, *Albert Thibaudet et la critique créatrice* (Paris: Boivin et Cie, 1953), p. 274.

24. *Physiologie de la critique*, p. 16.

25. *Réflexions sur le roman*, p. 206; ibid., p. 200.

book to his ideas, which he constantly sees, however, as a counterweight to his own preferences. The idea of rigidity, hardness, "muscle, vigor, density,"[26] permeates his discussion. Thibaudet cannot believe in the possibility of a return to classicism. Though he knew Greece and the Greeks and though he values classical tradition and training highly, he doubts that it is a panacea. The greatest French writers are not so deeply dependent on the classics as is often assumed. It may be true of Ronsard, Racine, and Chénier but not of Descartes, Corneille, and Pascal.

Thibaudet always tries to preserve a proper balance of judgment and taste. "It is a mark of intellectual cowardice to claim to understand everything while judging nothing, to let one's taste fall asleep and disappear, but one must also guard against launching, too indiscreetly and armed with an infallible blue pencil, an attack on authors."[27] Intelligence (meaning understanding) and judgment also must be kept in proper proportions. "A criticism of a Spinozistic kind, by which everything is understood as natural and necessary, would never judge, while a criticism which prides itself in pronouncing verdicts will play in the world of great works and great men the role of a comic Dandin. Criticism cannot but temper intelligence with judgment without going to the extreme of either one or the other."[28] Ultimately the critic will have to recognize the immense variety of literature which should be

26. *Trente ans de vie française, I: Les Idées de Charles Maurras* (Paris: NRF, 1920), p. 67.

27. "Si c'est une marque de lâcheté intellectuelle que de prétendre tout comprendre sans rien juger, de laisser s'endormir et disparaître son goût, il faut aussi se garder d'aller trop indiscrètement, armé d'un infaillible crayon bleu, à l'assaut des auteurs." *Réflexions sur la littérature*, pp. 136–37.

28. "Une critique à forme spinoziste par laquelle tout serait compris comme naturel et nécessaire ne jugerait jamais, et une critique qui ne s'attacherait qu'à rendre des arrêts jouerait dans le monde des grandes œuvres et des grands hommes le rôle d'un Dandin de comédie. La critique ne peut que tempérer l'intelligence et le jugement l'un par l'autre sans aller au bout ni de l'un ni de l'autre." *Intérieurs: Baudelaire, Fromentin, Amiel* (Paris: Plon-Nourrit, 1924), p. 132.

treated in two foci of interest not exclusive of one another. The unique, the individual, the differences among works is one leading theme; the other is a "certain social sense of the Republic of Letters," "a sense of resemblances and affinities,"[29] a grand net of comparisons. Criticism must attend both to the work and to its setting in history and society.

Much of Thibaudet's most original and—in its time and place—most meritorious work was an analysis of style in the widest sense which went beyond the mechanical scholastic classifications usual in academic work and beyond the impressionism of the daily critics. Thibaudet's pages on Flaubert's use of "le style indirect libre" (which led to a curious exchange of letters with Marcel Proust)[30] and the analysis of Mallarmé's metaphors,[31] are highlights of Thibaudet's criticism. The concentration on the work itself is, in such contexts, completely free of biographical or social considerations. Thibaudet criticizes Lemaître's book on Chateaubriand for neglecting such a study of style. It seems to him as unreasonable as if a book on Rubens were to give less space to his manner of painting than to his embassies and two wives. The most appropriate method for a book on Chateaubriand (and, we must assume, on any writer) would consist in seeing his person and life purely as a function of his work. Thibaudet's own book on Mallarmé observes this principle. He refers to the man only when he refers to the author. Thibaudet's *La Vie de Maurice Barrès*, in spite of its title, has little or nothing to say of his life. We are even told that Barrès took offense at Thibaudet for not calling on him for biographical information.[32] Nor did the usual psychological approaches to literature appeal to

29. "Un certain sens social de la République des Lettres . . . un sentiment des ressemblances, des affinités." *Réflexions sur la critique*, p. 244.

30. *Gustave Flaubert, 1821–1880: Sa vie, ses romans, son style*, pp. 229 ff.; *Réflexions sur la critique*, pp. 72–815; for Thibaudet's letter to Proust, see ibid., pp. 82–97; Proust's "A propos du style de Flaubert" may be found in the appendix, ibid., pp. 249–63.

31. *La Poésie de Stéphane Mallarmé: Etude critique* (Paris: NRF, 1926), pp. 106–7.

32. John C. Davies, *L'Oeuvre critique d'Albert Thibaudet* (Genève: E. Droz, 1955), p. 68n.

Thibaudet. He ridiculed some clumsy psychoanalytical studies as mere versions of the old method of allegorizing a text, and he is also wary of those who offer the "uncertainties" of scientific psychology as a solution to critical problems. Thibaudet does not believe in determinism: "In literature almost nothing happens which one could legitimately foresee."[33]

Still, this refusal to accept a biographical explanation of literature should not obscure the fact that Thibaudet actually wrote several intellectual biographies. The book on Flaubert—probably his best, and certainly his best-organized book—is based on a biographical outline which closely relates the work to the man, so closely indeed that the apocryphal saying "Madame Bovary c'est moi"[34] is taken as the key to the interpretation of the novel. Thibaudet's intense, sympathetic interest in Amiel is mainly concerned with his psychic and moral life. The fine sketch of Fromentin in *Intérieurs* is set in a biographical frame, as is the inferior late book on Stendhal. The unfinished volume on Montaigne devotes many pages to his biography and psychology. In the *History* a chapter sketching Hugo's life in heroic inflated terms is a curious example of Thibaudet's stylistic mimicry. He often (though not always) writes about an author under the discernible influence of his style.

Thibaudet was always wary of any social determinism. He rejected Taine's triad, *milieu*, *race*, and *moment*, as well as his *faculté maîtresse*. They seem to him all "logical and ideological substitutes for life."[35] Many times he shows his distrust of historical, political, and social explanations. He rejects, for instance, the obvious idea that the decline of Ronsard's reputation in the seventeenth century was due to the order established during the reign of Louis XIV. He ascribes it rather

33. "En littérature presque rien n'arrive de ce qu'on pouvait légitimement prévoir." *Réflexions sur la littérature*, p. 184.

34. The saying cannot be traced further back than to René Descharmes's *Flaubert avant 1857* (1909), where it is reported on distant hearsay. It seems highly improbable that Flaubert could have said it, considering the many contemporary pronouncements of his detachment and even distaste for the woman.

35. *Réflexions sur la critique*, p. 186; *Physiologie de la critique*, p. 220.

to "the internal life of French poetry," to the rise of "prosaic poetry" which he refuses—somewhat obtusely—to relate to any social causes.[36] He admits, quite generally, a coincidence of political and literary breaks but rejects an explanation by the action of politics on literature. It is explained rather "by the undercurrents they have in common, by a profound social trend in which they both partake and which they express in often quite discordant voices."[37]

Neither does Thibaudet believe in the idea of literature as an imitation of life. Art is creation; man is *homo faber*. "Poetic creation does not hold up a mirror to the universe, but adds to the existence of the universe."[38] Thibaudet rejects naturalism brusquely: "Talking of nothing but 'life,' it can picture only what in life anticipates death." Thibaudet tells the story of a clown who won applause at a country fair by imitating the squealing of a pig. Next time a peasant substituted for the clown but was hissed by the crowd. He then uncovered a live pig he had concealed under his coat and which he had pulled by the ears to make it squeal. Still, the crowd rightly preferred the performance of the clown. "The truth of art is not the truth of nature. The clown had to convey better than the pig the illusion of a pig."[39] In the book on Mallarmé Thibaudet ridicules those who criticized the poet for ignoring life. Life apparently meant "to some anarchist bombs, to others the purchase of some sociological books, to many more a salable novel or story, to certain others an administrative post and to the rest the forest of Fontainebleau."[40]

36. *Réflexions sur la littérature*, p. 22.

37. ". . . par des dessous qui leur sont communs, un élan social profond auquel ils participent également, et qu'ils expriment en des langages plutôt discordants." A manuscript dating from 1933 quoted by Davies, *L'Oeuvre critique*, p. 182.

38. "La création poétique . . . ne présente pas un miroir de l'univers, mais elle ajoute à l'être de l'univers." *Paul Valéry*, p. 92.

39. "N'ayant que la 'vie' à la bouche, il ne peut peindre de la vie que ce qui anticipe la mort." *Réflexions sur la littérature*, p. 155. "La vérité de l'art n'est pas celle de la nature. Le bouffon devait donner mieux que le cochon l'illusion d'un cochon." Ibid., p. 148.

40. "Par la Vie, les uns entendaient les bombes anarchistes, d'autres l'achat de quelques livres de sociologie, plusieurs de la

Again it would falsify Thibaudet's position if he were seen simply as a formalist, a defender of art for art's sake, of pure poetry and the ivory tower. Actually, he sees literature constantly in relation to society, studies it as an index of society and as a social institution. Thibaudet was greatly interested in the social standing of the writer in France, in such institutions as the French Academy and the Goncourt Academy, the press and the publishing business. A long paper, "Le Liseur des romans," traces a history of the novel from the point of view of the habitual reader of novels, and the reflections in *Physiologie de la critique* make much of the different kinds of criticism in social terms: spoken, spontaneous criticism, the criticism of journalists, of professors and of the creative writers. Thibaudet would like to study the effects of reading, the influence of criticism on taste, and, like any reviewer of novels, he cannot avoid the questions: Is it true to life? Is it true to what we conceive to be the nature of man? In the case of the novel Thibaudet seems even to assume a scale of approximation in the rendering of life. But he never accepts determinism and hardly, so far as I know, alludes to Marxism.

Thibaudet's concept of literary history is also social; he considers it a particular trait of French literature to be "eminently social and sociable."[41] The plan of his *History of French Literature* is based on a sequence of generations. This has been hailed as a great discovery, but it is nothing new in literary historiography; as early as 1812 Friedrich Schlegel based his sketch of the history of German literature on a carefully devised sequence of generations and since then the scheme has been worked out systematically for the nineteenth century in Germany.[42] Thibaudet himself reviewed a well-informed book by Mentré on the problem: he thought it rather

---

nouvelle ou du roman vendables, certains une sous-préfecture, et un reste la forêt de Fontainebleau." *La Poésie de Stéphane Mallarmé: Etude critique*, p. 445.

41. *Réflexions sur la littérature*, p. 137.

42. In his *Geschichte der alten und neuen Literatur*, lectures delivered in 1812, published in 1815; translated into French by William Duckett in 1829. See my *History of Modern Criticism* (New Haven: Yale University Press, 1955 and 1965), 2:24 ff.; 3:270 n. 7.

demonstrated the difficulties of the concept. He is not taken in by any mysterious mysticism of numbers and recognizes the main obstacle to any clear definition of a generation in history: the absence of a marked beginning and end, the continuity of life, the imperceptibility of its changes. He sees also that the breaks are not the same in different countries. Still, he is impressed by the apparent regularities quoted by Mentré from Otto Lorenz: 1615, the approximate beginning of the Thirty Years War; 1715, the death of Louis XIV; 1815, the fall of Napoleon; 1914, the outbreak of world war—which, thirty-three years later is followed by the series, 1548, 1648, 1748, 1848, all marking important historical events. But Thibaudet questions whether one can speak of "laws" and sees that within a generation there may be as deep divisions as there are between the generations themselves: each has its Right and its Left and even its extreme Left.[43]

In practice, in the *History* a generation is conceived as a group of people aged about twenty who have undergone the impact of a great historical event. Thus the generation with which Thibaudet's *History* begins consists of those who were about twenty in 1789: Napoleon—whom Thibaudet values highly also as a writer—Chateaubriand, and Madame de Staël. The next generation is the one aged twenty in 1820: the youth of Musset's *Confession* who first formulated the concept of generation, Hugo, and the other writers born around 1800. Similarly, there are the generations of 1850, 1885, and finally that of 1914. Examining the series soberly it seems obvious that only the dates 1789, 1848, and 1914 constitute real turning points in French (and European) history, while 1820 and 1885 are chosen rather arbitrarily for literary reasons: 1820 as the very approximate beginning of romanticism; 1885 as the date of the emergence of symbolism as a slogan. The series, we may conclude disappointedly, coincides with the divisions pre-romanticism, romanticism, realism, and symbolism, and is an old, rough, and ready scheme.

Thibaudet, however, somewhat obviates this objection by introducing the concept of a half-generation, which allows for

43. *Réflexions sur la littérature*, pp. 120 ff.

subdivisions in 1802, the return of the émigrés, in 1832, the assumption of conspicuous positions by professors and publicists such as Cousin, Villemain, and Guizot; and 1871, the year of the Commune. The second of these seems arbitrary and hardly significant enough. Thibaudet himself suggested, on another occasion, that the thirty-three years of a generation might well be divided into groups of eleven years.[44] As every writer who makes much of the birth year of his subjects, Thibaudet runs into trouble with authors who began to publish late or who remained unknown in their time but greatly affected a younger group. Stendhal, born in 1783, appears in the *History* with the generation of the twenties, since his first novel *Armance* appeared in 1826; while Mallarmé and Verlaine, born in 1842 and 1844 respectively, appear with the 1885 generation, and Proust, born in 1871, with that of the First World War. Such deviations give away the whole principle and show that one cannot make biological distinctions among a series of men born in 1800-1833-1866 from one born in 1801-1834-1867, etc. The only workable concept of a generation is a historical one, but this is hardly news. Thibaudet's *History* shows again that the historian has to struggle hard with the inescapable fact that he writes, so to say, in single file, one thing after another, though history is a process in which many things happen simultaneously. The literary historian has to make compromises between chronology and groupings by genres or other affinities and has to cut through chronology to accommodate a long-active figure such as Hugo. The idea of generations is only an organizational device.

In spite of such schematic divisions Thibaudet has a very strong sense of continuity, of flow, of imperceptible transitions, implied in his Bergsonism. On occasion he falls back on the concept of inexplicable genius, of sudden mutation, of "an accident of duration," when he reflects, for instance, on the emergence of Rabelais and Montaigne.[45] Often he labors, almost obsessively, the idea of doubles, contrasts, alternations

44. "Générations et expositions," *Nouvelles Littéraires*, 10 Oct. 1931; quoted by Davies, *L'Oeuvre critique*, p. 177.

45. *Réflexions sur la littérature*, p. 306.

either in sequence or in one single or approximately single time. Thibaudet picks these contrasts from almost anywhere. Some are metaphors as old as the succession of a golden age by a silver age, which seems to him a "law of nature."[46] Another is the rhythmic alternation of ages of feeling and intelligence which is only a version of the old double: romanticism-classicism. Thibaudet uses it expressly or assimilates it to a contrast between a stable order and a Heraclitean or Bergsonian flux. Romanticism is defined as the enemy of "the old Aryan root, the fundamental square root of duration, stability, being, which there is, like a metallic flow, in the plenitude of that word 'state.'"[47] In discussing some recent novels Thibaudet produces the distinction between a "really living work of art which is created as nature creates" and an "artificial, manufactured work of art as *homo faber* makes it." He confesses, obviously contradicting his usual vitalism, that he leans to the second side.[48] In the book on Mallarmé another distinction is developed at some length. Older poetry analyzes and describes human feelings, while the new poetry suggests and creates feelings. The writers of the seventeenth century were "experts of the human heart," while with the new symbolists, "poetry has become the human heart itself."[49] This seems an unnecessarily mystifying way of expressing an idea similar to that of the Nietzschean double of Apollonian and Dionysiac art. It is related to another fundamental dichotomy in Thibaudet's critical vocabulary: that of symbol and allegory.

Thibaudet knows that the distinction between symbol and allegory is of recent origin, and he quotes Kant's *Critique of Judgment* on the symbol. But he elaborates it very much in

46. *Réflexions sur la critique*, p. 46.

47. "La vieille racine aryenne, le $\sqrt{st}$ fondamental de durée, de stabilité, d'être, qu'il y a, comme une coulée métallique dans la plénitude de ce mot: l'Etat." *Réflexions sur la littérature*, p. 36.

48. "L'Oeuvre d'art vraiment vivante, qui est créée comme crée la nature . . . l'oeuvre d'art artificielle, fabriquée, comme l'*homo faber* fabrique." *Réflexions sur la littérature* II, p. 148.

49. "Connaisseurs du coeur humain . . . leur poésie est devenue le coeur humain lui-même." *La Poésie de Stéphane Mallarmé: Etude critique*, p. 119.

terms derived from Goethe and Carlyle. It is the contrast between mechanism and life. "Allegory presents itself to us in the form of a clear, precise, detailed intention while the symbol comes in the form of a free creation where idea and image are indiscernibly fused." He admits that all art has a tendency toward the symbolic, but insists that there is a difference. "The symbolic meaning of a work is the purer the more distant it seems from allegorical symmetry, the more it implies suggestion rather than expression." Besides, "the symbolic meaning of a work is the higher if the matter of the work, in its definition and concept, seems to carry less possibility of symbolization; the higher, then, if the symbol springs more directly from the particular, from the devices peculiar to an art, without the intervention of an intellectual generalization."[50] This contrast of symbol and allegory permeates the books on Mallarmé and Flaubert and organizes also much of Thibaudet's thought on the history of the novel from the *Roman de la rose* to his admired Giraudoux and Proust. Another related concept is type. Faust, Don Quixote, Don Juan are symbols or types of humanity. Somewhat desperately Thibaudet tries to make out of Madame Bovary a type which would be more than a social type. The creation of types is always high praise for a writer: Bel-Ami is a type, so are Candide and Pangloss and even Ubu Roi. Tom and Maggie Tulliver in the *Mill on the Floss* seem to him "the two types of the English soul."[51]

50. ". . . l'allégorie se présente à nous sous la forme d'une intention nette, précise, détaillée, le symbole sous la forme d'une création libre où l'idée et l'image sont indiscernablement fondues. . . . La portée symbolique d'une oeuvre est d'autant plus pure qu'elle paraît plus éloignée de la symétrie allégorique, qu'elle implique plus de suggestion et moins d'expression. La portée symbolique d'une oeuvre est d'autant plus haute que la matière de cette oeuvre paraissait, dans sa définition et son concept, comporter moins de possibilité de symbole,—d'autant plus haute que le symbole jaillit plus directement du particulier, des moyens propres à un art, sans l'intermédiaire d'une généralisation intellectuelle." *Réflexions sur le roman*, pp. 30–31.

51. *Réflexions sur la littérature*, pp. 227, 253, 277; ibid., p. 107; *Réflexions sur le roman*, p. 33.

Thibaudet pursues these dualisms even further. Each genre has two styles: one "sharp," the other "flat," one Doric, the other Ionic; one masculine, the other feminine. He contrasts Descartes and Pascal, Corneille and Racine, Bossuet and Fénelon, Voltaire and Rousseau, Lamartine and Hugo, and Balzac and George Sand, in these terms. Amusingly the couple Chateaubriand and Madame de Staël shows the same contrast with the literary and the real sex more or less inverted. There is only one exception, Molière. He remains alone in control of the realm of comedy.

This dualism seems to Thibaudet a feature peculiar to French literature, distinguished from the other great literatures of the West which are dominated by single figures: Dante, Cervantes, Shakespeare, and Goethe. Thibaudet constantly refuses to choose between the two contrasting series in French literature. He is for both Voltaire and Rousseau. "I have the feeling of inhabiting a literature which lives under the law of the many or the pair." [52] He disapproves of attempts to find the representative French author. He agrees with Charles Du Bos that Montaigne comes nearest to this idea but, in spite of great admiration, he feels that Montaigne is lacking in the exceptional and the heroic. Descartes, Corneille, Pascal furnish the rational and the tragic: they break with average human nature. Thibaudet always returns to this conviction: "A nation is what cannot be contained in a single formula or permit a single point of perfection." [53] Thus Nisard with his frozen ideal of the French spirit or Brunetière with his fixed concept of tradition falsify and petrify history. "We need the Maurrases and we need the Amiels, as we need the Barrèses and the Montaignes." [54] This universal tolerance, however, does not, Thibaudet insists, mean conciliation, a leveling of differences, a suppression of contradictions and conflicts which would only achieve a diminution of life. "In a world in agree-

52. "J'ai le sentiment d'habiter une littérature qui vit sous la loi du plusieurs, ou du couple." *Réflexions sur la littérature II*, p. 138.

53. "Une nation, c'est ce qui ne saurait tenir dans une formule unique, ni comporter un seul point de perfection." *Gustave Flaubert, 1821–1880: Sa vie, ses romans, son style*, p. 264.

54. *Réflexions sur la littérature*, p. 223.

ment with itself individuals would become a scandal, an infirmity of being. God has done well in choosing a world of individuals."[55] Contrasting *Anna Karenina* with Turgenev's *Smoke* he says characteristically: "In refusing to prefer one to the other, I do not surrender my judgment: there is something more beautiful than one or the other and that is one *and* the other, their opposition, and, hence, their harmony."[56] It is the same idea he expresses elsewhere even more strikingly: "In my impenitent bilateralism I refuse to choose, I do not abstain out of weakness, but with the firm decision not to decide."[57] It is not an ideal of synthesis, of universal amalgamation. It is rather the expression of the essence of historicism which recognizes all the fantastic variety of the world and enjoys it in its conflicts and contradictions. Thibaudet successfully combines the two sides of historicism: a strong sense of individuality, particularity, uniqueness, with a constant feeling for the large historical processes in time. It is still a view of literature and the world which is immensely fruitful for its understanding, however much it may run counter to the fanaticisms, limited preoccupations and the possibly profounder metaphysics of our time.

BIBLIOGRAPHY

WORKS BY THIBAUDET

La Poésie de Stéphane Mallarmé: Etude critique. Paris: NRF, 1912. New final edition, Paris: NRF, 1926.

Trente ans de vie française. Vol. 1: *Les Idées de Charles Maurras*. Paris: NRF, 1920.

55. "Dans un monde d'accord avec lui-même, les individus deviendraient un scandale, une infirmité de l'être. Dieu a bien fait de choisir un monde d'individus." *Réflexions sur la critique*, p. 190.

56. "En refusant de préférer l'un à l'autre, je n'abdique pas mon jugement: il y a quelque chose de plus beau que l'un ou que l'autre, c'est l'un et l'autre, c'est leur opposition, et, par suite, leur harmonie." *Réflexions sur le roman*, p. 19.

57. "Dans mon bilatéralisme impénitent je refuse de choisir. Je ne m'en abstiens pas par mollesse, mais avec la décision énergique de ne pas décider." *Réflexions sur la littérature II*, p. 59.

Trente ans de vie française. Vol. 2: *La Vie de Maurice Barrès*. Paris: NRF, 1921.

Gustave Flaubert, 1821–1880: Sa vie, ses romans, son style. Paris: Plon-Nourrit, 1922. New final edition; Paris: Gallimard, 1935. ("Madame Bovary." Translated by Paul de Man. In *Madame Bovary*, pp. 371–83. Edited by Paul de Man. Norton Critical Editions. New York: Norton, 1965.)

La Campagne avec Thucydide. Paris: NRF, 1922.

Trente ans de vie française. Vol. 3: *Le Bergsonisme*. 2 vols. Paris: NRF, 1923.

Paul Valéry. Les Cahiers Verts. Paris: Grasset, 1924.

Les Princes lorrains. Les Cahiers Verts. Paris: Grasset, 1924.

Intérieurs: Baudelaire, Fromentin, Amiel. Paris: Plon-Nourrit, 1924.

Etranger, ou Etudes de littérature anglaise. Geneva: Editions de la Petite-Fusterie, 1925.

Le Liseur de romans. Essais et Critiques. Paris: G. Grès et Cie., 1925.

Cluny. Portrait de la France. Paris: Editions Emile-Paul Frères, 1928.

Amiel, ou La Part du rêve. Le Passé Vivant. Paris: Hachette, 1929.

Mistral, ou la République du soleil. Le Passé Vivant. Paris: Hachette, 1930.

Physiologie de la critique. Les Essais Critiques. Paris: Editions de la Nouvelle Revue Critique, 1930.

Stendhal. Les Romantiques. Paris: Hachette, 1931.

Histoire de la littérature française de 1789 à nos jours. Paris: Stock, Delmain et Boutelleau, 1936. New edition. Paris: Stock, 1947. (*French Literature from 1795 to Our Era*. Translated by Charles Lam Markmann. New York: Funk and Wagnalls, 1967.)

Réflexions sur le roman. Paris: Gallimard, 1938.

Réflexions sur la littérature. Paris: Gallimard, 1938. ("Marcel Proust and the French Tradition." Translated by Angelo P. Bertocci. In *From the N.R.F.*, pp. 108–17. Edited by Justin O'Brien. New York: Farrar, Straus, and Cudahy, 1958. Reprinted as "Faces of Proust." In *Proust: A Collection of Critical Essays*, pp. 47–52. Edited by René Girard. Twentieth Century Views. Englewood Cliffs, N.J.: Prentice-Hall, 1962.)

Réflexions sur la critique. Paris: Gallimard, 1939.

Réflexions sur la littérature II. Paris: Gallimard, 1941.

Montaigne. Text established by Floyd Gray based upon manuscript notes. Paris: Gallimard, 1963.

Thibaudet also edited the Pléiade editions of Montaigne's *Essais* (Paris: Gallimard, 1933; new ed. 1950 and, jointly with Maurice Rat, 1963) and Flaubert's *Oeuvres*, 2 vols. (Paris: Gallimard, 1936; new ed. 1946).

SELECTED WORKS ON THIBAUDET

Hommage à Albert Thibaudet. Nouvelle Revue Française 46 (1936): 5–176. Contains tributes and articles by Valéry, Bergson, Alain, Jean Wahl, Ramón Fernández, E. R. Curtius, Benjamin Crémieux, and others. (Bergson's contribution: "Remarks on Thibaudet as Critic and Philosopher." Translated by J. Robert Loy. In *From the N.R.F.*, pp. 261–67. Edited by Justin O'Brien. New York: Farrar, Straus, and Cudahy, 1958.)

Blanchot, Maurice. "La Critique d'Albert Thibaudet." In *Faux pas*, pp. 334–38. Paris: Gallimard, 1943.

D.Z.H. "Thibaudet, or, The Critic as Mediator." *Yale French Studies* 2, no. 1 (Spring–Summer 1949): 74–78.

Davies, John C. *L'Oeuvre critique d'Albert Thibaudet*. Geneva: Droz, 1955. Bibliography. A solid thesis focusing on the criticism, more conventional than the Glauser entry below.

Devaud, Marcel. *Albert Thibaudet, critique de la poésie et des poètes*. Fribourg: Editions Universitaires, 1967.

Genette, Gérard. "Thibaudet chez Montaigne." *Critique* 20 (1964): 66–70. Reprinted as "Montaigne bergsonien." In *Figures*, pp. 139–43. Tel Quel. Paris: Seuil, 1966.

Glauser, Alfred. *Albert Thibaudet et la critique créatrice*. Paris: Boivin et Cie, 1952. Bibliography. Contains fine study of Thibaudet's style and imagery and pays much attention to him as a creative writer.

Spitzer, Leo. "Patterns of Thought in the Style of Albert Thibaudet." *Modern Language Quarterly* 9 (1948): 259–72, 478–91. Reprinted in *Romanische Literaturstudien*, pp. 294–328. Tübingen: Niemeyer, 1959. A brilliant analysis of Thibaudet's style concluding with praise of his "unfanatical, well-balanced, happy nature." Thibaudet, Spitzer argues, is no Bergsonian.

Alvin Eustis

5

The Paradoxes of Language: Jean Paulhan

Editor of the *Nouvelle Revue Française* after Rivière's death in 1925, Jean Paulhan was chiefly responsible for keeping the magazine abreast of the times. He opened its pages to young revolutionary movements like Dada and surrealism (spurned by Rivière, Gide, and the conservative wing of *NRF* critics) and accepted the first writings of authors as varied as Jean Giono, Julien Green, Jules Supervielle, André Malraux, Henri Michaux, Francis Ponge, Raymond Queneau, and Jean-Paul Sartre. In fact, his receptivity to experiment and innovation caused him to appear, superficially at least, a modern among moderns, unconcerned with tradition and those values of the past so dear to most members of the *NRF*, of whom, since he was born in 1884, he was an approximate contemporary. His dislike for conventional morality had led him to investigate the bypaths of sexual deviation; he championed the Marquis de Sade and wrote the preface to the scandalous *Histoire d'O*, which rumor immediately attributed to Paulhan himself.

Publication of the *Fleurs de Tarbes* in 1941 revealed, or should have revealed, how superficial was the emphasis upon that "fashionable" aspect of Paulhan. Several of the most influential critics in France today consider this book the most important critical work of the century. It is certainly one of the most ambitious, and most difficult; but when the reader finally grasps its import, Paulhan's goal during his years of relative silence, as well as the perspective in which his later major works would be composed, becomes clear. Paulhan's concern is with the aesthetics of literature and, more specifically, with criticism of criticism. His aim is the restoration to

French letters of a rhetoric reconciling past and present, rising above the warring traditions of classicism and romanticism, and permitting the establishment of a truly aesthetic criticism (i.e., neither historic nor pseudo-scientific). To attain that aim, however, Paulhan had consequently to create his own dialectical method. He confronts his reader with a complex, subtle, and paradoxical style in which, after an initial observation, he in effect states first that wrong is wrong, then that wrong is right, and, finally, that wrong is superseded by a superior truth integrating both right and wrong. The method obviously owes something to Hegel.

The only way into the *Fleurs de Tarbes* is to peel off layers. The work reposes on a double metaphor. In the southern city of Tarbes, Paulhan had been struck by a rather absurd sign at the entrance to the famous municipal gardens: "Visitors are forbidden to enter carrying flowers." The metaphor's figurative reference is to flowers of rhetoric. As the book develops, the sign reappears in revised form: "Visitors are forbidden to enter *not* carrying flowers." The reason for the revision must wait until we have reached the central argument. The second metaphor is contained in the subtitle, "Terror in Literature," an assimilation of the present state of French letters to the Reign of Terror under the Revolution, when purity and innocence were demanded of all citizens and professional competence of any kind was suspect. Confirmation of today's literary Reign of Terror is the book's point of departure.

That conception of literature depends, however, on a theory of language deriving from a number of factors: Paulhan's study of a primitive people's tongue, Malagasy; his searching examination into the form and content of maxims and proverbs; his analysis of the mental illusions revealed in the most ordinary criminal acts; and a family tradition. His father, an eminent psychologist, had published works on the phenomena of the mind and the two functions of language, denotative and connotative.

According to Paulhan, linguistic expression conceals a double paradox best formulated in the Italian saying, *Traduttore, traditore*. For language betrays us a first time when we try to translate to ourselves our thoughts and emotions (although, contrary to Bergson's assertion, they cannot exist prior to their formulation in spatial language) and again when we try to communicate them to others. There is furthermore some quirk in our mentality which prevents us, save in a few privileged moments, from grasping in a single insight both facets of language: the material word and its meaning. Our tendency to emphasize one at the expense of the other cannot be explained by linguistic science: phonetics is concerned only with the material aspect, semantics only with the meaning, and stylistics (as Paulhan conceived it) with the separation of thought or emotions from the words that express them.

Yet how can we seize thought except through language? Consequently, we dimly sense that they are but the two sides of a coin. Paulhan, who devoted his entire career to verification of that truth, quickly realized that Cartesian rationalism was an outmoded tool, destroying its object in the process of sifting out the parts. Only an oblique method, allowing for deformation by the subject, embracing the object in its totality, and examining the body of divergent opinions about the object, could discover the truth hidden in those opinions. In other words, the nature of language, he concluded, depends on how we look at it and what method we use.

In literary expression, the double paradox of language attains its greatest complexity; opinions are there most at odds. Paulhan notes in the *Fleurs de Tarbes* that the romantic revolution discredited rhetoric—the artistic use of words, rules in poetry and prose, a theory of genres—and put a premium on originality (innocence and purity of inspiration). Since then, generation after generation of practicing critics, together with writers theorizing on their own works, have demanded of literature a fresh point of view, a style owing nothing to tradition, even a solution to ethical, political, or metaphysical problems. Their efforts to free expression from the bondage of words and their pitiless denunciations of rhetoric (each generation finding the preceding one guilty of mouthing mere words) have led to hermetic texts, a flight from craftsmanship into ontology, and a state of anarchy and terror. Whence the Terrorist critics' anguished questions: What is literature? How can literature be possible? Why write? When the critics are not keeping their eyes fixed beyond literature and deign to look at individual works, they refuse to treat them as artifacts. Flirting with science (psychoanalysis or anthropology) or politics (dialectical materialism), they deemphasize the writer's product and relinquish their primary task (in Paulhan's eyes) of establishing values through judgment.

Paulhan felt that the time had come to apply common sense to the problem. Although the logical conclusion of Terrorist argument is silence, have not authors continued to write despite their guilty conscience revealed by various alibis? Has not each successive revolutionary movement, even surrealism (which at the outset was determined to destroy literature), culminated in some sort of rhetoric? The fact is that the Terrorists are victims of a series of illusions arising from the double paradox of language. They maintain that mind is superior to matter, that there is a difference between thought and language, that words constitute an obstacle to direct expression of emotions and ideas. They attack clichés and commonplaces as being nothing but words and consequently betraying mental laziness on the part of writers. Yet many of the offending expressions may show an effort at originality that they as readers have failed to perceive. Then who is guilty of laziness, if not the reader? Numerous commonplaces are strikingly ingenious—the opposite of common. Purple passages and words with vague or tendentious connotations—for example, liberty, communism, democracy—are contemptuously dismissed as rhetoric when the Terrorists do not support the causes that the words represent. However, a sincere desire to be understood may have dictated the utterance.

The Terrorists are in a sense right; but at the same time they are mistaken. If it is true that the less a style bears the stamp of personal invention, the more it has probably accepted conventional language, it is just as true that when one is looking for words and rhetoric, one invariably finds them, since language "thickens" and obtrudes itself upon our consciousness only where there is lack of communication. Again, if something is well written, we instinctively feel that it is contrived. Words chosen with care, however, are not always a barrier; a well-written book can transform our existence. The emotional impact of certain words of imprecise meaning does frighten us by seeming to call for violent action; but in authors with whose ideas the Terrorists agree, on the contrary, the words become transparent—communication is instantaneous.

This problem arises from the positions of writer and reader on opposite sides of expression, so to speak, with the result that what seems inspired to the first seems banal to the second (and vice versa). What solution can there be? Inasmuch as man appears incapable of comprehending both components of a word at once, would it not be best to accept language at its face value, admit that the unholy power of words ceases when we cease being preoccupied with it, and return to linguistic conventions, norms, and rhetoric as the art of writing? Words could once again have precise meanings, method and technique could be reinstated as creative values, tropes could furnish writers a means of exercising ingenuity, and some sense of aesthetic content could be restored. Criticism in turn could come back to an observation of the rules and thereby give authors back a sense of confidence in themselves. Then, truly, strollers in the gardens of Tarbes should be allowed to bring in flowers; if they had their own, they could not be accused of picking those in the gardens. The era of suspicion would be terminated, rule and freedom, soul and technique, would no longer be mutually exclusive terms, and literature would serve no ends but its own. Originality and inspiration might take care of themselves; it is of the nature of the paradox that rhetoric is verbalism when refused, and profound thought when accepted.

Obviously, in the *Fleurs de Tarbes*, the dialectical process has been brilliantly manipulated by the author. The arguments are loaded and Paulhan concludes in favor of a rhetoric conforming to the ideal of the *NRF*: that modern classicism of Gide (to whom the book is dedicated), Rivière, and their disciples, which seeks to integrate everything valid in modern civilization. So unqualified a statement, however, hardly does justice to Paulhan's scruples. What he considers valid encompasses much more than for any of his predecessors.

'I, too, have been a Terrorist,'' he confesses.[1] Also, the last pages of the book freely admit to Rhetoric's defects in both past and present. That is probably why Paulhan prefers a less tainted term: Maintenance, with its adherents designated as Maintainers. And the book's last sentence underlines the tentative nature of his conclusions, as well as his realization that the double paradox of language is operating for him, too, as author: "Let's leave it that I said nothing."[2] Judging by Paulhan's other major works, plus certain post-1941 articles presumably to be incorporated into a second volume (long announced, but never forthcoming) of the *Fleurs de Tarbes*, we may be certain that a similar dialectical process would have been applied to Rhetoric in that second volume as earlier to the Reign of Terror.

The superior truth transcending both Terror and traditional rhetoric may be conjectured from Paulhan's subsequent works. At the same time, he becomes more cautious in his method and the pros and cons are weighed more carefully. But the conclusions become firmer. In both *Clef de la poésie* (1944) and *Petite Préface à toute critique* (1951) Paulhan makes the following postulations: the problems to be examined are already solved; any solution has to be expressed in language and will of necessity be ambiguous; the method must be discrete from neither object nor solution; clear ideas cannot be fully comprehended until their aura of obscurity is restored to them; and, finally, he who poses a problem *is* (not *furnishes*) himself the answer. In both books, consequently, the reader upon reaching the end is temporarily disconcerted. They seem to hang in the air, without a conclusion, until the reader realizes that the point of arrival is in reality the point of departure and the form of the two books is the embodiment of Paulhan's method, in his parables and in his criticism.

Clef de la poésie sets out to render intelligible, inconceivable though it may be, the law governing poetry. Any explanation

1. "Comment ne pas faire ici l'aveu que j'étais, au fond, terroriste?" *Les Fleurs de Tarbes, ou La Terreur dans les lettres* (Paris: Gallimard, 1941), p. 155.

2. "Mettons enfin que je n'ai rien dit." Ibid., p. 177.

must take into account a mystery curiously like that of the surrealists' explanation: the heightened effect of poetic language, since coincidence of ideas-emotions and words is greater in poetry than in any other sort of language. Paulhan observes that opinions on poetry fall into two groups, some critics making content flow from form (e.g., Poe and Valéry) and others form from content (e.g., Apollinaire and Novalis). The paradox is that both opinions can be proved by facts, both are true in general, both are false in general. Therefore, there must be adhering to them a law that escapes us. Both groups of theorists (they are recognizable as Rhetoricians and Terrorists) use analogous principles. The first demand figures of speech and thought; the second, a technique of some sort. Both treat metaphor in the same manner. And the works of both groups are also similar according to Paulhan. Let us assume the contradiction (as one "assumes" the burden of proof) by concluding that the relationship between language and poetry, form and content, words and ideas-emotions is one of equivalence or indifference—but not of identity. And a poem will be poetic or prosaic according to the degree of complexity of word-emotion and idea, *each in its own order*. This final remark, as well as the refusal of the Hegel-Croce principle of identity of word and idea, reveals that there still lurks in the Germanic depths of Paulhan's method a spark of Gallic rationalism.

The *Petite Préface à toute critique* is in many respects Paulhan's most satisfactory piece of critical writing. In it he comes closest to formulating his ideal in rhetoric and criticism. The book is so positive in tone that one wonders whether a partial explanation of the lack of a sequel to the first volume of the *Fleurs de Tarbes* might not be that the *Petite Préface* has stolen many of its ideas. Paulhan states that rhetoric and criticism can be valid only as long as they remain faithful to the paradox of language, never losing sight of the indivisibility of ideas-emotions and words. Or, as he had put it in *Clef de la poésie*, faithful to "the . . . mystery . . . espoused and comprehended in the same act."[3] The *Petite Préface* also sets forth in detail

3. ". . . le . . . mystère . . . épousé dans le même temps que compris." *Clef de la poésie* (Paris: Gallimard, 1944), p. 59.

what Paulhan had meant in the *Clef* by a rhetoric "founded no longer on external tricks, but on a conviction deriving from inner feeling" and a criticism "whose point of departure is no longer rules and measures, but exact participation . . . in poetry's secret; in short a criticism knowing what it is about."[4]

Paulhan's point of departure in the *Petite Préface* is the observation that while creators can indeed theorize on their own works, not one has been able to offer a universally valid rhetoric. Yet criticism cannot be reformed until that rhetoric comes into being. The sciences of language are, once more, of no help, not only for the reasons with which we are familiar, but because they cannot make value judgments. On the other hand, the arts of language (traditional grammar and rhetoric) furnish no reasons for their norms. The solution is inescapable (since it is already present): an *equilibrium* between tradition and innovation. (One is reminded of Eliot's *Tradition and the Individual Talent*.) Rhetoric will accept, and criticism will enforce, the rules, but will allow room for experiment; they will accept and enforce usage, but will allow violation of usage. They will constantly be inspired by the living rhetoric found in literary masterpieces. Like the *Fleurs de Tarbes*, the *Petite Préface* might have been dedicated to André Gide (or rather, to his memory); the circle is complete, with the *NRF* movement at the end as it was at the beginning.

F.F. ou le critique (1945) comes as an anticlimax; contrary to the estimate of a number of critics, I feel that it is overrated. There are no new ideas; those present are invariably better developed elsewhere, and, given the author's usual dialectics, the writing is too clear to represent a serious effort at comprehension.

Paulhan's contribution to French criticism remains nevertheless enormous. Just as an earlier *NRF* critic, Albert Thibaudet, bridged the gap between two centuries by combining literary history with Bergsonian interest in contemporary literature and the creative process, so Paulhan effects a

4. ". . . qui parte à l'avenir, non plus de règles et de mesures, mais d'une exacte participation . . . du secret de la poésie: bref une critique en connaissance de cause." Ibid.

transition between the prewar period and today. Dubbed "dean of contemporary criticism," he anticipates some aspects of present-day French criticism but disapproves of others, as a few distinctions will make clear.

Paulhan reminds one of Dilthey and the French phenomenologists. He describes reality only as it presents itself to consciousness and eschews explanatory hypotheses, preferring to examine contradictory doctrines out of which the dialectical process forces hidden truth. He seems close to Maurice Blanchot's concern with ambiguities, paradoxes, and contradictions of literary language, and closer still to Roland Barthes's investigations into rhetoric. But affinities are outweighed by differences. In terms of Anglo-American criticism, he seems somewhat like an I. A. Richards beset by a number of Kenneth Burkes.

Paulhan is indeed postwar in having worked out a personal dialectic and in considering language the seat of the primary paradox of our existence. He has also created a metalanguage (to use Barthes's terminology) and perhaps a metacriticism. On the other hand, he has never ventured into metaphysics. His field is the psychology of language and aesthetics; there he is determined to remain. Most postwar critics appear to him as Terrorists. When Blanchot points out in *La Part du feu* that Paulhan is wrong in reducing literature to a question of language, the implication is obvious. Agitation of such metaphysical problems as being, death, solitude, and anguish, for Paulhan, can be symptomatic only of the disease of criticism—Terrorism. Nor does the existentialist concept of the Other occupy any place in his thought (save at most as the interlocutor, or *traditore*). The opposition between Paulhan and younger critics like Blanchot, Camus, or Sartre (the last soon forming his own review) was doubtless as inevitable as the disavowal by Paulhan's generation of Thibaudet's criticism.

At the end of the *Petite Préface* appears a scathing indictment of Sartre and Brice Parain, who use language as a pretext for metaphysical speculation; their solutions to problems, Paulhan feels, are consequently philosophical, not linguistic. Sartre particularly draws his fire for treating the silence of confrontation as a kind of language, reducing language to concrete action, and in general subordinating in such a cavalier fashion specific problems of language to the ontological problem of the existence of the Other. And in Sartre's applied literary criticism, Paulhan points, with some pleasure, to the passages where the philosopher accuses authors of verbalism. For had Sartre not professed that there was no difference between words and thought?

The same discrepancy can be found in Paulhan himself, for it is difficult to be both a traditionalist and a revolutionary. In his polemical writings, as distinguished from the category of works discussed in this essay, we find a different, sharper Paulhan. A rationalist and conceptualist, he separates problems into their component elements and even distinguishes words from the ideas or emotions that they express. Nevertheless, the body of Paulhan's writings remains an impressive effort to free French criticism from an excessive clarity.

BIBLIOGRAPHY

WORKS BY PAULHAN

Complete Works

Oeuvres complètes. Edited by P. Oster and J.-C. Zylberstein.

I. *Récits: Les Instants bien employés*. Paris: Cercle du Livre Précieux, 1966. Includes *Le Guerrier appliqué; Le Pont traversé; La Guérison sévère; Aytré qui perd l'habitude; De Mauvais Sujets*; and a postface by André Dhôtel.

II. *Langage I: La Marque des lettres*. Paris: Cercle du Livre Précieux, 1966. Includes *Entretien sur des faits divers; Les Hain-tenys; Expérience du proverbe; Jacob Cow le Pirate, ou Si les mots sont des signes; La Rhétorique renaît de ses cendres; La Demoiselle aux miroirs; Eléments; Traité des figures; Clef de la poésie; Petite Préface à toute critique; A Demain la poésie*, "Entretien à la radio avec Robert Mallet (1952)"; and a postface by Roger Judrin.

III. *Langage II: Le Don des langues*. Paris: Cercle du Livre Précieux, 1967. Includes *Les Fleurs de Tarbes*; "Sept Pages d'explications"; "Un Embarras de langage en 1817"; "La Rhétorique avait son mot de passe"; "Un Rhétoriqueur à l'état sauvage"; "Benda, le clerc malgré lui"; "La Preuve par l'étymologie"; "Les Douleurs imaginaires"; "Le

Clair et l'obscur''; ''La Conscience à midi''; and a postface by Maurice-Jean Lefebve.

IV. *Polygraphie I: Littérature. Sade et autres primitifs.* Paris: Cercle du Livre Précieux, 1969. Includes pieces on Montaigne, Sade, Rimbaud, Lautréamont, Vallès, Renard, Fénéon, Gide, Hamsun, Larbaud, Henry Church, Groethuysen, Ungaretti, Thibaudet, Ramuz, Hellens, Cingria, Chazal, Perse, Eluard, Devaulx, and Pauline Réage; ''Entretien avec Robert Mallet'' (continued); and a postface by André Pieyre de Mandiargues.

V. *Polygraphie II: La Tâche aveugle.* Paris: Cercle du Livre Précieux, 1970. Includes ''Braque le patron''; ''La Peinture cubiste''; ''Fautrier l'enragé''; ''L'Art informel''; ''Lettre à Jean Dubuffet''; ''Chagall à sa juste place''; ''L'Artiste moderne face à son public''; ''Petit Traité du pacifisme''; ''L'Abeille''; ''Les Morts''; ''Jacques Decour''; ''Slogans des jours sombres''; ''Patrie''; ''Modestie de l'occident''; *De la paille et du grain*; ''Lettre sur la paix''; ''Lettre aux directeurs de l'Europe''; ''Lettre aux directeurs de la Résistance''; ''Lettre à un jeune partisan''; postfaces by Jean Grenier and Jacques Debû-Bridel and a bibliography by Jean-Claude Zylberstein.

Selected Separate Works

1. The major works discussed in this chapter:

Les Fleurs de Tarbes, ou la Terreur dans les lettres. Paris: Gallimard, 1941.

Clef de la poésie. Paris: Gallimard, 1944.

F.F. ou le critique. Paris: Gallimard, 1945.

Petite Préface à toute critique. Paris: Editions de Minuit, 1951.

2. The minor works and articles revealing the formation of thought and method:

Le Guerrier appliqué. Paris: Sansot, 1915.

Le Pont traversé. Paris: Camille Bloch, 1920.

Jacob Cow le Pirate, ou Si les mots sont des signes. Paris: Au Sans Pareil, 1921.

''L'Expérience du proverbe.'' *Commerce*, no. 5 (Autumn 1925), pp. 23–77.

La Guérison sévère. Paris: Gallimard, 1927.

''Carnet du spectateur.'' *Nouvelle Revue Française* 32 (1929): 242–51, 380–94, 851–65.

Les Hain-tenys merinas, poèmes populaires malgaches. Revised edition. Paris: Gallimard, 1938.

Aytré qui perd l'habitude. Brussels: La Nouvelle Revue de Belgique, 1943.

Entretien sur des faits divers. Paris: Gallimard, 1945.

Préface. B. Grœthuysen. *Mythes et portraits*. Paris: Gallimard, 1947.

Le Marquis de Sade et sa complice, ou Les Revanches de la pudeur. Paris: Les Editions Lilac, 1951.

La Preuve par l'étymologie. Paris: Editions de Minuit, 1953.

Préface. Pauline Réage (anagram of Jean R. Paulhan?). *Histoire d'O*. Paris: J.-J. Pauvert, 1961. (*Story of O*. Translated by Sabine d'Estrée. The Traveller's Companion Series. Paris: Olympia, 1959. New York: Grove, 1966.)

De Mauvais Sujets. Paris: Estienne, 1962.

3. The minor works and articles indicating the probable orientation of what might have been the second volume of the *Fleurs de Tarbes* (together with "Querelle de l'image" and "Les Linguistes en défaut" from *Clef de la poésie*):

"Un Embarras de langage en 1817." *L'Arche*, no. 12 (December 1945–January 1946), pp. 3–19.

"La Rhétorique était une société secrète." *Les Temps Modernes* 1 (1946): 961–84.

"Un Rhétoriqueur à l'état sauvage [Paul Valéry], ou la littérature considérée comme un faux." *La Nef* 3 (July 1946): 3–12; (August 1946): 53–73.

"A demain la poésie." Préface. *Les Poètes d'aujourd'hui*. Texts assembled by Jean Paulhan and Dominique Aury. Paris and Lausanne: Clairefontaine, 1947.

De la Paille et du grain. Paris: Gallimard, 1948.

"Le Secret des poètes." *La Revue (des Deux Mondes)* 1 (January 1948): 158–70.

"Benda, le clerc malgré lui." *Critique* 4 (1948): 387–407, 499–513, 859–864.

"Les Figures ou la rhétorique décryptée." *Cahiers du Sud* 29 (1949): 361–95.

"Un papier-collé en littérature." *Nouvelle Nouvelle Revue Française* 1 (1953): 129–33.

4. Works edited and recent homages:

Ed. Albert Thibaudet: *Réflexions*. 3 vols. Paris: Gallimard, 1938–40.

"Enigmes de Perse." *Nouvelle Revue Française* 10 (1962): 773–89; 11 (1963): 74–83; 12 (1964): 6–17.

Ed. and Introduction. *Honneur à Saint-John Perse: hommages et témoignages littéraires*. Paris: Gallimard, 1966.

"Un héros du monde." *Nouvelle Revue Française* 15 (1967): 589–91.

On André Breton.

5. Interviews

"Entretien à la radio" (1952). By Robert Mallet. *Oeuvres complètes*, vol. 2, pp. 301–11, and vol. 4, pp. 463–514.

"Jean Paulhan." By Denise Bourdet. *Revue de Paris* 70 (March 1963): 119–24.

6. Bibliography

Zylberstein, Jean-Claude. *Oeuvres complètes* 5:497–545.

SELECTED WORKS ON PAULHAN

Berne-Joffroy, André. "Destin de la rhétorique: Stendhal, Valéry, Paulhan." *Cahiers du Sud* 31 (1950): 272–98.

Blanchot, Maurice. *Comment la littérature est-elle possible?* Paris: José Corti, 1942. Reprinted in *Faux pas*, pp. 97–107. Paris: Gallimard, 1943. By the question he raises in his title and by the way in which he conducts his analysis of *Fleurs de Tarbes*, Blanchot reveals that he is a Terrorist.

———. "Le Mystère dans les lettres." In *La Part du feu*, pp. 49–66. Paris: Gallimard, 1949. A general study of Paulhan's work as far as *Clef de la poésie*.

Bourgade, Pierre. "Jean Paulhan et les philosophes." *Nouvelle Revue Française* 14 (1966): 170–73. An amusing and sympathetic (to Paulhan) account of Paulhan's encounter with new "Terrorists" at the Société de Philosophie, 23 April 1966.

Bousquet, Joë. *Les Capitales, ou de Jean Duns Scot à Jean Paulhan*. Paris: Le Cercle du Livre, 1955. Superficial.

———. "A propos des *Fleurs de Tarbes*." *Cahiers du Sud* 26 (1939): 285–307. Also superficial.

Debû-Bridel, Jacques. "Jean Paulhan, citoyen." *Oeuvres complètes* 5:481–92.

Dhôtel, André. "Vers une science de l'illusion littéraire? La méthode de Jean Paulhan." *Critique* 4 (1948): 291–306. Another Terrorist who, in the midst of a generally sympathetic analysis of Paulhan's work, accuses him of being divorced from reality and tarrying among purely aesthetic considerations—the underlying attitude of the Bataille group.

Diéguez, Manuel de. "Jean Paulhan." In *L'Ecrivain et son langage*, pp. 124–32. Paris: Gallimard, 1960. Paulhan's place among postwar French critics.

Genette, Gérard. "La Rhétorique et l'espace du langage." *Tel Quel*, no. 19 (Autumn 1964), pp. 44–54.

Grenier, Jean. "Jean Paulhan critique d'art." *Oeuvres complètes* 5:261–66.

Guérin, Raymond. "Jean Paulhan, ou d'une nouvelle incarnation des lettres." In *Un Romancier dit son mot*, pp. 57–82. Paris: Corrêa, 1948.

Hommage à Jean Paulhan. Nouvelle Revue Française 17 (1969): 641–1055. Bibliography.

Judrin, Roger. *La Vocation transparente de Jean Paulhan*. Paris: Gallimard, 1961. Particularly valuable for the number of Paulhan letters published for the first time. Also points out the influence of Chesterton on Paulhan's use of paradox to defend orthodoxy.

———. "Le Poids du sanctuaire." *Oeuvres complètes* 2:331–41.

Lefebve, M.-J. *Jean Paulhan: une philosophie et une pratique de l'expression et de la réflexion*. Paris: Gallimard, 1949. Despite abusive interpolation, our best reference work.

———. "Paulhan qui perd l'habitude." *Cahiers du Sud* 61 (1966): 110–22.

———. "Un Possédé du réel." *Oeuvres complètes* 3:427–36.

Lévy, Yves. "Jean Paulhan, du jardin fleuri aux catacombes." *Preuves* 13, no. 153 (November 1963): 3–21.

Pieyre de Mandiargues, André. "J. P." *Oeuvres complètes* 4:515–24.

"Portrait de Jean Paulhan." *Les Cahiers des Saisons*, no. 10 (April–May 1957), pp. 263–307. A series of articles on the man and his work by Robert Mallet, Francis Ponge, Marcel Jouhandeau, Obaldia, J.-L. Curtis, Henri Thomas, Jean Grenier, Georges-Emmanuel Clancier, André Dhôtel, Bernard Groethuysen, Jacques Brenner, and Armand Robin.

Rolland de Renéville, André. "Jean Paulhan et l'expression poétique" (*Hain-tenys*). In *L'Univers de la parole*, pp. 133–42. Paris: Gallimard, 1944.

———. "Sur une nouvelle méthode critique" (*Les Fleurs de Tarbes*). Ibid., pp. 143–52.

Toesca, Maurice. *Jean Paulhan, ou l'écrivain appliqué*. Paris: Variété, 1948. Excellent biography; less good on the work.

Weidlé, Wladimir. "Sur la notion de procédé." *Cahiers du Sud* 32 (1950): 100–108.

Frederick Brown

6

Creation versus Literature: Breton and the Surrealist Movement

In the literary domain," wrote Breton on the eve of surrealism's birth, "I became infatuated by turns with Rimbaud, Jarry, Apollinaire, Germain Nouveau, and Lautréamont, but I owe my greatest debt to Jacques Vaché."[1] What sounds at first like a Dada spoof subverting semilegendary *poètes maudits* with Joe Blow was, on the contrary, a papal bull astutely combining truth and fable. Jacques Vaché, dead in 1919 from an overdose of drugs, survived as a kind of ideal absentee whose very absence gave surrealism its cohesion. Breton, alone among the surrealists to have known him at all well, explicated Vaché like a text, *the* text, whose authority nobody could dispute as Vaché himself had left behind no literary traces (excepting some few letters published under the title *Lettres de guerre*). "Jacques Vaché is surrealist in me"[2]—so he figures on the roster of surrealist precursors in Breton's *Manifeste du surréalisme*. Translating Vaché's silence into a vocation, expounding his mysteries like a hierophant, Breton created a poetic movement whose exemplar despised poets.

How then was the exemplar exemplary? Breton met him during World War I while interning at a hospital in Nantes.

1. "En littérature, je me suis successivement épris de Rimbaud, de Jarry, d'Apollinaire, de Germain Nouveau, de Lautréamont, mais c'est à Jacques Vaché que je dois le plus." *Les Pas perdus* (Paris: *NRF*, 1924), p. 9.

2. "Vaché est surréaliste en moi." *Manifestes*, Idées (Paris: Gallimard, 1963), p. 39.

Vaché, laid up with a wound, spent days drawing picture postcards for which he invented weird captions, or arranging and rearranging the few objects on his night table. Directly his leg mended, he got a job unloading barges in Nantes, otherwise amusing himself by day in various dock dives and bar-hopping or movie-hopping at night. Clothing particularly fascinated him; attired as an English army officer or an aviator or a doctor, he would parade through Nantes pretending not to recognize friends. At home, Louise, his companion, sat silent and motionless hours on end, stirring only to prepare tea for her master, a gesture rewarded (according to Breton) with a hand kiss; Vaché boasted that he had never made love to her. Afterward, in Paris, Breton saw him only four or five times, once during the intermission of Apollinaire's play *Les Mamelles de Tirésias* when suddenly Vaché appeared in the aisle waving a pistol which he threatened to empty into the audience. Returning to Nantes, he died, apparently a suicide, although his death, mirroring his life, remains a matter of conjecture. As for Vaché's literary views, he liked Jarry, whose incendiary humor, arising "from a sensation . . . of the theatrical (and joyless) futility of everything" answered his own. Otherwise Vaché professed total indifference toward art and artists, considering them play-actors who come to mistake their stage for life.

I concede a little affection for LAFCADIO because he doesn't read and produces only by amusing experiments, like the Murder—and then without any Satanic lyricism—my old rotten Baudelaire!—what he needed was a little of our dry air: machinery—presses with stinking oil—throb—throb—throb—whistle! Reverdy—the POHETE amusing, and boredom in prose; Max Jacob my old fraud—PUPPETS—PUPPETS—PUPPETS.[3]

It little matters that Vaché may have been a juvenile dandy, a foppish Anglophile, a frustrated painter. His alibis became archetypal virtues. As Breton would have it, Vaché promoted

3. "J'accorde un peu d'amour à LAFCADIO car il ne lit pas et ne produit qu'en expériences amusantes, comme l'Assassinat—et cela sans lyrisme satanique—mon vieux Baudelaire pourri!—Il fallait notre

life beyond its conventions by means of masks, confounding theater with itself, like Jarry's Ubu, whose very improbability keeps him alive. Being an outright marionette, he thus dodges the traps of illusion and verisimilitude. "Vaché was the first to insist on the importance of acts,"[4] wrote Breton. Jerking convulsively from "act" to "act" like some human non sequitur, he acted out his instincts, whose only law was their absolute lack of law. In other words Vaché, supremely the actor, became apotheosized as a nature god, a *force de la nature* whose manifold guises and apparent illogic ultimately signify his glorious self-coincidence. Exempted from psychology, his mind resembles a blind mechanism which, revved up beyond consciousness of itself, indifferently creates and destroys, as though creation and destruction were coefficients of instantaneity. Vaché's mythical speed goes hand in hand with his mythical status as a destroyer. "Jacques Vaché's swift journey across the sky of war," wrote Breton, "his appearing in every way extraordinarily rushed, this catastrophic haste which makes him obliterate himself."[5] Magnifying Vaché's mock massacre during *Les Mamelles de Tirésias*, Breton fancied it a metaphysical gesture; the simplest surrealist act, he proclaimed, would be emptying a revolver, aimlessly, into a crowd.

It is significant that the surrealists, bourgeois by upbringing, came of age between 1914 and 1918. The war, exercising a twofold effect, at once declassed them and afforded them *its* perspective. Identifying destruction with nature, they invented heroes whose heroism consisted in their magical

---

air sec un peu: machineries—rotatives à huiles puantes—vrombis—vrombis—vrombis—siffle! Reverdy—amusant le pohète, et ennui en prose; Max Jacob mon vieux fumiste—PANTINS—PANTINS—PANTINS . . ." Vaché, *Lettres de guerre*, Collection de Littérature (Paris: Au Sans Pareil, 1919), pp. 18–19. New edition, with four prefaces by Breton (Paris: K, 1949).

4. "Le premier . . . il insiste sur l'importance des gestes." *Les Pas perdus*, p. 18.

5. "Le passage rapide de Jacques Vaché à travers le ciel de guerre, ce qu'il y a en lui d'extraordinairement pressé, cette hâte catastrophique qui l'amène à s'anéantir." Ibid., p. 206.

metamorphism, their violence, their dark powers, their uncanny science. Vaché "mythologized" can hardly be distinguished from Fantômas the film villain (wildly acclaimed by the surrealists) whose knowledge of society's sham psyche allowed him to foil his pursuers, but Fantômas in turn descended from the romantic Lucifer. Exalted as "Master of Fright," "The Torturer," "The Emperor of Crime," he emerged as a latter-day avatar of Balzac's Vautrin, Maturin's Melmoth, Byron's Manfred, and Ponson du Terrail's Rocambole. At war with bourgeois mores, the surrealists thus inhabited an underworld even before taking up residence in the unconscious. Crime prefigured nature, one apocalyptic, *necessary* act sufficing to undermine the shaky foundations of Cartesian logic. But the surrealist underworld would be incomplete without its heroines who, like its hero, derived from films. "The idea an entire generation had of the world was formed in the movies," wrote Aragon in 1922, "and one film especially epitomized it, a serial. The young fell head over heels in love with Musidora, in the *Vampires*."[6] Surrealism enthroned the adventuress, by turns man-eating and man-creating, ambiguously virginal and sluttish, at the center of its sleep. Vaché had a female counterpart in Pearl White, whose fast-motion exploits if anything surpassed his own. As Pauline in *The Perils of Pauline*, she defied gravity, death, walls, leaping about with imbecile haste, infallibly coming out on top (in every sense)—the Artemis of her age. But vampire and adventuress merely foreshadowed the murderess.

In the first issue of *La Révolution Surréaliste*, one page bore penny-arcade snapshots of Freud, Breton, et al., littered about Germaine Berton who, a few months previously, had killed a proto-fascist named Marius Plateau. The caption reads: "Woman is the being who projects the greatest shadow of the greatest light in our dreams. Ch.B. [Charles Baudelaire]" Five years later, after the movement had suffered clamorous defec-

6. "L'idée que toute une génération se fit du monde se forme au cinéma, et c'est un film qui la résume, un feuilleton. Une jeunesse tomba tout entière amoureuse de Musidora, dans les Vampires." Aragon, unpublished manuscript, University of Paris, Bibliothèque Littéraire Jacques Doucet 7206–10.

tions and was reconstituting itself round Breton's second manifesto, the surrealists, eyes closed, posed again, their centerpiece this time not Germaine Berton but a nude woman, her head atilt like a madonna's and her right arm above her left breast as though giving it to suckle (or pledging allegiance). It would seem that they intended a kind of temporal collage. Superimposed, Berton and the nude amount to something like Parwati, the virgin mother of Hindu mythology who retires from the world during an age of troubles and tyranny, marrying Shiva the Destroyer. This ambiguous icon, resembling withal those depraved virgins so dear to art nouveau, the praying mantises and consumptive vampires who populate romantic literature, presided over the whole surrealist movement.

Surrealism was as much a mythopoeic adventure as it was a literary movement. "It couldn't escape me for long," wrote Aragon in *Le Paysan de Paris*, "that the nature of my thought, of its evolution, was a mechanism altogether comparable to the genesis of myths, and that I doubtless thought nothing without my mind straightaway forming a god." [7] But which god? It's as though the surrealists cast their lot with the daimones, rejecting outright the Olympians. Bent on bringing mankind back to its senses, literally, surrealism reawakened (in modern guise) the chthonic deities whose rule extends over the humanly ungovernable: nature, fate, and death. Everything—its loves and tantrums, its basic tenets and cant—pivoted about this original option. The surrealists, not by forfeit but through hope radically verging on despair (or vice versa) chose the choiceless, founding their movement on man's presumptive self-possession during moments of *lapse*. Anguished by the transparency of the conscious mind, they incorporated themselves around dreams or, more precisely, around one dream: of Being, foolproof and conclusive as death. Reckoning death

7. "Il ne put m'échapper bien longtemps que le propre de ma pensée, le propre de l'évolution de ma pensée était un mécanisme en tout point analogue à la genèse mythique, et que sans doute je ne pensais rien que du coup mon esprit ne se formât un dieu." Aragon, *Le Paysan de Paris* (Paris: Gallimard, 1926), p. 143.

not a measure of contingency but of the durable, Breton poured all his considerations on love, literature, mind into its mold. At the close of *Nadja*, for example, he recalls driving from Versailles to Paris when suddenly his companion jammed her foot down on his, covering his eyes with her hands:

What a test of life, indeed! Unnecessary to add that I didn't yield to this desire. It is known how I felt . . . about Nadja. I am no less grateful to her for revealing to me, in this overpowering way, what a common recognition of love would have committed us to at that moment. I feel less and less capable of resisting such a temptation *in every case*. I can do no less than offer thanks, in this last recollection, to the woman who has made me understand its virtual necessity.[8]

In writing, death figures as ultimate silence: the space invading print, the sum of everything unspoken and unwritten, the Absolute intercepting our rhetorical lines. "I love only unaccomplished things," wrote Breton in *Les Pas perdus*, resolving to begin each day by throwing himself out the window anew. Again in *Nadja*, Breton tells an anecdote whose esoteric meaning bears directly on the surrealist movement:

I was recently told such a stupid, grim, moving story! A man enters a hotel and asks to rent a room. He is shown up to number 35. As he comes down a few minutes later and deposits the key at the desk, he says: "Excuse me, I have no memory whatever. If you please, each time I come in, I'll tell you my name: Mr. Delouit. And each time you'll tell me my room number." Soon afterward he returns and, passing the desk, says, "Mr. Delouit"—"Number 35, Sir"—"Thank you." A moment later a man totally disheveled, his clothes splattered with mud, bleeding, his face scarcely a face, appears at the desk: "Mr. Delouit"—"What do you mean, Mr.

8. "Quelle épreuve pour l'amour, en effet. Inutile d'ajouter que je n'accédai pas à ce désir. On sait où j'en étais alors . . . avec Nadja. Je ne lui sais pas moins gré de m'avoir révélé, de façon terriblement saisissante, à quoi une reconnaissance commune de l'amour nous eût engagés à ce moment. Je me sens de moins en moins capable de résister à pareille tentation *dans tous les cas*. Je ne puis moins faire qu'en rendre grâce, dans ce dernier souvenir, à celle qui m'en a fait comprendre presque la nécessité." Breton, *Nadja*, Livre de Poche (Paris: Gallimard, 1964), p. 175.

Delouit? Don't try to put one over on us! Mr. Delouit has just gone upstairs!"—"I'm sorry, it's me. . . . I've just fallen out the window. Please, what is my room number?"[9]

Recommending daily defenestration as a way of life, Breton thus described the hotel called surrealism, full of exits and entrances but uninhabitable. Its virginal tenant gets his sleep shuttling dangerously between the window and the front door. Surrealist metaphysics observes this same eternal return, its antipodes beckoning one another, round a void; it lay, in fact, nowhere but at extremes, whose contradiction and identity provide the *merveilleux*—that sudden eruption of surreality—its perverse dynamics. Black humor, *amour fou*, the poetic image: all rely on the "marvelous." But these are its subsidiary occasions. At its absolute, it would bare the end in the beginning, some immovable point governing all the vagaries of consciousness, like a mathematical locus. Metaphysically, surrealist "movement" signifies displacement in opposite directions at once—the paradoxical line of fate carrying, for example, Oedipus toward birth even as he approaches death. Weaned on destruction, the surrealists at full maturity discovered its alter-image: creation. Creation as opposed to literature.

Literature pertains to reality, creation to surreality, the one descending from Aristotelian rationalism, the other from man's primitive unconscious. We have given a spatial image of

9. "On m'a conté naguère une si stupide, une si sombre, une si émouvante histoire. Un monsieur se présente un jour dans un hôtel et demande à louer une chambre. Ce sera le numéro 35. En descendant, quelques minutes plus tard, et tout en remettant la clef au bureau: 'Excusez-moi, dit-il, je n'ai aucune mémoire. Si vous permettez, chaque fois que je rentrerai, je vous dirai mon nom: Monsieur Delouit. Et chaque fois vous me répéterez le numéro de ma chambre.—Bien monsieur.' Très peu de temps après il revient, entreouvre la porte du bureau: 'Monsieur Delouit—C'est le numéro 35—Merci.' Une minute plus tard, un homme extraordinairement agité, les vêtements couverts de boue, ensanglanté et n'ayant presque plus figure humaine, s'adresse au bureau: 'Monsieur Delouit.—Comment, M. Delouit? Il ne faut pas nous la faire. M. Delouit vient de monter—Pardon, c'est moi. Je viens de tomber par la fenêtre. Le numéro de ma chambre, s'il vous plaît?'" Ibid., pp. 180–81.

surrealism. If one assigned each a temporal valence, literature would presuppose the calendar day, while creation elapses in an instant. But even this distinction won't hold, for the "instantaneous," that pivotal value of surrealist thought, underlying as it does automatic writing, effaces the temporal continuum whose absolute limit it represents. Instantaneity and eternity are obverse and reverse of the same coin. In other words, Breton, defining speed (his obsessive concern) by its limit, nurtured a dream of some atemporal mode of being, of Being. Vaché's exorbitant haste (as Breton imagined it), and his own, amount to a headlong plunge toward eternity. Amending the above statement, it might be said that literature and reality are correlatives of time, creation and surreality of timelessness. But what is time if not those tenses which, conjured forth by the mind's constitutional awareness of itself, erode us, the theatrical scheme regulating our conscious lives? Self-conscious, we cannot be ourselves without playing ourselves. Consciously—that is, time-creating—we mistake our total absenteeism for total self-possession; only the unconscious, its power "marvelously" generated during one privileged instant, will allow us to behold ourselves globally, as a totality, given above and beyond time. "What we want," wrote Aragon, "is the human equivalent of exterior things." By this, the surrealists did not favor obfuscation of the mind. Perforce *aware* (above all during that spasm called the "marvelous"), it cannot achieve the self-coincidence enjoyed by things unless aware so absolutely as to lose awareness *of*, a condition whose utopianism Breton acknowledges in the first manifesto, all the while maintaining its necessity as a goal. "How proud a thing it is to write," wrote Breton and Eluard in "Notes sur la poésie," "to write without knowing what language, words, comparisons, changes of ideas, of tone are: neither to conceive the *structure* of the work's duration, nor the conditions of its ends; no *why*, no *how*! To turn green, blue from being the parrot . . ."[10] From BEING. The "human

10. "Quelle fierté d'écrire, sans savoir ce que sont langue, verbe, comparaisons, changements d'idées, de ton; ni concevoir la *structure* de la durée de l'oeuvre, ni les conditions de sa fin; pas du tout le

equivalent of exterior things"—Being—connotes an openness and transparency the equivalent of a thing's absolute containment and opacity: like two mirrors mirroring one another ad infinitum. In fact Breton, in *L'Amour fou*, describes reciprocal love as an "arrangement of mirrors" reflecting the beloved and his own desire from every angle imaginable. But the substance by which he translated his dream was crystal, a mineral perfectly fixed yet perfectly transparent:

No higher artistic lesson seems to me possible than that of crystal. The work of art, like any fragment of human life considered in its gravest meaning, seems to me worthless if it doesn't afford the hardness, the rigidity, the regularity, the luster, on all its outer and inner surfaces, of crystal. Let it be understood that this affirmation stands in opposition, for me, in the most categorical, the most unwavering way, to everything that attempts, aesthetically and morally, to base formal beauty on a labor of voluntary improvement to which it would be a man's choice to commit himself. On the contrary, I am continually led to the apology for creation, for spontaneous action, and this to the very degree that crystal, by definition not ameliorable, is its perfect expression. The house I live in, my life, what I write: it is my dream that these should appear from a distance the way cubes of rock salt appear close by.[11]

---

pourquoi, pas du tout le *comment*! Verdir, bleuir, blanchir d'être le perroquet." Breton and Eluard, "Notes sur la poésie," *La Révolution Surréaliste*, no. 12 (15 December 1929), p. 54.

11. "Nul plus haut enseignement artistique ne me paraît pouvoir être reçu que du cristal. L'oeuvre d'art, au même titre d'ailleurs que tel fragment de la vie humaine considérée dans sa signification la plus grave, me paraît dénuée de valeur si elle ne présente pas la dureté, la rigidité, la régularité, le lustre sur toutes ses faces extérieures, intérieures, du cristal. Qu'on entende bien que cette affirmation s'oppose pour moi, de la manière la plus catégorique, la plus constante, à tout ce qui tente, esthétiquement comme moralement, de fonder la beauté formelle sur un travail de perfectionnement volontaire auquel il appartiendrait à l'homme de se livrer. Je ne cesse pas, au contraire, d'être porté à l'apologie de la création, de l'action spontanée et cela dans la mesure même ou le cristal, par définition, non améliorable, en est l'expression parfaite. La maison que j'habite, ma vie, ce que j'écris: je rêve que cela apparaisse de loin comme

"From a distance" the crystalline life would reflect itself, its very core having become an appearance, not superficial but pellucid. The crystalline life would be subject and object in one.

The words "concrete" and "necessary" stand totemlike at the center of surrealist ideology. Like Marxists (Koestler, in his autobiography, recalls that during the thirties German communists would invariably betray themselves by overusing the word "concrete"), surrealists couldn't make a crucial statement without resorting to one or the other of these words. "The taste, that taste of the divine which comes over me in every dizzy spell informed me once again that I was entering the concrete universe closed to passers-by; love was giving birth to the metaphysical spirit,"[12] wrote Aragon in *Le Paysan de Paris*. A compilation of all such instances would require a chapter by itself. In short, "concrete" signifies that wedlock of natural necessity and human *conscience* Breton called the surrealist state of grace: an objective order based not on history but on the convulsive instant. It does not imply political action but—and this owing to destruction, which gave surrealism its original fillip—(re)-creation. "Surrealism," wrote Roger Vailland, "was above all a common ground and meeting place of young petit-bourgeois intellectuals particularly aware of the futility of every activity expected of them by their background and their era."[13] Catapulted beyond the material world, the surrealist is a closer kin to, let's say, Sartre (hesitating on this side of materialism) than to the Marxist. While Breton and Sartre, both petit-bourgeois intellectuals, felt compelled now and again to take their bearings

---

apparaissent de près ces cubes de sel gemme." Breton, *L'Amour fou*, Métamorphoses (Paris: Gallimard, 1945), p. 16.

12. ". . . le goût, ce goût divin que je connais bien à tout vertige, m'avertissait encore une fois que j'entrais dans cet univers concret qui est fermé aux passants. L'esprit métaphysique pour moi renaissait de l'amour." *Le Paysan de Paris*, p. 245.

13. "[Le surréalisme] fut, avant tout, le lieu de rencontre de jeunes intellectuels petits-bourgeois particulièrement sensibles au caractère parfaitement dèrisoire de toutes les activités qui leur était proposées par leur époque ou par leur milieu." Roger Vailland, *Le Surréalisme contre la révolution* (Paris: Editions Sociales, 1948), p. 22.

from communism, their thought observes another dialectic. However discordant the one's mystical *élan* and the other's rationalism, they are strikingly comparable, the essential difference being that Breton allowed the possibility of a human atemporal, or what in Sartrean terms would amount to the *pour soi* congealed into an *en soi*, yet remaining *pour soi*. That would be the phenomenological translation of Breton's crystalline ideal. Revolting inseparably against the "theater" of bourgeois society and the theatrical optic imposed by the conscious mind, surrealism yearned for Being—objective, concrete, necessary, mineral-like, infinitely aware, eternally itself. It yearned to preside over Creation.

The surrealist view of literature hinged on this metaphysical attitude. Writing should not analyze, reconstitute, busy itself with semblances. The word must prevail like an unpremeditated act, of murder or of creation. It must exercise upon its author the compulsion of experience. Breton once said of acts that they carry within themselves their own justification, "radiating" beyond explanations and glossaries. Not that he impeached any one genre; rather, his attacks were directed against the universal abuse of language. Thus Sade and Lewis Carroll, enacting their fantasies, found grace while numerous poets found themselves consigned to hell. Ibsen didn't cross Breton's mind, whereas some neighborhood play he saw, its setting a girls' school whose mistress makes Sapphic overtures to one student (because one ambiguous act follows another, because the play amounts to its accumulated gestures and silence) haunted him. Just as "psychology" stands opposed to Being, the conscious mind obliging us to play ourselves, so psychological literature, observing its own logical prejudices, reducing life to theater, stands opposed to creation. But on the whole surrealism placed the major burden of guilt on the novel (not excepting Dostoevsky's and Proust's), investing its hope in poetry. Aragon put it succinctly when he said, "The concrete is the ultimate moment of thought and the state of concrete thought is poetry."[14] Before discussing the two

14. "Le concret est le dernier moment de la pensée, et l'état de la pensée concrète est la poésie." Aragon, "L'Ombre de l'inventeur," *La Révolution Surréaliste*, no. 1 (December 1924), p. 23.

poets who stood head and shoulders above all others in the surrealist pantheon, Rimbaud and Lautréamont, let us understand the repercussions of Being on language, what it was the surrealists meant by the concrete word.

In *Point du jour*, Breton asked two questions: "Doesn't the mediocrity of our world derive essentially from the way we use our power of speech? . . . What prevents me from muddling the order of words and thus dealing a blow to the wholly apparent existence of things?"[15] Most of the young poets of his generation—it is at the source of Aragon's *Traité du style*—were obsessed with the belief that the bourgeois had invested words with meanings agreeable to their class, so that speech had become the dictation of a ruling social order.[16] One contemporary of the surrealists and a signatory of the 1930 manifesto, Francis Ponge, inveighed against this crafty, congenital brainwashing, against the bourgeois republic which, by virtue of "speaking from within" its subjects and monopolizing their language, becomes a totalitarian regime. The surrealists' revolt against the commonplace signification of words, or against the word *as sign*, compelled them to dehumanize words in favor of things. Unlike Ponge who would evoke words from the thing, without denying its integrity, the surrealists dreamed of evoking a new world in speaking it, but both insist on the word's *materiality*; it is viewed as a kind of irreducible pit which signifies nothing because it bears its own evidence (a sign, if you wish, but signifying itself). In being hermetic or self-reflecting, the word strives for an equivalence with the muteness of objects. Whether or not the world signifies something, they felt, it nonetheless works.

15. "La médiocrité de notre univers ne dépend-elle pas essentiellement de notre pouvoir d'énonciation? . . . Qu'est-ce qui me retient de brouiller l'ordre des mots, d'attenter de cette manière à l'existence toute apparente des choses?" Breton, *Point du jour* (Paris: Gallimard, 1934), pp. 25, 26.

16. This section of the chapter is published here, slightly amended, with permission of the periodical where it originally appeared within my article entitled "On Louis Aragon: Silence and History," *Southern Review* 3 (1967): 311–21.

Thus, at their extreme points, idealism and materialism become confused with one another, as in Aragon's quest for "the human equivalent of exterior things." It was not his quest alone; the surrealists corporately felt that in some privileged state the mind would no longer be aware of words but press them out of itself: a thing expressing things. Words themselves being objects, the distance between subject and object would thereupon vanish; improbably, consciousness would cease to be consciousness *of*. In "Une Vague de rêves," one of the first essays about surrealism and its experiments, Aragon related how the group discovered that a written image could affect their senses, "lose its verbal aspect," and give rise to "phenomena" which they had thought it impossible to create. The word "phenomena," harking back to Kant, may prove misleading. It does not convey what lies at the heart of surrealism, the shamanic effort to make myths spring alive. Clearly this is what Aragon meant in calling mind not mind but "mental matter" (*matière mentale*), then stating that this matter consists of words. The surrealists, revolting against "given" speech, looked for substance in their metaphors—what Paul Nougé, a Belgian surrealist, called "the metaphor that lasts." Aragon's dictum that poetry is concrete thought brings to mind Ponge's apotheosis of the snail, whose expression, as he sees it, takes the form of dribble, clotting, drying, and establishing a silvery wake: "It does not have many friends. Nor does it need any to assure its happiness. It sticks so well to nature, revels so perfectly in its clasp; it is a friend of the ground, and kisses it with its whole body."[17] In the organism absolutely adequate to the earth, "awareness" as awareness *of* is dispelled. But ultimately surrealism was less the snail's clasp of earth than its containment, a kind of lyric self-embrace with mineral overtones, which may be understood as mind *hardening* into its images, like the snail ensconced in its shell. This comes out in Breton's essay on Picasso, whom he had a habit of considering one of his evangelists:

17. "Il n'a pas beaucoup d'amis. Mais il n'en a pas besoin pour son bonheur. Il colle si bien à la nature, il en jouit si parfaitement de si près, il est l'ami du sol qu'il baise de tout son corps." Ponge, *Le Parti pris des choses*, Métamorphoses (Paris, Gallimard, 1942), p. 31.

The plastic instinct, raised here by an individual to the apogee of its development, draws from the refusal, from the negation of everything that may distract it from a sense of itself, the means of reflecting upon itself. . . . With Picasso it is the sum of all these needs, these essays in disintegration, rendered with implacable lucidity. . . . it [the plastic instinct] is, to suppose the impossible, the spider devoting its attention to the design and substance of its web's polygon more than to the fly; it is the migratory bird peering over its wing in full flight to look at what it has left behind, or the bird seeking to recover itself in the labyrinth of its own song.[18]

The surrealist poem is on the same order as this: a locked, reflexive universe where language exists, to suppose the impossible, *on its own terms* (as Breton put it once, "words make love to one another"), conveying no feeling, no experience, no image felt, experienced, or imagined outside itself. The poem no longer derives from some intention or preconceived idea as in classical forms, but rather from the operations of pure chance—a kind of unconscious throw of the dice. Yet the results of this throw, of pure chance, are purely necessary in a way that only things, not ideas, can presume to be. Hence Breton's doctrine of "objective chance": the ellipses, the absence of rhetorical connectives, the dislocated clichés, the unforeseen meeting of rationally unjuxtaposable words, or sometimes the loneliness of a single word drumming through the poem, pivoting on itself in puns or disintegrating into its syllables form a material cryptogram of one's "mental matter," not a transparent sign dissolving into significance but a crystalline thing fixedly reflecting itself ("not oriented

18. "L'instinct plastique, porté ici individuellement au terme suprême de son développement, puise dans le refus, dans la négation de tout ce qui pourrait le distraire de son sens propre, le moyen de se réfléchir sur lui-même. . . . C'est, avec Picasso, la somme de tous ces besoins, de toutes ces expériences de désintégration qui va être faite avec une lucidité implacable. . . . c'est par impossible l'araignée qui va, plus qu'au moucheron, être attentive au dessin et à la substance du polygone de sa toile, l'oiseau migrateur qui en plein vol va tourner la tête vers ce qu'il quitte, l'oiseau encore qui va tenter de se retrouver dans le labyrinthe de son propre chant." Breton, *Point du jour*, pp. 196–97.

toward anything, just oriented, like a pearl,'' as Cocteau described Jules Lemaître). The surrealist poet, to the extent that he was liberated from society whose meanings would, were he not free, infiltrate whatever he wrote and wrench him into its own view, strove to create *an objective order*. And in what did this objective order consist? In word matter: in the resistant, disconnected word objects of the surrealist poem, in concrete metaphors bearing an imprint of the poet's ''true life'' on their inner face like a fossilized secret. Words become objects by virtue of their inhuman innocence. It remained for the poet, impossibly, to find his secret within the order he created, by chance—much as the bird striving ''to recover itself in the labyrinth of its own song.''

''I am stranded at your ear,'' Aragon once said to an audience of students in Madrid. Indeed he was, since surrealism hinged on the belief that mind is a thing-in-itself, therefore uncontingent, and that language, at its truest, is an innocent deposition of ''mental matter,'' an unconsciously dropped ''out-thereness'' of the mind. Surrealism, in other words, posited the existence of an objective ''I.'' But what are mind and language if mind is not consciousness of the world, thus separated from it, and if the word does not spring from this separation? The surrealists begged the question by defining one *as being* the other, as constituting the other's occult substance, so that ''pure'' language in their view would *be* the interned mind describing itself. Hence automatic writing, itself an ideal notion, whereby it was thought possible for the mind to become its own written object—the thing-in-itself which has placed itself in the world without being separated from its externalized self. Writing runs in a self-justifying circle leading from subject to object to subject—a kind of closed transcendence. An appropriate image of surrealist aesthetics might be that of someone looking out and seeing himself look in, someone endowed with the power to see, objectively, his own outside, to hear himself speaking through his own ears. Sartre was to designate this state of being as God. What the surrealists resented in the end was less the intrusions of the bourgeois mind than their own human condition, which may in part account for the impersonality, or centerlessness, of their poetry. Often this poetry reads like an attempted, unsuccessful silence: the only word totally pure, totally innocent of meaning, and totally knowing, is silence. It represents the logical consequence of Being. But God, the only Being, is the one writer who can afford silence, so the surrealists continued to write, those who didn't kill themselves. Equating mind and word in a substantial sense, they wished to short-circuit the world. Nowhere is their intention more boldly stated than in Breton's 1930 manifesto:

Everything leads one to believe that there exists a certain vantage point of the mind from which life and death, the real and the imaginary, the past and the future, the communicable and the incommunicable, the high and the low cease to be perceived as opposites. Well, you search in vain for any other motive to surrealist activity than the hope of determining this point. . . . It is clear . . . that surrealism is not seriously interested in whatever is being produced next door under the pretext of art, or of anti-art, of philosophy or of anti-philosophy, in a word, in anything whose end is not the annihilation of being in a flash, interior and blind. . . . What could those people who harbor some concern about the place they occupy *in the world* expect to gain from the surrealist experiment?[19]

Here, as in his above-quoted text on Picasso, Breton gives an image of the self, divided in the phenomenal world, recoiling upon itself, gaining the kind of absolute oneness which may be called the prerogative of matter on the one hand and of angels on the other. At times the surrealist would characterize words as matter materializing the self, like dreams of stone, at other times as a solvent dissolving it (Breton's image of "soluble

19. "Tout porte à croire qu'il existe un certain point de l'esprit d'où la vie et la mort, le réel et l'imaginaire, le passé et le futur, le communicable et l'incommunicable, le haut et le bas cessent d'être perçus contradictoirement. Or, c'est en vain qu'on chercherait à l'activité surréaliste un autre mobile que l'espoir de détermination de ce point. . . . Il est clair . . . que le surréalisme n'est pas intéressé à tenir grand compte de ce qui se produit à côté de lui sous pretexte d'art, voire d'anti-art, de philosophie ou d'anti-philosophie, en un mot de tout ce qui n'a pas pour fin l'anéantissement de l'être en un brillant, intérieur et aveugle," *Manifestes,* pp. 76–77.

fish''). The manifesto could have been published with two illustrations on facing pages, one being Magritte's tableau of a petrified man seated at a petrified table within petrified walls and the other a blank canvas on a blank page. Surrealist writings everywhere refer to an original unity of which man has been dispossessed but which he can regain in some new Creation, conceived alternately as a plenum and a void: the hallucinatory *thing* impacting the dreamer's mind, or a kind of all-dissolving word, a word that finally achieves silence. Poetry is crystalline or else ''a lack *created*.''

Of all the ''annunciatory'' figures surrealism rescued from semi-oblivion—Sade, Aloysius Bertrand, Rabbe, Germain Nouveau, Raymond Roussel—Rimbaud and Lautréamont must be accounted its most brilliant lights. Surrealistically speaking, both followed ideal careers, incanting themselves into Being, then lapsing the one into silence, the other into triumphant banality.

The will to create springing from an infinite aspiration, the creator cannot, by nature, remain within his own confines. Creation, that ultimately individualistic act, thus implies ultimate anonymity. Being—that is, the self extrapolated from time and consubstantial with itself—means being anonymous, being All. Hence, Rimbaud's astonishing equation: ''I is another.'' In that celebrated letter to Paul Demeny, Rimbaud described as follows his creative duplicity: ''Brass cannot be blamed for awakening as a clarion. One thing is clear: I witness the flowering of my thought; I observe it, I listen to it, I swing my baton downward and the symphony begins rumbling in the depths or else appears on stage with one leap.''[20] Himself and his spectator, the creator becomes transformed by his creation from a first person into a third, the impersonal ''one''; he creates himself (at once actively and passively) but,

20. ''Car *Je* est un autre. Si le cuivre s'éveille clairon, il n'y a rien de sa faute. Cela m'est évident: j'assiste à l'éclosion de ma pensée: je la regarde, je l'écoute: je lance un coup d'archet: la symphonie fait un remuement dans la profondeur, ou vient d'un bond sur la scène.'' Rimbaud, *Oeuvres*, ed. Suzanne Bernard (Paris: Garnier, 1960), p. 345.

by being himself and his own object, achieves objectivity, impersonality, oneness. So when Rimbaud inveighs against "all those old imbeciles" (meaning writers) for misconstruing the *moi* (the self), the *moi* properly construed would be the *soi* (the it-self). Writers stand accused of "egotism," while the creator or *voyant* remains innocent, his innocence representing the sum of all imagined and imaginable experiences. "Excruciating torture," wrote Rimbaud, "for which he needs superhuman faith, strength, by virtue of which he becomes the greatest invalid, the greatest criminal, accursed above all—and the supreme Knower."[21] The creative act, thus conceived, bears comparison with the religious mass, its magical effect being to make the believer's "I" surpass its nomenclature, to make the "I" become "One-Self" (as in Mallarmé's evocation of Poe: "Tel qu'en lui-même enfin l'éternité le change"); but instead of eating the body and soul of God, the poet dissolves into the Being he intones from his own depths, like Isidore Ducasse intoning his anonym, Lautréamont.

If anything, *Les Chants de Maldoror* and *Poésies* eclipsed *Une Saison en enfer* and *Illuminations* from surrealism's viewpoint, *Les Chants* having the sustained automatism, an immediacy of epic proportions which Rimbaud's prose poetry lacks. Heaping imprecations on "man and his Creator," Lautréamont fetches from underground Maldoror, whose "evil" will create a new world, like the gnostic demiurge except that his creation rivals Creation. It breaks the chain of Being, which brings us full circle, back to Maldoror's antecedent, the romantic Lucifer, and his scions, Fantômas and Vaché. Lautréamont describes him as follows:

He knew that the police, that shield of civilization, had for many long years persevered in its search for him, that a veritable army of agents and spies had continually been on his heels, without ever quite catching up. . . . He had the particular gift of assuming guises that fooled the wariest eye.

21. "Ineffable torture où il a besoin de toute la foi, de toute la force surhumaine, où il devient entre tous le grand malade, le grand criminel, le grand maudit,—et le suprême Savant!" Ibid., p. 346.

Superior disguises, I must say, speaking from an artistic viewpoint. . . . In this respect, he verged on genius.[22]

How then can one account for Lautréamont's *Poésies*, subtitled *Préface à un livre futur*, in which he declares that "poetry should have a practical end," that plagiarism is "necessary" (progress implying it), that mankind should cultivate its axioms, that "poetry should be made by all, not by a single person"? Is this a palinode, like Rimbaud's silence? Or the aftermath of apocalypse, like Rimbaud's silence? The surrealists chose the second, surmising rightly perhaps, as Lautréamont throughout the *Chants* alludes to its future sequel: "The first five narrations haven't been useless; they were the frontispiece of my work, the building's foundation, the prefatory explanation of my future poetics."[23] Here, as with Rimbaud, the poet, viewing himself as a demiurge, dares speak objectively. Having forfeited name and civil status, he thereby gains the creator's credentials: "one" or All. Doesn't the "all" in "Poetry should be made by all, not by a single person" signify first and foremost himself, whose poetry—"the indestructible thread of impersonal poetry," as he called it—will guide mankind toward corporate anonymity? It heralds not the proletarian state but the Second Creation. Breton congratulated Lautréamont as "an absolutely virgin eye" on the alert for the world's "scientific" perfection, viewing this "in the light of apocalypse." But apocalypse is by definition the last word. Perfection has no need to express itself, least of all by aphorisms. Lautréamont's future book (like Mallarmé's *Livre*) never saw the light of day, undone by

22. "Il savait que la police, ce bouclier de la civilisation, le recherchait avec persévérance, depuis nombre d'années, et qu'une véritable armée d'agents et d'espions était continuellement à ses trousses. Sans, cependant, parvenir à le rencontrer. . . . Il avait une faculté spéciale pour prendre des formes méconnaissables aux yeux exercés. Déguisements supérieurs, si je parle en artiste! . . . Par ce point il touchait presqu'au génie." Lautréamont, *Oeuvres complètes* (Paris, Corti, 1953), p. 324.

23. "Les cinq premiers récits n'ont pas été inutiles; ils étaient le frontispice de mon ouvrage, le fondement de la construction, l'explication préalable de ma poétique future." Ibid., p. 322.

its preface. Or perhaps, logically, it exists in its invisibility. "Maldoror's revolt," wrote Breton, "would not be the everlasting Revolt if it were to salvage one form of thought while disposing of some other; it must then, in *Poésies*, ruin itself in its own dialectical game."[24] This could serve as surrealism's epitaph. Determined by its own destructive genes, it was bound to espouse a poetry that stares at itself . . . in silence.

If surrealism collapsed as a literary movement in the 1930s, various members, recognizing the implications of their dogma, opted for communism (Aragon, Eluard) or for suicide (Rigault, Crevel). But perhaps Antonin Artaud proved himself the most clear-sighted apostate. Implicitly, the surrealist movement reached Mallarmé's conclusion, that "the world exists to end up as a theater." Revolting against the mind's innate theatricality, against literature for exacerbating that property, surrealism raised theater to an infinite exponent, miming Being. So Artaud, in *Le Théâtre et son double*, wrote its summa and its parody, not a preface to some future play but a postface to the surrealist movement itself. His players would convulse on stage, achieving the metaphysical concrete through automatic acting. "The theater," he wrote, "must become a kind of experimental demonstration of the profound identity between the concrete and the abstract."[25] Surrealism was this experiment. It resuscitated forgotten poets, it created some remarkable poetry of its own, it propagandized the unconscious, it reinstated the imagination, but it came to grief on Surreality. Supplanting theater with Theater, it followed a trajectory which carried it full circle, from one mad actor to another, from Vaché's hijinks to Artaud's program notes.

24. "La révolte de Maldoror ne serait pas à tout jamais la Révolte si elle devait épargner indéfiniment une forme de pensée aux dépens d'une autre; il est donc nécessaire qu'avec *Poésies*, elle s'abîme dans son propre jeu dialectique." Preface, ibid., p. 44.

25. "En un mot le théâtre doit devenir une sorte de démonstration expérimentale de l'identité profonde du concret et de l'abstrait." Antonin Artaud, *Oeuvres complètes* 4 (Paris: Gallimard, 1964): 129.

BIBLIOGRAPHY

SELECTED CRITICAL WORKS BY BRETON, ARAGON, AND OTHER SURREALISTS

The most important of Breton's contributions to *Littérature* (which ran from March 1919 to June 1924) were collected in *Les Pas perdus* (Paris: NRF, 1924; Gallimard, 1949), containing lengthy articles on Vaché, Jarry, Apollinaire, and Lautréamont.

Similarly, his major contributions to *La Révolution Surréaliste*, including "Discours sur le peu de réalité" and a penetrating piece on Picasso, were collected as *Point du jour* (Paris: Gallimard, 1934).

Breton and Aragon wrote some of their best observations on literature while making observations on painting, Max Ernst's collages in particular, as in Aragon's *La Peinture au défi* (Paris: Galerie Pierre, 1930; Paris: J. Corti, 1930), reprinted in *Collages*, pp. 35–71 (Miroir de l'Art, Paris: Hermann, 1965), and Breton's *Le Surréalisme et la peinture* (Paris: Brentano's, 1946; new ed., Paris: Gallimard, 1965).

Where Breton and Aragon are concerned, many of their remarks on literature lie buried in hodgepodges (a *genre* surrealism invented) containing libel, metaphysics, romance, dream interpretations, oneiric promenades, etc., dosed in unequal parts depending on the volume, the most important being:

Breton. *Nadja*. Paris: NRF, 1928. New ed. Paris: Gallimard, 1963. Livre de Poche. Paris: Gallimard, 1964. (Translated by Richard Howard. New York: Grove Press, 1960.)

———. *Les Vases communicantes*. Paris: Cahiers Libres, 1932. Paris: Gallimard, 1955.

———. *L'Amour fou*. Métamorphoses. Paris: Gallimard, 1937, 1945.

———. *Arcane 17 enté d'ajours*. Paris: Sagittaire, 1947. Reprinted, followed by Michel Beaujour's "André Breton, ou La Transparence." 10–18. Paris: Union Générale d'Editions. 1965.

Aragon. *Libertinage*. Paris: NRF, 1924.

———. *Le Paysan de Paris*. Paris: NRF, 1926. Livre de Poche. Paris: Gallimard, 1966. (*The Nightwalker*. Translated by Frederick Brown. New Library of French Classics. Englewood Cliffs, N. J.: Prentice Hall, 1970.)

———. *Traité du style*. Paris: NRF, 1928.

Breton's clearest statements about surrealism are his *Manifestes du surréalisme* (Paris: Sagittaire, 1955; Paris: J.-J. Pauvert, 1962; Idées, Paris: Gallimard, 1963), translated by Richard Seaver and Helen R. Lane, *Manifestoes of Surrealism* (Ann Arbor: University of

Michigan Press, 1969); the second of these manifestoes, however, which appeared in 1930, bogs down in metaphysical wrangling with communism. *Notes sur la poésie* (Paris: G.L.M., 1936), goes to the heart of surrealist aesthetics, trenchantly, owing perhaps to Paul Eluard's collaboration. Aragon's Urmanifesto of surrealism, "Une Vague de rêves," *Commerce*, no. 2 (Autumn 1924), pp. 91–122, is a crucial document.

Flagrant délit; Rimbaud devant la conjuration de l'imposture et du truquage (Paris: Thésée, 1949; Libertés, Paris: J.-J. Pauvert, 1964), a book inspired by the publication of several apocryphal poems of Rimbaud, contains Breton's most prolonged deliberation over *Illuminations*.

Breton's remarkably temperate conversations (his anger takes the form of omission: like the name Cocteau, not once mentioned) with André Parinaud—*Entretiens* (Le Point du Jour, Paris: NRF, 1953)—shed light on his early literary influences, Mallarmé in particular.

Some interesting articles by younger or peripheral figures in the surrealist movement appeared in *Surréalisme au Service de la Révolution*, successor of *La Révolution Surréaliste*. Among these, Roger Caillois, Paul Nougé, and Zdenko Reich.

Antonin Artaud's *Le Théâtre et son double* (Métamorphoses, Paris: Gallimard, 1938, 1944), also in *Oeuvres complètes* 4:11–171 (Paris: Gallimard, 1964), though written long after his "expulsion" from the movement, captures its essence: the sacramental, the gnostic sadism, the penchant for Oriental models. It was translated by Mary Caroline Richards, *The Theatre and Its Double* (New York: Grove Press, 1958); see also *Collected Works 1*, translated by Victor Corti (London: Calder and Boyars, 1968), and *Antonin Artaud: Anthology*, edited by Jack Hirschman (2d ed. rev., San Francisco: City Lights Books, 1965).

Among other critical works from within the movement one might add Julien Gracq's *André Breton* (Paris: J. Corti, 1948) and Pierre Reverdy's books of notes: *Le Gant de crin*, Roseau d'Or (Paris: Plon, 1927; Paris: Flammarion, 1968), *Le Livre de mon bord: Notes 1930–1936* (Paris: Mercure de France, 1948), and *En vrac* (Monaco: Editions du Rocher, 1956).

SELECTED WORKS ON SURREALISM

As for histories of the movement, Maurice Nadeau's *Histoire du surréalisme*, 2 vols. (Pierres Vives, Paris: Seuil, 1945), translated by Richard Howard, *History of Surrealism* (New York: Macmillan, 1965), gives a good general picture, the only one. Michel Sanouillet, in *Dada à Paris* (Paris: J.-J. Pauvert, 1965), covers the Dada period exhaustively; his appendixes include hitherto unpublished correspondence between Breton and Tzara. Rivière's "Reconnaissance à Dada" (*Nouvelle Revue Française* 15 [1920]: 216–37, included also in his *Nouvelles Etudes*, pp. 294–310 (Paris: Gallimard, 1947) and as "Gratitude to Dada" in *The Ideal Reader*, pp. 230–44, edited and translated by Blanche Price (New York: Meridian, 1960), written by a Dada sympathizer but not a subscriber, stands as one of the most acute appreciations of the movement. Tzara's *Le Surréalisme et l'après-guerre*, Littérature (Paris: Nagel, 1947), written from an erstwhile Dadaist's point of view, contains some good general observations. Roger Vailland's *Le Surréalisme contre la révolution* (Paris: Editions Sociales, 1948), in some ways the self-defense of one who opted not for the revolution but for the Establishment (Vailland belonged to a para-surrealist group which brought out *Le Grand Jeu*, its other editors being René Daumal and Roger Gilbert-Lecomte, the second of whom may well—as his surviving family releases his writings for publication—prove, along with Eluard, the most gifted poet produced by the period), gives the other side of the picture.

As for articles and books dealing with surrealism as literature and metaphysics, the following represents a bone-bare list:

Alquié, Ferdinand. *La Philosophie du surréalisme*. Bibliothèque de Philosophie Scientifique. Paris: Flammarion, 1955. (*The Philosophy of Surrealism*. Translated by Bernard Waldrop. Ann Arbor: University of Michigan Press, 1965.) Attempts to show the roots of surrealism in Descartes, on the basis of Descartes's dictum, *Mundus est fabula* (the world consists in our narration of it).

Balakian, Anna. *The Literary Origins of Surrealism: A New Mysticism in French Poetry*. New York: King's Crown Press, 1947.

Beaujour, Michel. "André Breton ou la transparence." Postface to 10/18 edition of Breton's *Arcane 17*. Paris: Union Générale d'Editions, 1965. Has the merit of pointing to Breton's essential image and category of being, i.e., transparency.

Blanchot, Maurice. "A propos du surréalisme." *L'Arche*, no. 8 (August 1945), pp. 93–104. Reprinted as "Réflexions sur le surréalisme." In *La Part du feu*, pp. 92–104. Paris: Gallimard, 1949. Penetrating essay on surrealist aesthetics.

———. *Lautréamont et Sade*. Propositions. Paris: Editions de Minuit, 1949. 10/18. Paris: Union Générale d'Editions, 1967. His essay on surrealist "precursors" which discloses a great deal about surrealism proper.

Carrouges, Michel. *André Breton et les données fondamentales du surréalisme*. Les Essais. Paris: Gallimard, 1950. Of the many books which adopt surrealist pronouncements whole-cloth and look at the world from Breton's eyes, which, in other words, follow the party line, this seems to me the best.

Caws, Mary Ann. *Surrealism and the Literary Imagination: A Study of Breton and Bachelard*. Studies in French Literature. The Hague: Mouton, 1966.

Champigny, Robert, "Analyse d'une définition du surréalisme." *PMLA* 81 (1966): 139–44. Included in *Pour une esthétique de l'essai: analyses critiques*, pp. 7–28. Situations. Paris: Lettres Modernes, 1967.

Raymond, Marcel. *De Baudelaire au surréalisme: Essai sur le mouvement poétique contemporain*. Paris: Corrêa, 1933. New edition. Paris: Corti, 1952, 1960. (*From Baudelaire to Surrealism*. Translated by G. M. The Documents of Modern Art. New York: Wittenborn, Schultz, 1949, 1950.) Places surrealism within the literary context of the avant-garde, without going very deeply into the connection between symbolism and surrealism.

Shattuck, Roger, *The Banquet Years: The Arts in France, 1885–1918: Alfred Jarry, Henri Rousseau, Erik Satie, Guillaume Apollinaire*. New York: Harcourt, Brace, 1958. New York: Doubleday, Anchor, 1961. Sets the scene better than any other book.

———. "On Love and Laughter: Surrealism Reappraised." Introductory essay to the Macmillan translation of Nadeau's book, cited above, making as it does the proper points and precautions, could serve as a hygienic introduction for someone not familiar with surrealist literature.

Sartre, Jean-Paul. "Qu'est-ce que la littérature?" In *Situations II*. Paris: Gallimard, 1948. (*What Is Literature?* Translated by Bernard Frechtman. New York: Philosophical Library, 1949). In a pages-long footnote and toward the end of this essay, Sartre takes some damning potshots at surrealist metaphysics; this represents the keenest criticism of surrealist thought, although Sartre gets waylaid from the essential (the dream and the solecism) by his own polemics.

One might add the following collections and *recensements*:

André Breton: Essais et témoignages. Edited by Marc Eigeldinger. Neuchâtel: La Baconnière, 1950.

André Breton (1896–1966) et le mouvement surréaliste: hommages—témoignages—l'oeuvre. *Nouvelle Revue Française* 15 (1967): 577–964.

Gershman, Herbert S. *A Bibliography of the Surrealist Revolution in France*. Ann Arbor: University of Michigan Press, 1968.

Hardré, Jacques. "Present State of Studies on Literary Surrealism." *Yearbook of Comparative and General Literature* 9 (1960): 43–46.

Surrealism. Edited with an introduction by Herbert Read. London: Faber and Faber, 1937. New York: Harcourt, Brace & Co., 1937. Breton and Eluard both contributed.

Surrealism. *Yale French Studies*, vol. 1, no. 2 (Fall–Winter 1948).

Surrealism. *Yale French Studies*, no. 31 (May 1964).

"Surréalisme." *Europe*, vol. 46, no. 475–76 (November–December 1968).

"Values in Surrealism." Edited by Nicolas Calas. *New Directions 1940*. New York: New Directions, 1940. Contributions by Herbert J. Muller, Nicolas Calas, Kenneth Burke.

Michel Beaujour

7

Eros and Nonsense: Georges Bataille

The essays of Georges Bataille, which identify literature with evil, must seem strangely wrongheaded. They do few of the things that criticism is supposed to do: they do not explain much and they interpret even less; they disregard the formal structure of individual works, and their own structure looks haphazard and fragmentary. Finally, their strictures resemble the most outdated forms of ethical criticism, but they praise only immoral works. Bataille's approach to the written word is perverse, his scorn for the greater part of literature, narrow and uncompromising.

A bizarre terminology borrowed from Hegel, political science, ethnology, economics, and mysticism disconcerts the reader who does not readily grasp its relevance to literary problems. On the other hand, Bataille ignores the technical terms derived from rhetoric, poetics, and linguistics which have brought some measure of lucidity to modern critical discourse.

Such key words as "sovereignty," "evil," "transgression," "excess," and "consummation," with their connotation of barbaric ritual, bespeak Bataille's refusal of "civilization": to him, literature belongs outside the law, it challenges order. Through writing, modern man attempts a return to the primitive darkness of violence and eroticism. Literature must seek the antipodes of reason and culture, or sink into nothingness.

As a writer, and a critic, Bataille himself tried to be an outlaw: his underground, pornographic novels constitute an aggression against taste, morality, and the regular uses of language. His criticism defies all lawful theories of literature and chooses to explore the wilderness of violence. The field of rational criticism begins where Bataille's meditation on the written word ends, and the two approaches do not readily meet in a unified field. Bataille does not yield to synthesizing efforts. Between Bataille and most other critics (with the exception of such outsiders as Blanchot, Klossowski, and Caillois), there lies a precipitous gap. Bataille's thought endangers all criticism.

Despite the undistinguished grayness of its style, Bataille's critical discourse slips the reader's reason. While they are partly due to the elusiveness of the concepts, to the skids which pull the essays now and again toward a kind of nonsense, the difficulties arise, in the last analysis, from the fundamental difference between Bataille's assumptions and those of common sense. Yet, it is not easy to grasp and define this difference, because the language of the essays is free from obvious distortions. Bataille takes his liberties with sense on the sly. Unlike his fiction, which is permeated with the gravest disorders of words and deeds, Bataille's critical essays run a dull course, where the whirlpools remain hidden from the eye that scans the surface. This superficial flatness, combined with a certain stylistic awkwardness (especially in the *Critique* version of the essays, before they were polished for publication as a book under the title *La Littérature et le mal*), delays our realization that the key concepts—belonging, somehow, outside the pale of rational discourse—have warped and sabotaged a thought which at first sounded like second-hand Hegelianism and derivative ethnology.

Bataille, like a very quiet lunatic, skips and hops imperceptibly over the boundaries of reason in his criticism. He uses and undercuts at the same time concepts which have become void of their usual sense as they are imperceptibly withdrawn from the full circle of dialectical reason.

The key concept of sovereignty, for instance, derives from the Hegelian dialectic of master and slave, but it does not settle within this dialectic. Endowed with Nietzschean connotations, the word drops out of history, it takes on an absolute meaning, it is immobilized in its transcendence over what is forever subordinate; yet, this sovereignty cannot be attained, it remains beyond man's reach, except in "timeless" moments of ecstasy. In other words, the concept of sovereignty might make sense within a theological context, but Bataille has once and for all rejected any belief in a sovereign Being. In Bataille, there is no theology, although some of his writings parody the approach of negative theologians. So there we are: if sovereignty does not refer to the dominance of one man over men, or to the transcendence of the Godhead, or, in any tangible, permanent sense, to the possibility for man to become like a god, the concept appears empty. Yet, although perfectly aware of these difficulties, Bataille kept insisting that man can experience sovereignty in the face of an Absence, that he had himself experienced it beyond the reach of words. He insisted further that literature, as he understood it, was one of the ways toward this impossible experience.

We cannot pin Bataille down; reading his essays is like wrestling with an elusive angel, or with an invader from a fourth dimension. To make matters worse, we are faced with Bataille's laughter, which punctuates his excursions into nonsense. Bataille laughs at himself and at the reader, signifying that man is the odd animal endowed with reason who can speak outside reason and still make a strange kind of sense—the only kind of sense that matters, perhaps, in view of man's tragic condition in a godless world.

If we define humanity as "what makes sense," then Bataille succeeds in stepping out of his humanity. He speaks senselessly, at times. Yet, unlike the madman, he always straddles the boundary of reason; Bataille does not make sense *only* to the psychiatrist trained to read and interpret the symptoms of his disorder. Insofar as any man can, he makes sense for himself and remains conscious of what others call the temporary absences of sense in his discourse. Bataille accepts what is alien and lawless within himself and his desires, while we hide from ourselves our otherness through the strategies of reason. He welcomes the strangeness which surges forth and stands revealed in transgressions of the law (of reason), in excess of sense unduly attributed to concepts and in ecstasy, when language altogether breaks down.

At this point, we realize that Bataille has turned the tables on us, for we are all here and yet not here, familiar in our sameness and alien in our difference, in turn law-abiding and yearning for a wilderness beyond the law. Like the insane among us, he raises, for the writer and the critic, the question of the locus of humanity, a humanity whose topology has become so shifting and uncertain that we are not sure whether it resides where it seemed to be, while we suspect ever more strongly that it is also located where it appeared not to be. Bataille is thus a critic who, at a high cost to himself and his readers, succeeds in weaving into the texture of his discourse those very questions which make criticism something more than a mere scholarly pursuit.

This self-defeating success results from Bataille's refusal of the dialectic which enables reason to swallow everything, turning the Other into the Same (e.g., literary criticism digesting the individual unconscious with its puns, its slips and its nonsense, and the "cultural" unconscious which shapes the very categories of our reasoning). There are limits which must remain limits, although, like all limits, these must repeatedly be overstepped, in fear and trembling. In other words, Bataille clings to guilt, he accepts his guilt, man's guilt. In a sense, guilt becomes a positive value. Primitive transgression, crime, evil are not swept under the rug of reason. On the contrary, Bataille founds the dignity of man—and his abjection—his difference from the rest of the universe, upon the permanence of transgression, of guilt, fear, and ecstasy. He opposes, ultimately, the modern sciences of man which, despite their pious talk of human dignity, tend to fuse man with the universe, submitting him ever more intimately to the laws of nature. Bataille, in his odd, perverse fashion, is a religious thinker who struggles against the imperialism of reason (defined as the realm of the lawful) which stretches its horizon to the point where it becomes all-encompassing.

Bataille's battlefield was language. The enemy was the Logos, since the imperialism of positivistic reason and the ambitions of rational discourse coincide in their permanent assault upon what used to be beyond their grasp. The order of the law is the order of language. This explains Bataille's central concern for poetry, although he manifested it in a marginal fashion. Poetry transgresses the law (of language). As our culture becomes increasingly rational, poetry becomes the only breach of order, the sole—metaphorical—transgression of reason's rule which dissolves man into what used to constitute the Outside. The violence necessary in order to maintain a difference takes its refuge in literature.

Breaking the law is *evil*; breaking the law is the only way for man to break out of the circle of *what is*, that is, of reason (a circle whose circumference is everywhere and the center nowhere). Evil, therefore, is the name given to man's effort to rise above his subordination, to distinguish himself from everything which *is*, to force his way for an uncertain moment into the Outside, which is nondialectical negativity, and thus achieve—although never really possessing—sovereignty.

What cannot be obtained within the law must be stolen at a capital risk: death is ever present in Bataille's criticism, in a vivid imagination of the "supreme moment," when everything is finally consummated. This moment, of which poetry can give us only a metaphorical approach, cannot be captured in language. Thus sovereignty cannot be separated from an ultimate denial of discourse. Only the conjunction of tears, sobs, and irrepressible laughter, or a wordless ecstasy, can express the supreme moment. Ultimately, the fulfillment of literature means the destruction of its medium.

In history and in his personal life, Bataille sensed the overwhelming menace of entropy, ever busy at paring away differences. All that had made human life both tragic and exhilarating since the dawn of *homo sapiens* was on the verge of being engulfed by the law. Excess, crime, and ecstasy would be eradicated. Monsters, which fascinated Bataille, were at least a sign that the law could occasionally break down, while the homogenizing tendency of the law was worse than death itself, since it deprived even the supreme moment of its meaning. Bataille was haunted by the idea of the end of history, which had perhaps come to pass; hence the need to substitute written words for acts, in order to retain at least a metaphorical difference of potential. Clearly, Bataille's ideas on literature were based on an analogical reading of the phases of French history. To him, the crucial moment was the passage from feudal—or aristocratic—violence, based on inequality, to the democratic leveling when the law supersedes privilege.

In this perspective, and in view of the crucial function of evil, it becomes easy to grasp why Sade is the pivotal figure in Bataille's vision of history and literature. The aristocrat who cannot assert anymore the exorbitant rights of his mastery through murder (and who is therefore unable to attain sovereignty) must resort to transgression in writing. Actual violence is transmuted into literary sadism. Thus the writer in search of sovereignty appears as the heir to the aristocrat, for like the nobleman of yore, he takes on mortal risks in order to rise above the leveling effects of rationality. Violence is limited to the exercise of language, and literature appears as the modern avatar of action. Writing supersedes the enactment of history. Yet, it is but a radical alibi for inaction.

If we think that literary criticism is an attempt to establish laws accounting for the transgressions of ordered discourse which constitute the essence of literature; if it is our mission to pull literature from its teetering balance on the outer limits of sense in order to place it squarely within the field of science; if we intend to roll back the limits so that they recede beyond our horizon, then Bataille cannot mean anything to us. Then again, his criticism might mark the limits of our success and be the measure of our perpetual defeat. Bataille's thought does not fit the ever spreading puzzle of academic eclecticism; actually, its function is to challenge our certainties.

Every critic knows that writing about literature cannot be seriously equated with science. Bataille underscores the fact that criticism is not knowledge, and in his extreme fashion he turns it into an identification with the writer's attempt to break free of the law's circle. Bataille's book on Nietzsche (*Sur Nietzsche*), perhaps his most central critical venture, embodies this philosophy and carries it to its ultimate consequences: oscillating between the journal and the essay form, the book remains spotty and fragmentary.

When Bataille recalls that "it is from the feeling of a community binding me to Nietzsche that the desire to communicate was born in me," we recognize a critical commonplace. Yet Bataille's decision to write on Nietzsche had to be absolutely banal and subtly different. Clearly, a feeling of community with Nietzsche implies a radical perversion and a precipitous break with common sense. Identifying with Voltaire, Jane Austen, or Longfellow is safe enough and can be accomplished within the requirements of a doctoral dissertation, whereas following Nietzsche into madness calls for a different kind of nerve. Granted, it cannot be done, but the very attempt is staggering. Criticism must choose between this deadly game and futility: "I had to write *with my life* this book on Nietzsche I had planned, a book in which I wanted to state and solve, if I could, the intimate problem of morals."[1] Writing with one's life, as the saint writes with his life a commentary on the Gospels: the attempt may be trite, and irrelevant to literature as we normally understand it. At any rate, this leads us out of the field of criticism and into the twilight where man makes a choice between sainthood, or crime, and literature; between poetry and madness. Yet the very existence of Bataille's book indicates that the choice never was made, for this twilight zone is ambiguous and pregnant with sudden reversals. Bataille—after Sade, Nietzsche, Strindberg, Artaud, and perhaps Pound—testifies to the ambivalence which constitutes literature against common sense. Obviously, this extreme conception of literature as a fatal risk cannot produce a full, viable form of criticism. Bataille's literary criticism is flawed, piecemeal, and elusive. He had courted the failure which also marks the work of the writers who attracted his attention.

Bataille's work defies the straightforwardness of an academic discourse and puts *his* critic on the spot. His criticism contains no positive information, and no usable message can be readily extracted from it. He stands alone: where can we fit him in the spectrum of contemporary French criticism? He seems to belong near the surrealists, but can there be such a thing as

1. "Pour cette raison, je ne pouvais qu'écrire *avec ma vie* ce livre projeté sur Nietzsche, où je voulais poser, si je pouvais, résoudre le problème intime de la morale." Georges Bataille, *Sur Nietzsche, volonté de chance* (Paris: Gallimard, 1945), p. 21.

surrealist criticism? And sometimes Georges Bataille seems to be Maurice Blanchot's soiled double. His thought has pervaded, and perhaps perverted, modern criticism, so that no survey would make sense without it, yet, as soon as we try to deal with it, we trip over the obstacles it puts in the way of rational discourse. Bataille's thought is the limit which defines and exacerbates the frustrations of contemporary approaches to the written word.

Let us attempt the biographical evasion, for the life of this slippery figure coincides with the highlights of recent French intellectual history. Yet, at every turn, Bataille stands outside the mainstream; his positions parallel but subtly contradict the dominant trends. Neither a poet nor a philosopher, he is both, and he conscientiously sharpens the contradictions which make his positions untenable, so that few can agree with him, or disregard his stance. Totally serious in his irresponsibility, he likes to appear as the Other, the devil of doubt and contradiction. And he is all the more respected for appearing ludicrous or repulsive at times.

A biography of Georges Bataille is yet to be written, but the significant elements are already well known; they are typical of a bourgeois revolutionary intellectual of the first half of this century. In other words, they shed some light on Bataille's major preoccupations, but they do not elucidate the peculiar obscurity of his work.

When Michel Leiris first met him in 1924,[2] Bataille, who had undergone a mystical crisis in adolescence, was spending his free time whoring, gambling, and drinking. Deeply influenced by Dostoevsky, Bataille was modeling himself on the "impossible" hero of *Notes from the Underground*. He was exploring vice and degradation. If God is dead, all is permitted. Bataille went beyond self-indulgence, beyond disgust and physical sickness, in search of those moments when exhaustion and repulsion seem to challenge the limits of man and induce a kind of negative ecstasy. He never strayed from a wayward

2. Michel Leiris, "De Bataille l'impossible à l'impossible *Documents.*" *Critique* 19 (1963): 685–93.

religious quest, for, in spite of God's shocking absence, man *had* to be more than mere man.

Through Michel Leiris, Bataille came into contact with the surrealists, who were also challenging the social and physical limits of man. Yet he never saw eye to eye with André Breton. Their disagreements were perhaps deeper than a superficial reading of the *Second Surrealist Manifesto* of 1929 (in which Bataille was violently attacked) might indicate. Bataille despised the idealism of the surrealists, as well as their exalted conception of love and their "puritanism." Although he and Breton agreed on the pivotal importance of Sade, the orthodox surrealists tended to view the latter as the supreme literary champion of love and freedom, while Bataille found in his writings the guideposts of a mystical "way."[3]

Bataille retained his independence. In 1929–30, he founded and edited *Documents*, a bizarre luxury review financed by the art dealer Wildenstein. Among the contributors were academic scholars and revolutionary artists. A forerunner of *Minotaure*, edited by Breton in the thirties, and of several recent reviews, *Documents* studied fantastic art, the grotesque and the erotic, with special emphasis on monstrosities which stagger the reason and challenge our belief in the lawfulness of Nature. Bataille's touch is apparent in the choice of topics, as it is in the scholarly approach to scabrous material and in the refusal to accept the limitations of "good taste." Wildenstein soon withdrew his support.

In the thirties, a political involvement was unavoidable. A militant anti-fascist, Bataille always steered clear of the Communist party. Nevertheless, he was drawn to the Cercle Communiste Démocratique, founded by Boris Suvarin. This small opposition group published a journal, *La Critique Sociale*, to which Bataille contributed. Raymond Queneau, a former surrealist, was also a member of this group, along with Michel Leiris. By that time, they were all versed in Marxism. Queneau and Bataille had studied Hegel's philosophy, taking courses under Alexandre Kojève, the founder of Hegelian

3. Bataille, "La Valeur d'usage de D.A.F. de Sade," *L'Arc*, no. 32 (1967), pp. 88–90.

studies in France. Up to the early thirties, Hegel was hardly taught at the Sorbonne, and there was no reliable translation of his works. Bataille's participation in the rebirth of Hegelian studies placed him in the mainstream of the philosophical awakening which paved the way for Sartre and Merleau-Ponty.[4]

Familiar with Hegel and the latest developments in German philosophy such as Husserl's phenomenology and the existentialism of Heidegger, Bataille might have become a professional philosopher. The influence of Nietzsche and a sense of futility killed this temptation.[5] Bataille remained a Hegelian, in the sense that to him Hegel's philosophy was ultimate philosophy, the very incarnation of the discourse of reason and knowledge. As we have seen, his thinking is an endless subversive play around Hegel's concepts, which brings the stately unfolding of dialectics to a standstill.

This work of corrosion, which never puts in doubt Hegel's *rightness*, was fed by the discovery of ethnology; it proved that man could be *wrong*, and *alive*, on the side of evil. For Bataille, the discovery of the Aztec culture, through his friend Alfred Métraux, was far more than an intellectual excursion into exoticism. He found in Aztec human sacrifices the very foundation of his ideas on transgression and consummation; there was the antithesis of our own culture based on production and accumulation. The American Indians provided Bataille with examples of reckless, almost superhuman generosity. He saw in their sacrificial destruction of human lives, their conspicuous waste of excess goods in the potlatch,[6] the signs of a sovereignty over human fate which stood in striking contrast to our West-

4. See Georges Bataille and Raymond Queneau, "La Critique des fondements de la dialectique hégélienne," *La Critique Sociale*, no. 5 (March 1932), pp. 209–14, reprinted in *Deucalion* 40, no. 5 (October 1955): 45–60.

5. Bataille's symbiosis with Nietzsche is evident in his *Sur Nietzsche, volonté de chance*. The book begins as an essay on Nietzsche and gradually becomes Bataille's own spiritual diary.

6. Bataille studied this form of economic exchange among the American Indians of the Northwest in his book on economics, *La Part maudite, essai d'économie générale. I. La Consumation* (Paris: Editions de Minuit, 1949), pp. 81–98.

ern emphasis on caution, on submission to material, subordinate ends. Ethnology became Bataille's constant frame of reference. Although he shunned cultural relativism, he found in primitive societies the living proof that the limits imposed upon man in Western society by the mystique of labor were neither a natural boundary nor an inescapable fate. Ethnology verified those surrealist beliefs which Bataille had always shared with Breton.[7]

No doubt, in his revolt and impatience, Bataille overstepped the limits of scientific prudence. Yet, only a total misunderstanding of his quest could lead us to judge from a scientific point of view the program of the Collège de Sociologie, an association which he founded in 1938. This Collège ought to be seen as a secret society, a kind of Gnostic sect, devoted to the creation of a new mythology.[8] Around Bataille and Michel Leiris were Roger Caillois, Jules Monnerot, Pierre Klossowski, and the painter André Masson. They sought to reinstate violence, eroticism, and ecstasy as central social values. The title of their short-lived review, *Acéphale*, expresses their distrust of Reason. Combining Nietzschean themes with ethnological evidence, they set out to transgress the inherent limitations of Western culture. Whether or not these men remained faithful to the ideology of the Collège de Sociologie, they gave general currency to its ideas. Such books as *La Poésie moderne et le sacré*, by Monnerot, or Caillois's *L'Homme et le sacré*, as well as Klossowski's meditation on Sade, can all be traced back to this fruitful association.

Beginning in 1938, Bataille undertook mystical experiments in the form of solitary meditations leading to ecstasy. A godless mystic, Bataille came "face to face" with an "absence," which he distinguished from "nothingness." His way was in

7. Michel Leiris became a professional ethnologist, and Antonin Artaud sought the solution of his own problems among the Taharumaras, a Mexican Indian tribe. The affinity is consistent. Even Claude Lévi-Strauss began by undergoing the influence of surrealism.

8. The manifesto of the group ("Pour un Collège de Sociologie," written by Bataille, Leiris, and Roger Caillois) appeared in the *Nouvelle Revue Française* 51 (1938): 5–54, 874–76. The title of Bataille's contribution is "L'Apprenti sorcier," pp. 8–25.

some respects close to that of Yoga, of which he became an initiate, and to Zen Buddhism, alternating the quest for an inner silence and the mental representation of unbearably painful images, such as the picture of a man whose flesh is being cut and torn from his live body. A record of these meditations, as well as an attempt to share his mystical experience of the unknown is to be found in *L'Expérience intérieure* and *Méthode de méditation*.[9]

Georges Bataille's criticism is but a continuation, through other means, of his spiritual quest. This is the secret of his influence in the postwar years when, as the editor of *Critique*,[10] he became the spokesman for those opposing a narrow, political interpretation of Sartre's call to commitment. One might argue that most French approaches to literature since World War II find themselves either under the aegis of Sartre's *What Is Literature?*[11] or of Bataille's articles in *Critique*. The two positions are not antipodal. But the difference is sharp: Sartre spurned imagination and the "privileges" of poetry, in which he saw not only a departure from the proper uses of language, but a wayward destruction of its significance, while Bataille praised in poetry a sacrifice of language, outside the

9. Bataille, *L'Expérience intérieure* (Paris: Gallimard, 1943); *Méthode de méditation* (Paris: Fontaine, 1947).

10. The first issue of *Critique* came out in June 1946. The aims and the format of the review were outlined in a foreword:

"*Critique* will publish essays on the books and articles which appear in France and abroad.

"These essays will go beyond mere reviews. Through them, *Critique* wishes to offer as complete a survey as possible of the various activities of the human mind in the domains of literary creation, philosophical research, as well as historical, scientific, political, and economic scholarship."

"*Critique* publiera des études sur les ouvrages et les articles paraissant en France et à l'étranger.

"Ces études dépassent l'importance de simples comptes-rendus. A travers elles, *Critique* voudrait donner un aperçu, le moins incomplet qu'il se pourra, des diverses activités de l'esprit humain dans les domaines de la création littéraire, des recherches philosophiques, des connaissances historiques, scientifiques, politiques et économiques."

11. Jean-Paul Sartre, "Qu'est-ce que la littérature?" *Situations* II (Paris: Gallimard, 1947).

requirements of pragmatism.[12] Beyond good and evil, poetry maintained man's primitive claim to sovereignty.

Bataille tried to discover what is specifically human in man. He was therefore fascinated by the primitive, and especially by the birth of man out of the pre-hominid. His view is expressed most elaborately in *Lascaux, or the Birth of Art.*[13] He sees the passage from sluggish *homo faber* to *homo sapiens* as the dawn of human sovereignty. *Homo faber*, the toolmaker, is not yet quite human, whereas *homo sapiens* is "the man who plays, plays above all the admirable game of art." Man the maker is engaged in a subordinate activity, while play is sovereign, that is, not subordinate to any other purpose. It exists for its own sake. And so art, "which frees us, if upon each occasion for a time only, from the oppressive yoke of grim necessity, and in some sort brings us nearer to that marvelous heritage, that shower of riches for which every one of us feels himself born,"[14] is ultimate play. But play involves risks: for "the fullness and reality of the game man plays are consequences of his overstepping what is prohibited."[15] So art is inseparable from transgression.

Man is caught between his desire to maintain the harmony of his world, in order to survive, and the impulse to disobey prohibition. This contradiction is partially resolved with the feast day, when the rules are no longer binding and a relative license ensues. Yet, transgression must, by its very nature, be an act committed knowingly, despite the toll it is certain to exact. Thus, in transgression, man experiences a profound distress, which is alleviated, in the revelry, by an intense

12. See, for example, "Baudelaire 'mis à nu.' L'Analyse de Sartre et l'essence de la poésie," *Critique* 2 (1947): 3–27. See also "Jean-Paul Sartre et l'impossible révolte de Jean Genet," *Critique*, 8 (1952): 819–32 and 946–61. Both articles were rewritten and enlarged for publication in Bataille's collection of critical essays, *La Littérature et le mal* (Paris: Gallimard, 1957).

13. Bataille, *Prehistoric Painting: Lascaux, or the Birth of Art*, translated by Austryn Wainhouse (Geneva: Skira, 1955). See also "Le Passage de l'animal à l'homme et la naissance de l'art," *Critique* 9 (1953): 312–30.

14. *Lascaux*, p. 36.

15. Ibid., p. 37.

excitement. Religious transgression engenders the ecstasy, and ecstasy is the core of religion. In traditional societies this connection is normally provided for and made manifest in sacrifice. Taking lives is the supreme transgression; the sacrificer is conscience-stricken, yet in front of the awed spectators he violates the ban on murder.

Art expresses the prohibition, and, with gravity, it also expresses the awe of and the need for sacrifice. It resolves this human dilemma. Art expresses the need and the fear, desire and transgression, it approaches the richer, more marvelous world of the sacred.

Bataille is aware that every work of art, beneath its sacred import, embodies a specific practical intention. We assume the Lascaux paintings may have been done to assuage dead animals or chase evil spirits, but this specific intention is subordinated to the supreme intention of marking the difference between animal and man. The implication is clear: the birth of man cannot be dissociated from the recognition of prohibitions, and it comes to pass with the transgression of such prohibitions:

> A work of art, a sacrifice, contain something of an irrepressible festive exuberance that overflows the world of work, and clashes with, if not the letter, the spirit of the prohibitions indispensable to safeguarding this world. Every work of art, in isolation, possesses a meaning independent of the desire for the prodigal, a desire each has in common with all the rest. But we may say in advance that a work of art in which the desire cannot be sensed, in which it is faint or barely present, is a mediocre work.[16]

Bataille places metaphysical criteria above formal ones. Characterizing man as a destroyer and a transgressor, Bataille chooses the side of evil. This extreme attitude makes short shrift of literature and aesthetics, insofar as these two values are related to the Good. Bataille's own books are an example of the limits of writing, and of the impossible burden that literature must carry in order to manifest man's desire. Each of his mystical meditations is an uneasy breach of silence, an

16. Ibid., p. 39.

approach to the speechless ecstasy and laughter which consume his rare moments of "sovereignty." These books, despite their brevity, are as monotonous as Sade's novels, for they endlessly circle around the instant when language breaks down, as it does in agony and orgasm. Language, the very stuff of our humanity, is both the means whereby we seek the absolute, through a perversion of its profane functions, and the sign of our tragic, time-bound fate. Language must explode beyond a certain point in our quest for the absolute, since it is the vehicle and the cause of the specialization in our usual life. Language is either the tool of action, or it becomes poetry. But action is limited to the possible, subjecting us to a subordinate purpose, while poetry, which challenges the practical uses of language, entails its own tragic failure; it is a mere representation of our quest for the "impossible" rather than a real, existential possession of the absolute. Inescapably, language embodies and manifests man's limits, while the transgression of limits which, from Sade to Artaud, has been the impossible dream of modern poets, remains beyond the grasp of words.

This concern with the dual function of language as a means and a limit permeates Bataille's criticism and places it in the mainstream of modern approaches to literature which recognize that the absence of an eternal Word vouching for the continuation of discourse beyond the last gasp of ecstasy places an exhilarating and tragic responsibility upon human speech. Man is wholly responsible for his words, and the writers who have dared to use language irregularly, in a spirit of Promethean revolt, are the only witnesses of man's quest for sovereignty.

Bataille was therefore foremost among those critics whom Jean Paulhan termed "Terrorists":

> . . . writers conscientiously bent on refusing literary artifice and the rules of the literary game, putting in their place an inexpressible event, which, they claim, is at once erotic and terrifying; intent on challenging creation at all times, dedicated to seeking the sublime within the loathsome, greatness within the subversive, demanding further that each work commit and compromise its author forever.[17]

17. Jean Paulhan, "La Douteuse Justine, ou les Revanches de la pudeur," 1946 preface to D.A.F. de Sade, *Les Infortunes de la vertu*

And indeed, only an enemy of literature could write: "To the extent that it retains a literary void, a sentence is doomed to gather dust in a museum."[18]

Bataille was faithful to the surrealist legacy and, beyond it, to Dada's critique of literature and to the cult of silence whose saints are Lautréamont, Rimbaud in the Harrar, and all the *poètes maudits*. Pitched against silence and ultimate self-destruction, criticism can lay no claim to innocence, and the critic may not recoil from total commitment. This radical conception of the critic's responsibility, implicit throughout Bataille's writings, is clearly expressed in the review of a book by an academic critic whose smug detachment called for an angry rebuttal:

Criticism is nothing (an exercise in literary history or an unruly dialogue with an author) when it is not the expression of a philosophy (one really ought to say, more generally: of—if not quite a religion—at least what one lives by). Viewing it humbly as a limited area of the mind's activity causes a reduc-

---

(reprinted; Paris: Pauvert, 1959), p. xiv. Paulhan was the first French critic to oppose the literary terrorism described here. The passage continues:

"... I wonder if in so extreme a reign of terror one must not recognize less an invention than a recollection, less an ideal than a memory, and in short, if our modern literature, in that part which seems the most vital—in any case the most aggressive—is not in fact entirely pointing backward, and, to be precise, determined by Sade."

"[Je me demande, quand je vois tant d'] écrivains, de nos jours, si consciemment appliqués à refuser l'artifice et le jeu littéraire au profit d'un événement indicible dont on ne nous laisse pas ignorer qu'il est tout à la fois érotique et effrayant, soucieux de prendre en toute circonstance le contre-pied de la création, et tout occupés à rechercher le sublime dans l'infâme, le grand dans le subversif, exigeant d'ailleurs que toute oeuvre engage et compromette à jamais son auteur . . . je me demande s'il ne faudrait pas reconnaître, dans une aussi extrême terreur, moins une invention qu'un souvenir, moins un idéal qu'une mémoire, et bref si notre littérature moderne, dans sa part qui nous semble la plus vivante—la plus aggressive en tout cas—ne se trouve pas tout entière tournée vers le passé, et très précisément déterminée par Sade."

18. "Toute phrase est vouée au musée dans la mesure où persiste un vide littéraire." *Sur Nietzsche*, p. 44.

tion of the works to dimensions that their nature undoubtedly exceeds. If one is agreed that a philosophy would remedy this, it is only under the condition that this philosophy appear from the start as a questioning of the possibilities of criticism. . . . Unless one possesses this fundamental awareness, he may believe he is discussing poetry (poetry in literature is the essential, the *moving* part of it) while he turns his back upon it.

> . . . the play of language, taken in the sense of an opening onto all that is possible, is *associated* by criticism with the efforts of discursive thought. Precisely, criticism describes the limits of this effort (its own effort), it places itself astride these limits, and it defines itself as the extreme possibility of philosophy.[19]

All criticism must eventually turn upon itself and become a critique of criticism. In the process, the limits of language are challenged, for criticism is a discursive attempt to determine how writers break their original silence, to see how their use of language for an approach to the unutterable will ultimately lead back to silence in self-destruction or death.

Bataille never was reconciled to the necessity of dealing with literature at all. Writing is a laughable substitute for the sacred

19. "La critique littéraire n'est rien (exercise d'histoire littéraire ou dialogue déréglé avec l'auteur) si elle n'est l'expression d'une philosophie (même on devrait dire, plus généralement, sinon d'une religion, d'un système de vie). Par modestie, vouloir l'envisager comme un domaine limité de l'activité de l'esprit a pour conséquence une réduction des oeuvres à des mesures que sans doute leur nature excède. Et s'il est vrai qu'une philosophie y remédierait, c'est à la condition justement qu'elle apparaisse dès l'abord comme une contestation des possibilités de la critique. . . . En *fait*, la formule que je donne répond à la méthode de Maurice Blanchot. Sans cette constatation fondamentale, on croit parler de poésie (la poésie, dans la littérature est l'essentiel, *ce qui touche*), on se détourne de la poésie.

". . . le jeu du langage, pris dans le sens d'une ouverture sur tout le possible, est *associé* par la critique à l'effort de la pensée discursive. Exactement, la critique décrit les limites de cet effort (qui est le sien), se situe sur ces limites et se définit comme l'extrême possibilité de la philosophie. (Cette méthode en un sens répond avec rigueur à des préoccupations que le surréalisme a formulées.)" A review of Victor Giraud, *La Critique littéraire. Le Problème. Les Théories. Les Méthodes* (Paris: Aubier, 1946), in *Critique* 2 (1947): 171–72.

trance, the word is but an image of the roaring revel—a symbolic sacrifice. True life is elsewhere. He keeps going back to the constituent flaw of literature:

Literature (fiction) has taken the place of spiritual life, poetry (a disorder of the *words*), that of *real* trance. Art forms a small free estate outside action, which pays for its freedom by renouncing the real world. . . . The domain of the arts does, in a sense, embrace the totality: yet, totality, inescapably, also gives it the slip.[20]

This is a variation on what he had written a few years earlier in "L'Apprenti sorcier":

But what is the meaning of the painted ghosts, of the written ghost conjured up in order to make the world into which we wake up less worthy of being haunted by our idle lives? Everything is *false* about the images of fancy.[21]

Literature occasionally does try to shake off its constituent falsehood by inserting itself into the real world. Knowing that it cannot be the true representation of the world that science is, literature will buy reality at the cost of its freedom. It subordinates its freedom to a commitment. But, subordinated to special interests, literature loses its capacity to embody the whole of human destiny. Effectual commitment results in an incapacity for literature to stretch itself out to the limits of the totality, since all action is fragmentary and fractional. More often, the commitment is incomplete, and literature is relegated to a limbo where it forfeits its sovereign freedom. Literature is fundamentally vitiated.

20. "La littérature (la fiction) s'est substituée à ce qu'était précédemment la vie spirituelle, la poésie (le désordre des *mots*) aux états de transe *réels*. L'art constitue un petit domaine libre en dehors de l'action, payant sa liberté de sa renonciation au monde réel. . . . Le domaine des arts en un sens embrasse bien la totalité: celle-ci néanmoins lui échappe de toute façon." *Sur Nietzsche*, p. 31.

21. "Mais que signifient ces fantômes peints, ces fantômes écrits suscités pour rendre le monde où nous nous éveillons un peu moins indigne d'être hanté par nos existences désoeuvrées? Tout est *faux* dans les images de la fantaisie." Bataille, "L'Apprenti sorcier," *Nouvelle Revue Française* 51 (1938): 11.

Nietzsche caught the whole man, and saved his enterprise: he was the first writer to express the extreme, unconditional aspiration of man, independently of a moral purpose. But Nietzsche himself could not overcome the fatal flaw of literature: "Zarathustra also is a poet, and even a literary fiction!"[22] The sole, but fundamental, difference between Nietzsche and other scribblers, is that *he never accepted*. He never accepted the writing condition, as he never accepted the human condition within the modern world.

He never accepted: this applies to Bataille the mystic, and to Bataille the critic. He never accepted that a book be but a work of art, a reflection of a fragment. The writers he did eventually study were all made of the same intractable stuff; they never accepted their art as a solace. They saw it rather as an insufferable fall from silence which ought to lead back to silence. They might all have said, along with Bataille himself:

What forces me to write, I believe, is the fear of going mad.

I suffer a burning, tormenting aspiration, which lingers inside me like an unfulfilled desire.

My tension, in a sense, resembles a great welling up of laughter, it is not unlike the burning passions of Sade's heroes, and yet, it is close to that of the martyrs, or of the saints.[23]

The significance of Bataille's criticism shifts according to its context. Within *Critique*, surrounded by articles on history and philosophy, on the natural and social sciences, his essays are a firm center, the refuge of humanity in language. They testify that while man makes history and discovers new scientific laws, he preserves within him a sanctuary. His eyes must sometimes turn away from the world and from the objectified part of himself; they must be rolled upward in meditation and seek

22. "Zarathoustra aussi est un poète, et même une fiction littéraire!" *Sur Nietzsche*, p. 32.

23. "Ce qui m'oblige d'écrire, j'imagine, est la crainte de devenir fou.

"Je subis une aspiration ardente, douloureuse, qui dure en moi comme un désir inassouvi.

"Ma tension ressemble, en un sens, à une folle envie de rire, elle diffère peu des passions dont brûlent les héros de Sade, et pourtant, elle est proche de celle des martyrs ou des saints." *Sur Nietzsche*, p. 12.

the dazzling night which founds his very being in the serious play of poetic language. In *La Littérature et le mal*, Bataille's essays bespeak the futility of all human speculation which does not attempt to enunciate man's identification with eroticism and death. They take on a tragic color. As we read through *La Littérature et le mal*, we become increasingly aware that all leads back to Sade's inaugural disclosure of the identity of man's eroticism with his Promethean fate in a godless world. Guilt and exhilaration, tears and spasms, abjection and triumph, all pertain to this nexus which defines the new man who makes evil his Good. All of Bataille's critical essays set out to find re-enactments of the Sadian transgression and assumption of sex. His language is largely the transposition, on the anthropological plane, of Sadian and Nietzschean metaphysics. If, in the context of *Critique*, his articles point up man's yearning for sovereignty in a convulsed world, in isolation these essays underscore man's guilt. Thus Bataille added the following paragraph to his *Critique* article on Baudelaire for its republication in *La Littérature et le mal*:

Although it is true that in many respects Baudelaire's attitude is miserable, berating him is the most inhuman course. Yet, we would be forced to do so, did we not take upon ourselves the unavowable attitude of Baudelaire, who deliberately refuses to act as a grown man, that is to say, as a prosaic man. Sartre is right: Baudelaire has chosen to be guilty, like a child. But before we decide that this choice is untenable, we must examine its nature. Was it made by default? Is it only a deplorable mistake? Or, on the other hand, was it made by excess? In a miserable fashion, no doubt, but decisively? I even wonder: is not this choice in its essence the very choice of poetry? Is it not *man's choice*?

This is the meaning of my book.[24]

24. "S'il est vrai qu'à bien des égards l'attitude de Baudelaire est malheureuse, l'accabler semble bien le parti le moins humain. Il le faudrait pourtant, si nous ne prenions à notre compte l'attitude inavouable de Baudelaire, qui, délibérément, refuse d'agir en homme accompli, c'est-à-dire en homme prosaïque. Sartre a raison: Baudelaire a choisi d'être en faute, comme un enfant. Mais avant de le juger malencontreux nous devons nous demander de quelle sorte de choix il s'agit. Se fit-il par défaut? n'est-il qu'une erreur déplorable? Au

Does this all add up to *criticism*? From the untroubled viewpoint of a "theory of literature," it obviously does not. No need to say that Bataille could not have cared less.

Like the surrealists, Bataille knew that all expository writing is a defeat and a fraud; the best summary of his dilemma is perhaps contained in a short review of Maurice Nadeau's books on surrealism:

> Of the "spot of intellectual blood," which is the rage to rationalize, Lautréamont said it could not be washed off. And, in fact, it cannot be, I succumb to the use of words: *being*, *fact*, *succumb*, *use*, all these assembled and chained words proclaim my servitude; and it is not enough that I recognize it to be rid of it. In fact, the writer, as averse to the discursive as he may be—to the "order of things" and to the servile language which expresses it—cannot limit himself to turning his back upon it; he is forced to express himself on the level of discourse, forced to have an intellectual position. It is painful to him: he does it unwillingly, he gnashes his teeth, he manifests his impatience. The consciousness that he ought to be silent incites him to play the prophet.[25]

To Bataille, criticism was but the reverse of an impossible silence.

Since the dominant school of contemporary criticism now turns squarely to science in an attempt to analyze literature

---

contraire eut-il lieu par excès? d'une façon misérable peut-être, décisive pourtant? Je me demande même: un tel choix n'est-il pas dans son essence, celui de la poésie? n'est-il pas *celui de l'homme*?

"C'est le sens de mon livre." *La Littérature et le mal*, p. 40.

25. "De la 'tache de sang intellectuelle,' qui est la rage de rendre raison, Lautréamont a dit qu'elle ne pouvait être lavée. Elle ne peut l'être en effet, je succombe à l'usage des mots: *être*, *effet*, *succomber*, *usage*, tous ces mots assemblés, enchaînés, annoncent ma servitude; et il ne suffit pas de la reconnaître pour qu'elle ne soit plus. En effet l'écrivain même le plus opposé au discours,—à l' 'ordre des choses' et au langage servile qui l'exprime,—ne peut se borner néanmoins à tourner le dos; il est contraint lui-même à s'exprimer sur le plan du discours, contraint d'avoir une position intellectuelle. Mais cela lui est pénible: il le fait à contrecoeur, en grinçant des dents, et il se laisse aller à l'impatience. La conscience qu'il devrait se taire l'engage à vaticiner." Bataille, "Le Surréalisme et Dieu," *Critique* 4 (1948): 844.

with tools adapted from linguistics, Bataille's breach of silence may look like a closed parenthesis. His efforts belong to a defunct metaphysical age whose vague verbiage ensured that the right, positive questions never got asked, and could not be answered.

Silence has not engulfed Bataille. On the contrary, his presence is felt acutely where it can be most influential: in *Critique*, which remains France's best forum for ideas, and in *Tel Quel*, the leading magazine of the present generation, despite the confused leanings of this group toward structuralism. Bataille's influence is at the root of some incisive questioning of the current positivism; it is also responsible for much pretentious pathos on language.

It is difficult to disentangle this influence from that of his friends and disciples, such as Blanchot and Klossowski, but it does seem dominant in the work of at least one major thinker, Michel Foucault, whose book *Madness and Civilization*, for instance, seems at times the brilliant elaboration in a prestigious style of Bataille's favorite themes.

The growing reputation of Jacques Derrida (*L'Ecriture et la différence* [Paris, Le Seuil, 1967]), probably the most gifted philosopher of the written word in our time, ensures that Bataille's thinking will remain a living presence and an active force on the unsettled borders of literary criticism. While the structuralists are engaged in mapping out the topology of literature, some thinkers will keep on trying to understand why modern man endeavours to turn himself into a god through the mysteries of literary creation. For those, Bataille remains a model, and the ultimate judge of their efforts, for he stands forever outside the certainties of Reason. So long as Sade, Nietzsche, and Artaud boggle our understanding, we shall not free ourselves from Bataille's ironical play with nonsense.

BIBLIOGRAPHY

WORKS BY BATAILLE

Complete Works

Oeuvres complètes. 4 vols. Paris: Gallimard, 1970–71.

Books of Criticism

Sur Nietzsche, volonté de chance. Paris: Gallimard, 1945.

La Part maudite, essai d'économie générale, I. *La Consumation*. Paris: Editions de Minuit, 1949. Bataille thought this his most important book; it contains the theoretical foundations of his ideas on excess energy that has to be consumed, on the ethics of labor, on preferring the instant to the future.

L'Expérience intérieure. Revised edition containing also *Méthode de méditation* and *Post-scriptum 1953*. Paris: Gallimard, 1954. Bataille's mystical quest.

La Peinture préhistorique: Lascaux, ou la naissance de l'art. Geneva: Skira, 1955. (An English language edition was published concurrently with a translation by Austryn Wainhouse.)

Manet. Le Goût de Notre Temps. Geneva: Skira, 1955. (Published also in an English translation by Austryn Wainhouse and James Emmons in New York.)

La Littérature et le mal. Paris: Gallimard, 1957. Contains essays on Emily Brontë, Baudelaire, Michelet, Blake, Sade, Proust, Kafka, Genet.

L'Erotisme. Paris: Editions de Minuit, 1957. 10/18. Paris: Union Genérale d'Editions, 1964. (*Death and Sensuality: A Study of Eroticism and the Taboo*. Translated by Mary Dalwood. London: Calder, 1962. New York: Walker, 1962.) The most complete discussion of transgression, the profane and the sacred.

Les Larmes d'Eros. Paris: J.-J. Pauvert, 1961.

Edited by G. B. *Le Procès de Gilles de Rais: Les Documents*. Paris: J.-J. Pauvert, 1965. A narrative and sourcebook for the famous criminal's career and trial.

Documents. Paris: Mercure de France, 1968. Collection of articles published in the review of the same name, 1929–30.

Selected Articles

"L'Apprenti sorcier," in "Pour un Collège de Sociologie." *Nouvelle Revue Française* 51 (1938): 8–25.

"La Morale de Miller." *Critique* 1 (1946): 3–17.

"Le Surréalisme et sa différence avec l'existentialisme." Ibid., pp. 99–110.

"De l'Age de pierre à Jacques Prévert." Ibid., pp. 195–214.

"La Méchanceté du langage." Ibid. 4 (1948): 1059–66. An essay on Raymond Queneau's novels *Saint-Glinglin* and *L'Instant fatal*.

"Le Bonheur, l'érotisme et la littérature." Ibid. 5 (1949): 291–306; 401–11.

"Lettre à René Char sur les incompatibilités de l'écrivain." *Botteghe Oscure* (Rome) 6 (1950): 172–87.

"Le Silence de Molloy." *Critique* 7 (1951): 387–96. An essay on Samuel Beckett's *Molloy*.

"René Char et la force de la poésie." Ibid., pp. 819–23. A review of René Char's *A une Sérénité crispée*.

"L'Art et les larmes d'André Gide." Ibid., pp. 919–36. An essay on Gide's *Et nunc manet in te*.

"Le Temps de la révolte." Ibid., pp. 1019–27; and ibid. 8 (1952): 29–41. Two essays on Albert Camus's *L'Homme révolté*.

"Hemingway à la lumière de Hegel." Ibid. 9 (1953): 195–210.

"Un Livre humain, un grand livre." Ibid. 12 (1956): 99–112. A review of Claude Lévi-Strauss's *Tristes Tropiques*.

WORKS ON BATAILLE

Hommage à Georges Bataille. *Critique* 19 (1963): 675–832. This issue of the periodical is the best source of information on Bataille's life and thought. It contains important articles by the following friends and disciples: Alfred Métraux, Michel Leiris, Raymond Queneau, André Masson, Jean Bruno, Jean Piel (the current editor of *Critique*), Maurice Blanchot, Pierre Klossowski, Michel Foucault, Roland Barthes, Jean Wahl, and Philippe Sollers. The issue also contains a bibliography of Bataille's books and articles, as well as a bibliography of secondary sources. This bibliography is completed and brought up to date in *L'Arc*, no. 32 (1967). *L'Arc*'s homage to Bataille is a collection of critical essays. The most important contributions are those of Michel Leiris, Jacques Derrida, and Denis Hollier. The issue also includes some of Bataille's own texts which had not previously been published.

Blanchot, Maurice. "L'Expérience intérieure de Georges Bataille." In *Faux pas*, pp. 51–56. Paris: Gallimard, 1943.

———. "Le Récit et le scandale." *Nouvelle Nouvelle Revue Française* 4 (1956): 148–50. Reprinted in *Le Livre à venir*, pp. 231–33. Paris: Gallimard, 1959.

Bounoure, Gabriel. "Georges Bataille, poète maudit." *Mercure de France* 347 (1963): 196–203.

Foucault, Michel. "Préface à la transgression." *Critique* 19 (1963): 751–69.

Hollier, Denis. "Le Matérialisme dualiste de Georges Bataille." *Tel Quel*, no. 25 (Spring 1966), pp. 41–54.

Klossowski, Pierre. "Le Corps du néant. L'Expérience de la mort de Dieu chez Nietzsche et la nostalgie d'une expérience authentique chez Georges Bataille." In *Sade mon prochain*, pp. 153–83. Pierres Vives. Paris: Seuil, 1947.

———. "La Messe de Georges Bataille." In *Un si funeste désir*, pp. 121–32. Paris: Gallimard, 1963.

Limbour, Georges. "Bibliothécaire à Carpentras." *Mercure de France* 349 (1963): 752–58.

Réda, Jacques. "Georges Bataille." *Cahiers du Sud* 54 (1963): 280–86.

Sartre, Jean-Paul. "Un nouveau mystique." In *Situations I*, pp. 143–88. Paris: Gallimard, 1947.

Robert Champigny **8**

Gaston Bachelard

Most of Gaston Bachelard's works can be classified either as studies of the scientific spirit or studies of the "poetic" spirit, in a broad sense of the word. It is with the latter that we are mainly concerned here. They include five studies which take as their main themes the four traditional elements of physical nature: *La Psychanalyse du feu* (1938), *L'Eau et les rêves* (1942), *L'Air et les songes* (1943), *La Terre et les rêveries de la volonté* (1948), *La Terre et les rêveries du repos* (1948). To these works may be added *La Poétique de l'espace* (1957), *La Poétique de la réverie* (1961), and a short study of Lautréamont (1939).

In *La Psychanalyse du feu*, Bachelard, who had already written books on modern physics and chemistry and on the "formation of the scientific spirit," approaches the subject of what he calls "material imagination" through prescientific texts where chemistry is still confused with alchemy. His interest is mostly negative: he considers what the texts say as vagaries, as errors. When he adopts a psychological point of view, he is content to refer to a Freudian type of interpretation. Epistemologically, this maneuver amounts to substituting one prescientific language for another.

However, the perspective begins to shift toward the latter part of the book. The change will be accomplished in the second book of the series, *L'Eau et les rêves*. From now on, the illustrations are examined with sympathy rather than with irony. Their range is broader, most of them being excerpts from literary texts of the nineteenth and twentieth centuries. For their interpretation, Bachelard often takes his cue from the romantic philosophy of Nature.

His change of attitude may thus be interpreted as a kind of romantic conversion. The romantic exaltation of dream and imagination came at a time when, through mathematization, the sciences of Nature had broken with common language, when, through analysis, the basic elements of chemistry were becoming abstract.

This conversion, however, is not complete. Epistemologically, Bachelard remains on the side of science and "reason." He does not brandish "poetry" and "imagination" as flags for a holy war. He is not an advocate of mythic "truth." Rather, he adopts and recommends "a total separation between rational life and oneiric life," "a dual situation."[1] "The function of the real" and the "function of the unreal" should not be confused, nor should one be sacrificed to the other. They should rather be developed separately to achieve a healthy balance.

This semiconversion is enough to bring him into close affinity with the major ideological movements in France between the two world wars: surrealism and existentialism, insofar as they are both offshoots of the romantic philosophy of Nature. In the field of existential phenomenology, the perceptive analyses which can be found in Eugène Minkowski's *Vers une cosmologie* (Paris: Aubier, 1936) should be given a special mention, in view of their kinship with Bachelard's studies.[2]

1. *Le Matérialisme rationnel* (Paris: Presses Universitaires de France, 1953), p. 19.

2. Bachelard borrows from Minkowski the notion of *retentissement* (resonance in depth):

"Very often, then, it is in the opposite of causality, that is, in *resonance*, which has been so subtly analyzed by Minkowski (cf. Eugène Minkowski, *Vers une cosmologie*, chapter IX), that I think we find the real measure of the being of a poetic image. In this resonance, the poetic image will have a sonority of being. The poet speaks on the threshold of being. Therefore, in order to determine the being of an image, we shall have to experience its resonance in the manner of Minkowski's phenomenology." *The Poetics of Space*, translated by Maria Jolas (New York: Orion, 1964), p. xii.

"C'est donc bien souvent à l'inverse de la causalité, dans le *retentissement*, si finement étudié par Minkowski, que nous croyons trouver les vraies mesures de l'être d'une image poétique. Dans ce retentissement, l'image poétique aura une sonorité d'être. Le poète parle au seuil de l'être. Il nous faudra donc pour déterminer l'être

Bachelard's books on "material imagination" are divided into chapters which develop various themes. Thus, in the second book about the Earth there are sections on the house, the cave, the maze, the snake, the vine. Sometimes the name of a character or of a writer is used to label the theme. Thus, in the book on Water we find the Ophelia complex, the Swinburne complex. Sometimes Bachelard stays with a writer for several pages; most often he jumps from one writer to another, from a descriptive paragraph to a poetic line, from an aphorism to a legend. Between quotations, his developments are a motley flow of amplifications, analogies, confidences, humorous allusions. He is partial to rhetorical questions, lyrical exclamations. Rather than definitions he prefers an accumulation of suggestive labels. The introductory chapters of the various books do not clearly isolate a method, a point of view. A precise, stable terminology is never adopted.

Gaston Bachelard was a brilliant, exciting lecturer with contagious gusto. He writes much as he spoke. The voice is gone; yet there are echoes. He should be read as he was listened to. In no definite genre, whether it be ontology, epistemology, psychology, aesthetics, can his works pass as polished products. But they offer a remarkably rich mine of possibilities. Gaston Bachelard was an inspiring teacher; his writing can still be inspiring.

The purpose here is to determine the significance of his works in the domain of literary criticism: stylistics and the philosophy of literature. The perspective is thus narrowed; we are not concerned with dreams, but with language. More precisely, the interest lies in the bearing which Bachelard's works may have on the study of the aesthetic uses of language as such. It is the poetic conversion of language which we have to keep particularly in mind, in view of Bachelard's frequent use of the term *poetry*. He himself warns that his "poetics of reverie" should not be mistaken for a "poetics of poetry."

---

d'une image en éprouver, dans le style de la phénoménologie de Minkowski, le retentissement." *La Poétique de l'espace* (Paris: Presses Universitaires de France, 1957), p. 2.

But he also intimates that the former might serve as a proper introduction to the latter.

Let us start with the opposition between *reason* and *imagination*. These two terms have often been used in different contexts at different times. Their accumulated meanings are vague and incoherent. In the case of Bachelard, what is meant by *reason* is, fortunately, not traditional: he means the rationality which is at work in contemporary physics and chemistry. Stylistically, then, *reason* refers to a type of language whose logic is mathematical and whose meaning is abstract, more abstract than the meaning of analytical prose; thus, the time variable is more abstract than the concept of time.

The uses which Bachelard makes of the word *imagination* are less simple and stable. But the stylistic meaning which has just been given for *reason* can help us do the same for *imagination*. Let us say, to begin, that Bachelard is interested in a type of language which "speaks to the imagination," an evocative language, whose vocabulary is "concrete." He is interested more precisely in "material imagination" and "dynamic imagination" as opposed to "formal imagination." This eliminates description and narration in as much as they give set "pictures" of spatio-temporal individuals. Bachelard is interested in a language evocative of substantiality and energy, which is specifically what is no longer evoked by the language of modern physics and chemistry.

It is to be noted that, though the texts which Bachelard quotes are often rich in metaphors and "images," these devices are not characteristic of the type of language which interests him. And the same thing could be said about the fantastic. On the other hand, he shows great interest in metamorphoses such as he finds in Lautréamont, because they prevent the evocation of shape from setting and masking the evocation of substance and energy.

At least in part of the first book on the cosmic elements, Bachelard adopts an epistemological point of view. In this perspective, language appears as cognitive, as being either true or false. This gives us another meaning for *imagination*: imaginary, or unreal, is what is posited by a false declarative language. This perspective cannot serve to isolate the aesthetic aspect of language. Rather, it rules it out of existence. In order to consider language aesthetically, one must first consider it neither true nor false. One must abandon both an attitude of belief and an attitude of disbelief, the two being correlative.

This epistemological perspective has left a few traces in the subsequent books: thus the phrases "function of the unreal" and "function of the real." But, on the whole, it has been abandoned. The perspective to which Bachelard has shifted can be called "psychological," or "phenomenological." He uses the label of phenomenology to set himself apart from professional psychologists.[3] It also has the advantage of being even vaguer and of leaving him perfectly free.[4] Sometimes he views the texts which he quotes as documents of the temperament

3. Thus, in *The Poetics of Space*, pp. xiii–xiv:

". . . In all psychological research, we can, of course, bear in mind psychoanalytical methods for determining the personality of a poet, and thus find a measure of the pressures—but above all of the oppressions—that a poet has been subjected to in the course of his life. But the poetic act itself, the sudden image, the flare-up of being in the imagination, are inaccessible to such investigations. In order to clarify the problem of the poetic image philosophically, we shall have to have recourse to a phenomenology of the imagination. By this should be understood a study of the phenomenon of the poetic image when it emerges into the consciousness as a direct product of the heart, soul and being of man, apprehended in his actuality."

". . .Certes on peut, dans des recherches psychologiques, donner une attention aux méthodes psychanalytiques pour déterminer la personnalité d'un poète, on peut trouver ainsi la mesure des pressions —surtout de l'oppression—qu'un poète a dû subir au cours de sa vie, mais l'acte poétique, l'image soudaine, la flambée de l'être dans l'imagination, échappent à de telles enquêtes. Il faut en venir, pour éclairer philosophiquement le problème de l'image poétique, à une phénoménologie de l'imagination. Entendons par là une étude du phénomène de l'image poétique quand l'image émerge dans la conscience comme un produit direct du coeur, de l'âme, de l'être de l'homme saisi dans son actualité." *La Poétique de l'espace*, p. 2.

4. *Phenomenology* and *imagination* are Protean terms. The diversity of their meanings can be sampled by comparing Sartre's *L'Imaginaire* (Paris: Gallimard, 1939) with Bachelard's studies. The two pheno-

of a writer, but most often of human nature in general. In either case, it would seem that his psychological or phenomenological point of view is quite irrelevant to literary criticism proper. The very vagueness of the word *phenomenology*, however, is a warning against a summary dismissal.

From our point of view, Bachelard's way of dealing with texts offers some negative advantages over the attitude of the psychiatrist, or of the psychoanalyst. Generally, he does not interpret what the texts say as pathological symptoms. And he does not interpret what they state as symbolic of what they do not state. His comments do not decode: they amplify and link. Except in his first book on material imagination, the evocation of substantiality is not taken as symbolic of interhuman relations. In existentialist terms, he does not consider *being-in-the-world* as less basic than *being-with-others*. Thus, if we follow him, we shall not interpret *water* as symbolic of *mother*; rather, we shall say that the maternal is a possible dimension, or quality, of water. In this way, we shall substantialize the maternal, instead of humanizing and socializing the natural element. As a whole, Bachelard's approach does not encourage a confusion between symbolic and aesthetic values.

The very lack of conceptual structure in Bachelard's works may also be regarded as a negative advantage. The variety of themes which he brings out does not constitute a closed, hierarchic classification. Thus, there is little danger, in this case, that a psychological system might serve as a set of in-

---

menologists of the imagination appear to be treating different subjects in different ways. In Sartre's essay, phenomenology is still a recognizable method. The same can hardly be said in Bachelard's case. In *La Poétique de l'espace* (see note 3 above), he endorses the term; in *La Terre et les rêveries de la volonté* (Paris: J. Corti, 1948), he rejects it:

"In the long run, material imagination is not the object of a phenomenology but, as we will show in a good number of instances, of a dynamology."

"L'imagination matérielle finalement ne relève pas d'une phénoménologie, mais, comme nous le montrerons dans bien des occasions, d'une dynamologie" (p. 117).

In *L'Etre et le néant* (Paris: Gallimard, 1943), Sartre praises Bachelard's books on Fire and Water (pp. 690–91). But he objects to his use of the term *imagination*.

appropriate criteria for aesthetic judgments: judgments of authenticity, or depth, for instance. Even the four cosmic elements hardly appear in the role of archetypes.[5] In the last two books, *La Poétique de l'espace* and *La Poétique de la rêverie*, they are no longer used as a basis at all.

5. It is probably in the following passage (*L'Eau et les rêves* [Paris: J. Corti, 1942], p. 7) that Bachelard comes closest to setting up the four elements in the role of archetypes:

"So you can understand that to a material element such as fire may be attached a kind of reverie governing the beliefs, the passions, the ideal, the philosophy of a whole life. There is a sense in speaking of the aesthetics of fire, of the psychology of fire and even the ethics of fire. All these precepts are brought together in a poetics and a philosophy of fire. The two of them constitute this prodigious, ambivalent precept which upholds the convictions of the heart by the instructions of reality and which, vice versa, makes the life of the universe understandable by the life of our heart.

"All the other elements are rich in similar, ambivalent certainties. They suggest secret disclosures and display striking images. All four have their believers or, more precisely, each of them is already profoundly and materially a *system of poetic loyalty*. In singing of them one believes he is being loyal to a favorite image; one is, in reality, being loyal to a primitive, human feeling, to a primary organic reality, to a fundamental oneiric temperament."

"On comprend donc qu'à un élément matériel comme le feu, on puisse rattacher un type de rêverie qui commande les croyances, les passions, l'idéal, la philosophie de toute une vie. Il y a un sens à parler de l'esthétique du feu, de la psychologie du feu et même de la morale du feu. Une poétique et une philosophie du feu condensent tous ces enseignements. A elles deux, elles constituent ce prodigieux enseignement ambivalent qui soutient les convictions du coeur par les instructions de la réalité et qui, vice versa, fait comprendre la vie de l'univers par la vie de notre coeur.

"Tous les autres éléments prodiguent de semblables certitudes ambivalentes. Ils suggèrent des confidences secrètes et montrent des images éclatantes. Ils ont tous les quatre leurs fidèles, ou, plus exactement, chacun d'eux est déjà profondément, matériellement, un *système de fidélité poétique*. A les chanter, on croit être fidèle à une image favorite, on est en réalité fidèle à un sentiment humain primitif, à une réalité organique première, à un tempérament onirique fondamental."

What Bachelard's studies do demonstrate is that, *in certain cases and from a certain standpoint*, the four elements may serve as the most revealing principles of classification.

But Bachelard's phenomenological studies also offer a positive contribution to the philosophy of literature. It is remarkable that he constantly attempts to present material imagination as conducive to joy, if not to a romantic type of ecstasy. The satisfying aspect of this kind of imagination can easily be seen; it can provide what is missing in abstract thought and in social relations, even if they are harmonious. And it is understandable that Bachelard should venture to see in it a kind of therapy. Yet, cannot one's reaction be one of horror as well as joy, or the intimate disgust which invades the hero of Sartre's *La Nausée*?

Bachelard's own temperament has to be taken into account, also the fact that his childhood was spent where Champagne meets Burgundy, rather than in Paris or the Kalahari desert. But what matters is that his studies of material imagination are derived from texts, from language. He considers material imagination in the domain of linguistic creation, or re-creation. He himself makes it clear that he is mainly interested in the creative aspect of material imagination.[6] And where

6. In *L'Eau et les rêves* (p. 6), Bachelard acknowledges that material imagination can be associated with pain as well as joy:

"... Beside the psychoanalysis of dreams there must therefore be a psychophysics and a psychochemistry of dreams. This very materialistic psychoanalysis will go back to the old precepts that sought the cure of *elementary sicknesses* through *elementary medicines*. The material element is a determinant for the malady as it is for the cure. We suffer by dreams and we are cured by dreams."

"... A côté de la psychanalyse des rêves devra donc figurer une psychophysique et une psychochimie des rêves. Cette psychanalyse très matérialiste rejoindra les vieux préceptes qui voulaient que les *maladies élémentaires* fussent guéries par les *médecines élémentaires*. L'élément matériel est déterminant pour la maladie comme pour la guérison. Nous souffrons par les rêves et nous guérissons par les rêves."

Suffering by dreams goes with passivity, as in the case of Sartre's Roquentin, whom Bachelard examines in *La Terre et les rêveries de la volonté* (pp. 112–14). To be cured by dreams, one has to make imagination active and creative, either through the medium of words or not: "For us, the material imagination of pulpy matter is essentially industrious"; "Pour nous, l'imagination matérielle de la pâte est essentiellement travailleuse." Ibid., p. 115.

there is creation, or re-creation, there is joy. Bachelard's subject thus appears more precise: substance and force as aesthetically experienced; material imagination as "fuel" for linguistic creation. The outlook remains psychological, but we are at least dealing with a psychology of linguistic creation and aesthetic experience.

The accent on creativity is also characteristic of Bachelard's books on science. He emphasizes theoretic creativity in contemporary physics: we are far from a language of observation. It has its correlative in technical creativity: the relevant facts cannot be observed directly; and they are not given, they are made by the apparatus. Physics has become metaphysical; the so-called elementary *particles* are not spatio-temporal individuals.

Water, Earth, Air, and Fire are "cosmic" elements. The conception of them was the material out of which the Greek cosmologists made the world, or rather their worlds. The connection between the idea of creation and the idea of world is not lost in Bachelard. It increases the aesthetic relevance of his studies. They point to one basic desire: the desire for a world, a cosmic desire. This desire is the proper impulse of aesthetic creation. For the world is not a fact, but it can be a goal, or an ideal. If the world were a fact, then aesthetic creation would be devoid of a *raison d'être*.

To understand this, we must put aside pejorative or neutral uses of the term, such as *the world of politics*, or *the world in which we live*. We should rather start from the cosmic—or cosmicity—as an ideal, as the aesthetic ideal. Then we might say that anything is a world, is cosmic, to the extent that it is an autonomous and coherent whole, in other words, to the extent that it is possessed of cosmicity.

Immediate, passive, or practical experience does not constitute a cosmos. It is not closed; it is disparate; it is not coherent; it deserves the name *apeiron*. What is cosmic has to be built, and since it cannot embrace or reduce life, the cosmic can be achieved only in a limited and multiple manner. Insofar as it remains one, it remains purely ideal.

Understood in this way, in correlation with the accent on creativity, the idea of the cosmic brings together Bachelard's interests in scientific and nonscientific language. He contrasts the solitude of the artist with the scientific community. Each work of art, insofar as it is aesthetically successful, is a world. The scientists, on the other hand, cooperate in the task of composing one cosmos, *the* world, rather than worlds.

But, to remain one, the cosmic has to remain ideal: the ideal of Leibnitz's *mathesis universalis.* As he concentrates his attention on physics and chemistry, Bachelard tends to underestimate the plurality of scientific disciplines, languages, world projects. And even if we remain in the field of physics, we are faced with several world models whose plurality echoes the multiplicity of the old metaphysical systems. Whatever their cognitive value, they can be enjoyed aesthetically.

These world models, and the entities which compose them, escape the grasp of *formal* imagination, of an imagination which tends to picture *its* world as a big box containing much smaller boxes, such as human beings. In its own way, *material* imagination helps break the spell of this common picture. According to this model and to a normal descriptive style, the basic entities are individuals linked spatially, temporally, and, perhaps, socially. A mathematized language turns individual entities into *points*; relation is what is basic. Bachelard's studies of material imagination suggest instead a conversion to quality.

Take the example of the spatial relation *in* holding between two individuals: a human being and a house. A text may posit this relation between the individuals; it may also posit a feeling of intimacy as somehow contained in the smaller of the two entities. But it may instead liberate this *property* and present it as a pervading atmosphere. Finally, by blurring the evocation of the two individuals and of their spatial relation, the text may signify the quality of intimacy as what is basic.

Texts which primarily signify substances and forces, that is to say, qualities, invite the reader to dismiss the picture of individuals in the world as small boxes in a big box. Poetic biology and cosmology are one and the same; air is breathing, rather than what a body breathes. Instead of conflicts between individuals, the text will evoke a tension between forces; the relation *against* becomes the quality of againstness, for a relation between qualities is also a quality. Bachelard labels himself "a philosopher of the adjective." His studies also show how prepositions can be converted into concepts of qualities.

The texts which he quotes, and his own developments, may be judged anthropomorphic. But this presupposes a definition of man as an individual or a class of individuals. And it presupposes that certain qualities are to be classified as attributes of these individuals. In short it presupposes the adoption of a kind of logic and ontology which does not fit the case. The conversion to the perspective of quality can take place only in aesthetic experience. To the degree that experience is practical, we do not, for instance, experience againstness as a quality; we have to conceive of it as a relation between individuals or groups. And it is againstness, the Heraclitean *polemos*, not conflict between certain individuals, which can serve as a basic cosmic element.

In the preceding paragraphs, an attempt has been made to gather and distill what Bachelard's studies yield on the subject of the cosmic. In the process, his perspective has been somewhat altered. I remember him saying humorously, "I create a cosmos every morning." His Burgundian accent and flowing beard tended to produce a Jovian impression. But there was no hubris in his words. The sentence should be interpreted as a clue to his main interest. He was more interested in creativity than in creative achievement, in the process more than in the result, in the cosmic impetus more than in set structures. To this extent, he was in the line of Bergson. In his works, he tries to catch this cosmic *élan*, some of its modes and moods. He is not concerned about the value of the works from which he quotes as finished products, as worlds.

There remains the problem of determining the relevance of Bachelard's outlook to a theory of poetry, rather than to literature in general. The difference between the two has been suggested in the development on the cosmic; a conversion to the logic of quality is not likely to serve equally well the various types of literary worlds: essay, play, novel, poem.

If Bachelard had been a philosopher of history or sociology, he might have been drawn, on the literary side, to the novel or the drama. But the most likely literary counterpart of mathematical physics and chemistry is poetry: logic of quantitative relation on one side, logic of quality on the other. Bachelard draws almost no example from plays. His quotations from novels are numerous, but his examples are taken from "poetic" novels.

This in itself tends to show that the meaning which he generally gives to *poetry* is too vague to be significant for a theory of the genres. But there are passages in which he seizes upon what can turn poetry into a specific genre: the exploitation of phonetic qualities. These passages are not technical analyses of meter and harmony. And it is to be noted that, at the time when Bachelard begins to write on material imagination, prosody was spurned by most writers who considered themselves poets, from Claudel to the surrealists; counting syllables would have demeaned a prophet of God or a liberator of Man. In these circumstances, a professor in the philosophy of science could hardly have been expected to be interested in the theory of meter and harmony. Yet the passages in which Bachelard considers the phonetic aspect of language do manage to touch upon something which is basic to poetry, understood not simply as something atmospheric but as a definite genre, with its own way of using language. This happens in particular at the end of *L'Eau et les rêves* and *L'Air et les songes*.

The poetic exploitation of phonetic qualities extends the application of Bachelard's ideas to another aspect of language. We are now considering the substantiality and dynamics of language itself, not of what it means. As the poem is recited, quality is invoked rather than evoked. And it may be questioned whether the term *imagination* still fits the case. It tends to make us confuse the experience of reciting a poem with the experience of reading a comment on its phonetic aspect; the prose of the commentary translates invocation into evocation.

However this may be, it appears that a poem can provide an aesthetic experience of substance and force, even if its themes are not of the kind which Bachelard studies. For poetry does not name things; it things names. Since Bachelard uses linguistic documents to illustrate his studies it can be argued that the "materiality" which should be considered as basic is the materiality of language itself. In this way, we can extend the relevance of Bachelard's outlook to the theory of poetic language.

On the semantic side, the same result can be achieved by inquiring further into the distinction between *formal* and *material* imagination. Formal imagination, as I understand the concept, is the imagination which visualizes, pictures, represents, objectifies. Formal imagination is the imagination *of* form. Material imagination, on the other hand, cannot be the imagination *of* substance and force. Material imagination is not imagination *of* qualities, but qualitative imagination, for that is the proper way to "imagine" qualities. In other words, qualities as such cannot be represented; they can but be felt, experienced. We shall say that a language is poetic insofar as, both phonetically and semantically, it lets us experience qualities aesthetically, instead of pragmatically.

Understood in this way, Bachelard's concept of material imagination can be used to define the poetic mode of meaning. For it suggests that the proper way of signifying qualities as such differs from the proper way of signifying individuals and from the proper way of signifying concepts (concepts of qualities, for instance). And the mode of meaning goes with a mode of composition; the logic of qualities differs from the logic of individuals and from the logic of concepts. Bachelard's concept of material imagination can thus be used to distinguish between poetry and the various genres of literary or philosophical prose.

It must be pointed out, however, that Bachelard himself does not go so far. His studies are a possible introduction to a theory of poetry. But they cannot pass, nor are they intended to pass, for such a theory. Their style and their mode of composition are not designed to bring out a specifically poetic value in the texts which they quote.

Commentaries on poems have to make explicit what the poem, insofar as it is poetic, has to make implicit. This is inevitable and there is no risk of confusion between the value of the poem as poetry and the value of the commentary as prose if the style and composition of the commentary and the text to be studied are strikingly different. Bachelard's studies do not offer a clear contrast. The texts which he quotes are, stylistically, a motley crowd. And his own comments are amplifications rather than stylistic analyses. His choice of themes is such that formal images tend to overshadow concepts of qualities: thus the image of the house instead of the concept of intimacy. The result is that the texts which emerge best from Bachelard's developing bath are likely to be those which are the poorest in poetic value: puffed up phrases, complacent descriptions which make *material imagination* appear better suited to the art of publicity than to the art of poetry. This shows, more generally, the inadequacy of a psychological approach to literature, even when it is as open-minded and sensitive as that of Bachelard.

His studies are rich in insights which should be valuable to the literary critic.[7] But the approach has to be changed. Otherwise, literary criticism might be confused with psychological gloss. Bringing out psychological themes can be as pointless aesthetically as the more traditional study of characters. Such themes are likely to find more conformist illustrations in texts which are aesthetically worthless than in texts which are aesthetically worthy. Psychological considerations should have a peripheral, rather than central, role in literary criticism.

The question of the relation between stylistics and ontology is another matter. Bachelard's studies tend to show that this relation is basic, especially if his works on scientific creation are taken into account. With the exception of *La Psychanalyse du feu*, they can also help us reject the traditional confusion between epistemology and ontology. The mode of meaning determines the mode of being, whether language is used cognitively or not. To be sure, language does not create being. But the mode of meaning and composition determines the type of entities and, accordingly, the type of world.

7. Bachelard's influence on literary criticism is widespread, but diffuse and mixed with others. The absence of a strict method precluded the formation of a Bachelardian school of criticism. *Eluard et Claudel* (Paris: Le Seuil, 1945), by Michel Carrouges, provides an early example of Bachelard's influence; Michel Guiomar's *Inconscient et imaginaire dans Le Grand Meaulnes* (Paris: Corti, 1964), a recent one.

BIBLIOGRAPHY

CRITICAL BOOKS BY BACHELARD

On the subject of material imagination, *La Terre et les rêveries de la volonté* (Paris: J. Corti, 1948), is Bachelard's best book. I should group next *L'Eau et les rêves* (Paris: J. Corti, 1942); *L'Air et les songes* (Paris: J. Corti, 1943); *La Terre et les rêveries du repos* (Paris: J. Corti, 1948).

La Psychanalyse du feu (Paris: Gallimard, 1938) is a work of transition. In *La Poétique de l'espace* (Paris: Presses Universitaires de France, 1957) and *La Poétique de la rêverie* (Paris: Presses Universitaires de France, 1961), the treasure chest shows signs of exhaustion. Add to this less important group the *Lautréamont* (rev. ed., Paris: J. Corti, 1956).

For an epilogue, see *La Flamme d'une chandelle* (Paris: Presses Universitaires de France, 1961). Or *Le Droit de rêver* (A la Pensée, Paris: Presses Universitaires de France, 1970).

La Formation de l'esprit scientifique (Paris: Vrin, 1938) and *Le Matérialisme rationnel* (Paris: Presses Universitaires de France, 1953) show the links between Bachelard's two main interests.

La Dialectique de la durée (Paris: Presses Universitaires de France, 1936) presents Bachelard's position on the subjects of time and self: his reaction against Bergson prepares the reaction of Sartre, yet differs from it.

Several of the books on material imagination are available in English: the *Psychoanalysis of Fire*, translated by Alan C. M. Ross (Boston: Beacon Press, 1964); *The Poetics of Space*, translated by Maria Jolas (New York: Orion Press, 1964); and *The Poetics of Reverie*, translated by Daniel Russell (New York: Orion Press, 1969). There is also a volume of selections: *On Poetic Imagination and Reverie*, translated with an introduction by Colette Gaudin, The Library of Liberal Arts (Indianapolis and New York: Bobbs-Merrill, 1971).

Pierre Quillet's *Gaston Bachelard* (Paris: Seghers, 1964) includes a comprehensive presentation and a good selection of texts.

Jean Lescure has given some last reminiscences in "Le Dernier Cours de Gaston Bachelard," *Le Figaro Littéraire*, no. 861 (20 October 1962), and "Paroles de Gaston Bachelard: Notes sur les derniers cours de Gaston Bachelard à la Sorbonne," *Mercure de France* 348 (1963): 118–30.

WORKS ON BACHELARD'S CRITICISM

One might consult the following books and monographs:

Caws, Mary Ann. *Surrealism and the Literary Imagination: A Study of Breton and Bachelard*. Studies in French Literature. The Hague: Mouton, 1966.

Dagognet, François. *Gaston Bachelard, sa vie, son oeuvre*. Paris: Presses Universitaires de France, 1965.

Gagey, J. *Gaston Bachelard ou la conversion à l'imaginaire*. Paris: Rivière, 1969.

Ginestier, Paul. *La Pensée de Bachelard*. Pour Connaître la Pensée. Paris: Bordas, 1968.

Mansuy, Michel. *Gaston Bachelard et les éléments*. Paris: J. Corti, 1967.

Pire, François. *De l'Imagination dans l'oeuvre de Gaston Bachelard*. Paris: J. Corti, 1968.

Therrien, Vincent. *La Révolution de Gaston Bachelard en critique littéraire*. Paris: Klincksieck, 1970.

Articles dealing with various aspects of Bachelard's works can be found in the following special issues and publications:

Annales de l'Université de Paris 33 (1963): 5–47.

L'Arc, no. 42 (1970).

Cahiers du Sud 57 (1964): 179–206.

Critique 20 (1964): 3–51.

Etudes Philosophiques 18 (1963): 395–427.

Hommage à Gaston Bachelard, Etudes de Philosophie et d'Histoire des Sciences. Paris: Presses Universitaires de France, 1957.

Revue de Métaphysique et de Morale 70 (1965): 1–54.

Revue Internationale de Philosophie 17 (1963): 419–504. Includes an extensive bibliography, compiled by Jean Rummens (pp. 492–504). Lists Bachelard's publications and books, articles, reviews devoted to him in part or in whole.

A selection of other articles might include:

Blanchot, Maurice, "Vaste comme la nuit." *La Nouvelle Nouvelle Revue Française* 7 (1959): 684–95.

Christofides, G. C. "Gaston Bachelard's Phenomenology of the Imagination." *Romanic Review* 52 (1961): 36–47.

———. "Bachelard's Aesthetics." *Journal of Aesthetics and Art Criticism* 20 (1962): 263–71.

Diéguez, Manuel de. "Gaston Bachelard." In *L'Ecrivain et son langage*, pp. 221–33. Paris: Gallimard, 1960.

Ehrmann, Jacques. "Introduction to Gaston Bachelard." *Modern Language Notes* 81 (1966): 572–78.

Gaudin, Colette. "L'Imagination et la rêverie: Remarques sur la poétique de Gaston Bachelard." *Symposium* 20 (1966): 207–25.

Hyppolite, Jean. "L'Epistémologie de Gaston Bachelard." *Revue d'Histoire des Sciences et de leurs Applications* 17 (1964): 1–11.

———. "Gaston Bachelard ou le romantisme de l'intelligence." *Revue Philosophique* 144 (1954): 85–96.

Jones, Emmet. "Gaston Bachelard." In *Panorama de la nouvelle critique en France*, pp. 39–76. Paris: Société d'Edition d'Enseignement Supérieur, 1968.

Kushner, Eva M. "The Critical Method of Gaston Bachelard." In *Myth and Symbol*, pp. 39–50. Lincoln: University of Nebraska Press, 1963.

Poulet, Georges. "Bachelard et la critique contemporaine." In *Currents of Thought in French Literature: Essays in Memory of G. T. Clapton*, pp. 353–57. Oxford: Basil Blackwell, 1965. New York: Barnes and Noble, 1966.

Fredric Jameson

9

Three Methods in Sartre's Literary Criticism

It is safe to say that Sartre's work as a whole has left its mark on every French intellectual experience of the last twenty-five years; its enormous ideological impact may be measured by the position of Sartre in French intellectual and literary life today, a position that has no equivalent in any other recent national experience.

Yet it would be wrong to assume that this personal authority is at one with the influence of Sartrean existentialism. Indeed, the purely existential strain in Sartre's thought, which finds its most intense expression in *Nausea*, has always been limited by the presence of other modes of thinking and may be most clearly observed at work in what we may call works of *applied* existentialism, such as the book on anti-Semitism or Simone de Beauvoir's *Second Sex*. For in these works the principal instrument of analysis (or *method*, as it will be called here) remains the notion of anxiety in the face of freedom, of a flight into the reassuring conducts of bad faith, whether in woman's submission to the comfortable and secondary role of an object for a masculine freedom, or in the justification by the anti-Semite of his own unjustifiable existence through the "thingification" of Jews. Yet even here, the concept of objectification, from which the concrete character of these analyses derives, is not really existential in origin. From this point of view, Sartre's literary criticism offers a privileged and relatively closed realm within which to identify the other strands in his thinking, and it will be our thesis in the present essay that these are not so much existential as dialectical in character. The intellectual coherence which will be demonstrated here is less that of a unified theory than one of a basic attitude toward literary material; Sartre is the meeting place between a linguistic optimism, a conviction as to the unlimited expressive possibilities of language, and a formal pessimism, a feeling that literary forms, insofar as they always stylize lived experience, are always distortions of it.

Sartre's originality, among contemporary critics of style, lies in his treatment of literary style as an objective rather than a subjective phenomenon. As against those for whom the work of art is the privileged occasion of contact with some deeper force, with the unconscious, with the personality, with Being, or with language, Sartre takes his place among the rhetoricians. The work of art is a construct designed to produce a certain effect; the style of the work of art is the instrument with which a certain illusion of time is conveyed. The objectivity of style in the work of art shows up most clearly in its accessibility to pastiche and imitation, for pastiche remains the best way of trying on the lens of a strange new style, of seeing what the world looks like through it.[1]

But this objectivity brings in turn another form of objectivity with it; if style is a model of time, a certain kind of optical illusion of temporality, then the number of possible styles must be in some sense limited by the number of ways time itself can be deformed or projected. And in this light Sartre's early essays on style in modern writers[2] turn out to be, not principally reviews or occasional articles, but rather chapters of a phenomenology of different attitudes toward, different models of, narrative time.

The basic problem of narrative time is that of the event and the way the novelist disposes his raw material into events,

1. See the pastiches of Dos Passos, *Situations I* (Paris: Gallimard, 1947), p. 23, and of Genet, *Saint Genet, comédien et martyr* (Paris: Gallimard, 1952), p. 472; and see also Simone de Beauvoir's discussion of the use of Dos Passos's style as a critical instrument, *La Force de l'âge* (Paris: Gallimard, 1960), pp. 143–44.

2. Written for the *Nouvelle Revue Française* and for *Cahiers du Sud* from 1938 to 1944, they are collected in *Situations I*, to which all references are made.

preparation for events, consequences leading from them. At this point the nature of the raw material, of the content of the novel, is of less importance, although ultimately that content—the legendary gestures of Faulkner, the social ambitions in Dos Passos, the sexual guilt of Mauriac—comes to seem symbolic of the way the story is told, emblematic of the kind of time registered in its style.

But initially style is felt as being a structure imposed on a relatively formless raw material; it is somehow an addition to it, a rearranging or reordering of it. If, in the existential formula, existence precedes essence, style, or a certain temporal structure, functions precisely as an essence with respect to the directionless unformed lived existence of the story material. For real time is, according to Sartre, a synthesis of all three temporal dimensions at once; and memories, remembered moments, carry their dead future with them, just as anticipated moments in the future are projected, not in a void, but as the future of somebody with a clearly defined past. But when we try to narrate our experiences, to put time into words, inevitably we do violence to this temporal synthesis, and we lay stress on one dimension of time to the exclusion of the others.[3] Stylistic innovation implies precisely this new way of telling events, or rather the invention of a new illusion of the passage of time, a new projection of the temporal synthesis.

Faulkner's world, for example, is a world without a future; in it, events do not happen, they *have* happened already, they are already legendary, frozen, immobilized. Everyone recognizes the distinctive quality of those stunned and breathless evocations of suspended gestures, the way the Faulknerian sentence rises toward the Event and hangs in midair as though mesmerized by it, in a stillness in which only the words, adjectives and present participles, continue to pile up vainly, in their very obstinacy conveying something of the irrevocability of the act itself. For where the future as a temporal dimension does not exist, the present also loses its force,

3. The most revealing discussion of this incommensurability of words to lived time is to be found in the chapter on adventures in *La Nausée* (Paris: Gallimard, 1938), pp. 57–59.

becomes an already-past; and the Faulknerian present, amputated of its future, resembles nothing quite so much as those images of space that the idiot Benjy watches unwinding on either side of him as he rides along backwards in the carriage. The characteristic of this present is a repetition, an *enfoncement*, a succession like the ticking of a clock, in which events move into the past, growing tinier and tinier in the distance like objects receding. And from this primary apprehension of time, a Faulknerian grammar can be constructed, in the light of which his other stylistic peculiarities find their place and perspective (the fresh starts, the "becauses" and "so's," dangling "and's" and "or's," the use of negation to reinforce the single isolated gesture, the attempt to conjure up a fresh present with the repeated sound of the word "now").

The temporal progression in Dos Passos presents certain affinities with that of Faulkner. Here also events have been transformed into things; here also a storytelling voice has warped experience from the very start, converting it into anecdotes and stories, lending it solidity, objectivity, the appearance of a kind of destiny. But where the narrative voice of Faulkner was an epic one, finding its source in the very point at which gestures are turned into legends, the voice of Dos Passos is that of gossip, and for it all events are to be retailed like so many items in a social column, with the same breathless enthusiasm, the same vacuity and distraction. The style of Dos Passos is therefore the very embodiment of the "objective spirit" of our society, of inauthenticity become public opinion. The narrator of the novels of Dos Passos is the "everybody" of Heidegger, the German "man" or French "on," the anonymous degraded consciousness of mass man; and there is in his narration a radical discrepancy between the stylization of events, the impersonal accounts of anonymous destinies, and the lived events themselves.

But in Dos Passos the narrating voice does not fully identify itself with any one of the temporal dimensions as Faulkner's did with the past. Rather, the time of Dos Passos is the time of History in which the present dominates—not our lived present, but a present already past, a succession of events which have solidified and taken on permanency without quite becoming incorporated into a massive official past, which remain somehow halfway between living events and stale, finished ones, which we surprise in the moment of turning past. The peculiar pathos of Dos Passos is that in his optic we can see events from two different temporal perspectives at once: both in the naive excitement and freshness they have for those living them in the moment, and, over a great distance, in that dreary statistical objectivity that the youthful experiences of old people take on for later generations.

At this point in Sartre's analyses two different types of value judgment intervene. First, what might be described as a purely aesthetic one: both of these styles are *invented* and not premeditated, they don't describe a new way of looking at things, they produce it as a kind of optical illusion in the reader's mind. This is the meaning of the judgment on François Mauriac: in Mauriac's novels also, as in Faulkner and Dos Passos, the freshness of lived experience was converted into a kind of destiny, was seen from the outside like a thing. In Mauriac also we are unable to live a genuine present of events on account of the intervention of a view of them from above, from outside the action itself, on account of the superposition of another perspective. Mauriac, says Sartre, takes the point of view of God on his characters; hence his well-known conclusion: "God isn't an artist; neither is M. Mauriac."[4]

But the difference between Mauriac on the one hand, and Faulkner and Dos Passos on the other, is precisely that Mauriac has not invented a new stylization of time. He does not embody his contradictory vision of the world in a new formal principle, a new method of storytelling. Instead, he simply intervenes in his own narration; interrupts the thoughts of his characters to place an author's appreciation; into their subjective reality drops the "fateful" hint as to their predestined fates.[5] It is not the ideology of Mauriac which Sartre objects

4. "Dieu n'est pas un artiste; M. Mauriac non plus." *Situations I*, p. 57. (All translations are mine.)

5. This point is related to the ideological criticism elsewhere in *Situations I* of Bataille, Ponge, and Renard, all of whom introduce the external and objective categories of scientism into their subjective experience and thereby deform it.

to; the worlds, the world views, of Faulkner and Dos Passos were equally contradictory, represented analogous distortions of lived experience. Faced with this contradiction, however, Mauriac does not attempt to overcome the contradiction in his material by stylistic means: he merely alternates his two methods of looking at his characters instead of imposing a new illusion of time through his language. He does not invent; he merely cheats.

There is a second type of value judgment implicit in these early essays, one which will become more pronounced later on. This kind of judgment is precisely an ideological one, a way of evaluating the various kinds of effects resulting from the different modern stylistic innovations. In a general way, one can say that these effects are right-wing or left-wing, tend to give revolutionary or conservative views of the world. But it is not so much the view of the world which counts in this judgment (both Dos Passos and Faulkner present basically *false* pictures of time), but rather the effect this world view has on the reader, the way it makes him think of himself and his life, and of the society around him. Faulkner's time is inhuman because it perpetuates a view of the world in which the future is dead, in which action is impossible. And no doubt such a picture has profound symptomatic value. Faulkner's integrity as an artist reveals a genuine dimension of things, lives without futures, change without hope: "We're living in a time of impossible revolutions, and Faulkner uses his extraordinary art to describe this world dying of old age and our own suffocation."[6] Yet Faulkner's art tends to mesmerize us, to cause us to be fascinated with our own impotence and with the immobility of the world. His legendary gestus invites us to become fixated on the past, his dreamy, urgent, and hypnotic sentences encourage us to dwell in the intolerable.

The stylization of Dos Passos on the other hand has the immediate effect of disgusting us with ourselves, of making self-complacency impossible. The rather obvious and awkward

6. "Nous vivons au temps des révolutions impossibles, et Faulkner emploie son art extraordinaire à décrire ce monde qui meurt de vieillesse et notre étouffement." *Situations I*, p. 80.

intrusions of history into *U.S.A.* in the form of the biographies and the Camera Eye are only the most external symptoms of a reality in the very texture of the style. In the movement of the narrative sentences we are able to watch our subjective experience transformed into the substance of history itself, into inauthentic collective representation; we watch our own private feelings turn into those of anybody at all, and the process has something of the horror of the absorption by viscosity described in *L'Etre et le néant*.[7] Thus the reader of Dos Passos through the process of reading discovers his own inauthenticity, his own inextricable involvement in history. His reaction is evidently not a political one; yet it touches that vision of ourselves and the world which is the very source of political action.

What we have said about the distortion of narrative time in favor of the past could be shown equally with respect to the present as well. The world of Giraudoux, for example, this world of Aristotelian essences, is a perpetual present, a present of fresh beginnings, a morning world without any genuine past or future, in which change takes the form of a replacement of one image by another, like leafing through the pages of a family album. Its optimism is no doubt as false as Faulkner's pessimism; yet it is a genuine stylization and represents one of the extreme possibilities of that deformation which narration brings to lived time.

The events of *L'Etranger* seem at a far remove from this fairy-tale universe; yet it also is a succession of pure presents, and in it the *passé composé* has the effect of camouflaging the passage of time, the Hemingway-like succession of bald sentences making each present seem a complete unit in itself, a self-sufficient moment that needs links with neither past nor future. It is in this way, through the movement of the style, that Camus's notion of the absurdity of abstraction and of hope, of any kind of existence beyond the bounds of the present instant, is demonstrated, not as an abstract idea, but as an experience lived by the reader sentence by sentence.

7. See *L'Etre et le néant* (Paris: Gallimard, 1943), pp. 695–704.

It is significant that the essay on Camus should close with a question of terminology. Sartre is reluctant to describe *L'Etranger* as a novel; he would rather see it in the tradition of the *conte philosophique* that goes back to Voltaire. Indeed, the principal tendency of everything that has preceded may be described as a defense of the *novel* against that rival form which the French call the *récit* ("narrative" or "tale" are not altogether satisfactory English equivalents). The genuine novel is for Sartre that form of narration which emphasizes, in its temporal stylization, neither the past nor the present, but rather the future. The novel exists as a form when we are thrown into the minds and experiences of characters for whom the future, for whom destiny, has not yet taken shape, who grope and invent their own destinies, living blindly within the entanglement of one another's unforeseeable actions and under the menace of history's unforeseeable development. In this perspective, the future is that which is sought passionately through the present, that which will ultimately return upon the events narrated to give them their meaning. Such a form requires an absolute nonintervention on the part of the novelist; but its open perspective, the blankness stretching before reader and character, can paradoxically be conveyed either through a completely objective or a completely subjective mode, as long as either is applied systematically throughout the work. The novelist can show us the entire stream of events through his characters' eyes, making us share their limits of vision, the imperfection of their points of view, as is the case in Joyce or Henry James; or he can withhold this subjective, psychological reality entirely and give us nothing but the external actions, the words and gestures, of his characters, in the manner of the American "behavioristic" novel of the thirties, the novel of Hemingway or Dashiell Hammett.

It is evidently difficult to draw a clear line between this genuine novel and the mixed practice of the *récit*. But it seems clear that if for Sartre the modern American novel stands as a kind of privileged model for what the open form ought to be, it is the French realistic tradition of the nineteenth century which furnishes the classic illustration of the motivation behind the *récit*.

Beneath the objective surface of the nineteenth-century novel the old-fashioned storyteller lies hidden. This is the secret truth of the form, the key to its distance from experience and to the deformation it imposes on lived events. In order to grasp the significance of the techniques of the *récit*, we must first understand the experience of storytelling itself, its meaning as a social phenomenon in its own right. Here is a description of the most typical storytelling situation, the framework of a Maupassant novella:

First the listeners are presented to us, generally some brilliant and socially distinguished group which has come together in the salon at the conclusion of a dinner. It's night, and night cancels everything out, weariness as well as passions. The oppressed sleep, the rebels sleep also; the world is shrouded, history catches its breath. All that remains, a globe of light within the surrounding nothingness, is this watchful élite absorbed in its ceremonies. If intrigues are going on between its members, loves, hatreds, we don't know about it, and in any case desires and rages have been stilled for the moment; these men and women are absorbed by the task of *preserving* their culture, their customs, and of exchanging ritual *recognition* with each other according to the forms. They stand for order at its most refined: the stillness of the night, the silence of passions, everything in this scene bears witness to the stabilized bourgeoisie of the late nineteenth century, which thinks that nothing further will ever take place, which believes in the permanence of capitalist organization. Hereupon the narrator is brought forward: an older man, somebody who "knows life" and has a thing or two to say about it, a doctor, a military man, an artist or a Don Juan. He has reached that point in life when, according to a respectful and convenient myth, man is freed from his passions and looks back on those he has known with indulgent lucidity. His heart is as calm as the night; he is utterly detached from the story he is about to tell; if once he suffered from it, now that suffering is sweet, he looks back on it and contemplates it in its truth, that is to say *sub specie aeternitatis*. It's true that once upon a time something painful took place, but all that has long since been over and done with; the people involved are all dead or married or consoled. Thus the adventure is a brief disorder which has been repealed. It's told from the point of view of experience and wisdom, listened to from the point of view of order. Order triumphs, order is everywhere, and contemplates an ancient and abolished disorder much as the peaceful water of a summer day might preserve the memory of the ripples that had once passed over it.[8]

It is in the light of this basic situation that the principal techniques of the nineteenth-century novel are to be understood: the recapitulation of the past history of the characters or the place of the action; the omniscient narrator; the secondary narrative figure who, drawn by rumor and legend, approaches closer and closer to the truth of the story; the use of social values (sentiment, judgment on adultery) as channels of conventional expectation; and so forth. The living voice is the

8. "On nous y présente d'abord l'auditoire, en général société brillante et mondaine qui s'est réunie dans un salon, à l'issue d'un dîner. C'est la nuit, qui abolit tout, fatigues et passions. Les opprimés dorment, les révoltés aussi; le monde est enseveli, l'histoire reprend haleine. Il reste, dans une bulle de lumière entourée de néant, cette élite qui veille, tout occupée de ses cérémonies. S'il existe des intrigues entre ses membres, des amours, des haines, on ne nous le dit pas et d'ailleurs, les désirs et les colères se sont tus: ces hommes et ces femmes sont occupés à *conserver* leur culture et leurs manières et à se *reconnaître* par les rites de la politesse. Ils figurent l'ordre dans ce qu'il a de plus exquis: le calme de la nuit, le silence des passions, tout concourt à symboliser la bourgeoisie stabilisée de la fin du siècle, qui pense que rien n'arrivera plus et qui croit à l'éternité de l'organisation capitaliste. Là-dessus, le narrateur est introduit: c'est un homme d'âge, qui a 'beaucoup vu, beaucoup lu et beaucoup retenu,' un professionel de l'expérience, médecin, militaire, artiste ou Don Juan. Il est parvenu à ce moment de la vie où, selon un mythe respectueux et commode, l'homme est libéré des passions et considère celles qu'il a eues avec une indulgente lucidité. Son coeur est calme comme la nuit; l'histoire qu'il raconte, il en est dégagé; s'il en a souffert, il a fait du miel avec sa souffrance, il se retourne sur elle et la considère en vérité, c'est-à-dire *sub specie aeternitatis*. Il y a eu trouble, c'est vrai, mais ce trouble a pris fin depuis longtemps: les acteurs sont morts ou mariés ou consolés. Ainsi l'aventure est un bref désordre qui s'est annulé. Elle est racontée du point de vue de l'expérience et de la sagesse, elle est écoutée du point de vue de l'ordre. L'ordre triomphe, l'ordre est partout, il contemple un très ancien désordre aboli comme si l'eau dormante d'un jour d'été conservait la mémoire des rides qui l'ont parcourue." *Situations II* (Paris: Gallimard, 1948), pp. 180–81.

source of these later, more sophisticated formal developments and remains imminent in them, like the *gestus* of the Roman orator in later rhetoric, or the traditional gestures and mimicry of the Russian *skaz* which Eichenbaum found preserved and transformed in *The Overcoat* of Gogol.[9] It represents a choice of the past, or of the timeless, as against the uncomfortable present; but unlike the innovations of the modern writers we have examined, this choice is not an individual one, but one inscribed in the very values of society itself, and of the middle class which dominates it. This narrative style is therefore the appropriate reflection of the historical moment in which it originated, and becomes problematical, in the twentieth century, when that moment is itself at an end.

In the early 1950s a new motif makes its appearance in Sartre's work: the distinction between an *act* and a *gesture*, between the *real* and an attitude toward it which seems to drain it of its reality, transform it into mere appearance, *irrealize* it, to use Sartre's term.

The groundwork for this theme had already been laid in one of Sartre's most technical and impersonal writings, *L'Imaginaire* (1940), which demonstrated the basic incompatibility between the act of perceiving and the act of imagining. Both are ways of relating to external objects, but in the second mode the object is apprehended as being *absent*, and my relationship to it is precisely a kind of absence. The implication of this thesis is that, contrary to popular belief, I am never in any danger of mistaking imaginary phenomena (hallucinations, obsessions, dream-images) for real ones. There is a radical difference in quality between the two experiences, the imaginary one is always known to be unreal. I therefore dispose of two possible ways of living the real world: in the first I stand in an active, practical relationship to its objects; in the second I put their reality between parentheses and live with their absence, with their idea or image. These two modes of existence point to two fundamentally opposed passions; for

9. *Théorie de la litérature*, ed. T. Todorov (Paris: Seuil, 1965), pp. 212–33.

there can be a passion for the unreal, for the imaginary, which leads its subject to prefer imaginary feelings to real ones, psychological satisfactions to genuine ones, gestures to acts. It is in this sense that Sartre can say of a writer like Mallarmé[10] that his literary creation is the equivalent of a destruction of the world; such a passion for the imaginary has as its motivation a kind of resentment against the real, and finds its satisfaction in a symbolic revenge upon it.

The starting point of this theory of the imaginary is, however, a theory of the real, which can be briefly summed up as follows: consciousness is basically activity; our primary relationship to the world is not a contemplative or static one, not one of knowledge but one of action and work; the "world" in the phenomenological sense is not motionless space spread out before me, but rather time, "hodological" space, a network of paths and roads, a complex organization of means and ends and projects, unveiled through the movement of my own adventures and desires. This notion, with its emphasis on the primacy of work over mere abstract knowledge, may seem Marxist in origin, indeed provides the connecting link between existentialism and Marxism in Sartre's later works; but in fact it originates directly in Heidegger.[11] For the latter we apprehend objects first as tools and only later on as things-in-themselves, as static substances. For human reality, involved in its projects, each object is primarily a frozen project, an immobile imperative, a thing-to-be-used-in-a-certain-way—*zuhanden*, available, lying to hand in case of need. And just as scientific objectivity is a later, more sophisticated development among human attitudes toward the world, so also is the apprehension of the thing or object as *vorhanden*, as simply being there, as an entity with no evident relationship to myself.

Heidegger's theory of art is based on these two dimensions of the object itself;[12] for him the work of art causes us to suspend

10. Preface to *Poésies* of Mallarmé, Poésie (Paris: Gallimard, 1966).

11. *Sein und Zeit* (Tübingen: Niemeyer Verlag, 1957), pp. 66–88. And see the discussion of Marxism as an ontology in *Über den Humanismus* (Frankfurt am Main: V. Klostermann, 1947).

12. *Der Ursprung des Kunstwerkes*, Universal-Bibliotheck (Stuttgart: Reclam, 1960).

our preoccupation with things as tools, to step back from our immediate involvement in them, and to grow aware of them as vessels of Being. But his illustrations are mainly poetry (Hölderlin, Trakl) and painting (Van Gogh), and his theory lays stress primarily on the content of literature (objects as revelatory of Being itself) rather than on its forms. In this respect Sartre's theory of literature is more exhaustive.

For Sartre the principal distinction between poetry and prose is that the reader takes a utilitarian attitude toward the latter. In it language functions as a system of signs, and the reader's mind is primarily involved, not with the signs themselves, but beyond them, with the things signified. The relationship of the reader to prose language is therefore an active, practical, transcendent one; he uses it, and like all tools it dictates by its own structure the operations necessary to use it properly. For the prose writer also language is the instrument of an act, a secondary or indirect mode of action which Sartre calls action by revelation (*dévoilement*). By naming things, by constructing verbal models for experiences which until then had remained formless and inchoate, the writer acts on his readers, makes it impossible for them to live as they had before (if they wish to continue to be unaware of a given feeling, for example, they must now, after it has been named, *deliberately* avoid thinking about it; they can no longer enjoy the uncompromised innocence of the ignorant).

Poetry on the other hand is distinguished from prose in that in it language intervenes between the reader and the abstract meanings; in poetry it is the words which are primarily apprehended, the meanings in turn become mere pretexts for an awareness of language in its materiality. Thus in poetry a practical, utilitarian attitude toward language is replaced by a contemplative one, for a doing is substituted a being. This is why for Sartre the history of modern poetry is, in terms of the lives of the poets and of their relationship to society, not one of accomplishment but one of failure:[13] When I succeed, I pass from one practical goal to another, the means go unnoticed in the effortless progress from end to end. But when I

13. *Situations II*, pp. 85–88, n. 4.

fail, when my racket misses the ball suddenly, then the means stand out in all their materiality; I become conscious of my own body in its awkwardness, of the racket, of the disposition of space around me. So with the poet: he is able to apprehend the materiality, the being, of language with intensity only against the background of the collapse of his own real projects and of the failure of language as an instrumental means toward an end.

This distinction between an object taken as a means and one taken as an end in itself can be prolonged into the very structure of the poetic image. In the beginning Sartre tends to consider the poetic image in a relatively static fashion, as the symbol and reflection of the consciousness which conceives it. Following Bachelard, he sees the sensation, or the poetic image, as an "objective symbol of being and of the relationship of human reality to that being."[14] Thus the images of Baudelaire are characterized by a certain *spiritualized* quality: objects "which can be apprehended by the senses and yet resemble consciousness. The entire effort of Baudelaire was to recuperate his consciousness, to possess it and hold it like a thing in the palm of his hands, and this is why he seizes on anything that has the look of consciousness objectified: perfumes, muffled lights, distant music, so many little closed mute consciousnesses, so many images of his unattainable existence at once taken into himself, consumed like hosts."[15]

But here the relationship between consciousness and its product (the image, the poem, the sensation) remains one of mere reflection; later on, Sartre will conceive of it as a more dynamic interaction, particularly in those suggestive pages of *Saint Genet* (1952) in which he distinguishes two basic types of

14. "Le symbole *objectif* de l'être et du rapport de la réalité humaine à cet être." *L'Etre et le néant*, p. 693.

15. "Qui se laisse saisir par les sens et qui ressemble le plus à la conscience. Tout l'effort de Baudelaire a été pour récupérer sa conscience, pour la posséder comme une chose dans le creux de ses mains et c'est pourquoi il attrape au vol tout ce qui offre l'apparence d'une conscience objectivée: parfums, lumières tamisées, musiques lointaines, autant de petites consciences muettes et données, autant d'images aussitôt absorbées, consommées comme des hosties, de son insaisissable existence." *Baudelaire* (Paris: Gallimard, 1947). p. 203.

modern images, the expansive and the retractile.[16] In the first a single object ("l'aube") is felt to be an expanding multiplicity ("comme un peuple de colombes"). In such an image, basically inanimate space or externality has been apprehended as an arrested glimpse of an explosion in progress; what is lifeless and measurable has been suddenly endowed with energy and movement, felt to be a moment of a universal and dynamic progress.

The other type of image is one in which existing multiplicities are reduced to unity, in which a movement which was outward-exploding becomes circular, cyclical, in which the chaos of external objects are subordinated to the hierarchical order of the closed image. (Sartre's examples are the restaurant scene in *A l'Ombre des jeunes filles en fleur*, where the tables and the people at them, the waiters and the entire surroundings, are transformed into a single unified planetary system; as well as certain hermetic images of Mallarmé and of Genet himself.)

These two poles of spatial configuration, which are not unlike Jakobson's opposition between metaphor and metonymy, reintroduce into the heart of the poetic image the distinction already described above between the practical/transcendent, the vision of the thing as a frozen use or potential project, and the irrealizing/contemplative, the category of the self-sufficient thing-in-itself. In the first kind of image the reader feels reflected back to him his own energy and generosity, his own transcendent power, "the unity which human work imposes by force on the disparate"; in the second the "whole world is represented according to the model of a hierarchical society."[17] It is characteristic of Sartre that he sees in these two kinds of imagination a fundamental opposition between left-wing and right-wing thinking, between an open revolutionary type of thought and a closed one which wishes to contemplate permanence or eternity in the flux of things themselves. But it is no less characteristic that he furnishes a psychological explanation as well. The first, exploding type of imagery is a figure of freedom itself, of the projection of con-

16. *Saint Genet*, pp. 429 ff.

17. "Le premier vise à représenter l'unité que le travail humain impose de force au disparate; le second à figurer le monde entier sur le type d'une société hiérarchisée." Ibid., p. 430, n. 1.

sciousness out into the world of things, of the transcending of anxiety through choice and activity; the second attempts to conjure anxiety away by suggesting perfect order, by situating consciousness, not in a dangerous indeterminacy, but in the midst of a world in which everything has its appointed place, in which values are inscribed in things themselves.

In the novel, where the attitude toward language is a relatively straightforward, practical one, the distinction we have been developing finds its application in content, in the treatment of the objects of the novel's world, in their relative distance from characters and novelist. Static description, for example, that characteristic of the nineteenth-century novel, is to be understood in the light of this opposition between the practical/transcendent and the contemplative:

Since Schopenhauer it's an accepted fact that objects stand forth in their fullest dignity when man silences the will to power in his own heart: their secrets are disclosed only to those who consume them at their leisure; you're supposed to *write* about them only at those moments when there's nothing to *do* with them. The fastidious descriptions of the last century are a rejection of practical use: you don't touch the universe, you swallow it raw, through the eyes; the writer, in opposition to bourgeois ideology, chooses that privileged instant to tell us about things when all the concrete relationships that linked him to them are broken save for the tenuous thread of vision itself, when they separate beneath his look, sheafs of exquisite sensations come apart.[18]

But this technique, in which a whole life style is inculcated through an apparently natural and harmless description of sur-

18. "Depuis Schopenhauer, on admet que les objets se révèlent dans leur pleine dignité quand l'homme a fait taire dans son coeur la volonté de puissance: c'est au consommateur oisif qu'ils livrent leurs secrets; il n'est permis d'en *écrire* que dans les moments où l'on n'a rien à en *faire*. Ces fastidieuses descriptions du siècle dernier sont un refus d'utilisation: on ne touche pas à l'univers, on le gobe tout cru, par les yeux; l'écrivain, par opposition à l'idéologie bourgeoise, choisit pour nous parler des choses la minute privilégiée où tous les rapports concrets sont rompus, qui l'unissaient à elles, sauf le fil ténu du regard, et où elles se défont doucement sous sa vue, gerbes dénouées de sensations exquises." *Situations II*, p. 263.

roundings, is only one distortion among the many possible when the object of the practical world passes through into the mirror world of art.

The unique optical illusion of Kafka's world, for example, is created by the emphasis on means at the expense of ends, on a monstrous instrumentality of things which points everywhere and leads nowhere: "The means soaks up the end like a blotter soaking up ink."[19] Purpose is implicit in every manufactured thing, in every item of the city's inventory; but normally, absorbed in the passage from one end to another, from one project to another, we fail to notice this structure of the objects around us. Kafka makes us intensely aware of it by suddenly concealing the second term, masking the teleological purposes which would make the objects around us comprehensible and natural to us; and at once they stand out starkly in their instrumentality, with astonishment we see for the first time that dimension of human reality which is activity, which brings tools into being around it. Sartre is careful to distinguish this unique vision from the apprehension of the absurd, as it takes place in Camus for instance; for the absurd is the awareness of a world in which ends simply do not exist and never have, in which there are no tools, no point to any activity, in which it is not teleology that surprises us but precisely the opposite of it.

Yet it should be noted that Kafka's world is not a lived experience but an artistic projection, a technical feat made possible by a rearrangement of the structure of his raw material. For if in real life such a substitution of means for ends was possible in some of the inventions of the surrealists (Duchamp's sugar cubes suddenly turning out to be heavy bits of marble), such moments, being contradictions in terms, rapidly disintegrate, and the stable world of cause and effect quickly takes shape around us once again.

Hence the great interest of the experiment of Genet, who by his position as an outsider *within* our practical world succeeds in undermining its objects, in *irrealizing* them and sub-

19. "Le moyen a bu la fin comme le buvard boit l'encre." *Situations I*, the essay on Maurice Blanchot's *Aminadab*, p. 131.

stituting for our practical attitude toward them a demoralizing aesthetic and contemplative one, replacing action with the aesthete's values, with Beauty or the Imaginary.

For an object can be neutralized with respect to its practical functions and transformed into something magical, into an image, by the rearrangement of the time scheme in which it is perceived. Genet is struck by red velvet armchairs, gilt mirrors, abandoned in a field.[20] For the utilitarian mind these objects are understood as moments in a process, their position can be deciphered by consulting the future: housecleaning is a project, the preservation of the empty lot for its investment value is also a project, the image itself is nothing but a momentary juxtaposition of prosaic, wholly unmysterious activities. But for Genet the visual intensity of the juxtaposition is everything, the present takes precedence over past history or future destinations, and indeed the latter become mere pretexts for the former; whatever the mysterious sign which these abandoned armchairs are trying to convey to him, the woman of the house picked that day to move them out *in order for* Genet to witness it. In this reversal of the real and the imaginary it is the practical project which is appearance, illusion, and the visual image which is reality.

And as it is in the world of material objects, so also with those objects which are words: the latter shed their practical uses, drift up into Genet's mind like strange and fascinating fragments of an exotic reality, a single odd-sounding term or expression becomes a poem in itself. So also with human behavior: the vision obsessed with the imaginary rather than the real tends to retain isolated gestures for their own sake rather than operations comprehensible only in the light of some larger practical purpose, to see the human world as a discontinuous series of instants (the "Divinarianes" of *Notre-Dame des Fleurs*), of striking or characteristic remarks or anecdotes. And evidently in a kind of "motivation of the device" this stylistic predilection ends up producing the kind of content which can best satisfy it; seen principally through the lens of isolated gestures, the characters of Genet turn out to be people whose

20. *Saint Genet*, p. 256.

lives are led *in order to* make gestures, whose principal value is the acting out of their creator's aesthetic, who are themselves aesthetes, transvestites, exhibitionists, criminals.[21]

To this characteristic selection of content corresponds a peculiar quality of the typical Genet image; its essence is "toc," the sham, the fake, that which shows garish bad taste. The older literary criticism analyzed function, structure, and tone and had as its basic presupposition that the image *worked* in some way (otherwise the work in question was faulty or not worth analyzing). Here the point is that Genet does not want his images to work; the solid coherent image is taken as a reality by the reader, what was imaginary in the writer's mind becomes a feature or component of a world which enjoys a certain objective existence outside him. But since Genet's passion aims at the symbolic destruction of the world, at an undermining of its solidity, he cannot afford to tolerate this paradox or dialectic of the literary process, this density or materiality which is the end-product of his unreal daydreaming. So he sabotages his own art, he short-circuits his material so that it will remain purely imaginary for the reader as well, he creates images which are visual in appearance but which the reader is at a loss to visualize. (The flower images come to mind—"There exists," decrees Genet, "a close relationship between flowers and convicts: the fragility, the delicacy of the former are of the same nature as the brutal insensitivity of the latter.")[22] Such images call for the performing of mental operations which are contradictory, which the reader cannot complete.

This prolongation of the unreal to the very heart of the literary image itself is repeated on the level of the plot as a

21. Criminality, the choice of evil, involves for Sartre an analogous withdrawal from Being and from the real, a similar and equally contradictory attempt to destroy what is at the same time affirmed (theft is inconceivable without the institution of private property against which it is directed); evil, like Beauty, is *parasitic*.

22. "Il existe donc un étroit rapport entre les fleurs et les bagnards. La fragilité, la délicatesse, des premières sont de même nature que la brutale insensibilité des autres." *Journal du voleur* (Paris: Gallimard, 1949), p. 9.

whole. Genet's characters and story do not have the objective self-sufficiency of the conventional work of fiction. They are instead quite clearly products of his desire, wish-fulfillments, fantasies, and at every moment they threaten to vanish away and leave us face to face with the lonely dreaming consciousness from which they sprang. Genet alone is the hero of all his books, his novels are books about novel-writing, about the imagining of characters and stories, and in them we watch desire trying out its voice and inventing the forms in which it is symbolically to satisfy itself: first images, faces, phrases, anecdotes; then the willful setting in motion of the wish-fulfillment itself; finally those moments when the dream seems to *take*, and scenes unfold which are somehow external to the dreamer, have their own terrible autonomy and logic (as in the murder and trial scenes of *Notre-Dame des Fleurs*). Thus the entire work remains profoundly imaginary in its very core, is not drawn by the reader out into a kind of objectivity but instead draws him into its irreality, contaminates his mind with the imaginary. Genet's revenge against the real world thus falls on the reader as well.

This peculiar relationship to the object and to its image is not an exclusively literary invention on Genet's part. Just as Kafka's objective situation as a government functionary put him in a position to explore the predominance and proliferation of means over ends, and to do so objectively, without any personal intervention, so the very situation of Genet as orphan and thief, as social outcast, places him at distance from ordinary utilitarian objects and activities, causes him to stare at them from the outside and to invent a whole system of values (beauty, the importance of the gesture) and a whole rearrangement of time (the hallucinatory present) in order to live them in a contemplative mode, all practical, transcendent relationships to them being closed to him.

Both Kafka and Genet represent artistic deformations of our lived experience of the world. Their value is first of all artistic, in the invention of new techniques through which to project their contradictory vision of things, and secondly ethical, in the way the former brings us to a heightened awareness of the practical structure of our world, in the way the latter forces us to look at ourselves and our society through the eyes of its outcasts, its functional rejects. But it is characteristic of Sartre that he should feel, along with these value judgments, a certain impatience with the artifices and detours, with the formal untruths, which art entails; and that he should at the same time sketch out a program for an art in which this deformation of lived reality would be overcome.

Such an art was to have been the "literature of *praxis*" or of *production* described at the end of *Qu'est-ce que la littérature?*[23] The model for such a literature was the novel of aviation developed by Saint-Exupéry, work centering on the technical relationship of men to things, in which objects are neither described in an objective, contemplative way nor irrealized, but transcended toward their use, revealed by their position in the human project itself. And the aesthetic formula behind such a work is neither that of static description nor of poetic irrealization but rather that expressed as an artistic law by Valéry, namely, that the density of a literary object is in direct proportion to the multiplicity of relationships it entertains with the other elements of the work. But this literature, which presents striking similarities with the theory of socialist realism (and with works such as the early films of Eisenstein), was never brought into being by Sartre and his generation.[24] It was a utopian ideal, one dependent in the long run on the nature of the writer's society, on the possibility in it of experiencing objects, not as alienated commercial wares, but rather as tools or as the products of human work; on the possibility of addressing readers who feel themselves engaged in activity, rather than those passively enmeshed in routines and systems that are beyond their control. In this sense, the idea of a literature of praxis remains a negative, a critical one: one which reminds us of the ultimate and authentic relationship to objects within the free project, as tools to be transcended toward a future, as crystallized human activity.

23. *Situations II*, pp. 264–66.

24. A few of the works of this period give an idea what such a literature might have been like, in particular those whose characters are working-class people, as in the two movie scenarios, *Les Jeux sont faits* and *L'Engrenage*, and in Simone de Beauvoir's *Le Sang des autres*.

The dynamic element in Sartre's existentialism is a Hegelian graft, the idea of the Other and of Otherness. It is this concept which completes the idea of freedom with a description of the way freedom objectifies and alienates itself in its objects. (Flaubert's *Madame Bovary* is for example misappropriated by his contemporaries, and transformed into an object unrecognizable to him.) It is this notion which permits the free consciousness of *L'Etre et le néant* to escape from its isolation in the monad, to discover its dimension of Being-for-other-people and its inextricable involvement in an intersubjective world. Later on, the notion of Otherness serves as a means of accounting for the relationship between the self and the institutions around it with which it must come to terms; in particular, it accounts for the paradoxical phenomenon of the divided self, the Hegelian unhappy consciousness, in which people are obliged to choose themselves as Other for Other people, to feel their center of gravity outside the self.[25] Finally, Otherness is the source of the optical illusion of Good and Evil, of the ethical manichaeanism which results in justification for the Self and condemnation of the Other (anti-Semitism, anti-communism, racism, social stereotypes of the insane and the criminal, and so forth).

But dialectical thinking involves the setting into relationship with each other of two incommensurable realities, two phenomena which cannot be thought in the same conceptual framework. The scandal of Otherness is precisely this revelation of an underside of existence, a dimension which is out of reach, which cannot be dissolved by ordinary analytical thought, and which always *turns* it, reckons it into the account beforehand. (Imagine someone with a horror of other people's judgments; to escape them he always does the opposite of what people expect; at length a superior judgment falls, imprisoning him this time in a larger perspective: he is simply *capricious*.) The scandal of literary Otherness for literary critics is this obligation to go outside the neat world of the single conceptual

25. See in particular *Saint Genet*, *Réflexions sur la question juive* (Paris: Morihien, 1946), and Beauvoir, *Le Deuxième Sexe* (Paris: Gallimard, 1949).

framework, to make a dialectical leap from the comfortable, imminent system of forms and purely formal analysis to an unpleasantly external reality. For Marxism this external reality is the economic and social situation, the historical form which material conditions take; and the Marxist literary dialectic involves the disagreeable reminder that the major part of writers' and readers' lives is spent in the preoccupation with material questions, that the work of art, in appearance self-sufficient and above history, is conditioned (even more radically than by the purely literary history of its form and content) by such external and absolutely nonliterary phenomena as the state of book publishing in the period, the increasing enrichment and leisure of certain classes of the society, and so forth.

Merleau-Ponty has pointed out[26] that the originality of Sartre's view of literature with respect to this materialistic dialectic is that for him the work of art is not felt to be retrospective, a product of a certain social background, but rather prospective, itself a way of choosing the social group to which it speaks and of which it will eventually become emblematic. The Otherness of the work of art for Sartre is constituted not so much by the *milieu* in which it originates as by the *public* which it calls forth for itself.

For the theory of prose was based on the idea that an appeal to the reader was built into the very structure of prose language: the words of the novel are signs rather than material objects; they require certain mental operations in order to be completed, to be endowed with signification. The writer cannot himself complete the signs which he prepares for the reader; he knows their meaning too well already, he cannot approach them with uncertainty and groping experimentation, against an open future; he can never see his own work with the eyes of an outsider; as operations to perform, his own words remain for him a dead letter.

Thus on the most basic level all prose requires the cooperation of a reader to come into being, does not exist until a reader has somehow re-created it and brought it to being with

26. *Les Aventures de la dialectique* (Paris: Gallimard, 1955), pp. 209 ff.

his own freedom (by living *through* the characters, by agreeing momentarily to lend the novel's signs his own personal experience, his own memories, his own expectations and solidity). But the reader is implied on a more specific level as well; the kinds of signs chosen by the writer tend to limit his readers to a certain group or class, to imply a certain kind of background knowledge in them which limits the availability of the work to initiates only. An American writer would for example feel he had to explain to a European audience allusions which Americans would grasp without comment on his part. But literature is primarily allusion; a work in which everything is explained, justified intellectually, accounted for, is quite inconceivable, so that all works of literature in one way or another speak to a closed group of people at the expense of others.

Beside the formalist or the social and biographical methods, there is thus a place for a new type of examination which would describe the work of art in terms of the public which it implies; and it is this new type of literary history which Sartre writes in *Qu'est-ce que la littérature?* (1948). The logic of his position distinguishes two kinds of public, the *real* (that group implied by the background required to read the work), and the *virtual* (those groups deliberately or implicitly shut off from access to it). The various possible relationships of literature to its public will therefore tend to be governed by two kinds of possible opposition: one between real and virtual publics, the other between two different possible real publics, both of which may happen to be available to the writer at that moment of history. Sartre's history of literature amounts to a working out of the various possible combinations and permutations of these terms.

His central distinction corresponds to the more fundamental Hegelian one between abstract and concrete;[27] for Sartre the work of art becomes concrete only to the degree

27. It is this insistence on the primacy of the concrete, its relationship to the historical development of society at a given moment, rather than their actual estimates of past literary history, which Sartre shares with the Lukács of the *Theorie des Romans*; see Beauvoir, *La Force des choses* (Paris: Gallimard, 1963), p. 130, n. 1.

that it approaches an ever widening public, one which tends toward universal readership as an outside limit. For the writer who must limit his readership severely must also limit the range of experiences treated; must translate them into the terms understood by the group; must therefore practice symbolism and abstraction as a habit of mind developed and imposed by his confining situation as a writer in a certain society. The archetype of this abstract literature is that of the Middle Ages, in which the reading of literature was limited primarily to the writers themselves, to the clerical caste which possessed the specialized technique of the written word. In such a situation, where the virtual public extends for all practical purposes to the whole of society at large, the subject matter of literature shrinks to an almost modern purity; the only available content is the literary activity itself in the form of pure spirituality, at its most abstract, in other words, religion, a symbolic apparatus in which the entirety of the concrete world is present in inverted reflection, transformed into abstraction or pure idea.

The ideal counterpart to this moment in which the virtual public eclipses the real public is of course one in which the two are identical, in which the real public includes all of humanity. This utopia of literature is difficult to imagine, but clearly presupposes a literature from which all abstraction has been eliminated, in which ideas as separate entities no longer exist, and in which every kind of subject matter possesses its intrinsic importance and meaning. The history of modern philosophy offers perhaps the most convenient analogy, where little by little, and through its own self-criticism, philosophy as system, as an independent structure of abstractions, has been replaced by the various sciences (logic and linguistics, history and economics, sociology, psychology) into which its own concrete content evolved. The movement in literature would be the reverse of that described in medieval times, where writing was a technique like any other, and for that very reason separated off from all the others into its own closed guild or caste. Here writing as an action becomes in a world of unalienated work the symbol of any other kind of human energy or transcendence, serves as a relationship of analogy and similarity rather than the sign of inequality and unlikeness which it had been in the earlier period.

Between these two extreme moments, all the other forms which a literature can take, which French literature has taken: the property of a ruling class which was its real reading public (during the seventeenth century), a mediation between two different real publics, the nobility and the bourgeoisie (in the eighteenth century), the possibility of an appeal to the oppressed class (during the nineteenth century), the possibility once again of a mediation between two classes, the workers and the bourgeoisie (in the twentieth century), and finally, a refusal of any public, the reduction to the public of the clericature of the Middle Ages, to a public of other writers, posterity and the great literary dead (our own literature, modernism, the religion of art from its beginnings in the nineteenth century). It is clear from this scheme that the dialectic of literary development is not always a logical or predictable one; the privileged position of the eighteenth-century writer, for instance, who could speak to two classes and be imprisoned by neither, should in the nature of things present itself again in our time, except that the influence of the Communist party over the workers makes it impossible to address them directly. The literature of the nineteenth century ought to have been once again a literature designed for a ruling class, as in the seventeenth century, except that the best writers refused this kind of service and took refuge in dandyism, hatred of the bourgeois, and art for art's sake. To explain why this was so would involve an analysis of the specific nature of bourgeois, as opposed to earlier feudal, values. Indeed, it has not been sufficiently noticed how significant a part of Sartre's life work has been given over to a portrait and an analysis of the French middle class;[28] this is perhaps his most important contribution to the history of ideas behind literature, as opposed to the purely literary examination of forms, and there is implicit in his work as radical a revision of modern French social and intellectual

28. From the "salauds" of *La Nausée* to the analysis of the generations of the bourgeoisie in *Critique de la raison dialectique* (Paris: Gallimard, 1960), pp. 687–734, and to the recent biography of Flaubert.

history as that which Lukács undertook for modern Germany.

It is characteristic that with the possibility of disengaging himself from his own class (as in the eighteenth century) ruled out, Sartre should turn to the kind of "internal emigration" represented by the example of Genet. The appeal to the reader was built into the very linguistic structure of Genet's work; Sartre shows in concrete detail how his poetry (pure materiality of language) is infected and undermined by an instinctive prose (a system of signs, organization by paraphrasable significations).[29] For the appeal to the Other was at the very source of Genet's creative impulse; victim of an initially verbal trauma (accusation, being *named* a thief), he first experiences words as impenetrable objects, as Otherness, and his attempt as a writer is to recapture this dimension of language for himself, either to see himself from the outside as others see him, or to make them go through the same strange contradictory experience themselves, that of being looked at from the outside, of being unable to seize from the inside the language of their writer-accuser. The favorable judgment on Genet is therefore similar to that passed on Dos Passos; such literature has a value of contestation, reflects back to the middle classes their own truth in all its ugliness as seen, not from the vantage point of another class, but from a point on the very margin of their own, in Genet's case through the eyes of a criminal and outcast.

It should be added that besides this "prospective" criticism, there is also in Sartre, particularly in the existential biographies, a "retrospective" criticism as well, one which evaluates the effect of his background, his *situation*, on the writer. Thus both Genet and Giraudoux present medieval characteristics, have basically medieval imaginations,[30] but this is not to be attributed to their sharing in one of those Platonic abstractions such as the medieval world view which German idealistic literary criticism used to favor. Rather, the medieval world view was itself the expression of an agricultural society, and it

29. *Saint Genet*, pp. 402–11.

30. *Saint Genet*, pp. 435–42; and the essay on Giraudoux in *Situations I*, esp. pp. 96–98.

is to the degree that Genet's background, his life situation, was by accident agricultural in a predominantly industrial society, that certain objective similarities appear between his way of thinking and those of medieval times.

It is in the light of this reduction to the lived situation of the writer that the much discussed notion of *engagement* (commitment) is to be understood. The emotional logic of this idea is characteristic of Sartre: if in fact we *are* our situation, it seems to run, then we ought to *choose* to be it, with all its limitations, we should prefer a lucid awareness of it to imaginary evasions and the mystification with abstract or unreal issues. Indeed, the whole bias of Sartre's philosophy is against placelessness and against the kind of introspection in which I lose my own limits, in which I forget my observer's position in the universe and come to identify myself with privilege, absolute spirit, or whatever justification subjectivity invents in order to persuade itself of its isolation from other people, its implied superiority over other people. In literary history the form that this passion for privilege has taken is the religion of art, the attempt to escape one's own historical moment by associating one's self mentally with eternity in the form of the confraternity of art, the great tradition, or posterity. *Engagement* is therefore not a political notion, or a call to propaganda, but serves a primarily negative function: that of cutting away all the imaginary dimensions we give ourselves in an effort to avoid awareness of our concrete historical condition.

From a positive point of view, the idea of engagement can be seen as a theory of living literature. Already the notion of a public and the mechanism of alienation had seriously restricted the immediacy of the literature of the past; if Flaubert's *Madame Bovary* is not one but a whole series of different literary phenomena nesting inside one another (the book Flaubert wrote, the one his contemporaries read, that of the naturalists, of the subsequent generations, etc.), then we cannot so much read it directly as decipher it, separating the various historical objects of our attention. Perhaps one might express this death of past literature in a different way by saying that it is for the modern reader exotic, just as foreign works are exotic. For implicit in the idea of *engagement* is a limitation to the given national society itself, inasmuch as the various nations of the world have developed at unequal rates, have different social structures and face dissimilar problems, in short present different kinds of content to the writers who must work in them. *Engagement* thus involves a reduction to the present, both in space and time, and the advantage it holds forth is that of an immediate contact with the problems and lives of its readers in the present. The ideal is political only insofar as any really complete picture of the present in all its contradictions would ultimately have to emerge into a political dimension of things; and the criticism of engaged literature as occasional literature and mere propaganda is only a caricature of a more accurate criticism that might be made of it, namely, that it imprisons the writer perhaps too dramatically in the present, neglects the passage of time required between conception and execution as well as the lag between generations, and ultimately that it tends to reduce art to a relationship between two people of common background and situation, that is, to return the work of art to that direct interpersonal relationship which was its origin.

There is no doubt that Sartre's attitude toward literature is an ambiguous one, full of suspicion of its duplicities and illusions, its necessary indirection. Yet at the same time literature is a crucial form of self-consciousness, one which we do without only at the risk of sinking back into the animal kingdom: "Through literature the collectivity turns to reflection and mediation, it acquires an unhappy consciousness of itself, an unstable reflection which it perpetually attempts to modify and to ameliorate."[31]

The source of this ambiguity can be found in Sartre's idea of consciousness in general. Consciousness is a not-being, a nothingness, a withdrawal from the solid world of things and Being and a distance from it; here the value of consciousness is

31. "Par la littérature . . . la collectivité passe à la réflexion et à la médiation, elle acquiert une conscience malheureuse, une image sans équilibre d'elle-même qu'elle cherche sans cesse à modifier et à améliorer." *Situations II*, p. 316.

negative, and all our acts of consciousness in their various ways (desire, work, knowledge, imagination) constitute a negation of the given object and a heroic activity with respect to the latter's mindless passivity. But at the same time, as we have already seen in connection with the idea of engagement, Sartre is passionately unwilling to preach withdrawal from the world or refuge in the purely subjective, the mystical, the imaginary. Thus slowly the value judgment shifts around to the other side and comes to adhere to that consciousness which chooses, not negation of the world in general, but negation of that *particular* given object; in other words, which chooses not so much withdrawal as attachment to the immediate world around it and to its immediate objective situation.

This double movement is visible in his literary criticism as well. He visibly prefers an art which challenges society, which shows it a hostile portrait of itself, to an art at one with its public, sharing its values implicitly, serving as apologia for them. Yet in a larger sense all art is contestation in its very structure; the basest flattery forces its subject to see himself, to take the first step on the road to reflection and self-consciousness, so that the first internal judgment on various works of art as compared with one another seems to fall before this second, more global one as to the structure of art in general. In the same way, he clearly prefers an art which insists on human activity and on the practical structure of things, rather than one in which a contemplative, poetic, irrealizing relationship to them is encouraged; yet it is obvious in a larger perspective that all art is imaginary, and that even the literature of praxis represents a momentary withdrawal from the real world of means and ends. Finally, a model of the world in which the future is alive is to be preferred to one in which an exaggerated attachment to the present or past seems to shut off human possibilities. On the other hand, if all language is essentially a deformation of experience, an essence imposed on existence, then even the future-oriented style is an optical illusion, does not genuinely reflect the world but merely conveys a striking and persuasive caricature of it, in its way defends a kind of thesis. Perhaps the most fundamental example of this antinomy is to be found in the idea of freedom itself, in the apparent opposition between the structural fact that all consciousnesses *are* free and the moral imperative to them to *become* free, the implication that only some of them have done so.

The attitude that we have just described probably accounts for the gradual retirement of Sartre from the writing of novels and plays.[32] Even the interest in Genet is characteristic in this respect, if we compare it with the earlier interest in Dos Passos: the latter was thought of as an artist and praised for his art. The former can be considered an autobiographical writer, both in the content he uses, and in the form, which as we have seen takes the shape of the satisfaction of personal desires on the writer's part. Genet's works, therefore, if they show great artistry, can also be felt to have the solidity of documents, of fact.[33]

In his own work it is increasingly clear that for Sartre the novel is simply not capable of doing justice to the complexities of lived experience; hence the existential biography as a more adequate form, one which is able better to unify the various isolated and interconnecting dimensions of a given life (childhood, death, the body, social class, etc.):

The novelist shows us now one, now another of these dimensions in the form of "thoughts" which alternate in the hero's mind. But he's lying to us: these dimensions don't (or don't necessarily) have anything to do with "thoughts" as such, and they all coexist together, man is imprisoned *inside* them, at every moment he stands in relationship to *all* the walls that surround him at once, he doesn't cease for a moment to *know* that he's imprisoned. All these walls make a single prison, and this prison is a single life, a single act; the significance of each wall changes, changes all the time, and its transformation in

32. This process of disintoxication with literature is of course the explicit subject of Sartre's autobiography, *Les Mots* (Paris: Gallimard, 1964).

33. Other indications of this increasing refusal of the artistic and predilection for the real, the document, can be found in the remark on the *anti-novel* in the Preface to Nathalie Sarraute's *Portrait d'un inconnu* (*Situations IV* [Paris: Gallimard, 1964]) and in the Preface to André Gorz's autobiography *Le Traître* ("Des rats et des hommes," *Situations IV*).

turn has repercussions on all the others. What a totalization therefore must reveal is the multidimensional unity of the act; this unity is the basic condition for the reciprocal interpenetration as well as the relative autonomy of the various dimensions, and our old habits of thought tend to oversimplify it; language in its present state is ill-equipped to perform such a unification.[34]

It is well that these absolute demands should be made on art, that this ultimate challenge be addressed to the novel as a form. It is well that Sartre should force us to pass an absolute judgment on literature as a whole, as well as relative ones. But at the same time we should not forget the earlier Sartre, the one who evaluated literature not in terms of an impossible totality but in the light of what it could best do, how it could best be used, the philosopher of freedom who only recently described again the kind of liberation which the ordinary man owes to literature:

If once he has lived this instant of freedom, if for an instant in other words he has managed to escape—by means of the book—from the forces of alienation or oppression all around him, you can be sure that he won't forget it. And I think that literature can have that effect, or at least that a certain kind of literature can.[35]

34. "Le romancier nous montrera tantôt l'une, tantôt l'autre de ces dimensions comme des pensées qui alternent dans 'l'esprit' de son héros. Il mentira: il ne s'agit pas (ou pas nécessairement) de pensées et toutes sont données ensemble, l'homme est enfermé *dedans*, il ne cesse d'être lié à *tous* ces murs qui l'entourent ni de *savoir* qu'il est emmuré. Tous ces murs font *une seule prison* et cette prison, c'est *une seule vie, un seul acte*; chaque signification se transforme, ne cesse de se transformer et sa transformation se répercute sur toutes les autres. Ce que la totalisation doit découvrir alors, c'est *l'unité* pluridimensionnelle de l'acte; cette unité, condition de l'interpénétration réciproque et de la relative autonomie des significations, nos vieilles habitudes de pensées risquent de la simplifier; la forme actuelle du langage est peu propre à la restituer." "Question de méthode," *Critique de la raison dialectique*, p. 74.

35. "S'il a vécu ce moment de liberté, c'est-à-dire si pendant un moment il a échappé—et par le livre—aux forces d'aliénation ou d'oppression, soyez sûrs qu'il ne l'oubliera pas. Cela, je crois que la littérature le peut, ou du moins une certaine littérature." *Que peut la littérature?* edited by Yves Buin (Paris: L'Herne, 1965), p. 127.

BIBLIOGRAPHY

CRITICAL WORKS BY SARTRE

Baudelaire. Paris: Gallimard, 1947. (Translated by Martin Turnell. London: Horizon, 1949.)

L'Etre et le néant. Paris: Gallimard, 1943. (*Being and Nothingness*. Translated by Hazel Barnes. New York: Philosophical Library, 1956.)

L'Idiot de la famille: Gustave Flaubert de 1821 à 1857. 2 vols. Bibliothèque de Philosophie. Paris: Gallimard, 1971.

L'Imaginaire. Paris: Gallimard, 1940. (*Psychology of Imagination*. Translated by Bernard Frechtman. New York: Philosophical Library, 1948.)

"Question de méthode." *Critique de la raison dialectique*, I. *Théorie des ensembles pratiques*. Bibliothèque des Idées. Paris: Gallimard, 1960. Reprinted: Idées. Paris: Gallimard, 1967. (*Search for a Method*. Translated by Hazel E. Barnes. New York: Alfred A. Knopf, 1963.)

Saint Genet, comédien et martyr. Paris: Gallimard, 1952. (*Saint Genet, Actor and Martyr*. Translated by Bernard Frechtman. New York: Braziller, 1964.)

Situations I. Paris: Gallimard, 1947. Essays on Faulkner, Dos Passos, Mauriac, Camus, etc. (*Literary and Philosophical Essays*. Translated by Annette Michelson. London: Rider & Co., 1955. Collier Books. New York: Macmillan, 1966.)

Situations II. Paris: Gallimard, 1948. Contains "Qu'est-ce que la littérature?" (*What Is Literature?* Translated by Bernard Frechtman. London: Methuen, 1950.)

Situations IV. Paris: Gallimard, 1964. Contains essays on Nathalie Sarraute, Paul Nizan, Merleau-Ponty, and others, as well as on visual arts, principally Tintoretto. (The literary sections are in *Situations*. Translated by Benita Eisler. New York: Braziller, 1965. Essays on the arts in *Essays in Aesthetics*. Translated by Wade Baskin. New York: Philosophical Library, 1963.)

SARTRE BIBLIOGRAPHY

Contat, Michel, and Michel Rybalka. *Les Ecrits de Sartre: chronologie, bibliographie commentée*. Paris: Gallimard, 1970.

WORKS ON SARTRE'S CRITICISM AND AESTHETIC THEORIES

Bataille, Georges. *La Littérature et le mal*. Paris: Gallimard, 1957. Subtle replies to and appreciations of the books on Baudelaire and Genet.

Champigny, Robert. *Stages on Sartre's Way*. Bloomington: Indiana University Press, 1959. Excellent chapters on the aesthetic theories.

Cumming, Robert. "The Literature of Extreme Situations." In *Aesthetics Today*. Edited by Morris Philipson. New York: Meridian, 1961. Revealing study of the "aesthetic" versus the "practical" in Kierkegaard and Sartre.

Diéguez, Manuel de. "Jean-Paul Sartre." In *L'Ecrivain et son langage*, pp. 234–93. Les Essais. Paris: Gallimard, 1960.

Douglas, Kenneth. "Blanchot and Sartre." *Yale French Studies* 2, no. 1 (Summer–Spring 1949): 85–95.

Erlich, Victor. "A Note on Sartre's Poetics." *Bucknell Review* 9 (1960): 123–29.

Girard, René. "Existentialism and Criticism." *Yale French Studies*, no. 16 (Winter 1955–56), pp. 45–52. Reprinted in *Sartre: A Collection of Critical Essays*, pp. 121–28. Edited by Edith Kern. Twentieth Century Views. Englewood Cliffs: Prentice-Hall, 1962. Traces the influence of Sartre's critical methods among the newer critics.

Hahn, Otto. "L'Oeuvre critique de Sartre." *Modern Language Notes* 80 (1965): 347–63.

Kaelin, Eugene F. *An Existentialist Aesthetic: The Theories of Sartre and Merleau-Ponty*. Madison: University of Wisconsin Press, 1962.

Kohut, Karl. *Was ist Literatur? Die Theorie der "littérature engagée" bei Jean-Paul Sartre*. Marburg: Druck von Gg. Nolte, 1965. Contains useful material and bibliographies.

Leiris, Michel. "Sartre et Baudelaire." In *Brisées*, pp. 120–24. Paris: Mercure de France, 1966.

Magny, Claude-Edmonde. *Les Sandales d'Empédocle: Essai sur les limites de la littérature*. Etre et Penser. Neuchâtel: La Baconnière, 1945.

Manser, Anthony. *Sartre: A Philosophical Study*. London: Athlone Press, 1966. One of the rare works to contain a separate chapter on Sartre's various observations on language.

Morpurgo-Tagliabue, Guido. *L'Esthétique contemporaine*. Milan: Marzorati, 1960. Relevant material translated in *Sartre: A Collection of Critical Essays* (see Girard entry above). Discusses the philosophical and literary sources of Sartre's opposition of prose to poetry.

Paulhan, Jean. "M. Jean-Paul Sartre n'est pas en bons termes avec les mots." *Table Ronde* 35 (1950): 9–20. Interesting as an application of Paulhan's own linguistic paradoxes to Sartre's critical practice.

Pouillon, Jean. *Temps et roman*. La Jeune Philosophie. Paris: Gallimard, 1946.

———. "Sartre et Lévi-Strauss: Analyse/Dialectique d'une relation dialectique/analytique." *L'Arc*, no. 26 (1965). pp. 55–60.

"Sartre aujourd'hui." *L'Arc*, no. 30 (1966).

Sontag, Susan. "Sartre's *Saint Genet.*" In *Against Interpretation,* pp. 93–99. New York: Farrar, Straus, and Giroux, 1966.

Suhl, Benjamin. *Jean-Paul Sartre: The Philosopher as Literary Critic.* New York: Columbia University Press, 1970.

Neal Oxenhandler

10

Literature as Perception in the Work of Merleau-Ponty

Maurice Merleau-Ponty wrote in 1945 that the tasks of literature and philosophy could no longer be separated. Both modes of expression attempt to seize the "originary" experiences of human subjectivity in its act of life and incarnate them in speech. The upsurging or streaming forth of the "I" into the world calls into being our categories of space, time, the visible, the self, the other, etc. The grasp of reality which these categories give us is elusive, and the philosopher finds that the world is no longer easily conceptualized: "The world is such that it cannot be expressed except in 'stories' and, as it were, pointed at."[1] The philosopher, then, must "point at" landmarks on a kind of map which charts the "sedimentation of meaning" that he has drawn from his own life experience; the symbols on his map must function as resonant analogues of the reader's own life experience. Such a concept of philosophy is remarkably close to the concept of literature that we find in a poet such as Valéry or a novelist such as Proust; and, indeed, Merleau-Ponty was a philosopher who wrote like a poet.

The philosophy of Merleau-Ponty is poetic because of a hidden poetic structure—a use of repetition, leitmotif, metaphor, paradox, ambiguity, rhythm. Equally important, the writing is emotional, that is, it attempts to evoke a response

1. *Sense and Nonsense* (Evanston, Ill.: Northwestern University Press, 1964), p. 28. "Le monde est fait de telle sorte qu'il ne puisse être exprimé que dans des 'histoires' et comme montré du doigt." "Le Roman et la métaphysique," *Sens et non-sens* (Paris: Nagel, 1948), p. 55.

in the reader, a response through which the reader may intuit the very phenomenon (e.g., time, anguish, contingency) under discussion. Finally, Merleau-Ponty discusses in an unusually dense and contextual way such major themes of modern literature as sexuality, history, myth, violence, and freedom.

Yet there is this difference between philosophy and literature, that while the first *speaks* to us *about* "originary" or preconceptual experience, while it *presents* or *points at* Cézanne's attempt to grasp things in their immediate revelation to perception or Balzac's discovery of the structure and meaning of chance, the artist allows us to relive the experience in its unfolding. While the philosopher maintains always a certain distance, a certain reserve (Merleau-Ponty was perennially accused of aloofness; he was called a *monstre sacré* or, after his appointment to the Collège de France, an "academic"), the writer speaks from the intersubjective center.

It is the writer, Merleau-Ponty suggests, who invents a new "rapport with self" (*rapport à soi*), who replaces the "I" or "he" of conventional speech with a new kind of personal pronoun, a new vision of self. We can only grasp Michel Butor's use of these new self-concepts if we understand that "language is a being, a world, [and] it is the Word that is the circle."[2] The word, especially the incarnate word of literature, is the circle, that is, the revelation of that transparent obscurity, of that concealing givenness which is man's presence to himself, to others, and to the world.

Since literature has always been a phenomenology, it is not surprising that criticism, in becoming one also, has made a great leap forward and taken on new powers. Much of the new critical expressiveness shows the influence of Merleau-Ponty. Several commentators on Merleau-Ponty have attempted to derive an aesthetic or a criticism from his work (see Bibliography); yet we find that his work makes only scattered comments about literature. Still, if we raise the perennial problems of literature while we are, so to speak, in the

2. "Le langage est un être, un monde, . . . c'est la Parole qui est le cercle." "Cinq Notes sur Claude Simon," *Médiations*, no. 4 (1961), p. 6.

"aura" of the work, we will find these problems illuminated in an original way. Merleau-Ponty, who has written much less than Sartre about literature, may ultimately prove to have made as great a contribution to criticism, and this not because of anything explicit in his thought but because his way of philosophizing is closer to the activity of the true poet than is Sartre's. There is something of the ideologue in Sartre, and his reverence for the eighteenth century as the writer's "lost paradise" is not accidental. Many of his novels and plays are clearly ideological, closer to *Candide* and *Jacques le fataliste* than contemporary models. Sartre's style of philosophizing is quite different from that of Merleau-Ponty, who avoids absolute concepts, never becoming prisoner of categories; nor does Merleau-Ponty substitute for history his description of it. In his reflection on the act of philosophizing or on being a man, in his search for the fundamental, Merleau-Ponty illuminates the activity of the artist by analogy and implication, while the whole context of critical thought is renewed.

It is paradoxical that so little has been written about Merleau-Ponty as a man, since his philosophy is essentially a vast introspection, one that ranks in depth of insight with the *Confessions* of Rousseau or *A la Recherche du temps perdu*, yet it is an introspection that conceals the man as much as it reveals him. His statement about Montaigne applies: "But perhaps in the end he finds in this ambiguous *self*—which is offered to everything, and which he never finished exploring—the place of all obscurities, the mystery of all mysteries, and something like an ultimate truth."[3]

The long essay which Sartre devoted to Merleau-Ponty in the commemorative number of *Les Temps Modernes* tells us something of Merleau-Ponty, the man, while recounting the story of a friendship that seemed to "fail" in a human sense, yet enriched them both:

3. *Signs* (Evanston, Ill.: Northwestern University Press, 1964), p. 198. "Mais, dans ce *soi* ambigu, offert à tout, et qu'il n'a jamais fini d'explorer, peut-être trouve-t-il finalement le lieu de toutes les obscurités, le mystère de tous les mystères, et quelque chose comme une vérité dernière." "Lecture de Montaigne," *Signes* (Paris: Gallimard, 1960), p. 251.

Too individualistic to work together, we became reciprocal while resting separate. Alone, each one would have too easily been persuaded that he had grasped the phenomenological idea; together, we incarnated its ambiguity for one another: for each grasped as an unexpected deviation from his own work the alien, sometimes adversary project of the other. Husserl became at the same time our distance and our friendship. On this terrain we were merely, as Merleau so well said of language itself, "differences without term or rather terms engendered by the differences which appear among them." He retained a subtle memory of our conversations. Basically, he wanted only to deepen himself and discussion annoyed him. . . . I don't know if he profited from these discussions: sometimes I doubt it. But I don't forget what I owe to them: an aerated mind. In my opinion, this was the purest moment of our friendship.[4]

The relationship, as Sartre has described it, was marked by a wary attitude on the part of Merleau-Ponty. On the one hand, the two were in close collaboration as co-directors of *Les Temps Modernes*. Indeed, Sartre has said that, by becoming editor-in-chief and political director, Merleau-Ponty "saved" the review. But, on the other hand, Merleau-Ponty became more and more critical of Sartre's philosophy, which he had attacked directly in *La Phénoménologie de la perception* (1945). In "Un Auteur scandaleux" (1948), Merleau-Ponty wrote an effective piece of journalism in defense of Sartre; but the con-

4. "Trop individualistes pour mettre en commun nos recherches, nous devînmes réciproques en restant séparés. Seul, chacun se fût trop aisément persuadé d'avoir compris l'idée phénoménologique; à deux, nous en incarnions l'un pour l'autre l'ambiguïté: c'est que chacun saisissait comme une déviation inattendue de son propre travail le projet étranger, parfois ennemi, qui se faisait en l'autre. Husserl devenait à la fois notre distance et notre amitié. Sur ce terrain nous n'étions, comme Merleau l'a bien dit à propos du langage, que 'des différences sans termes ou plutôt des termes engendrés par les différences qui apparaissent entre eux.' Il a gardé de nos entretiens un souvenir nuancé. Dans le fond, il ne voulait que s'approfondir et les discussions le dérangaient. . . . Je ne sais s'il tira profit de ces discussions: parfois j'en doute. Mais je n'oublie pas ce que je leur dois: une pensée ventilée. A mon avis ce fut le moment le plus pur de notre amitié." Jean-Paul Sartre, "Merleau-Ponty vivant," *Les Temps Modernes* 17 (1961): 307–8.

clusive work was "Sartre et l'ultra-bolchevisme," published in 1953, the year after his resignation from *Les Temps Modernes*. This long essay, an elaborate refutation of Sartre's theory of liberty and related matters, was ignored by Sartre at the time but answered by Simone de Beauvoir in a violent counter-attack. In the light of these events, one might attribute a certain pathos to the following words, again from the essay on Montaigne: "Far from La Boétie's friendship having been an incidental feature in his life, we would have to say that Montaigne and the author of the *Essays* were born of this friendship, and that for him, in sum, existing meant existing in the eyes of his friend."[5]

Merleau-Ponty, the man, has disappeared behind the work, and the work begins now to speak more totally, to respond with greater resonance, as more and more voices begin posterity's dialogue with it.

Merleau-Ponty's principal theme is the prereflexive or preconscious life of the self, expressed bodily in an environing world. He locates this theme in his earliest essays, pursuing it somewhat desultorily at first, as he concerns himself primarily with aesthetic or political questions. In his first major book, *La Structure du comportement* (1942), he prepares the examination of this theme by attacking the assumption of causal explanation by which empirical science has traditionally explained the behavior of plants, animals, and men. But it is in his masterpiece, *Phénoménologie de la perception* (1945), that he finally treats his chosen theme directly and with great mastery of expression. Later collections of essays as well as the fragmentary posthumous work *Le Visible et l'invisible* (1964), represent a falling off in intensity, a failure to deepen and pursue the theme to a satisfactory conclusion. Merleau-Ponty anticipated such criticisms of incoherence and incom-

5. Translation with some revisions, *Signs*, p. 207. "Loin que l'amitié de La Boétie ait été un accident [de] sa vie, il faudrait dire que Montaigne et l'auteur des *Essais* sont nés de cette amitié, et qu'en somme, pour lui, exister, c'est exister sous le regard de son ami." Merleau-Ponty, *Signes*, p. 262.

pleteness when he said, in his inaugural lecture at the Collège de France, that a philosopher was primarily the witness of his own inner disorder.

Merleau-Ponty's philosophy has been called "a philosophy of the ambiguous."[6] He has been seen as a philosopher who gives us "a knowing permeated with not-knowing," since the "realm of existence is a chiaroscuro and has no room for Cartesian clear and distinct ideas."[7] "In morality as in art there is no solution for the man who will not make a move without knowing where he is going and who wants to be accurate and in control at every moment."[8] The philosopher "goes against every unqualified affirmation of truth and values. . . . he is unable to surrender unqualifiedly to anything whatsoever."[9]

Merleau-Ponty's thought develops in an almost uninterrupted series of pulsating movements. Its structure is often antithetical, as in the following passage: "Love is not only of the body since it seeks someone, and it is not only of the mind since it seeks him in his body."[10] Such antithetical language reflects the paradox of man—the fact that he is a "body-subject," that is, a material being thrown into the world of history and action; yet he is also a center of reflective or subjective existence. Merleau-Ponty writes in such a way that the two aspects of man appear simultaneously in each moment of his thought. His ambiguity is further traceable to the effort to make his statements as totally contextual as possible, to force into them, by image, metaphor, qualification, rhythm,

6. Title of the book by Alphonse de Waelhens.

7. Remigius C. Kwant, *The Phenomenological Philosophy of Merleau-Ponty*, trans. Henry J. Koren, Duquesne Studies, Philosophical Series (Pittsburgh: Duquesne University Press, 1963), p. 8.

8. *Sense and Nonsense*, p. 4. "En morale comme en art, il n'y aurait pas de solution pour celui qui veut d'abord assurer sa marche, rester à tout instant juste et maître absolu de soi-même." Merleau-Ponty, *Sens et non-sens*, p. 9.

9. R. Kwant, *The Phenomenological Philosophy of Merleau-Ponty*, p. 82.

10. My translation; for context, see *Signs*, p. 201. "L'amour n'est pas du corps seulement puisqu'il vise quelqu'un, et il n'est pas de l'esprit seulement puisqu'il le vise dans son corps." "Lecture de Montaigne," *Signes*, p. 254.

as much of the situated or lived reality of each human moment as possible.

Merleau-Ponty's approach is to accumulate antithetical or conflicting data from introspective experience or from the experience of the writer or artist discussed (his essays on Cézanne, on Montaigne, on Claudel are based on carefully selected anecdotes). The meditation moves slowly, in a symphonic way. Themes appear, are developed, vanish, only to reappear later on. The philosopher does not merely speak, he listens to himself speak. He does not seek to attain the solution of a problem or even a total description of a subject but rather, to use a phrase employed by Paul Ricoeur, he seeks to attain "a certain point of unresolved tension." (These "unresolved tensions" echo and reinforce each other in a musical way. When extracts from an essay or book are given, they are necessarily mutilations of a thought which has full resonance only in context.)

Merleau-Ponty's thought appears at each moment as paradoxical, since it attempts to maintain the two contraries which define man—his situational or historical aspect and his inner or subjective aspect. Thus as Merleau-Ponty's gaze or rumination becomes more and more diffused in the shadowings and crosshatchings of his introspection, there is a corresponding illumination of history and the shared zone of human experience. For the subjective life is also the locus of our relations with others. "For the value is there. It consists of actively being what we are by chance, of establishing that communication with others and with ourselves for which our temporal structure gives us the opportunity and of which our liberty is only the rough outline."[11]

These are the last words of an essay in defense of Simone de Beauvoir, but a veiled reference to Sartre's theory of the absolute freedom of the *pour soi* is unmistakable. In contrast to Sartre, Merleau-Ponty emphasizes mutuality, interdependence,

11. *Sense and Nonsense*, p. 40. "Car la valeur est là. Elle consiste à être activement ce que nous sommes par hasard, à établir cette communication avec autrui et avec nous-mêmes dont notre structure temporelle nous offre la chance et dont notre liberté n'est que l'ébauche." "Le Roman et la métaphysique," *Sens et non-sens*, p. 80.

interrelatedness. "The communicative world [is not] a network of parallel consciousnesses. Our traces mix and intermingle; they make a single track of 'public temporality.'"[12]

It is in history, in this track of shared meaning, that Merleau-Ponty considers expression. All forms of art, including film and the plastic arts, express the artist both as individual and as *intermonde* or community of shared meanings. Because of the thematic closeness of "history" and "expression" we find Merleau-Ponty criticizing Sartre's view of literary expression in a lengthy critique of the latter's philosophy of history:

He [Sartre] is the same philosopher who, analyzing the act of reading, finds nothing between the writer's scrawl, the book in its physical existence and the meaning that the reader's consciousness puts into it. The interval [*entre-deux*], that is, the book taken according to its conventional interpretation, and the variations throughout time of that reading, and the way in which these layers of meaning accumulate and displace or indeed complete each other, in other words, the "metamorphosis" of the book and the history of its meaning, and my reading reinserted in that history, taken up by it, inserted by it as the book's provisional truth, none of all this, for Sartre, prevents the canonical meaning of the book from being that which I myself create while reading, nor that my reading, taken formally, becomes the criterion of all others. We cannot prevent ourselves from inserting into the leaves of the book lying on the table the thoughts that we have formed in reading it, and this makes it what we call a cultural object; on a higher plane, we imagine Julien Sorel like a phantom traveler who haunts one generation after another, different for each one, and we write literary history that attempts to connect these apparitions and to constitute the truth of Julien Sorel, the genesis of his total meaning. But, for Sartre, this universe of literature or of culture is an illusion: there is only the Julien Sorel of Stendhal, *and* that of Taine, *and* that of

12. My translation; for context, see *Signs*, p. 19. "Le monde communicatif n'est [pas] un faisceau de consciences parallèles. Les traces se brouillent et passent l'une dans l'autre, elles font un seul sillage de 'durée publique.'" *Signes*, p. 28.

Léon Blum, *and* that of Paul Bourget, and they represent as many irreducible absolutes.[13]

It is therefore in "the communicative world," in "the single track of public temporality," in the *entre-deux* of our shared existence with others that language is born. We may now narrow our gaze, from the field of total expression, to look more closely at the phenomenon of language itself. Once again, an antithetical construction, expressed by a pulsating rhythm of thought, is found.

Man signifies his presence to the world by speech, the typical act of incarnated consciousness as creator of meaning. Merleau-Ponty uses an ancient metaphor to convey the value of speech: he sees it as the illumination of being whose very reaching out toward the world is less a groping after objects in the dark than the seeking of light. Speech is the metaphor of the human "mixture," since it is in the concrete universal of

13. "Il est le même philosophe qui, analysant l'acte de lecture, ne voyait rien entre le grimoire, le livre dans son existence physique et le sens que la conscience du lecteur y met. L'entre-deux, c'est-à-dire le livre pris selon la signification qu'on lui donne d'ordinaire, et les changements avec le temps de cette lecture, et la manière dont ces couches de sens s'accumulent ou se déplacent l'une l'autre, ou même se complètent, bref la 'métamorphose' du livre et l'histoire de son sens, et ma lecture replacée dans cette histoire, comprise par elle, insérée par elle dans une vérité provisoire de ce livre, rien de tout cela pour Sartre, n'empêche que la forme canonique du sens soit celle que je fais être en lisant, moi, et que ma lecture, formellement considérée, soit la mesure de toute autre. Nous ne pouvons pas nous empêcher de mettre dans les feuillets du livre posé sur la table les pensées que nous avons formées en le lisant, et c'est ce qu'on appelle un objet culturel; à un niveau supérieur: nous imaginons Julien Sorel comme un fantôme baladeur qui hante les générations, toujours autre en chacune, et nous écrivons une histoire littéraire qui essaye de relier ces apparitions et de constituer une vérité de Julien Sorel, une genèse de son sens total. Mais, pour Sartre, cet univers de la littérature ou de la culture est une illusion: il n'y a que le Julien Sorel de Stendhal, *et* celui de Taine, *et* celui de Léon Blum, *et* celui de Paul Bourget, et ce sont autant d'absolus incompossibles." Merleau-Ponty, "Sartre et l'ultra-bolchevisme," *Les Aventures de la dialectique* (Paris: Gallimard, 1955), pp. 189–90.

language that we realize "we are indivisibly within and without."[14]

Language is the founding act of human communality:

There is one particular cultural object which is destined to play a crucial role in the perception of other people: language. In the experience of dialogue, there is constituted between the other person and myself a common ground; my thought and his are interwoven into a single fabric. . . . We have here a dual being, where the other is for me no longer a mere bit of behavior in my transcendental field, nor I in his; we are collaborators for each other in consummate reciprocity. Our perspectives merge into each other, and we co-exist through a common world.[15]

Within the communicating world, Merleau-Ponty distinguishes between the "spoken word" (*parole parlée*) and the "speaking word" (*parole parlante*), the first being the one whose meaning has been constituted by custom and usage, the language of *being*. The speaking word, which builds on the acquired meanings of the spoken one, is the language of *existence*.

Taught to speak by the spoken word in him, the artist expresses by his speaking word the reality at a specific historical moment of human consciousness which appears as an "openness" or, to use Sartre's term, a "hole in being." But while Merleau-Ponty considers the act of expression as partially negating prior spoken words, he insists far more than Sartre on the dependency, the continuity, the interrelatedness of this

14. *Signs*, p. 205. "Nous sommes indivisiblement au-dedans et au-dehors." *Signes*, p. 259.

15. *Phenomenology of Perception* (London: Routledge and Kegan Paul; New York: Humanities Press, 1962), p. 354. "Il y a, en particulier, un objet culturel qui va jouer un rôle essentiel dans la perception d'autrui: c'est le langage. Dans l'expérience du dialogue, il se constitue entre autrui et moi un terrain commun, ma pensée et la sienne ne font qu'un seul tissu. . . . Il y a là un être à deux, et autrui n'est plus ici pour moi un simple comportement dans mon champ transcendantal, ni d'ailleurs moi dans le sien, nous sommes l'un pour l'autre collaborateurs dans une réciprocité parfaite, nos perspectives glissent l'une dans l'autre, nous coexistons à travers un même monde." *Phénoménologie de la perception* (Paris: Gallimard, 1945), p. 407.

act. Language builds upon itself like a wave, projecting into the future specific forms or modes of expression which nonetheless remain open to forces of consciousness and creativity.

If we move from the consideration of the totality of expression as spoken word to the question of specific literary forms and genres, we can begin to envisage possibilities which no other aesthetic has allowed. A sonnet, a tragedy, a satire speak of the very incarnation of literary sensitivity in a context of expression. Each work, by the fact of what it is, evokes with it the multitude of all the forms it is not, all the options refused which yet remain as virtualities of the work, so that its speaking to us in a particular way is also a silent dialogue with the totality of the tradition. Notions such as "classic" and "romantic" describe equilibrium points at which the speaking word stands in a relation of opposition to the spoken word—innovation defines itself against tradition; yet also, through the silent dialogue, includes tradition. "Even when it is possible to date the emergence of a principle which exists 'for itself,' it is clear that the principle has been previously present in the culture as an obsession or anticipation, and that the act of consciousness which poses it as an explicit form does no more than render its long period of incubation operative."[16] The constant in tradition is the human body, and this is the primordial element which plays out against history to produce the changing yet interrelated forms of art. "Like the functioning of the body, that of words or paintings remains mysterious to me: words, lines, colors which express my thoughts come from me like my gestures; they are forced from me by what I want to say as my gestures are by what I want to do."[17]

16. Translation with a few revisions, *Signs*, p. 16. "Même quand il est possible de dater l'émergence d'un *principe pour soi*, il était auparavant présent dans la culture à titre de hantise ou d'anticipation, et la prise de conscience qui le pose comme signification explicite ne fait qu'achever sa longue incubation dans un sens opérant." "Le Langage indirect et les voix du silence," *Signes*, p. 52.

17. "Comme l'opération du corps, celle des mots ou des peintures me reste obscure: les mots, les traits, les couleurs qui m'expriment sortent de moi comme mes gestes, ils me sont arrachés

In a lengthy study of Cézanne, Merleau-Ponty shows the development of the painter's art as a dialectical encounter between tradition and the specificity of the body-subject. Cézanne's art attempts the apparently impossible reconciliation of the classical impulse to "imitate nature" with the impressionist aesthetic of sensation; but, according to Merleau-Ponty, Cézanne succeeds by fusing these two irreconcilables in a rendering of authentic perception which arises in the field of awareness generated by an incarnated spirit. Cézanne is a great painter precisely because he shows us how meaning appears as form, mass, contour, and color on the margins of physical existence; he shows us how the shape of an object or the expressiveness of a face arises mysteriously out of the chaos of sensation. Although Cézanne was a withdrawn and somewhat schizoid personality, his art creates a human community; it converts into "visible object" that viscous and equivocal reality which had previously remained locked in individual human spirits. So it is that art joins disparate lives, and the artist's private delirium becomes the basis of a shared world.

It is in his essay on Cézanne that Merleau-Ponty has best shown how doubt, as an intentional structure, becomes the basis for a new and authentic vision. Cézanne is the artist who feels at an early age the commitment of a vocation, yet doubts that vocation because it contradicts the "natural attitude," that is, it must measure itself against the power of an already achieved tradition which has articulated clear and distinct ideas; yet the vocation is no more than a confused obsession, a delirium or a dream. With no more to go on than a "vague fever," the artist proceeds, over a period of many years, to create not merely a personal vision but (despite his intense reserve and the public's hostility) the experience that will embed this vision in other spirits. Returning to the comparison we used at the outset: Cézanne was forced not merely to

---

par ce que je veux dire comme mes gestes par ce que je veux faire." "Le Langage indirect et les voix du silence," *Les Temps Modernes* 8 (1952): 83, quoted by Kaelin, *An Existentialist Aesthetic: The Theories of Sartre and Merleau-Ponty* (Madison: University of Wisconsin Press, 1962), p. 278.

create the map of an unknown world but to provide landmarks that would generate an echo of recognition and an emotional response in others. Despite his success, Cézanne continued to the end a prisoner of doubt, since he was (as was Merleau-Ponty himself) a creator who believed that truth is essentially the unknown if not the unknowable. What Merleau-Ponty said of Cézanne might apply to the philosopher himself: "Only one emotion is possible for this painter—the feeling of strangeness—and only one lyricism—that of the continual rebirth of existence."[18]

From Merleau-Ponty's descriptions, we can move to a better understanding of the artistic or literary work as constitutive of a human presence, to be understood as a sector of intersubjectivity which no single stream of discourse can define or exhaust. We realize that there is finally no "explanation" of the work but only a ceaseless referring back through it to its source in consciousness.

There is a constant unity of attitude in all of Merleau-Ponty's statements about the arts, although this attitude faces in different directions and is elaborated into a large number of descriptions. This attitude is implied in the statement quoted at the outset on the convergence of literature and philosophy. Merleau-Ponty does not see the work of art as something "made" but as the vehicle through which perceptions assume a form wherein they can be communicated and described. Art, described as "giving speech to what is perceived" (*faire parler ce qui est senti*) is, with introspection, the major source for data about perception; Merleau-Ponty's lectures at the Collège de France were studded with illustrations from Proust, Stendhal, Balzac, and contemporary writers such as Michel Butor and Claude Simon.

Merleau-Ponty first discussed the perception of time in literature apropos of *L'Invitée* of Simone de Beauvoir, using temporality as the category through which the principal character, Françoise, came to experience her contingency.

18. *Sense and Nonsense*, p. 18. "Pour ce peintre-là, une seule émotion est possible: le sentiment d'étrangeté, un seul lyrisme: celui de l'existence toujours recommencée." "Le Doute de Cézanne," *Sens et non-sens*, p. 33.

Every being suffers a "perpetual malaise." This malaise arises from awareness of the existence of others: "And so we try to subdue the disquieting existence of others."[19] He shows us how Françoise attempts to escape this destiny by the construction of an unworkable "dual being" ("être à deux") in her relationship with Pierre. But the arrival of Xavière (the "invitée" of the title) shatters this false happiness. Françoise is then plunged back into contingency, into temporality, and the critic comments:

The future ceases to be the natural extension of the present, time is fragmented, and Françoise is no more than an anonymous being, a creature without a history, a mass of chilled flesh. She now knows there are situations which cannot be communicated and which can only be understood by living them. There was a unique pulsation which projected before her a living present, a future, a world, which animated language for her—and that pulsation has stopped.[20]

The essay concludes with a further attempt to convey temporality, the mode in which Françoise experiences contingency:

Her book shows existence understood between two limits: on the one hand, there is the immediate closed tightly upon itself, short of any word and any commitment (Xavière); and, on the other, there is an absolute confidence in language and rational decision, an existence which grows empty in the effort to transcend itself (Françoise at the beginning of the book). Between these fragments of time and that eternity which erroneously believes it transcends time, there is an actual existence which unfolds in patterns of behavior, is organized like a

19. *Sense and Nonsense*, p. 29. "Nous essayons donc de mettre en sommeil l'inquiétante existence d'autrui." "Le Roman et la métaphysique," *Sens et non-sens*, p. 58.

20. *Sense and Nonsense*, p. 33. "L'avenir cesse d'être le prolongement naturel du présent, le temps se fragmente, Françoise n'est plus qu'un être anonyme, sans histoire, une masse de chair transie. Elle sait maintenant qu'il y a des situations incommunicables et qu'on ne peut comprendre qu'en les occupant. Il y a une pulsation unique qui projetait devant elle un présent vivant, un avenir, un monde, qui animait pour elle le langage—et cette pulsation a cessé. *Sens et non-sens*, p. 65.

melody, and, by means of its projects, cuts across time without leaving it. There is undoubtedly no *solution* to human problems; no way, for example, to eliminate the transcendence of time, the separation of consciousnesses which may always reappear to threaten our commitments; no way to test the authenticity of these commitments which may always, in a moment of fatigue, seem artificial conventions to us. But between these two extremes at which existence perishes, total existence is our decision by which we enter time in order to create our life within it. All human projects are contradictory because they simultaneously attract and repel their realization. One only pursues a thing in order to possess it, and yet, if what I am looking for today must someday be found (which is to say, passed beyond), why bother to look for it? Because today is today and tomorrow, tomorrow.[21]

Merleau-Ponty writes with a certain opacity here, perhaps because he is not able to fully transmute Simone de Beauvoir's ontology into his own. More luminous and complete are those descriptions of temporality given in *Phénoménologie de la perception*.

21. Translation with a few revisions, *Sense and Nonsense*, pp. 39–40. "Son livre montre l'existence comprise entre deux limites, d'un côté l'immédiat fermé sur lui-même, en deçà de toute parole et de tout engagement,—c'est Xavière,—de l'autre une confiance absolue dans le langage et dans les décisions rationnelles, une existence qui se vide à force de se transcender, c'est Françoise au début du livre. Entre ce temps morcelé et cette éternité qui croit faussement transcender le temps, se trouve l'existence effective, qui se déploie en cycles de conduite, s'organise à la facon d'une mélodie et par ses projets traverse le temps sans le quitter. Sans doute il n'y a pas de *solution* aux problèmes humains: aucun moyen d'éliminer la transcendance du temps, la séparation des consciences, qui peuvent toujours reparaître et menacer nos engagements, aucun moyen de vérifier l'authenticité de ces engagements, qui peuvent toujours, dans un moment de fatigue, nous apparaître comme des conventions factices. Mais entre ces deux limites ou elle périt, l'existence totale est la décision par laquelle nous entrons dans le temps pour y créer notre vie. Tout projet humain est contradictoire, puisqu'il appelle et repousse à la fois sa réalisation. On ne chercherait jamais rien si ce n'était pour l'obtenir, et pourtant, si ce que je recherche aujourd'hui doit être un jour atteint, c'est-à-dire depassé, pourquoi le rechercher? Il faut le rechercher parce que aujourd'hui est aujourd'hui et demain, demain." *Sens et non-sens*, pp. 79–80.

If consciousness, throughout the writings of Merleau-Ponty, might be defined as that which always remains itself while becoming other, the most crucial form of this behavior is manifested in regard to time, which is a ceaseless *rétention* or reaching back coupled with a ceaseless *protension* or reaching forward. The Husserlian terms, *rétention* and *protension*, together create a present time at which juncture the self emerges. But the self is maker of meanings, and hence we are not surprised to read that "time and meaning are identical," thereby completing a typically circular series of definitions.

To clarify his discussion of time, Merleau-Ponty gives as example the appearance of jealousy as one phase of Swann's love for Odette. Commenting on the appearance of jealousy as an apparently *new* phenomenon, he maintains that the notion of causality does not apply in the domain of the psychic. Swann's love cannot be shown to change into jealousy by any precise mechanism; rather, that love *is* jealousy from its very beginning. Swann's jealousy is not an accident of character, arising in time, but is the very structure of his existence. Thus do past, present, and future ceaselessly imply and "conjugate" each other. This is not to imagine any transcendental or absolute time but only to look closely at the temporal dimension of subjectivity.

It is clear from the examples given that Merleau-Ponty does not use time as a category to "explain" the novels of Simone de Beauvoir or Proust but takes the novelistic situation as a concrete demonstration of a reality beyond concepts not to be otherwise clarified. His procedure thus differs from that of Georges Poulet, whose *Etudes sur le temps humain* (1949) moves in the same mode as *Phénoménologie de la perception*. As does Merleau-Ponty, Poulet uses time as the central category to understand consciousness; he is perhaps even guilty of a certain hyperbole, since time becomes a category that devours all the others. Merleau-Ponty, the trained philosopher, is more rigorous in distinguishing the categories of consciousness, while Poulet tends to assimilate them all to *durée*; on the other hand, Poulet shows vastly more sensitivity to the texture of literary works. These have a largely exemplary function for Merleau-Ponty; it appears that he does not, in fact, make the effort of submission to and reconstruction of their temporal structure.

When the category of the temporal is chosen as the key to subjectivity, there is an inevitable heightening of the dramatic and absurd fact of contingency. Merleau-Ponty envisages contingency—that is to say, Death—through the eyes of Montaigne:

Death is *the act of one person alone*. In the confused mass of being, death cuts out that particular zone which is ourselves. It puts in matchless evidence that inexhaustible source of opinions, dreams, and passions which secretly gave life to the spectacle of the world. And thus it teaches us better than any episode of life the fundamental accident which made us appear and will make us disappear.[22]

In an even more extraordinary text, Merleau-Ponty analyzes the intuition of death as an aesthetic effect:

Like a painting, a novel expresses tacitly. Its subject, like that of a painting, can be related. But Julien Sorel's trip to Verrières and his attempt to kill Mme de Rênal after he has learned that she has betrayed him are not as important as that silence, that dream-like journey, that unthinking certitude, and that eternal resolution which follow the news. Now these things are nowhere said. There is no need of a "Julien thought" or a "Julien wished." In order to express them, Stendhal had only to insinuate himself into Julien and make objects, obstacles, means, and hazards appear before our eyes with the swiftness of the journey. He had only to decide to narrate in one page instead of five. That brevity, that unusual proportion of things omitted to things said, is not even the result of a *choice*. Consulting his own sensitivity to others, Stendhal suddenly found an imaginary body for Julien which was more agile than his own body. As if in a second life, he made the trip to Verrières according to a cadence of cold

22. *Signs*, pp. 201–2. "La mort est *l'acte à un seul personnage*. Elle découpe dans la masse confuse de l'être cette zone particulière qui est nous, elle met dans une évidence sans seconde cette source inépuisable d'opinions, de rêves et de passions qui animait secrètement le spectacle du monde, et ainsi elle nous enseigne mieux qu'aucun épisode de la vie le hasard fondamental qui nous a fait paraître et nous fera disparaître." "Lecture de Montaigne," *Signes*, p. 255.

passion which itself decided what was visible and what was invisible, what was to be said and what was to remain unspoken. The death urge is thus not in the words at all. It is between them, in the hollows of space, time, and signification they mark out, as movement at the cinema is between the immobile images which follow one another.

The novelist speaks for his reader, and every man to every other, the language of the initiated—initiated into the world and into the universe of possibilities confined in a human body and a human life. What he has to say he supposes known. He takes up his dwelling in a character's behavior and gives the reader only a suggestion of it, its nervous and peremptory trace in the surroundings. If the author is a writer (that is, if he is capable of finding the elisions and caesuras which indicate the behavior), the reader responds to his appeal and joins him at the virtual center of the writing, *even if neither one of them is aware of it*. The novel as a report of events and an announcement of ideas, theses, or conclusions—as manifest or prosaic meaning—and the novel as expression of a style—as oblique and latent meaning—are in a simple relationship of homonymy.[23]

23. Translation with a few revisions, *Signs*, p. 76. "Un roman exprime tacitement comme un tableau. On peut raconter le sujet du roman comme celui du tableau. Mais ce qui compte, ce n'est pas tant que Julien Sorel, apprenant qu'il est trahi par Mme de Reynal, aille à Verrières et essaie de la tuer—c'est, après la nouvelle, ce silence, ce voyage de rêve, cette certitude sans pensées, cette résolution éternelle. Or cela n'est *dit* nulle part. Il n'est pas besoin de 'Julien pensait,' 'Julien voulait.' Il suffit, pour exprimer, que Stendhal se glisse en Julien et fasse paraître sous nos yeux, à la vitesse du voyage, les objets, les obstacles, les moyens, les hasards, Il suffit qu'il décide de raconter en une page au lieu de raconter en cinq. Cette brièveté, cette proportion inusitée des choses omises aux choses dites, ne résulte pas même d'un choix. Consultant sa propre sensibilité à autrui, Stendhal lui a trouvé soudain un corps imaginaire plus agile que son propre corps, il a fait comme dans une vie seconde le voyage de Verrières selon une cadence de passion sèche qui choisissait pour lui le visible et l'invisible, ce qu'il y avait à dire et à taire. La volonté de mort, elle n'est donc nulle part dans les mots: elle est entre eux, dans les creux d'espace, de temps, de significations qu'ils délimitent, comme le mouvement au cinéma est entre les images immobiles qui se suivent. Le romancier tient à son lecteur, et tout homme à tout homme, un langage d'initiés au monde, à l'univers de possibles que détient un corps humain, une vie humaine. Ce qu'il a à dire, il le suppose connu, il s'installe dans la conduite d'un per-

The passage begins with the statement of an apparent commonplace: "A novel expresses tacitly . . ." To illustrate, he turns to a scene from *Le Rouge et le noir*. What counts here are unspoken qualities ("nowhere said") which he describes as "silence . . . dream-like journey . . . unthinking certitude . . . eternal resolution." But how is the *tacit* communication achieved? What is happening when Stendhal communicates tacitly? Merleau-Ponty insists that the novel is its author's subjectivity: "Stendhal had only to insinuate himself into Julien . . ." Next, a series of observations enumerates with great rapidity the intuitive calculations of the author, who is simultaneously himself (Stendhal), the character (Julien), and the reader ("his own sensitivity to others"). This calculation is carried on by Stendhal in an imaginary body, hurtling along the road to Verrières. Behind his "cold passion" there is "the death urge." A metaphysical category now begins to arise from what had been but a moment before description of places, objects. Merleau-Ponty continues with a series of statements that reverberate in both the philosophic and the aesthetic dimensions: literature is a system of signs, operating in an intersubjective sector where meanings are given, yet where signs create a center of attraction which is the very communication of reader and author. The work then is a gift, an act of generosity, but more than that, a call, a solicitation to the most total kind of intersubjective intimacy.

Merleau-Ponty insists that the work has a privilege of truth, that the "being for others" which begins in language is carried in literature to a point at which the very completeness of communication makes communication more difficult. The

---

sonnage et n'en donne au lecteur que la griffe, la trace nerveuse et péremptoire dans l'entourage. Si l'auteur est écrivain, c'est-à-dire capable de trouver les élisions et les césures qui signent la conduite, le lecteur répond à son appel et le rejoint au centre virtuel de l'écrit, *même si l'un ni l'autre ne le connaissent*. Le roman comme compte rendu d'événements, comme énoncé d'idées, thèses ou conclusions, comme signification manifeste ou prosaïque, et le roman comme opération d'un style, signification oblique ou latente, sont dans un simple rapport d'homonymie." "Le Langage indirect et les voix du silence," *Signes*, pp. 95–96.

generosity of the work is somehow inhuman. This is the paradoxical movement once again, the swinging back of the pendulum. The intimacy, the *entre-deux*, of literary expression is true and false, an affirmation and a denial.

As for the writer, he well knows that there is no common measure between his rumination of his life and the clearest, most readable things it has been able to produce; that the comedy here would consist in playing the oracle; that after all, if those who take a fancy to him want to meet him, he has already made a rendezvous with them in his books; that the shortest way towards him leads through them; and finally that he is a man who works at living and can give no one a dispensation from the work of reading and the labor of living.[24]

The work stands as an enigma, saying more and less than we can understand. Excess and deficiency, light and shadow, solipsism and gift. "Solitude and communication cannot be the two horns of a dilemma, but two 'moments' of one phenomenon."[25] The enigma communicates, and in the writings of Merleau-Ponty it becomes the norm of all communication. In an age of the absurd, where irrationality has seized the instruments of human expression in a death grasp, Merleau-Ponty's aesthetic of doubt may prove to be the basis of a new affirmation.

BIBLIOGRAPHY

WORKS BY MERLEAU-PONTY

La Structure du comportement. Bibliothèque de Philosophie Contemporaine. Paris: Presses Universitaires de France, 1942. Preface, "Une

24. Translation with a few revisions, *Signs*, p. 318. "L'écrivain, lui, sait bien qu'il n'y a pas de commune mesure entre la rumination de sa vie et ce qu'elle a pu produire de plus clair et de plus lisible, que la comédie serait ici de jouer les oracles, qu'après tout, si l'on veut le rencontrer, il a déjà donné rendez-vous aux amateurs dans ses livres, que le plus court chemin vers lui passe par eux, enfin qu'il est un homme qui travaille à vivre, et ne peut dispenser personne du travail de lire et du travail de vivre." "Sur Claudel," *Signes*, pp. 396–97.

25. *Phenomenology of Perception*, p. 359. "La solitude et la communication ne doivent pas être les deux termes d'une alternative, mais deux moments d'un seul phénomène." *Phénoménologie de la perception*, p. 412.

philosophie de l'ambiguïté," by Alphonse de Waehlens. (*The Structure of Behavior*. Translated by Alden Fisher. Foreword by John Wild. London: Methuen; Boston: Beacon Press, 1963.) A study of the physical and physiological basis of behavior, leading to a critique of scientific anthropology and psychology. Development of a new *gestalt* theory or theory of forms. Distinction of orders of reality: the physical, the vital, the human.

Phénoménologie de la perception. Bibliothèque des Idées. Paris: Gallimard, 1945. (*Phenomenology of Perception*. Translated by Colin Smith. International Library of Philosophy and Scientific Method. London: Routledge and Kegan Paul; New York: Humanities Press, 1962.) The preface is a brief statement of Merleau-Ponty's view of phenomenology. The first part of the book considers bodily existence as giver of meaning; the second part studies the categories of perception. In this book Merleau-Ponty gives "a way of seeing the world and of seeing himself within the world" (Paul Ricoeur).

Humanisme et terreur. Les Essais. Paris: Gallimard, 1947. A study of communism. Merleau-Ponty asks if Marxism has an inhuman character. (One part of *Humanisme et terreur*: "The Yogi and the Proletarian." Translated by Nancy Metzel and John Flodstrom. In *The Primacy of Perception and Other Essays on Phenomenological Psychology, the Philosophy of Art, History, and Politics*. Edited, with an introduction, by James M. Edie. Northwestern Studies in Phenomenology and Existential Philosophy. Evanston, Ill.: Northwestern University Press, 1964. Besides the translation of other essays, indicated below, this volume includes an unpublished text by Merleau-Ponty: "A Prospectus of His Work." Translated by Arleen B. Dallery.)

"Le Primat de la perception et ses conséquences philosophiques," *Bulletin de la Société Française de Philosophie* 41 (1947): 119–53. ("The Primacy of Perception and Its Philosophical Consequences." Translated by James M. Edie. In *The Primacy of Perception and Other Essays*.)

Sens et non-sens. Pensées. Paris: Nagel, 1948. (*Sense and Nonsense*. Translated, with a preface, by Hubert L. Dreyfus and Patricia Allen Dreyfus. Northwestern University Studies in Phenomenology and Existential Philosophy. Evanston, Ill.: Northwestern University Press, 1964.) Contains essays on Cézanne, Simone de Beauvoir, Sartre, and film in the first section titled "Ouvrages."

Eloge de la philosophie. Paris: Gallimard, 1953. Inaugural Lecture, Collège de France. (*In Praise of Philosophy*. Translated with a preface by John Wild and James M. Edie. Northwestern University Studies in Phenomenology and Existential Philosophy. Evanston, Ill.: Northwestern University Press, 1963.)

Les Aventures de la dialectique. Paris: Gallimard, 1955. Contains the essay, "Sartre et l'ultra-bolchevisme," which studies Sartre's attempt to rethink communism. "Where communism places dialectics in an inhuman nature, Sartre deduces communist action from a dictate of free will. . . . Sartre disregards true history and knows only the history conceived by him, in which Marx, Lenin, Stalin and Duclos can no longer be distinguished from one another or even from Sartre himself. Sartre is the absolute thinker, for whom everything becomes an object and who, therefore, is able neatly to gather everything in a coherent and clear synthesis" (Kwant, *The Phenomenological Philosophy of Merleau-Ponty*, p. 212). (One part of *Les Aventures de la dialectique*: "The Crisis of the Understanding." Translated by Nancy Metzel and John Flodstrom. In *The Primacy of Perception and Other Essays*.)

Editor. *Les Philosophes célèbres*. La Galerie des Hommes Célèbres. Collaboration of Ferdinand Alquié et al. Paris: L. Mazenod, 1956. Contains sections by Merleau-Ponty: "Christianisme et philosophie," "Le Grand Rationalisme," "La Découverte de l'histoire," "La Découverte de la subjectivité," etc.

Signes. Paris: Gallimard, 1960. These essays, published the year before Merleau-Ponty's death, represent his mature thought and are the best introduction to his work. Of special interest are "Le Langage indirect et les voix du silence," his most complete statement on the aesthetics of language, and "Lecture de Montaigne," in which Merleau-Ponty draws his own portrait using Montaigne as a *persona*. (*Signs*. Translated, with an introduction, by Richard C. McCleary. Northwestern University Studies in Phenomenology and Existential Philosophy. Evanston, Ill.: Northwestern University Press, 1964. McCleary's introduction represents the best brief statement in English on Merleau-Ponty.)

Les Relations avec autrui chez l'enfant. Les Cours de Sorbonne. Paris: Centre de Documentation Universitaire, 1960. ("The Child's Relations with Others." Translated by William Cobb. In *The Primacy of Perception and Other Essays*.)

Les Sciences de l'homme et la phénoménologie. Les Cours de Sorbonne. Paris: Centre de Documentation Universitaire, 1963. ("Phenomenology and the Sciences of Man." Translated by John Wild. In *The Primacy of Perception and Other Essays*.)

"Cinq Notes sur Claude Simon," *Médiations*, no. 4 (1961), pp. 5–10. Brief but illuminating notes on perception in the novel with reference to Butor and Claude Simon.

L'Oeil et l'esprit. Paris: Gallimard, 1964. ("Eye and Mind." Translated by Carleton Dallery. In *The Primacy of Perception and Other Essays*.)

Le Visible et l'invisible: suivi de notes de travail. Edited by Claude Lefort. Paris: Gallimard, 1964. The book on which Merleau-Ponty was working at the time of his death. (*The Visible and the Invisible*. Translated by Alphonso Lingis. Northwestern University Studies in Phenomenology and Existential Philosophy. Evanston, Ill.: Northwestern University Press, 1968.)

"Pages d' 'Introduction à la prose du monde.'" Edited by Claude Lefort. *Revue de Métaphysique et de Morale* 72 (1967): 139–53.

Résumés de cours, Collège de France, 1952–1960. Paris: Gallimard, 1968. (*Themes from the Lectures at the Collège de France, 1952–1960*. Translated by John O'Neill. Northwestern University Studies in Phenomenology and Existential Philosophy. Evanston, Ill.: Northwestern University Press, 1970.)

L'Union de l'âme et du corps chez Malebranche, Biran et Bergson. Notes taken at Merleau-Ponty's course, edited by Jean Deprun. Bibliothèque d'Histoire et de Philosophie. Paris: J. Vrin, 1968.

The Essential Writings of Merleau-Ponty. Edited by Alden L. Fisher. New York: Harcourt, Brace and World, 1969. Anthology, with bibliography.

SELECTED STUDIES ON MERLEAU-PONTY

Books and Special Numbers

Deguy, Michel. "Le Visible et l'invisible." *Nouvelle Revue Française* 12 (1964): 1062–72.

Donato, Eugenio. "Language, Vision and Phenomenology: Merleau-Ponty as a Test Case." *Modern Language Notes* 85 (1970): 803–14.

Doubrovsky, Serge. *Pourquoi la nouvelle critique*. Paris: Mercure de France, 1966. A closely reasoned polemic in defense of the new criticism. Parts II and III draw extensively on the position of Merleau-Ponty.

Hyppolite, Jean. *Sens et existence dans la philosophie de Maurice Merleau-Ponty*. The Zaharoff Lecture. Oxford: Clarendon Press, 1963.

Kaelin, Eugene F. *An Existentialist Aesthetic: The Theories of Sartre and Merleau-Ponty*. Madison: University of Wisconsin Press, 1962. A thoroughgoing work which studies the aesthetic implications of Merleau-Ponty's phenomenology. Of special interest is the comparison with Croce.

Kwant, Remigius C. *The Phenomenological Philosophy of Merleau-Ponty*. Translated from the Dutch by Henry J. Koren. Duquesne Studies, Philosophical Series. Pittsburgh: Duquesne University Press, 1963.

This highly readable book simplifies Merleau-Ponty's thought without undue loss of content. It represents the best available introduction to his work in English.

"Présence de Merleau-Ponty." *Critique* 20 (1964): 1007–64 (articles by Jules Vuillemin, André Green, and Pierre Kaufman).

Robinet, André. *Merleau-Ponty, sa vie, son oeuvre, avec un exposé de sa philosophie*. Philosophes. Paris: Presses Universitaires de France, 1963.

Spiegelberg, Herbert. In *The Phenomenological Movement, II*, pp. 516–62. Phaenomenologica. The Hague: M. Nijhoff, 1960. 2d ed. 1965.

Les Temps Modernes 17 (1961): 193–436. Special number devoted to Merleau-Ponty. (Selected articles listed individually below name of author.)

Thévenaz, Pierre. *What Is Phenomenology? And Other Essays*. Translated by James M. Edie, Charles Courtney, and Paul Brockelman. Edited with an introduction by James M. Edie. Preface by John Wild. Chicago: Quadrangle Books, 1962. Part on Merleau-Ponty (pp. 83–89). Excellent brief introduction to phenomenology, translated from the writings of the Swiss philosopher.

Waelhens, Alphonse de. *Une Philosophie de l'ambiguïté: l'existentialisme de Maurice Merleau-Ponty*. Bibliothèque Philosophique de Louvain. Louvain: Publications Universitaires de Louvain, 1951. A. de Waelhens is the outstanding interpreter of Merleau-Ponty. This eloquent work not only expounds Merleau-Ponty's philosophy but responds to it. An attempt is made to base an aesthetic on the writings about Cézanne and Simone de Beauvoir.

Zaner, Richard M. *The Problem of Embodiment: Some Contributions to a Phenomenology of the Body*. Phaenomenologica. The Hague: M. Nijhoff, 1964.

Articles

Beauvoir, Simone de. "Merleau-Ponty et le pseudo-sartrisme." *Les Temps Modernes* 10 (1955): 2072–2122. Reprinted in *Privilèges*, pp. 201–72. Les Essais, Paris: Gallimard, 1955. Response to Merleau-Ponty's essay on Sartre in *Les Aventures de la dialectique*. A violent attack on Merleau-Ponty, which is also a good exposé of Sartre's ontology. Mme. de Beauvoir accuses Merleau-Ponty of delirium and bad faith in his critique of Sartre; she herself is not exempt in these pages from the former of these vagaries.

Hyppolite, Jean. "Existence et dialectique dans la philosophie de Merleau-Ponty." *Les Temps Modernes* 17 (1961): 228–44.

Lacan, Jacques. "Maurice Merleau-Ponty." *Les Temps Modernes* 17 (1961): 245–54. A Mallarmean tribute to Merleau-Ponty by the psychoanalyst with whom Merleau-Ponty discussed many of his theories.

Lefort, Claude. "L'Idée d' 'être brut' at d' 'esprit sauvage.'" *Les Temps Modernes* 17 (1961): 255–86.

Lewis, Philip E. "Merleau-Ponty and the Phenomenology of Language." *Yale French Studies*, no. 36–37 (1966), pp. 19–40.

McCleary, Richard C. Introduction to *Signs* (see above).

Pontalis, J.-B. "Note sur le problème de l'inconscient chez Merleau-Ponty." *Les Temps Modernes* 17 (1961): 287–303.

Pariente, Jean-Claude. "Lecture de Merleau-Ponty." *Critique* 18 (1962): 957–74, 1067–78.

Ricoeur, Paul. "Hommage à Merleau-Ponty." *Esprit* (1961), pp. 1115–20. A tribute to Merleau-Ponty by the philosopher who best continues his themes and style of thought.

Said, Edward W. "Labyrinth of Incarnations: The Essays of Maurice Merleau-Ponty." *Kenyon Review* 29 (1967): 54–68.

Sartre, Jean-Paul. "Merleau-Ponty vivant." *Les Temps Modernes* 17 (1961): 304–76. Reprinted as "Merleau-Ponty." In *Situations IV: Portraits*, pp. 189–287. Paris: Gallimard, 1964. (In *Situations*, pp. 225–326. Translated by Benita Eisler. New York: Braziller, 1965.) Sartre's tribute to his fellow philosopher takes the form of an "existential psychoanalysis" which finds the secret of Merleau-Ponty in the despair of a man whose childhood had been too perfect, a man unable to free himself from the past and work with conviction for the future.

Waehlens, Alphonse de. "Situation de Merleau-Ponty." *Les Temps Modernes* 17 (1961): 377–98. A statement by the outstanding authority on Merleau-Ponty, especially valuable for the concise distinction of the philosophical bases of Merleau-Ponty's two major works.

Wahl, Jean. "Cette Pensée . . ." *Les Temps Modernes* 17 (1961): 399–436.

Paul de Man **11**

Maurice Blanchot

Since the end of the war, French literature has been dominated by a succession of quickly alternating intellectual fashions that have kept alive the illusion of a fecund and productive modernity. First came the vogue of Sartre, Camus, and the humanistic existentialism that followed immediately in the wake of the war; then came the experimentalism of the new theater, which was succeeded in turn by the advent of the *nouveau roman* and its epigones. These movements are, to a large extent, superficial and ephemeral; the trace they will leave on the history of French literature is bound to be slighter than it appears within the necessarily limited perspective of our own contemporaneity. Not all the more significant literary figures have definitely remained aloof from these trends; several took part in them and fell under their influence. But the true quality of their literary vocation can be tested by the persistence with which they kept intact a more essential part of themselves, a part that remained untouched by the vicissitudes of a literary production oriented toward public recognition, arcane and esoteric as this "public" may have been. In some, like Sartre, this self-assertion took the form of a frantic attempt to maintain a firm inner commitment in open and polemical contact with the changing trends. But others kept themselves more consciously out of the reach of the surface waves and were carried by a slower and deeper current, closer to the continuities that link French writing of today to its past. When we are able to observe the period with more detachment, the main proponents of contemporary French literature may well turn out to be figures that now seem shadowy in comparison with the celebrities of the hour. And none is more likely to achieve future prominence than the little-publicized and difficult writer Maurice Blanchot.

Even the fashionable trends to which we alluded are characterized by a constant intermingling of literary practice and critical theory. Sartre and his group were the theoretical exponents of their own stylistic devices, and the affinities between structuralist criticism and the *nouveau roman* are obvious. In Blanchot, the same interplay occurs, in a more complex and problematic way, between his work as a writer of narrative prose and his critical essays. An intensely private figure who has kept his personal affairs strictly to himself and whose pronouncements on public issues, literary or political, have been very scarce, Blanchot is known primarily as a critic. A sizable group of readers have followed his essays, often appearing in the form of topical book reviews in various journals, none of them particularly esoteric or avant-garde: the *Journal des Débats*, *Critique*, more recently the *Nouvelle Revue Française*, to which Blanchot used to contribute a monthly article. These essays have been gathered in volumes—*Faux-pas* (1943), *La Part du feu* (1949), *L'Espace littéraire* (1955), *Le Livre à venir* (1959)—that bring out an almost obsessive preoccupation with a few fundamental concerns, thus reducing their apparent diversity to an implacably repetitive uniformity. The influence of the critical work has been far-reaching. More philosophical and abstract than Charles Du Bos and less conducive to practical application than Bachelard's theories of material imagery, Blanchot's criticism has remained aloof from recent methodological debates and polemics. Yet his already considerable impact is bound to increase; rather than directly affecting existing critical methods, his work questions the very conditions basic to all critical discourse and thus leads the reader toward a level of awareness that no other contemporary critic has reached.

It is clear that Blanchot derives much of his insight into the work of others from his own experience as a writer of narrative prose.[1] Up to now, his novels and *récits* have remained

1. Some of these fictions are called novels, such as the original version of *Thomas l'obscur* (1941), *Aminadab* (1942), *Le Très-haut* (1948), while others are called *récits*: *Thomas l'obscur*, new version (1950), *Au Moment voulu* (1951), *Celui qui ne m'accompagnait pas* (1953).

nearly inaccessible in their labyrinthine obscurity. All that has to be said about them, in an article dealing with the critical work, is that it is fortunately a great deal easier to gain access to the fiction of Blanchot through his criticism than the other way around. The crux of the interpretation of this writer, one of the most important of the century, lies no doubt in a clarification of the relationship between the critical and the narrative part of his work; a description of the movement of his critical mind is a valid preliminary to such an inquiry.

Reading Maurice Blanchot differs from all other reading experiences. One begins by being seduced by the limpidity of a language that allows for no discontinuities or inconsistencies. Blanchot is, in a way, the clearest, the most lucid of writers. He steadily borders on the inexpressible and approaches the extreme of ambiguity, but he always recognizes them for what they are; consequently, as in Kant, the horizon of our understanding remains clearly circumscribed. When we read him on one of the poets or novelists he happens to choose for a theme, we readily forget all we had assumed we knew about this writer. This does not happen because Blanchot's insight necessarily compels us to modify our own perspective; this is by no means always the case. Returning afterwards to the author in question, we will find ourselves back at the same point, our understanding barely enriched by the comments of the critic. Blanchot, in fact, never intended to perform a task of exegesis that would combine earlier acquired knowledge with new elucidations. The clarity of his critical meditations is not due to their exegetic power; they seem clear, not because they penetrate further into a dark and inaccessible domain, but because they suspend the very act of comprehension. The light they cast on texts is of a different type. Nothing, in fact, could be more obscure than the nature of this light.

For how are we to understand a reading process which, in Blanchot's words, is located "before or beyond the act of understanding"?[2] The difficulty of defining this conception

2. ". . . au delà ou en deçà de la compréhension." *L'Espace littéraire* (Paris: Gallimard, 1955), p. 205.

indicates how much it differs from our ordinary assumptions about criticism. Blanchot's critical reflections offer us no personal confessions or intimate experiences, nothing that would give immediate access to another person's consciousness and allow the reader to espouse its movements. A certain degree of inwardness prevails in his work and makes it into the very opposite of an objective narrative. But this intimacy does not seem to belong to a particularized self, for his prose reveals nothing about his private experience. The language is as little a language of self-confession as it is a language of exegesis. And, even in the articles that are obviously inspired by topical literary considerations, it is least of all a language of evaluation or of opinion. In reading Blanchot, we are not participating in an act of judgment, of sympathy, or of understanding. As a result, the fascination we experience is accompanied by a feeling of resistance, by a refusal to be led to a confrontation with something opaque on which our consciousness can find no hold. The ambivalence of this experience can be somewhat clarified by Blanchot's own statements.

> The act of reading does not change anything, nor does it add anything to what was already there; it lets things be the way they were; it is a form of freedom, not the freedom that gives or takes away, but a freedom that accepts and consents, that says yes. It can only say yes and, in the space opened up by this affirmation, it allows the work to assert itself as the unsettling decision of its will to be—and nothing more.[3]

At first sight, this passive and silent encounter with the work seems to be the very opposite of what we usually call interpretation. It differs entirely from the subject-object polarities involved in objective observation. The literary work is given no objective status whatever; it has no existence apart from that constituted by the inward act of reading. Neither are we dealing with a so-called intersubjective or interpersonal act,

3. "La lecture ne fait rien, n'ajoute rien; elle laisse être ce qui est; elle est liberté, non pas liberté qui donne l'être ou le saisit, mais liberté qui accueille, consent, dit oui, ne peut que dire oui et, dans l'espace ouvert par ce oui, laisse s'affirmer la décision bouleversante de l'oeuvre, l'affirmation qu'elle est—et rien de plus." Ibid., p. 202.

in which two subjects engage in a self-clarifying dialogue. It would be more accurate to say that the two subjectivities involved, that of the author and that of the reader, cooperate in making each other forget their distinctive identity and destroy each other as subjects. Both move beyond their respective particularity toward a common ground that contains both of them, united by the impulse that makes them turn away from their particular selves. It is by means of the act of reading that this turning away takes place; the possibility of being read transforms, for the author, his language from a mere project into a work (and thus forever detaches it from him). In turn, it brings the reader back for a moment, to what he might have been before he shaped himself into a particular self.

This conception of reading seems to differ altogether from interpretation. "It adds nothing to what was already there," says Blanchot, whereas it seems to be of the essence of interpretation to generate a language at the contact of another language, to be a kind of over-language added to that of the work. But we must not be misled by concepts of interpretation that derive from objective and intersubjective models. Blanchot expects us to understand the act of reading in terms of the work and not in terms of the constitutive subject, although he carefully avoids giving the work an objective status. He wants us "to take the work for what it is and thus to rid it of the presence of the author." What we are reading is located closer to its origin than we are and it is our purpose to be attracted by it to the place from where it issued forth. The work has an undeniable ontological priority over the reader. It follows that it would be absurd to claim that in reading we "add" something, for any addition, be it in the form of an explication, a judgment, or an opinion, will only move us further from the real center. We can only come under the true spell of the work by allowing it to remain what it is. This apparently passive act, this "nothing" that, in reading, we should *not* add to the work, is the very definition of a truly interpretative language. It designates a positive way of addressing the text, noticeable in the positive emphasis of the passage quoted from *L'Espace littéraire*, a rare example of affirmation in an author not prone to positive statement. The urge to let a work be exactly what it is requires an active and unrelenting vigilance which can be exercised only by means of language. In this manner, an interpretative language originates in contact with the work. To the extent that reading merely "listens" to the work, it becomes itself an act of interpretative understanding.[4] Blanchot's description of the act of reading defines authentic interpretation. It transcends in depth descriptions of interpretation that derive from the study of things or from the analysis of individual subjects.

Yet Blanchot feels the need to qualify his definition by an all-important reservation. The act of reading, by means of which the authentic dimensions of a work can be revealed, can never be performed by the author on his own writings. Blanchot frequently states this impossibility, perhaps most clearly at the beginning of *L'Espace littéraire*:

> The writer can never read his own work. It is, for him, strictly inaccessible, a secret which he does not wish to confront. . . . The impossibility of self-reading coincides with the discovery that, from now on, there is no longer room for any added creation in the space opened up by the work and that, consequently, the only remaining possibility is that of forever writing the same work over again. . . . The particular loneliness of the writer . . . stems from the fact that, in the work, he belongs to what always precedes the work.[5]

The remark is of central importance for an understanding of Blanchot. At first sight, it seems convincing enough: we can find many examples in literary history of the estrangement experienced by writers who handle their language seriously, when they face the expression of their own thought. And Blanchot links this estrangement with the difficulty of re-

4. See Martin Heidegger, "Logos," in *Vorträge und Aufsätze* (Neske: Pfullingen, 1954), pp. 215 ff.

5. "L'ècrivain ne lit jamais son oeuvre. Elle est pour lui, l'illisible, un secret, en face de quoi il ne demeure pas. . . . L'impossibilité de lire est cette découverte que maintenant, dans l'espace ouvert par la création, il n'y a plus de place pour la création—et, pour l'écrivain, pas d'autre possibilité que d'écrire toujours cette oeuvre. . . . La solitude de l'écrivain . . . viendrait alors de ce qu'il appartient, dans l'oeuvre, à ce qui est toujours avant l'oeuvre." *L'Espace littéraire*, p. 14; see also ibid., p. 209.

nouncing the belief that all literature is a new beginning, that a work is a sequence of beginnings. We may believe that the greater proximity to origin confers upon the work some of the "firmness of beginnings" that Blanchot is willing to grant to the work of others. But this strength is only an illusion. The poet can start his work only because he is willing to forget that this presumed beginning is, in fact, the repetition of a previous failure, resulting precisely from an inability to begin anew. When we think that we are perceiving the assertion of a new origin, we are in fact witnessing the reassertion of a failure to originate. Acceding to the work in its positivity, the reader can very well ignore what the author was forced to forget: that the work asserted in fact the impossibility of its own existence. However, if the writer were really reading himself, in the full interpretative sense of the term, he would necessarily remember the duplicity of his self-induced forgetfulness, and this discovery would paralyze all further attempts at creation. In that sense, Blanchot's *noli me legere*, the rejection of self-interpretation, is an expression of caution, advocating a prudence without which literature might be threatened with extinction.

The impossibility for a writer to read his own work sharply distinguishes the relationship between work and reader from that between work and author. Reading, as well as criticism (conceived as the actualization in language of the potential language involved in reading), can grow into a genuine interpretation, in the deepest sense of the term, whereas the relationship between author and work would be one of total estrangement, refusal and forgetting. This radical distinction raises several questions. It seems primarily motivated by caution, a virtue that is not typical of the almost ruthless audacity of Blanchot's thought. Moreover, the study of Blanchot's later work reveals that the process of forgetting, itself deeply linked with the impossibility of the author's reading his own work, is, in fact, a much more ambiguous matter than may have appeared at first sight. The positive assertion of the work is not merely the result of a complicity between reader and author that enables the one to ignore what the other is willing to forget. The will to forget enables the work to exist and becomes a positive notion leading to the invention of an authentic language. Blanchot's recent work compels us to become aware of the full ambivalence of the authenticating power contained in the act of forgetting. It reveals the paradoxical presence of a kind of anti-memory at the very source of literary creation. If this is so, can we still believe that Blanchot refuses to read his work and dodges confrontation with his literary self? The remembrance of a forgetting can occur only while reading the work, not in the course of its composition. The reading that allows Blanchot to move from the first to the second version of his early novel *Thomas l'obscur* could still be explained as an attempt "to repeat what was said earlier . . . with the power of an increased talent." But the dialogue of the late text entitled *L'Attente l'oubli* could only be the result of a relationship between the completed work and its author. The impossibility of self-reading has itself become the main theme, demanding in its turn to be read and interpreted. A circular movement seems to take the writer, at first alienated in the work, back to himself, by means of an act of self-interpretation. In Blanchot, this process first takes the form of his critical reading of others as preparatory to the reading of himself. It can be shown that Blanchot's criticism prefigures the self-reading toward which he is ultimately oriented. The relationship between his critical work and his narrative prose has to be understood in these terms, the former being the preparatory version of the latter. A complete study of Blanchot should illustrate this by means of several examples; we have space for one instance only, the sequence of articles he wrote on Mallarmé. This may suffice to indicate that the movement of Blanchot's critical mind reflects the circular pattern that can be found in all acts of literary invention.

Mallarmé is one of the writers that have constantly solicited Blanchot's attention; the poet of *Un Coup de dés* reappears as one of his main topics at every stage of his development. Since Blanchot writes in the traditional French format of the periodical review, his choice of subject matter is not always dictated by a deeper affinity with the book he criticizes; it may be inspired by current fashion or by the pressure of literary events. In accordance with his conception of criticism, he is not interested in the discovery of new talent or in the revaluation of established names. In his selection of topics, he is generally content to follow a cosmopolitan current of opinion that is well informed but lays no claim to originality. There are, however, a few figures that recur as the true centers of his concern. Mallarmé is undoubtedly one of them; the presence of the other writers that influenced Blanchot may often remain hidden, but Mallarmé is explicitly discussed on various occasions.

Above all, Mallarmé fascinates Blanchot by his claim to absolute impersonality. The other main themes of Mallarmé's work, the large negative themes of death, ennui, and sterility, or even the self-reflection by which literature "scrutinizes its very essence" all take second place to the *gageure* of letting the work exist only by and for itself. Blanchot frequently quotes the statement of Mallarmé which he considers of central importance: "The book, when we, as authors, separate ourselves from it, exists impersonally, without requiring the presence of a reader. Know that, among all human entities, it is the one that comes into being by itself; it is made, and exists, by itself."[6] Impersonality means, in the first place, the absence of all personal anecdotes, of all confessional intimacies, and of all psychological concerns. Mallarmé eschews such forms of experience, not because he considers them devoid of importance, but because the generality of poetic language has moved far beyond them. Hence the naiveté of reductive critical methods that try to gain access to Mallarmé's poetry by tracing it back to actual private experiences. One is never so far removed from the center as when one assumes one has recaptured the origin of the self in an empirical experience that is taken to be the cause. Blanchot is not likely to be misled

6. "Impersonifié, le volume, autant qu'on s'en sépare comme auteur, ne réclame approche de lecteur. Tel, sache, entre les accessoires humains, il a lieu tout seul: fait, étant." "L'Action restreinte," *Variations sur un sujet*, *Oeuvres complètes*, Pléiade (Paris: Gallimard, 1945), p. 372.

in this direction: his negative comments on Charles Mauron's first psychoanalytical study of Mallarmé, dating as far back as 1943, are still altogether valid and topical.

Mallarmé's impersonality cannot be described as the antithesis, or the compensatory idealization, of a regressive obsession, as a strategy by means of which the poet tries to free himself from haunting emotional or sexual trauma. We do not find in him a dialectic of the empirical and the ideal self, as Freud describes it in the Narcissus essay. More than all other critics who have written on Mallarmé, Blanchot stressed most emphatically, from the start, that the impersonality of Mallarmé does not result from a conflict within his own person. It stems instead from a confrontation with an entity as different from himself as non-being differs from being. Mallarmé's alienation is neither social nor psychological, but ontological; to be impersonal does not mean, for him, that one shares a consciousness or a destiny with a number of others but that one is reduced to being no longer a person, to being no one, because one defines oneself in relation to being and not in relation to some particular entity.

In an article that dates back to 1949, Blanchot stresses that, for Mallarmé, the only medium by means of which such impersonality can be achieved is language. "Many striking points [about Mallarmé's conception of language] are to be remembered. The most remarkable is its impersonality, the autonomous and absolute existence that Mallarmé is willing to grant language. . . . this language supposes neither a speaker, nor a listener: it speaks and writes *by itself*. It is a kind of consciousness without a subject."[7] The poet thus encounters language as an alien and self-sufficient entity, not at all as if it were the expression of a subjective intent with which he could grow familiar, still less a tool that could be made to fit his needs. Yet it is well known that Mallarmé always used

7. "Il serait à retenir plusieurs points frappants [sur le langage]. Mais de tous le plus remarquable est le caractère impersonnel, l'espace d'existence indépendante et absolue que Mallarmé lui prête. . . . Ce langage ne suppose personne qui l'exprime, personne qui l'entende: il *se* parle et il *s*'écrit. . . . Il est une sorte de conscience sans sujet." *La Part du feu* (Paris: Gallimard, 1949), p. 48.

language in the manner of the Parnassian poets, the way a craftsman uses the material in which he is working. Well aware of this, Blanchot adds: "But language is also an incarnate consciousness that has been seduced into taking on the material form of words, their life and their sound, and leading one to believe that this reality can somehow open up a road that takes one to the dark center of things."[8] This important qualification leads us at once to the heart of the Mallarmean dialectic. For it is true that Mallarmé always conceived of language as a separate entity radically different from himself, one which he was incessantly trying to reach; the model for this entity, however, was always for him the mode of being of a natural substance, accessible to sensation. Language, with its sensory attributes of sound and texture, partakes of the world of natural objects and introduces a positive element in the sheer void that would surround a consciousness left entirely to itself. The double aspect of language, capable of being at the same time a concrete, natural thing and the product of an activity of consciousness, serves Mallarmé as the starting point of a dialectical development that runs through his entire work. Nature, far from representing the satisfaction of a happy, unproblematic sensation, evokes instead separation and distance; nature is for him the substance from which we are forever separated. But it is also "la première en date, la nature" and, as such, it precedes all other entities and occupies a privileged position of priority. This assumption is of determining importance for the genesis and the structure of Mallarmé's work. The symbols of failure and of negativity that play such an important role in his poetry must be understood in terms of the underlying polarity between the world of nature and the activity of consciousness. Reacting against the natural world in an attempt to assert his autonomy, the poet discovers that he can never free himself from its impact. The final image of Mallarmé's work shows the protagonist of *Un Coup de dés* sinking into the "ocean" of the natural world.

8. "Mais [le langage] est aussi une conscience incarnée, séduite à la forme matérielle des mots, à leur sonorité, à leur vie et donnant à croire que cette réalité nous ouvre on ne sait quelle voie vers le fond obscur des choses." Ibid.

Nevertheless, in a gesture that is both heroic and absurd, the will to consciousness keeps asserting itself, even from beyond the catastrophic event in which it was destroyed. The persistence of this effort keeps carrying the work forward and engenders a trajectory that seems to escape, to some extent, from the chaos of indetermination. This trajectory is reflected in the very structure of Mallarmé's development and constitutes the positive element that allows him to pursue his task. The work consists of a sequence of new beginnings that are not, however, as for Blanchot, identical repetitions. The eternal repetition, the *ressassement* of Blanchot is replaced, in Mallarmé, by a dialectical movement of becoming. Each successive failure knows and remembers the failure that went before, and this knowledge establishes a progression. Mallarmé's self-reflection is rooted in experiences that are not altogether negative but that nevertheless maintain a certain measure of self-awareness, "a recognizable clarity, the only thing to remain."[9] Subsequent works can start on a higher level of consciousness than their predecessors. There is room, in Mallarmé's world, for some form of memory; from work to work, one is not allowed to forget what went before. A link is maintained, despite the discontinuities, and a movement of growth takes place. The impersonality is the result of a dialectical progression, leading from the particular to the universal, from personal to historical recollection. The work depends for its existence on this dialectical substructure, which is itself rooted in an obscure assertion of the priority of material substances over consciousness. Mallarmé's poetics remain founded on the attempt to make the semantic dimensions of language coincide with its material, formal attributes.

Such an attempt should not be confused with Blanchot's experiments. When the latter speaks, in the passage previously quoted, of language as an "incarnate form of consciousness" (adding at once that this may well be a delusion), he is describing a conception of language that differs altogether from his own. Blanchot's writing lingers very seldom over the

9. ". . . la clarté reconnue, qui seule demeure," *Igitur*, *Oeuvres complètes*, p. 435.

material qualities of things; without being abstract, his language is rarely a language of sensation. His preferred literary form is not, as for René Char, to whom he is often compared, that of a poetry oriented toward material things, but rather the *récit*, a purely temporal type of narrative. It should not surprise us, therefore, that his presentation of Mallarmé at times misses the mark. This is particularly true of the sections of *L'Espace littéraire* in which Blanchot deals with the theme of death as it appears in Mallarmé's prose text *Igitur*. However, when Blanchot returns to Mallarmé later, in the articles now included in *Le Livre à venir*, his observations lead to a general view that is a genuine interpretation.

What is missing, perhaps deliberately, in Blanchot's commentaries on *Igitur*, is precisely this sense of dialectical growth by means of which the particular death of the protagonist becomes a universal movement, corresponding to the historical development of human consciousness in time. Blanchot translates the experience at once in ontological terms and sees it as a direct confrontation of a consciousness with the most general category of being. Igitur's death then becomes for him a version of one of his own main obsessions, what he calls "la mort impossible," a theme more closely affiliated with Rilke and one that does not fully coincide with Mallarmé's chief concern at the time of *Igitur*. The distortion is in keeping with Blanchot's deeper commitments; Mallarmé's theme of the universal historical consciousness, with its Hegelian overtones, is of slight interest to him. He considers the dialectic of subject and object, the progressive temporality of a historical growth, as inauthentic experiences, misleading reflections of a more fundamental movement that resides in the realm of being. Later, when Mallarmé has pursued his own thought to its most extreme point, he will at last convey the oscillatory movement within being that Blanchot prematurely claims to find stated in *Igitur*. It is at this point that a real encounter between Blanchot and Mallarmé can take place.

Blanchot's final interpretation of Mallarmé occurs in the essays from *Le Livre à venir* that deal with *Un Coup de dés* and with the preparatory notes which Jacques Scherer edited in 1957 under the title *Le "Livre" de Mallarmé*. In *Hérodiade*,

Igitur, and the poems that follow these texts, Mallarmé's main theme had been the destruction of the object under the impact of a reflective consciousness, the near dissolution ("la presque disparition vibratoire") of natural entities and of the self, raised to an advanced level of impersonality when, in the mirror of self-reflection, it becomes the object of its own thought. But in the process of depersonalization, the self could, to some degree, maintain its power; enriched by the repeated experience of defeat, it remained as the center of work, the point of departure of the spiral that grew out of it. Later on, in *Un Coup de dés*, the dissolution of the object occurs on such a large scale that the entire cosmos is reduced to total indetermination; "la neutralité identique du gouffre," an abyss in which all things are equal in their utter indifference to the human mind and will. This time, however, the conscious self participates in the process to the point of annihilation: "The poet disappears under the pressure of the work, caught in the same movement that prompted the disappearance of the reality of nature."[10] Pushed to this extreme point, the impersonality of the self is such that it seems to lose touch with its initial center and to dissolve into nothingness. It now becomes clear that dialectical growth toward a universal consciousness was a delusion and that the notion of a progressive temporality is a reassuring but misleading myth. In truth, consciousness was caught unawares within a movement that transcends its own power. The various forms of negation that had been "surmounted" as the work progressed—death of the natural object, death of the individual consciousness in *Igitur*, or the destruction of a universal, historical consciousness destroyed in the "storm" of *Un Coup de dés*—turn out to be particular expressions of a persistent negative movement that resides in being. We try to protect ourselves against this negative power by inventing stratagems, ruses of language and of thought that hide an irrevocable fall. The existence of these strategies reveals the supremacy of the negative power they are

10. "Le poète disparaît sous la pression de l'oeuvre, par le même mouvement qui fait disparaître la réalité naturelle." *Le Livre à venir* (Paris: Gallimard, 1959), p. 277.

trying to circumvent. For all his apparent lucidity, Mallarmé was mystified by this philosophical blindness until he recognized the illusory character of the dialectic on which he had founded his poetic strategy. In his last work, consciousness as well as natural objects are both threatened by a power that exists on a more fundamental level than either of them.

And yet, even beyond this destruction of the self, the work can remain in existence. In Mallarmé's final poem, survival is symbolized in the image of a constellation that seems to escape from the destruction to which everything else has succumbed. Interpreting the image of the constellation, Blanchot states that in the poem, "Dispersion takes on the form and appearance of unity."[11] The unity is first stated in spatial terms: Mallarmé literally depicts the typographical, spatial disposition of the words on the page. Creating a highly complex network of relationships between the words, he gives the illusion of a three-dimensional reading analogous to the experience of space itself. The poem becomes "the material, sensory assertion of the new space. It is this space become poem."[12] We have a late, extreme version of the attempt to make the semantic and the sensory properties of language coincide. As the words in the poem that designate a ship are grouped in the shape of a sinking sailboat, the meaning of language is represented in a material form. In *Un Coup de dés*, however, such experimentations come very close to being a deliberate hoax. If we have actually moved beyond the antithesis between subject and object, then such pseudo-objective games can no longer be taken seriously. In a very typically Mallarmean form of irony, the spatial resources of language are exploited to the full at the very moment that they are known to be completely ineffective. It is no longer valid to speak, with Blanchot, of the earth as a spatial abyss that, reversing itself, becomes the corresponding abyss of the sky in which "words, reduced to space,

11. "La dispersion prend forme et apparence d'unité." Ibid., p. 286.

12. ". . . affirmation sensible de ce nouvel espace. Il est cet espace devenu poème." Ibid., p. 287.

make this space shine with the pure light of stars."[13] The idea of a reversal, however, is essential, provided one understands the reversal no longer in a spatial but in a temporal sense, as an axis around which the metaphor of space revolves to disclose the reality of time.

Blanchot participates in the reversal as he gradually discovers the temporal structure of *Un Coup de dés*. The central articulation of this poem is very clearly marked: near the middle of the text, Mallarmé shifts from roman type to italics and inserts an extended episode beginning with the words "comme si." At that moment, we change from a temporality that follows the course of an event, presented as if it were actually taking place, to another, prospective temporality that exists only as fiction, strictly in the mode of "comme si." The fictional time is included in the historical time like the play within the play of the Elizabethan theater. This enveloping structure corresponds to the relationship between history and fiction. The fiction in no way changes the outcome, the destiny of the historical event. In the terms of Mallarmé's poem, it will not abolish the random power of change; the course of events remains unchanged by this long grammatical *apposition* that continues over six pages. The outcome is determined from the start by the single word "jamais," pointing to a past that precedes the beginning of the fiction and to a future that will follow it. The purpose of the fiction is not to intervene directly; it is a cognitive effort by means of which the mind tries to escape from the total indetermination that threatens it. The fiction influences the mode of abolition of consciousness, not by opposing it, but by mediating the experience of destruction; it interposes a language that accurately describes it. "History," says Blanchot, "is replaced by hypothesis."[14] Yet this hypothesis can derive its statement only from a knowledge that was already given and that asserts precisely the impossibility of overcoming the arbitrary nature of this knowledge. The verification of the hypothesis confirms the impossibility

13. "Des mots ne restant que leur espace, cet espace rayonne en un pur éclat stellaire." Ibid., p. 288.

14. "L'histoire est remplacée par l'hypothèse." Ibid., pp. 291–92.

of its elaboration. Fiction and the history of actual events converge toward the same nothingness, the knowledge revealed by the hypothesis of fiction turns out to be a knowledge that already existed, in all the strength of its negativity, before the hypothesis was construed. Knowledge of the impossibility of knowing precedes the act of consciousness that tries to reach it. This structure is a circular one. The prospective hypothesis, which determines a future, coincides with a historical, concrete reality that precedes it and that belongs to the past. The future is changed into a past, in the infinite regression that Blanchot calls a *ressassement*, and that Mallarmé describes as the endless and meaningless noise of the sea after the storm has destroyed all sign of life, "l'inférieur clapotis quelconque."

But does this knowledge of the circular structure of fictional language not have, in its turn, a temporal destiny? Philosophy is well acquainted with the circularity of a consciousness that puts its own mode of being into question. This knowledge complicates the philosopher's task a great deal, but it does not spell the end of philosophical understanding. The same is true of literature. Many specifically literary hopes and illusions have to be given up; Mallarmé's faith in the progressive development of self-consciousness, for example, must be abandoned, since every new step in this progression turns out to be a regression toward a more and more remote past. Yet it remains possible to speak of a certain development, of a movement of becoming that persists in the fictional world of literary invention. In a purely temporal world, there can be no perfect repetition, as when two points coincide in space. As soon as the reversal described by Blanchot has taken place, the fiction is revealed as a temporal movement, and the question of its direction and intent must again be asked. "Mallarmé's ideal Book is thus obliquely asserted in terms of the movement of change and development that expresses perhaps its real meaning. This meaning will be the very movement of the circle."[15] And elsewhere: "We necessarily always write the

15. "Le Livre est ainsi, discrètement, affirmé dans le *devenir* qui est peut-être son sens, sens qui serait le devenir même du cercle." Ibid., p. 296.

same thing over again, but the development of what remains the same has infinite richness in its very repetition."[16] Blanchot is very close here to a philosophical trend which tries to rethink the notion of growth and development no longer in organic but in hermeneutic terms by reflecting on the temporality of the act of understanding.[17]

Blanchot's criticism, starting out as an ontological meditation, leads back to the question of the temporal self. For him, as for Heidegger, Being is disclosed in the act of its self-hiding and, as conscious subjects, we are necessarily caught up in this movement of dissolution and forgetting. A critical act of interpretation enables us to see how poetic language always reproduces this negative movement, though it is often not aware of it. Criticism thus becomes a form of demystification on the ontological level that confirms the existence of a fundamental distance at the heart of all human experience. Unlike the recent Heidegger, however, Blanchot does not seem to believe that the movement of a poetic consciousness could ever lead us to assert our ontological insight in a positive way. The center always remains hidden and out of reach; we are separated from it by the very substance of time, and we never cease to know that this is the case. The circularity is not, therefore, a perfect form with which we try to coincide, but a directive that maintains and measures the distance that separates us from the center of things. We can by no means

16. "Ce que nous écrivons est nécessairement le même, et le devenir de ce qui est le même est, en son recommencement, d'une richesse infinie." Ibid., p. 276 n.

17. See, for example, Hans-Georg Gadamer, *Wahrheit und Methode*, 2d ed. (Tübingen: J. C. B. Mohr [P. Siebeck], 1960), pp. 250 ff. In *Sein und Zeit*, Heidegger is certainly one of those who have laid the groundwork for this form of thought in our century. The affinity between Blanchot and Heidegger, despite the divergence in their subsequent development, should be studied more systematically than has been done up to now. The French philosopher Emmanuel Levinas, in his opposition to Heidegger and in his influence on Blanchot, would have a prominent part in such a study. There exists a brief article on Blanchot and Heidegger by Levinas, "Maurice Blanchot et le regard du poète," published in the now defunct review *Monde Nouveau*, no. 98 (March 1956), pp. 6–19.

take this circularity for granted; the circle is a path that we have to construct ourselves and on which we must try to remain. At most, the circularity proves the authenticity of our intent. The search toward circularity governs the development of consciousness and is also the guiding principle that shapes the poetic form.

This conclusion has brought us back to the question of the subject. In his interpretative quest, the writer frees himself from empirical concerns, but he remains a self that must reflect on its own situation. As the act of reading "had to leave things exactly as they were," he tries to see himself the way he really is. He can do this only by "reading" himself, by turning his conscious attention toward himself and not toward a forever unreachable form of being. Blanchot finally reaches this same conclusion with reference to Mallarmé:

> How can the Book assert itself in conformity with its constitutive rhythm, if it does not manage to get outside itself? To correspond with the intimate mobility that determines its structure, it must achieve an outside distance that will allow it to make contact with this very distance. The Book needs a mediator. The act of reading performs the mediation. But not just any reader will do. . . . Mallarmé himself will be the voice of this essential reading. He has been abolished and has vanished as the dramatic center of his work, but this very annihilation has put him into contact with the appearing and disappearing essence of his Book, with the incessant oscillation which is the main statement of the work.[18]

The necessity for self-reading, for self-interpretation, reappears at the moment when Mallarmé rises to the level of insight that allows him to name the general structure of all literary con-

18. "Comment [le Livre] pourra-t-il s'affirmer selon le rythme qui le constitue, s'il ne sort pas en quelque manière de lui-même et s'il ne trouve pas, pour correspondre à l'intimité mobile qui est sa structure, le dehors où il sera en contact avec sa distance même? Il lui faut un médiateur. C'est la lecture. Cette lecture n'est pas celle d'un lecteur quelconque. . . . Mallarmé sera la voix de cette lecture essentielle. Disparu et supprimé comme auteur, il est, par cette disparition, en rapport avec l'essence apparaissante et disparaissante du Livre, avec son oscillation incessante qui est sa communication." *Le Livre à venir*, pp. 294–95.

sciousness. The suppression of the subjective moment in Blanchot, asserted in the form of the categorical impossibility of self-reading, is only a preparatory step in his hermeneutic of the self. In this way, he frees his consciousness of the insidious presence of inauthentic concerns. In the ascesis of depersonalization, he tries to conceive of the literary work, not as a thing, but as an autonomous entity, a "consciousness without a subject." This is not an easy undertaking. Blanchot must eliminate from his work all elements derived from everyday experience, from involvements with others, all reifying tendencies to equate the work with natural objects. Only when this extreme purification has been achieved, can he turn toward the truly temporal dimensions of the text. This reversal implies a return to a subject that, in fact, never ceased to be present. It is significant that Blanchot reaches this conclusion only with reference to an author like Mallarmé who came upon it obliquely and whose actual itinerary needs to be revealed by interpretation, the way a watermark becomes visible only by transparency. When he is dealing with writers who have given a more explicit version of the same process, Blanchot refuses them his full understanding. He tends to rate explicit forms of truth with other inessential matters that serve to make everyday life bearable—such as society, or what he calls history. He prefers hidden to revealed truth. In his critical work, this theoretician of interpretation prefers to describe the act of interpretation rather than the interpreted truth. He wanted, in all likelihood, to keep the latter in reserve for his narrative prose.[19]

BIBLIOGRAPHY

CRITICAL WORKS BY BLANCHOT

Books

Comment la littérature est-elle possible? Paris: Corti, 1942. Reprinted in *Faux pas*.

Faux-pas. Paris: Gallimard, 1943.

19. This essay, commissioned for the present volume, appeared in a shorter form as "La Circularité de l'interprétation dans l'oeuvre critique de Maurice Blanchot," *Critique* 22 (1966): 547–60.

La Part du feu. Paris: Gallimard, 1949.

Lautréamont et Sade. Paris: Editions de Minuit, 1949. New ed. Arguments. Paris: Editions de Minuit, 1964.

L'Espace littéraire. Paris: Gallimard, 1955.

Le Livre à venir. Paris: Gallimard, 1959.

L'Attente l'oubli. Paris: Gallimard, 1962.

L'Entretien infini. Paris: Gallimard, 1969.

Articles

A bibliography of Blanchot's articles published in *Critique* appears in the special issue of this periodical devoted to Blanchot (*Critique* 22 [1966]: 592). A large number of articles appeared in the *Nouvelle Revue Française*, but a comprehensive listing of Blanchot's articles is not available at this date.

SELECTED ARTICLES ON BLANCHOT

General introductions to the critical work:

Douglas, Kenneth. "Blanchot and Sartre." *Yale French Studies* 2, no. 1 (Summer–Spring 1949): 85–95.

Egebak, Niels. "Orpheus' Blik: Maurice Blanchots Aesthetik." *Ord och Bild* 74 (1965): 514–18.

Hartman, Geoffrey. "The Fulness and Nothingness of Literature." *Yale French Studies*, no. 16 (1955), pp. 63–78.

———. "Maurice Blanchot: Philosopher-Novelist." *Chicago Review* 15 (1961): 1–18.

Lawall, Sarah N. "The Negative Consciousness: Maurice Blanchot." In *Critics of Consciousness: The Existential Structures of Literature*, pp. 221–65. Cambridge, Mass.: Harvard University Press, 1968.

Oxenhandler, Neal. "Paradox and Negation in the Criticism of Maurice Blanchot." *Symposium* 16 (1962): 36–44.

Parret, Herman. "Lectuur en literaire Kritiek volgens Maurice Blanchot." *Het Franse Boek* (Groningen), vol. 38 (1968).

Picon, Gaëtan. "L'Oeuvre critique de Maurice Blanchot." *Critique* 14 (1956): 675–94 and 836–54. Reprinted in *L'Usage de la lecture*, pp. 199–238. Paris: Mercure de France, 1960.

Poulet, Georges. "Maurice Blanchot, critique et romancier." *Critique* 22 (1966): 485–97.

Sartre, Jean-Paul. "*Aminadab*, ou du Fantastique considéré comme un langage." In *Situations I*, pp. 122–42. Paris: Gallimard, 1947.

More specialized articles written by authors whose own thought is close to or influenced by Blanchot:

Bataille, Georges. "Le Monde où nous mourons." *Critique* 13 (1957): 675–84.

Foucault, Michel. ''La Pensée du dehors.'' *Critique* 22 (1966): 523–46.

Klossowski, Pierre. ''Sur Maurice Blanchot.'' *Les Temps Modernes* 4 (1949): 298–314. Reprinted in part in *Un si funeste désir*, pp. 159–83. Paris: Gallimard, 1963.

Levinas, Emmanuel. ''Maurice Blanchot et le regard du poète.'' *Monde Nouveau*, no. 98 (March 1956), pp. 6–19.

———. ''La Servante et son maître.'' *Critique* 22 (1966): 514–22.

Starobinski, Jean. ''*Thomas l'obscur*, chapitre premier.'' *Critique* 22 (1966): 498–513.

J. Hillis Miller 12

The Geneva School: The Criticism of Marcel Raymond, Albert Béguin, Georges Poulet, Jean Rousset, Jean-Pierre Richard, and Jean Starobinski

Consciousness of consciousness, literature about literature—all six of the critics to be discussed here would accept in one way or another these definitions of literary criticism. The similar assumptions of these critics about the nature of criticism may justify speaking of them as a "school," in spite of the important differences among them. Moreover, all but two (Georges Poulet and Jean-Pierre Richard) have been formally associated with the University of Geneva, and close ties of friendship and reciprocal influence have linked all six.

The members of the Geneva school share common sources in earlier criticism. Their work stems directly from that of the critics of the *Nouvelle Revue Française*, especially Jacques Rivière and Charles Du Bos, and the filiation may be extended behind them through Proust to mid-nineteenth-century writers like Pater and Ruskin, and so back to romantic criticism. Moreover, the older members of the Geneva school, especially Marcel Raymond and Georges Poulet, were strongly influenced in their development by the work of two German critics who continued the romantic and historicist traditions: Wilhelm Dilthey and Friedrich Gundolf. The presuppositions of the criticism of the Geneva school may therefore be defined as a unique version of attitudes toward literature and criticism which are our heritage from romanticism.

Literature about literature—such a definition of criticism sharply differentiates the work of the Geneva critics from that of those scholars—French structuralists, Russian formalists, or American new critics—who tend to think of criticism as a mode of objective knowledge. For such critics criticism is one of the "human sciences," and therefore, like anthropology, history, or sociology, part of the university-based enterprise of analysis and description which works toward a definitive conceptualization of the world. The Geneva critics, on the other hand, consider literary criticism to be itself a form of literature. It is a form which takes as its theme not that experience of natural objects, other people, or supernatural realities about which the poet and novelist write, but those entities after they have been assimilated into the work of some author. Literary criticism is literature at a second degree. It reaches the subject matter of literature by way of the intercession of poems, novels, plays, journals, and letters which others have written. In order to attain this subject matter, literary criticism must not describe from the outside, as a scientist describes a flower or an atom. It must extend, complete, and constitute in a new form the themes which are already present in literature. It therefore makes the same use of language as literature does, and it expresses the same kinds of reality.

This means, among other things, that the literary critic, like the novelist or poet, is pursuing, however covertly or indirectly, his own spiritual adventure. He pursues it not by way of his own experience, but by the mediation of the experience of others. His work is far from disinterested or detached. "The most valuable criticism," says Albert Béguin, "is . . . that criticism . . . in which the writer continues his own private adventure in his writing, in which through the very finding of the words he enacts one of the stages of his own personal spiritual adventure. Subjective criticism seems to me entirely justifiable and defensible."[1]

1. "La critique la plus valable est tout de même cette critique . . . où l'écrivain court sa propre aventure en écrivant, où dans l'invention même des mots il opère l'un des stades de son aventure personnelle et spirituelle. La critique subjective me semble entièrement justifiée et défendable." "Entretiens avec Albert Béguin," *Esprit* 26 (1958): 763.

It is therefore proper that Georges Poulet should have written a number of his most important recent essays on the work of other members of his own group: Raymond, Béguin, and Starobinski. This is not some final rarefying of criticism, the mirror mirroring the mirror. It is significant evidence that for the Geneva critics criticism is a form of literature and may itself be criticized in turn. If the work of these critics is literature about literature, it might be best to define it not in terms of its relation to other kinds of literary criticism but as a special form of that literature of meditation, reverie, or spiritual quest which is historically associated with Switzerland and most often with Geneva. One thinks of Rousseau, of Senancour, of Constant, of Amiel, of Ramuz. The Geneva critics continue in a new way this native tradition.

If criticism is literature about literature, what then is literature? The definition will determine not only the nature of the subject matter of criticism but also the nature of criticism itself. For the Geneva critics literature is a form of consciousness. This conception of literature once more separates these critics from many current kinds of criticism. For Poulet or Raymond literature is neither an objective structure of meanings residing in the words of a poem or novel, nor the tissue of self-references of a "message" turned in on itself, nor the unwitting expression of the hidden complexes of a writer's unconscious, nor a revelation of the latent structures of exchange or symbolization which integrate a society. Literature, for them, is the embodiment of a state of mind. In the language of a text from Rousseau's *Rêveries*, a poem by Hugo, or a novel by Balzac a certain mode of consciousness has been brought into the open in a union of mind and words. This union incarnates the consciousness and makes it available to others.

Criticism must therefore begin in an act of renunciation in which the critic empties his mind of its personal qualities so that it may coincide completely with the consciousness expressed in the words of the author. His essay will be the record of this coincidence. The "intimacy" necessary for criticism, says Georges Poulet, "is not possible unless the thought of the critic *becomes* the thought of the author criticized, unless it succeeds in re-feeling, in re-thinking, in re-imagining the author's thought from the inside. Nothing could be less objective than such a movement of the mind . . . for what has to be reached is a *subject*, that is to say a spiritual activity which cannot be understood unless the critic puts himself in its place and makes it play again within him its subjective role.''[2]

For the Geneva critics, then, criticism is primordially consciousness of the consciousness of another, the transposition of the mental universe of an author into the interior space of the critic's mind. Therefore these critics are relatively without interest in the external form of individual works of literature. Often the subject of one of their essays is the total work of an author, including his notes, his diaries, his unfinished works, his fragmentary drafts. Such incomplete writings may allow better access to the intimate tone or quality of a mind than a perfected masterpiece. ''Subjectively,'' says Poulet, ''there is nothing formal about literature. It is the reality of a thought which is always particular, always anterior and posterior to every object.''[3] A living mind is a protean energy which can never express itself fully in any objective form. ''It is characteristic of a work,'' says Poulet, ''at once to create its structures and to transcend them, I should even say to destroy them. So the work of an author is certainly the collection of texts which he has written, but in the sense that as they follow one another, each replaces the last and reveals thereby a movement toward a liberation from structures.''[4] Even Jean Rousset, the critic among the group most concerned with the form of

2. ''Or il me semble qu'une telle intimité n'est possible que dans la mesure où la pensée critique *devient* la pensée critiquée, où elle réussit à re-sentir, à repenser, à ré-imaginer celle-ci de l'intérieur. Rien de moins objectif qu'un tel mouvement de l'esprit. . . . car ce qui doit être atteint, c'est un sujet.'' ''Réponse,'' *Les Lettres Nouvelles*, no. 17 (24 June 1959), p. 10.

3. *La Distance intérieure* (Paris: Plon, 1952), p. ii.

4. ''C'est le propre de l'oeuvre à la fois d'inventer ses structures et de les dépasser, je dirai même de les détruire. Ainsi l'oeuvre d'un auteur, c'est bien l'ensemble des oeuvres qu'il a écrites, mais dans la mesure où, se succédant les unes aux autres, elles se remplacent les unes les autres et révèlent par là-même un mouvement qui est l'affranchissement des structures.'' ''Réponse,'' *Les Lettres Nouvelles*, no. 17 (24 June 1959), p. 12.

individual works, defines *structures* in literature as "formal constants" or "relationships" whose function is precisely to reveal a "mental universe."[5] A mental universe, however, has a structure of its own, and the critics of the Geneva school do not altogether reject structures in literature. Rather, they replace a concern for the objective structure of individual works with a concern for the subjective structure of the mind revealed by the whole body of an author's writings.

Though the Geneva critics would agree that literature is a form of consciousness, they would disagree in their assumptions about what consciousness is. The differences here are more than nuances within a single tradition of criticism. The varying intuitions of the nature of consciousness in the Geneva critics manifest fundamental oppositions within current thought and art, oppositions which suggest that we are living at the point of intersection of several incompatible conceptions of the nature of man. If the aim of literary criticism is to reach a coincidence of the critic's mind and the mind of the author, the nature of this experience will be determined by the nature of consciousness itself. What does one reach when one reaches the mind of another person and relives from the inside, by way of his writing, his thoughts and emotions? To identify the differing answers to this question among the critics of the Geneva school will be to specify the particular quality of the work of each.

Born in 1897, Marcel Raymond has recently retired after many years as a professor at the University of Geneva. He may be considered the founder and senior member of the Geneva school. No criticism could fulfill better than his the requirement that criticism should be consciousness of consciousness. Criticism begins for him with "a sort of ascesis." The critic must "enter into a state of profound receptivity in which his being becomes extremely sensitized." This preliminary state must "yield bit by bit to a penetrating sympathy." Only such a "sympathie pénétrante" will allow the critic to accomplish his primary task, which is to "relive from the inside,"[6] by a

5. *Forme et signification* (Paris: J. Corti, 1964), p. xii.
6. *Le Sens de la qualité* (Neuchâtel: La Baconnière, 1948), pp. 33, 45.

sort of "knowledge from within," the experience of the author as it is embodied in his words. The critic's job is to "transform states of existence into states of consciousness."[7] He must "re-create" the work of art "within himself, but in conformity to itself." The work must be born anew within him, rising up again in his mind by means of an act which is fundamentally to be defined as "creative participation."[8]

Raymond distinguishes two kinds of knowledge. There is intellectual, scientific, or objective knowledge, knowledge which holds everything at arm's length, separating the mind from its objects and all objects from one another, and there is that inward, affective knowledge in which the mind and its objects become one, or rather, in the case of criticism, in which the critic's mind and the mind expressed in the work become one. This experience is not so much intersubjective as introspective, for the mind of the author must be as much interior to the critic as his own sense of himself. Raymond's genius as a critic has depended on an extreme inner plasticity which has allowed him to duplicate within himself the affective quality of the mind of each of his authors', that profound note of self-hood which persists as the same throughout the work of each. Repeating it within himself, he is able to reproduce it with marvelous economy in a brief quotation or in an image of his own.

This admirable dispatch, which gets to the heart of an author in an instant, is essential to the atmosphere of Raymond's criticism and makes it very different from that of his immediate predecessors, Jacques Rivière and Charles Du Bos. In Raymond's work there is neither Rivière's hesitating approach to the mind of an author (which Georges Poulet has called "asymptotic")[9] nor Du Bos's tendency to be led to digressive

7. *Génies de France* (Neuchâtel: La Baconnière, 1942), pp. 110, 33.

8. "Le but dernier [est] de la recréer [l'oeuvre d'art] en soi, mais conforme à elle-même. Une valeur n'existe pleinement que dans l'acte qui la fait naître, ou resurgir dans l'esprit. En sorte qu'il n'y a de tradition vivante que là où il y a participation créatrice." *Le Sens de la qualité*, p. 49.

9. "La Pensée critique de Marcel Raymond," *Studi di Filologia Moderna* 3: *Saggi e Ricerche di Letteratura Francese* (1963), p. 210.

expansion by way of his coincidence with the mind of a writer. For a great many authors, especially those of the baroque period and those of the period which begins with Rousseau and extends to surrealism, Raymond has performed the basic critical act of reproducing in the words of his essay the unique affective quality of the mind of the writer. Raymond's masterpiece, *From Baudelaire to Surrealism*, inaugurated in 1933 a new epoch in French criticism. Its greatness lies as much in its succinct presentations of a multitude of individual poets as in its grasp of the inner unity of modern French poetry. With unrivaled sympathy and tact he identifies distinguishing characteristics in the work of Baudelaire, Rimbaud, and Mallarmé, and then traces the development from these fathers of modern French poetry in brief essays on Valéry, Apollinaire, Breton, Eluard, and many other twentieth-century poets.

Raymond's insight into the unity of what he calls "the modern myth of poetry" is, however, no less important than his ability to identify what is unique in each poet he discusses. What qualities does Raymond most often find in the authors he admires? A text in *From Baudelaire to Surrealism* will give the answer: "While the classical writer, anxious to know himself, relied on introspection and transposed the result of his observations to the plane of discursive reasoning, the romantic poet, renouncing any form of knowledge which was not at the same time a feeling and an enjoyment of himself—and a feeling of the universe, experienced as a presence—charged his imagination with the task of composing a metaphoric or symbolic portrait of himself in his metamorphoses."[10] The two elements which Raymond finds essential in authentic poetry are here neatly

10. My translation, as elsewhere below. See also, for this passage: *From Baudelaire to Surrealism*, trans. G.M. (New York: Wittenborn, Schultz, 1950), p. 8. "Ainsi, tandis que l'écrivain classique, désireux de se connaître, se fiait à l'introspection et transposait le résultat de ses observations sur le plan de l'intelligence discursive, le poète romantique, renonçant à une connaissance qui ne serait pas en même temps un sentiment et une jouissance de soi—et un sentiment de l'univers, éprouvé comme une présence—charge son imagination de composer le portrait métaphorique, symbolique, de lui-même en ses métamorphoses." *De Baudelaire au surréalisme* (Paris: J. Corti, 1940), pp. 14–15.

juxtaposed: "feeling of the self" and "feeling of the universe, experienced as a presence."

The self-consciousness of others with which Raymond seeks to identify himself is neither that lucid awareness of the self in its isolation and distinctness dear to Descartes and the intellectualist tradition, nor is it a mind filled to brimming with the various objects and thoughts which occupy it. It is rather a primitive sense of existence, preceding the identification of any distinct objects, a state of mind more emotive than rational, scarcely differentiated as that of one particular self. Expressions for this quality of mind run all through Raymond's work. It is "the feeling of existence in what it can have that is most elementary and least differentiated," or "the feeling of our profound life," or "the elementary and quasi-mystical feeling of existence," or "a general sense of existence," or "an apprehension or a presentiment of the nebulous, irrational opacity—or of existence as such—which subsists beyond knowledge by means of the intellect."[11]

Only this "nébuleuse opaque, irrationnelle" can break down the barriers which rational consciousness sets up between the mind and the world and give the critic, by way of the words of the poet, an experience of the universe as a communion of all objects and persons in an intimate overlapping. Such an interpenetration of all things will be pervaded throughout by a fugitive spiritual reality, "a mysterious presence . . . seductive and overwhelming, like a miracle." The ultimate goal of all true poetry is to reach this state. Raymond's criticism seeks in its turn to capture in poetry this mysticism of immanence, a "confused and delicious feeling of existence" in which "the sense of the self and the sense of the whole can no longer be distinguished." "Dream of a magical universe," says Raymond, "in which man would not feel himself to be distinct from things."[12]

11. Ibid., pp. 125, 287; *Jean-Jacques Rousseau: la quête de soi et la rêverie* (Paris: J. Corti, 1962), p. 119; *Paul Valéry et la tentation de l'esprit* (Neuchâtel: La Baconnière, 1946), p. 119; *De Baudelaire au surréalisme*, p. 354.

12. *De Baudelaire au surréalisme*, pp. 339, 14, 15.

Since 1950 the instinctive mysticism of this earth in Raymond, closer perhaps to primitive or pre-logical forms of participation than to Platonic or Christian mysticism, has been modified by the sudden appearance of a more traditional form of religious experience. This has to some degree cut Raymond off from his earlier attitudes and has opened the way for him to the confrontation of a transcendent personal divinity. The extremely beautiful and moving account of this experience in "La Maladie et la guérison,"[13] however, reaffirms Raymond's conviction that the supreme joy, whether in this world or in another, consists in a free communion of all objects and persons by way of a supreme being or spiritual power. Poetry, for Raymond, is still in its essence a testimony to the possibility of this fusion.

Albert Béguin was born in 1901 and died in 1957. In his youth he taught for several years in Germany and was then appointed to a chair at Basel. In 1950 he succeeded Emmanuel Mounier as editor of the distinguished Catholic magazine *Esprit*. He remained with *Esprit* until his death. He was the friend and, in early years, the disciple of Marcel Raymond, and his greatest book, *L'Âme romantique et le rêve* (1937) was presented as a dissertation at the University of Geneva.

Like Raymond, Béguin affirms that authentic literary criticism is only possible "if the commentator situates himself in the interior of the universe created by the author." The critic must "coincide with the spiritual adventure of the poet." But in place of the self-effacement and reticence characteristic of Raymond, Béguin is willing to say that the critic should be overtly "interested, engaged in an adventure, pursuing, under the guardianship of his familiar poets, a continuous research."[14] The poets and novelists about whom he has written—Pascal, the German and French romantics, Nerval, Balzac, Claudel,

13. *Revue de Théologie et de Philosophie* 11 (1961): 1–18.

14. "Limites de l'histoire littéraire," *Esprit* 23 (1955): 169; *L'Âme romantique et le rêve* (Marseille: Cahiers du Sud, 1937), 1: xix; "Péguy ou la fin du jansénisme," *Une Semaine dans le Monde* no. 45 (22 March 1947), p. 12.

Péguy, Bloy, Bernanos, Ramuz, Supervielle—are in his criticism openly encountered as intercessors. They are mediators who make it possible for him to reach, through their works, a physical and spiritual reality which might otherwise be unattainable. *L'Âme romantique et le rêve* was not undertaken as a work of objective scholarship, though it is in fact a landmark in the interpretation of romanticism. Béguin's encounter with the work of Hamann, Saint-Martin, Novalis, Tieck, Hoffmann, and the rest, and the intimate re-creations of the spiritual adventures of each in his book, were crucial stages in his own religious quest. He does not show the same sympathy for writers who do not help him in the quest and has, for example, great distaste for the idealism, the icy subjectivism, of a writer like Mallarmé. Béguin's identification with the consciousness of a poet has value for him only if that consciousness is one which participates in a transcendent reality of a certain kind.

"To restore in their integrity a contemplation characterized by *wonder* and the primary *presence of things*"[15]—this phrase expresses concisely Béguin's definition of true poetry. The poet is a man who by way of dream, or reminiscence, or a heightened sensitivity to physical objects can break through the veil of familiarity which hides reality from us and return to the naiveté of infancy. The theme of childhood recurs throughout Béguin's criticism—childhood of the individual, but also childhood of the race, time of the beginning of things and of myth. His interest in this theme determines not only his approach to the romantic writers but also his admiration for a twentieth-century author like Bernanos. His study of Bernanos, one of the most important of his later books, is organized around the analogous themes of childhood innocence, the vocation of the priesthood, and the vocation of the writer. For Béguin, as for Bernanos or Dostoevsky, each human being contains hidden somewhere within himself, amid the distractions and corruptions of adulthood, a portion of the immaculate purity of a child. This secret purity is his true self. If he is granted grace to recover even for a moment the innocence of the buried self he will recover at the same time the golden age

15. *L'Âme romantique et le rêve*, 1:106.

of our first parents, and with it a perfect openness to the natural world and to other people.

Such openness is the special virtue of childhood for Béguin. It is characterized by a sudden recognition of the concrete existence of physical objects. "On returning from the world of dreams," says Béguin in the admirable recapitulation of the adventure of romanticism at the end of *L'Âme romantique et le rêve*, "human vision is capable of that amazement which one experiences when suddenly things take on for an instant their primal novelty. I am born to things; they are born to me. The exchange is re-established as in the first minutes of existence; this astonishment endows the world again with its marvelous appearance of fairyland."[16]

This text will allow a further distinction to be made between Béguin's criticism and Raymond's. The concrete presence of substantial objects so cherished by Béguin in the work of the writers he admires is very different from the "nébuleuse opaque, irrationnelle" of Raymond. Raymond prizes a vague indistinction, a state in which all things and persons seem to melt into one another. Béguin, on the other hand, most values a state of lucid astonishment in which each thing is distinctly present to the contemplating mind in all its exact weight and texture and can be incarnated in the words of the poet. He praises the work of Claudel, for example, for its "strong taste of life": "The robust language of the poet is completely charged with the savor of terrestrial things. Things which are delectable and solid, loved in their solidity, things which keep, in their verbal evocation, their entire force of presence, their full weight."[17]

16. "Au retour du rêve, le regard humain est capable de cet émerveillement que l'on éprouve lorsque soudain les choses reprennent pour un instant leur nouveauté première. Je nais aux choses; elles naissent à moi. L'échange se rétablit, comme aux premières minutes de l'existence; l'étonnement restitue au monde sa merveilleuse apparence féerique." Ibid., 2:439.

17. "D'un bout à l'autre de l'oeuvre de Claudel, ce goût violent de la vie est reconnaissable. La langue du poète, avec sa robustesse, est toute chargée de la saveur des choses terrestres. Choses délectables, solides, aimées dans leur solidité, et qui gardent, dans l'évocation verbale, leur entière force de présence, leur pesanteur totale."

This *force de présence* which the child and the poet can see in things is, however, by no means limited to their physical pressure on the senses. In the presence of objects the poet also encounters the presence of the Creator who has everywhere incarnated himself in his creation. The word *presence* is the key word in Béguin's criticism. It names both the physical tangibility of objects and the habitation of God within that tangibility. The notion of Incarnation is at the center of his concept of poetry, and for him all true poetry has as its goal a revelation of "the presence of the spiritual in the terrestrial." Poetry must, as he puts it in a succinct formulation, "touch in the concrete the presence of the Invisible."[18]

Béguin finds in all the poets he admires something like the analogical symbolism of the Middle Ages or the Renaissance which allows an object to express some specific quality of the divine life without ceasing to be itself. The paradise poetry glimpses is characterized by resonance at a distance. All three realms—divine, natural, and human—vibrate musically together in the diapason of creation. Of the work of all the poets Béguin most loves he could say what he says of the "profound realism" of Péguy: "At every moment, in every object named, it evokes, demonstrates, installs the unique Presence; and before this, on its side, like every believer at the hour of prayer, it performs an *act of presence*. Presence of God to the world and to man; presence of the soul to God; presence of man to his universe."[19]

To this "triple witness" must be added two more forms of presence. These will complete the system of musical accords Béguin finds in poetry. The first is language itself, the instrument of poetic revelation and the indispensable means of his

---

Poésie de la présence (Neuchâtel: La Baconnière; Paris: Seuil, 1957), p. 227.

18. Ibid., pp. 197, 94, 95.

19. "A tout instant, en tout objet nommé, elle évoque, constate, installe la présence unique; et en face d'Elle, de son côté, comme tout fidèle à l'heure de la prière, elle fait *acte de présence*. Présence de Dieu au monde et à l'homme; présence de l'âme à Dieu; présence de l'homme à son univers." *La Prière de Péguy* (Neuchâtel: La Baconnière, 1942), p. 93.

"act of presence." The words of the poet stand in the middle, facing in turn toward the poet's consciousness, toward God, and toward the objects of the creation. Poetic language incarnates the affinities and harmonies of the other three realms, for the poet is the man who knows how to "call things by their true names, by their secret names,"[20] and his words bring into the open the hidden presence of God in things.

There is, finally, the presence of all the men and women of history to one another and to the world. The writers Béguin came especially to admire—Bernanos, Bloy, Claudel, Péguy—are those Catholic writers who recognize most clearly the communion of mankind in suffering which is a perpetual reenactment of the Incarnation and Crucifixion. "All the saints—and all the faithful, and all the sinners," says Béguin, "form through the ages a continuous chain."[21] To this brotherhood of pain poetry presents evidence of the possibility of redemption, evidence of a sacred freshness still present beneath the surface of things and uncorrupted by the long centuries since the Fall. Béguin's criticism, in the end, is an apologetic addressed to all men in their solidarity in suffering. It brings them the precious witness poetry offers of God's presence in the Creation.

Georges Poulet was born in Belgium in 1902 and was educated at the University of Liège. From 1927 to 1952 he taught at the University of Edinburgh; in 1952 he became professor of French at the Johns Hopkins University; from 1958 until recently he has been professor of French literature at the University of Zurich. He is now a professor at the University of Nice.

Like the other members of his group, Poulet thinks of criticism as beginning and ending in a coincidence of the mind of the critic and the mind of the author. There must be what he calls an "absolute transparency with the soul of the other." Poulet differs from the rest, however, in his unwillingness to use this transparency as a means to reach some further end.

20. *Poésie de la présence*, p. 288 (about Supervielle's poetry).
21. *La Prière de Péguy*, p. 40.

His "criticism of pure identification"[22] is an end in itself. This means that Poulet is somewhat broader in his sympathies than either Raymond or Béguin. Seeking nothing beyond consciousness in consciousness, he has been able to concern himself with a wide variety of authors, from the church fathers through the writers of the Middle Ages, the poets, dramatists, and religious thinkers of the seventeenth century, the sensationalists of the eighteenth century, and a multitude of nineteenth- and twentieth-century writers. He can take the same interest, for example, in Casanova as in Pascal or Mallarmé. As long as some specific quality of inner experience is successfully expressed in the work of a writer, Poulet will find it worthwhile to relive that quality from within. The aim of each of his critical essays is to re-create as precisely as possible the exact tone which persists in a given writer throughout all the variety of his work.

For this reason he puts great value on defining the *cogito* of each writer. The *cogito* is the primary moment of the revelation of the self to itself in "an act of self-consciousness" separating the mind from everything which may enter it from the outside. All those exterior things are for Poulet somewhat accidental and unimportant. The affective quality of a consciousness is the source of everything else in a writer. It is an invariant element, present as a necessary coefficient of all the things the consciousness is conscious of. A moment of self-consciousness is therefore the "invariable starting point of every human existence perceived from within." The aim of criticism must be to disengage the mind of the writer from everything extraneous to it, to catch it "in the surging forth and genetic action of its power," when it exists "in a nearly virginal state, not yet invaded and as it were masked by the thick mass of its objective contents."[23] One of Poulet's most recent books, a study of a group of twentieth-century writers, is called *Le Point de départ*. In each essay in this book, as in the rest of his criticism, he attempts to "go back in the work of the author all the way

22. "La Pensée critique de Jean Starobinski," *Critique* 19 (1963): 408.

23. "La Pensée critique de Marcel Raymond," *Studi di Filologia Moderna* 3: *Saggi e Ricerche di Letteratura Francese* (1963), pp. 208, 209.

to that act from which each imaginary universe opens out."[24]

This concern for the intimate texture of each writer's mind explains Poulet's special admiration for a writer like Amiel, whose journal lets one hear in its purity the murmur of "the original and final activity of the human consciousness, which consists in thinking itself, and again, and always, in thinking itself."[25] Or it explains his fondness for Joubert, whose *Pensées* bring clearly into the open something different from any specific thought they may express, that is, the "interior distance" of the mind, that transparent space of "pure vacancy and latency" whose luminous expanses offer themselves to everything the mind may come to think.[26]

Poulet's commitment to the idea that consciousness is the living source of literature distinguishes his work from all that criticism which presupposes a Husserlian conception of consciousness. For Husserl, for Martin Heidegger, for Maurice Merleau-Ponty, for Gaston Bachelard, for Jean-Pierre Richard, and for many other contemporary thinkers and artists, consciousness is always consciousness *of* something or other. For such men there is never an act of self-consciousness in which the mind is aware of nothing but its own native affective tone. However far back one goes, however seemingly far away from the world, no state of mind can be encountered which is not already an inextricable interpenetration of subject and object, mind and things. This categorical rejection of any complete division of consciousness and the world, so fecund in recent developments in philosophy and art, is fundamentally anti-Cartesian. It rejects the idea of a *cogito* in which the mind knows nothing but itself. Poulet, on the other hand, maintains the traditional dualism and affirms the priority of consciousness as the genetic energy in literature. This commitment appears clearly in an important letter of 1961. Distinguishing the presuppositions of his criticism from those of his friend and follower Jean-Pierre Richard, Poulet here rejects all that

24. *Trois Essais de mythologie romantique* (Paris: J. Corti, 1966), p. 11.

25. Introduction to H. F. Amiel, *Journal intime: l'année 1857*, 10/18 (Paris: Union Générale d'Editions, 1965), p. xvi.

26. Introduction to Joseph Joubert, *Pensées*, 10/18 (Paris: Union Générale d'Editions, 1966), p. xv.

modern tradition of thought which may be called phenomenological and states his allegiance to the tradition of Descartes:

> I should readily consider that the most important form of subjectivity is not that of the mind overwhelmed, filled, and so to speak stuffed with its objects, but that there is another [kind of consciousness] which sometimes reveals itself on this side of, at a distance from, and protected from, any object, a subjectivity which exists in itself, withdrawn from any power which might determine it from the outside, and possessing itself by a direct intuition, infinitely different from the self-knowledge which is the indirect result of our relations with the world. In other words, I should say that subjectivity is the consciousness of the critic coinciding with the consciousness of the thinking or feeling person, located in the heart of the text (of every literary text), in such a way that this double consciousness appears less in its multiplicity of sensuous relations with things than prior to and separate from any object, as self-consciousness or pure consciousness. . . . As you have seen, in this I remain faithful to the Cartesian tradition.[27]

Poulet's criticism, then, may more exclusively be defined as "consciousness of consciousness" than either the religiously oriented criticism of Raymond and Béguin or the thematic criticism of Bachelard and Richard. For Poulet neither the dense substance of physical objects nor any extra-human presence within them is as important as the consciousness of

27. "Je considérerais volontiers que la subjectivité qui importe le plus, n'est pas cette subjectivité pâmée, comblée et comme gavée par ses objets, mais qu'il en est une autre qui se découvre parfois en deçà, à distance et à l'abri de tout objet, une subjectivité qui existe en elle-même, soustraite à tout pouvoir de détermination extérieure, et se possédant par une intuition directe, infiniment différente de la connaissance de soi qui est l'effet indirect de nos rapports avec le monde. En d'autres termes, je dirai que la subjectivité est la conscience du critique coïncidant avec la conscience du sujet pensant ou sentant, placé au coeur du texte (de tout texte littéraire), de telle façon que cette double conscience apparaisse, moins dans ses multiples relations sensibles avec les objets, qu'en deçà et à l'écart de tout objet, comme conscience de soi ou conscience pure. . . . Comme vous l'avez bien vu, je reste par là dans la tradition cartésienne." From an unpublished letter of 25 November 1961.

the writer who describes them. If anything other than consciousness enters for him as an essential element into literature, it is something located not beyond or outside the mind, but precisely at its deepest center, for "the profundity of the interior [of consciousness] is such that one can never see the edge or the end of it, and, as in the case of Pascal, there is a transcendence of the center." This transcendence is reached not by going outside the minds of the writers criticized but by "prolonging in its very interiority the spirituality of all authors." In doing this "one comes to glimpse something which transcends them, to establish a convergence." [28]

The notion that the minds of all authentic authors converge toward a transcendent point which is the hidden center of every human consciousness is in part the rationale of the essays in *Les Métamorphoses du cercle* in which Poulet re-creates not the mind of a single author, but the mind of an age. For him, all human minds form a living whole, and the history of literature may therefore be defined as "a history of the human consciousness." [29]

The idea of a transcendence at the center also explains Poulet's interest in authors like Pascal, Maurice de Guérin, or Nerval, for whom writing is the quest for a goal which can never be reached in this world. A transcendent presence is one which always remains beyond and unattainable. "I am above all attracted," says Poulet, "by those for whom literature is—by definition—a spiritual activity which must be gone beyond in its own depths, or, which, in failing to be gone beyond, in being condemned to the awareness of a nontranscendence, affirms itself as the experience and verification of a fundamental defeat." [30]

28. "La profondeur du dedans est telle qu'on n'en voit jamais le bout ni la fin, et, comme dans le cas de Pascal, il y a transcendance du centre"; "en prolongeant dans son intériorité même la spiritualité de tous les auteurs"; "l'on arrive à pressentir quelque chose qui les dépasse, à constater une convergence." From a letter of 1963.

29. "Réponse," *Les Lettres Nouvelles*, no. 17 (24 June 1959), p. 12.

30. "Je suis surtout attiré par ceux pour qui la littérature est—par définition—une activité spirituelle qui doit être dépassée dans sa profondeur même, ou, qui ne pouvant l'être, étant condamnée à la

The dialectical development of each critical essay by Poulet follows a writer in his attempts to reach the depths of his mind. His encounters with things other than that mind are often important in these attempts. Poulet tries to clarify these encounters as much as possible, to put them in order according to their interconnections. Order and transparence are two fundamental aspects of his criticism. Transparence is attained by seeing through an author, by bringing to light the intimate reason for each quality of the consciousness expressed in his works. Though Poulet likes a consciousness which is semiopaque, a half-darkness penetrated with difficulty, this may be because such a mind is a challenge to his powers of clarification. Even when he talks about darkness or irrationality, he transforms muddle into clarity by demonstrating its plausibility. To show its plausibility means to show its connection to all the other salient motifs in the author's work. Order is attained in criticism through a demonstration of the mutual implication of all the characteristics of the consciousness being criticized. All the contents of the bubble of consciousness must be shown to be acting and reacting on one another, in reciprocal interchange.

Though Poulet concerns himself with the ways his authors have assimilated parts of the world into their writings, nevertheless his essential aim is to detach each mind from its contents. In relation to the characteristic texture or grain of a writer's interior space, the objects which happen to traverse it seem, to Poulet, more or less "a matter of indifference." [31] Marcel Raymond may have been the first to use the concept of the *cogito* in literary criticism, but Poulet's most important accomplishment is his extensive and deliberate investigation of the variations from writer to writer and from century to century in the ways men have come to self-consciousness. From the mobile self-awareness of Montaigne to the intellectualist *cogito* of Descartes, the sensationalist *cogito* of Rousseau,

---

conscience d'un non-dépassement, s'avère comme l'expérience et la constatation d'un fondamental échec." From a letter of 1963.

31. Introduction to H. F. Amiel, *Journal intime: l'année 1857*, p. xvi.

or the voluntarist *cogito* of Balzac, down to contemporary forms of self-consciousness in Proust, Claudel, Eluard, Char, and many others, Poulet has distinguished the manifold ways in which the human mind has become aware of its own "indescribable intimacy."[32]

Jean Rousset was born in Geneva in 1910. After studies at Geneva he was a lecturer in various German universities, and then returned to the University of Geneva, where he is now professor of French literature. Disciple and colleague of Marcel Raymond, also close friend of Georges Poulet, his work differs somewhat from theirs in its concern for structure in works of literature, and in the fact that he often devotes an essay to a single work—to a play by Corneille, or to a novel by Flaubert or Proust. Raymond too affirms that "it is impossible to escape from forms,"[33] but he tries to go as much as possible beyond them in order to reach the obscure sense of existence which is at the heart of each author's work. Rousset, on the other hand, is, in his interest in individual works, much closer to American new criticism, to Russian formalism, or to a French critic like Gaëtan Picon. For Rousset each work has its own unique form. This form brings into existence meanings which could become articulated in no other way. *Madame Bovary*, for example, "constitutes an independent organism, an absolute which is entirely self-sufficient, a whole which can be understood and clarified in itself."[34]

Unlike Picon, however, or the Anglo-Saxon formalists, Rousset affirms that the new presence which an authentic work brings into the world is not something impersonal, but is precisely the identity of its creator. If form for Poulet is something external which masks the consciousness that created it, Rousset sees in form the indispensable means by which a mind emerges from indistinction and becomes aware of itself in its individuality. The true structure of a work is nothing

32. "La Pensée critique de Marcel Raymond," *Studi di Filologia Moderna* 3: *Saggi e Ricerche di Letteratura Francese* (1963), p. 209.
33. Quoted in Jean Rousset, *Forme et signification*, p. xvi.
34. Ibid., p. xx.

like a superficial framework or shape, for "in art there is no form which is not experienced and worked out from the inside." Only such an interior form can be one in which the artist discovers himself in the process of making his work. "The writer," says Rousset, "does not write in order to say *something*, he writes in order to *say himself*, as the painter paints in order to express himself in paint." "It is not before or after, it is by way of his creation that [the artist] becomes the person he is," and therefore the writing of *Madame Bovary* "reveals to Flaubert what he could know only through it: Flaubert himself."[35]

Rousset's most important theoretical statement, the introduction to *Forme et signification*, makes explicit the presupposition of his critical studies, the notion that a work of literature is "the simultaneous development of a structure and of a way of thinking, the amalgamation of a form and of an experience which are interdependent in their genesis and growth." The critic must reverse this process, and "seize the dream by way of the form." For this reason Rousset is most interested in those structural themes or motifs in a work which seem to converge toward what Claudel calls its "dynamic source," "the foyer from which all the structures and meanings radiate."[36] Examples of such themes in Rousset's criticism are the motifs of windows and views from above in *Madame Bovary*, or the motif of the separating screen in the plays of Claudel. This desire to reach through structural motifs to the spiritual quality at the origin of form may also explain Rousset's interest in moving, unstable forms, forms behind which one can see the shaping experience at work. In *La Littérature de l'âge baroque en France* he describes with delicate sensitivity and great refinement of taste the development of a multitude of such forms in baroque art.

Jean-Pierre Richard was born in 1922. Though he has been strongly influenced by the older members of the Geneva school, particularly by Poulet, he stands a little apart from the

35. Ibid., pp. v, vi, ix.
36. Ibid., pp. x, xi, xv.

others. He was educated at the Ecole Normale Supérieure and at the Sorbonne, and he also followed Georges Poulet's courses at the University of Edinburgh. He has taught at the French Institute in London and in Madrid. Now he is a professor at the University of Paris (Vincennes). His work derives as much from the criticism of Gaston Bachelard as it does from the Geneva critics. He has applied to the work of individual writers the insights into poetic language which Bachelard expressed for that universal poetry diffused in the work of all the poets.

Like Bachelard, like Merleau-Ponty, Richard believes that there is no originating moment when consciousness is empty of any content but the presence of the self to itself. Like Bachelard, Richard affirms that the origin of poetry is material images, phrases or passages which express one or another of the thousands of ways in which subject and object can be joined by way of a bodily sensation. "It is in sensation that everything begins," says Richard; "flesh, objects, moods, compose for the self a primal space, a horizon of density or dizzying emptiness." Since everything, literature included, starts with sensation, Richard has in his criticism attempted, "by way of obsessive landscapes or visibly preoccupying reveries, a direct study of sensation" in literature.[37] His aim is to remain as close as possible to the primary physical level from which forms and ideas in literature are born. This aim implies Richard's conviction that ideas and forms are in fact less fundamental than sensations, material images, or obscure reveries in which the soul marries itself by way of the body to some objective quality. "I have tried," he says, "to seize [the *fundamental project* of the author] at its most elementary level, that at which it affirms itself with the greatest humility, but also most openly: level of pure sensation, of crude emotion, or of the image in the process of being born."[38]

37. *Littérature et sensation* (Paris: Seuil, 1954), text on cover; "Quelques aspects nouveaux de la critique littéraire en France," *Filologia Moderna*, no. 3 (April 1961), p. 14.

38. ". . . j'ai essayé de le saisir à son niveau le plus élémentaire, celui où il s'affirme avec le plus d'humilité, mais aussi avec le plus de

This is Richard's intention in criticism, but the intention does not prepare one for the great richness and weight of his critical language, his astonishing ability to re-create in the words of his essay the most evasive bodily or vegetative forms of life, the patient way in which he takes the reader through the network of recurrent physical images which organizes the work of Nerval or Flaubert, Baudelaire or Rimbaud, Mallarmé or Char. In each of Richard's essays certain fundamental images are shown to embody, in carnal concreteness, one writer's search for a "happy relation" to the world, his attempt to find an "experienced joy" in which "the most contradictory needs come to be satisfied together."[39] *L'Univers imaginaire de Mallarmé* is Richard's most challenging work. It brings to light an entirely new Mallarmé, not the cold symbolist seeking to capture "nothingness" in words but a poet enamored of the substances of this earth and seeking his happiness there.

Littérature et sensation, the title of Richard's first book, gives a name to one orientation of his criticism. *Poésie et profondeur*, the title of his next book, names another. Poetry for him must have depth as well as sensations. The writers he most admires seek to reach through sensations something secretly present in sensations, something glimpsed in an emptiness or limitless depth which opens beneath them, something which is the ground of them all, the "being" which is present in each sensation because it so substantially *is*. "Figures of a being at once radiant and withdrawn," says Richard. "Separation here becomes the very proximity of the distant. The void opens to reveal that there is something there, or rather to reveal the ground, the *foundation of things* which allows all things to be, to be in the distance which divides them from their depths."[40]

---

franchise: niveau de la sensation pure, du sentiment brut, ou de l'image en train de naître." *Poésie et profondeur* (Paris: Seuil, 1955), p. 10.

39. Ibid., p. 9; *L'Univers imaginaire de Mallarmé* (Paris: Seuil, 1961), p. 27.

40. "Chiffres d'un être à la fois fulgurant et retiré. . . ." "L'écartement y devient la proximité même du lointain. Le vide y ouvre à quelque chose, ou plutôt à ce sol, ce fond des choses qui permet à toutes choses d'être, d'être dans la distance qui les sépare de

This fugitive being which is the ground of things is not to be identified with the divine presence which Béguin and Raymond find. Richard's "being" is more closely tied to the physical substance of things. It is something present in them and absent from them at the same time. His interest in this theme in poetry connects his work, in this way at least and in spite of great differences in tone and atmosphere, to the criticism of Maurice Blanchot or to the philosophical thought of Heidegger. Unlike Blanchot or Heidegger, however, Richard always seeks to glimpse being by way of the concrete and intensely specific images in poetry which reveal it, as, for example, in a recent book, *Onze études sur la poésie moderne*, a series of essays on contemporary French poets, Reverdy, Perse, Ponge, Du Bouchet, Jaccottet, and others.

Jean Starobinski, the last critic to be discussed here, was born in Geneva in 1920 and educated at the University of Geneva. He completed medical as well as literary studies. From 1954 to 1956 he taught at the Johns Hopkins University. Since 1958 he has been at the University of Geneva, where he now holds a professorship.

Starobinski sides with Husserl and Merleau-Ponty in his conception of consciousness. "Consciousness exists," he says, "because it appears to itself. But it cannot appear to itself without bringing into existence a world to which it is indissolubly connected."[41] The locus of this connection is the body and its behavior. "We perceive, we express ourselves," says Starobinski, "by our body, by our gestures, by our words. . . . Our consciousness is from the beginning engaged in a body and in an experienced situation. . . . Merleau-Ponty refuted the presuppositions . . . of intellectualism, which endows with

leur fond." *Onze études sur la poésie moderne* (Paris: Seuil, 1964), pp. 7, 8.

41. From "Montaigne ou la conversion à la vie," cited in Georges Poulet, "La Pensée critique de Jean Starobinski," *Critique* 19 (1963): 391.

special privileges a consciousness entirely separated from the world and from the body."[42]

Though Starobinski agrees with the phenomenologists that the mind is always inextricably intermingled with a body and with a world which it knows by way of the body, nevertheless he has been haunted since his earliest writing by the dream of a perfect intellectualization of the body and of the world's density. In this transformation the mind becomes a limpid transparency open to a world also made transparent. This is "the illusion of a sovereign look, which would encounter no obstacle and for which the universe would be a palace of crystal." This state is most nearly made real in literature, for Starobinski, in those ecstatic reveries in which Jean-Jacques Rousseau "enjoys his own transparency by way of the presence of a universe which makes everything transparent." Such an ecstasy fulfills man's desire to "destroy the obstacle of material passivity," to "escape from his carnal condition and make himself an angel."[43] Starobinski's book on Rousseau is a brilliantly detailed analysis of the alternation in Rousseau's work between expressions of a paradisaical openness to the world and descriptions of the various barriers which may isolate a man from the world and from other people.

Back and forth, in Starobinski's interpretations of literature, human existence swings between a state of dense incarnation and a state of angelic intellectualization in which everything becomes so pellucid that it can be pierced by a single look. Among the obstacles which may resist this look are other persons. More than any other of the critics discussed here Starobinski is interested in the theme of intersubjective rela-

42. "Nous percevons, nous nous exprimons par notre corps, par nos gestes, par nos paroles. . . . Notre conscience est d'emblée engagée dans un corps et dans une situation vécue. . . . Merleau-Ponty réfutait les présupposés . . . de l'intellectualisme, qui privilégie une conscience entièrement séparée du monde et du corps." "Je ne peux pas sortir de l'être," *Gazette de Lausanne* no. 122 (27 May 1961), p. 13.

43. *Montesquieu par lui-même*, Ecrivains de Toujours (Paris: Seuil, 1953), p. 36; *Jean-Jacques Rousseau: la transparence et l'obstacle* (Paris: Plon, 1957), p. 323; "Mallarmé et la tradition poétique française," *Les Lettres* 3, special no. (1948): 40; "Le Divertissement précieux," *Labyrinthe* no. 7 (15 April 1945), p. 3.

tions in literature. This interest associates his work not only with that of Jean-Paul Sartre but also with the work of Georges Blin, who has, especially in his books on Stendhal,[44] investigated interpersonal relations in literature. Starobinski himself, in long sections of *Jean-Jacques Rousseau: la transparence et l'obstacle* and in the various essays in *L'Oeil vivant*, has made admirably concrete analyses of the interplay between consciousness and consciousness as it is expressed in literature by means of motifs like the mask, the look, the secret witness, or the village festival.

For Starobinski literary criticism is also a form of intersubjectivity, and, as he explains in the important theoretical chapter prefixed to *L'Oeil vivant*, criticism too must live in a movement between proximity and distance, opacity and transparency, "a total complicity with the creative subjectivity" and a "panoramic look from above."[45] Understanding the work of literature alternately from the inside and from the outside, the critic may come to attain what is otherwise unavailable to him, a full understanding of himself. Starobinski, in affirming this, is consistent with his description of himself as a man for whom "there will be no access to himself except by way of the world."[46]

For all the critics of the Geneva school criticism is fundamentally the expression of a "reciprocal transparency"[47] of two minds, that of the critic and that of the author, but they differ in their conceptions of the nature of consciousness. From the religious ideas of human existence in Raymond and Béguin, to the notion in Poulet's criticism that what counts most is "the proof, the living proof, of the experience of inner spirituality as a positive reality,"[48] Rousset's belief that the

44. *Stendhal et les problèmes de la personnalité* (Paris: J. Corti, 1958); *Stendhal et les problèmes du roman* (Paris: J. Corti 1954).

45. *L'Oeil vivant* (Paris: Gallimard, 1961), pp. 25, 26.

46. "Pour un portrait," *Les Lettres*, no. 6 (December 1944), p. 44.

47. *Jean-Jacques Rousseau: la transparence et l'obstacle*, p. 8.

48. ". . . la preuve, la preuve vivante, de l'expérience de la spiritualité intérieure comme réalité positive." Unpublished letter of 25 November 1961.

artist's self-consciousness comes into existence only in the intimate structure of his work, the unquestioning acceptance of an overlapping of consciousness and the physical world in Richard's criticism, and the fluctuation between incarnation and detachment in the work of Starobinski, these six critics base their interpretations of literature on a spectrum of dissimilar convictions about the human mind.

BIBLIOGRAPHY

This bibliography lists the major writings of each of the critics of the Geneva school and a few of the essays on their work.

WORKS BY MARCEL RAYMOND

L'Influence de Ronsard sur la poésie française, 1550–1585. 2 vols. Paris: E. Droz, 1927. New edition in Travaux d'Humanisme et Renaissance, Geneva: E. Droz, 1965.

De Baudelaire au surréalisme. Paris: Corrêa, 1933. New edition. Paris: J. Corti, 1940. (*From Baudelaire to Surrealism*. Translated by G. M. New York: Wittenborn, Schultz, 1950. London: Peter Owen, 1961.) Raymond's most important book, a seminal work for the Geneva school. It is a study of a multitude of poets, from Baudelaire, Rimbaud, and Mallarmé to Pierre-Jean Jouve and Jules Supervielle.

Henri Ghéon. Montreal: Editions du Cep, 1939.

Génies de France. Neuchâtel: La Baconnière, 1942. Contains essays on Montaigne, Agrippa d'Aubigné, La Fontaine, Racine, Montesquieu, Lamartine, Hugo, Baudelaire, and Bergson.

Paul Valéry et la tentation de l'esprit. Neuchâtel: La Baconnière, 1946. New edition. 1964. A study of the detached spirituality in Valéry which, for Raymond, is the worst temptation of the mind.

Le Sens de la qualité. Propos sur la culture et la situation de l'homme. Neuchâtel: La Baconnière, 1948. Contains some of Raymond's most important statements about criticism.

Editor. *Anthologie de la nouvelle française*. Lausanne: Guilde du Livre, 1950. Additional collections edited for the same publisher: Ronsard, Rimbaud, Verlaine, Baudelaire, Rousseau.

Trans. (with Claire Raymond). H. Woelfflin. *Les Principes fondamentaux de l'histoire de l'art*. Paris: Plon, 1953. Paris: Gallimard, 1966.

Baroque et renaissance poètique. Paris: J. Corti, 1955. Essays on Ronsard, Malherbe, and French baroque literature.

Commentaries. J.-J. Rousseau. *Oeuvres complètes*. Pléiade. Paris: Gallimard, 1959.

"La Maladie et la guérison: 1950–1957." *Revue de Théologie et de Philosophie* 11 (1961): 1–18. A record of Raymond's religious experience of 1950 and the years following.

Jean-Jacques Rousseau: la quête de soi et la rêverie. Paris: J. Corti, 1962. A collection of Raymond's various essays on Rousseau.

Vérité et poésie: études littéraires. Neuchâtel: La Baconnière, 1964. Essays on Pascal, Pierre Bayle, Rousseau, Senancour, Verlaine, Mallarmé, Rimbaud, and C.-F. Ramuz.

Senancour: Sensations et révélations. Paris: J. Corti, 1965. A full study of the thought of this Swiss meditative writer.

Fénelon. Les Ecrivains devant Dieu. Paris: Desclée de Brouwer, 1967. An admirable essay on this seventeenth-century quietist, whose thought has certain affinities with Raymond's own habit of mind in his criticism.

Etre et dire: études. Neuchâtel: La Baconnière, 1970.

WORKS ON RAYMOND

Lespire, Roger. "Réflexions sur la critique de Marcel Raymond." *Cahiers du Nord* 22, no. 90–91 (1950–51), pp. 365–74.

Poulet, Georges. "La Pensée critique de Marcel Raymond." *Studi di Filologia Moderna* 3: *Saggi e Ricerche di Letteratura Francese* (1963), pp. 203–29.

Rousset, Jean. "L'Oeuvre de Marcel Raymond et la nouvelle critique." *Mercure de France* 348 (1963): 462–70.

WORKS BY ALBERT BÉGUIN

L'Âme romantique et le rêve: essai sur la romantisme allemand et la poésie française. 2 vols. Marseilles: Cahiers du Sud, 1937. Another edition in 1 vol. Paris: J. Corti, 1939. Béguin's masterpiece, another of the generative books of the Geneva school. Studies of the important pre-romantic and romantic writers in Germany and France.

Gérard de Nerval, followed by *Poésie et mystique.* Paris: Stock, 1937. Revised and enlarged edition. Paris: J. Corti, 1945.

La Prière de Péguy. Neuchâtel: La Baconnière, 1942.

Léon Bloy l'impatient. Fribourg: Egloff, 1944. (*Léon Bloy: A Study on Impatience.* Translated by Edith M. Riley. New York and London: Sheed and Ward, 1947.)

Faiblesse de l'Allemagne. Paris: J. Corti, 1945.

Balzac visionnaire. Geneva: Skira, 1946.

Translation and preface (with Paul Zumthor). *Saint Bernard de Clairvaux: Choix de textes.* Le Cri de la France. Fribourg-Paris: Egloff, 1947.

L'Eve de Péguy. Paris: Labergerie, 1948. New edition. Paris: Seuil, 1955.

Léon Bloy, mystique de la douleur. Paris: Labergerie, 1948. New edition. Paris: Seuil, 1955.

Patience de Ramuz. Neuchâtel: La Baconnière, 1950.

L'Inde, les Indes. Neuchâtel: La Baconnière, 1953.

Pascal par lui-même. Ecrivains de Toujours. Paris: Seuil, 1954. In certain pages of this book Béguin finds Pascal alien to the sense of history and community in modern Catholicism.

Bernanos par lui-même. Ecrivains de Toujours. Paris: Seuil, 1954. A study of the theme of childhood in Bernanos and of the relation between the vocation of the priesthood and the vocation of writing.

Poésie de la présence: de Chrétien de Troyes à Pierre Emmanuel. Neuchâtel: La Baconnière. Paris: Seuil, 1957. A collection of Béguin's most important essays. Studies of Chrétien de Troyes, Maurice Scève, Corneille, Racine, Jean Paul, Hugo, Nodier, Baudelaire, Alain-Fournier, Verlaine, Claudel, Reverdy, Jacob, Supervielle, Saint-John Perse, Breton, Eluard, and Emmanuel.

"Limites de l'histoire littéraire." *Esprit* 23 (1955): 166–70.

"Note sur la critique littéraire." *Esprit* 23 (1955): 447–51.

Balzac lu et relu. Pierres Vives. Paris: Seuil, 1965.

WORKS ON BÉGUIN

Special Issues

Essais et témoignages: Etapes d'une pensée rencontrée. Edited by Marc Eigeldinger. Cahiers du Rhône. Neuchâtel: La Baconnière, 1950. Articles by Benjamin Péret, Jean Paulhan, Michel Carrouges, A. Rolland de Renéville, Julien Gracq, and others.

Essais et temoignages. Cahiers du Rhône. Neuchâtel: La Baconnière. Paris: Seuil, 1957. Contains important letters by Albert Béguin, as well as essays on his work by Julien Green, Raymond, Rousset, Poulet, Jean Cayrol, among others.

Esprit 26 (1958): 753–964. This issue contains many articles on Béguin, texts of letters and essays by him, and a full bibliography of his work, including a multitude of reviews and uncollected essays in periodicals.

Revue de Belles-Lettres, vol. 83, no. 6 (November–December 1958).

Cahiers du Sud 48, no. 360 (1961): 171–231. Contains essays on Béguin, as well as letters from Béguin to Marcel Raymond and two previously unpublished texts by Béguin. See especially Georges Poulet's essay, "La Pensée critique d'Albert Béguin," pp. 177–98.

Esprit 35 (1967): 979–1026, Articles by J.-M. Domenach, Camille Bourniquel, and others.

Articles and Books

Demorest, Jean-Jacques. "Albert Béguin: Le Salut par les poètes." *Modern Language Notes* 78 (1963): 453–70.

Diéguez, Manuel de. "Albert Béguin." In *L'Ecrivain et son langage*, pp. 204–20. Les Essais. Paris: Gallimard, 1960.

Franck, Dorothée-Juliane. *La Quête spirituelle d'Albert Béguin*. Neuchâtel: Paul Attinger, 1965. A dissertation on Béguin presented at the University of Zurich.

Grotzer, Pierre. *Les Ecrits d'Albert Béguin. Essai de Bibliographie*. Langages-Documents. Neuchâtel: La Baconnière, 1967.

WORKS BY GEORGES POULET

Etudes sur le temps humain. Edinburgh: University of Edinburgh Press, 1949. Paris: Plon, 1950. (*Studies in Human Time*. Translated by Elliott Coleman. Baltimore: Johns Hopkins Press, 1959.) Poulet's first book is, along with Raymond's *De Baudelaire au surréalisme* and Béguin's *L'Âme romantique et le rêve*, one of the seminal masterworks of the Geneva school. It contains essays on the experience of time in Montaigne, Descartes, Pascal, Molière, Corneille, Racine, Madame de La Fayette, Fontenelle, L'Abbé Prévost, Rousseau, Diderot, Benjamin Constant, Vigny, Théophile Gautier, Flaubert, Baudelaire, Valéry, and Proust. The appendix of the English translation contains brief essays on time in Emerson, Hawthorne, Poe, Thoreau, Melville, Whitman, Emily Dickinson, Henry James, and T. S. Eliot.

La Distance intérieure: Etudes sur le temps humain II. Paris: Plon, 1952. (*The Interior Distance*. Translated by Elliott Coleman. Baltimore: Johns Hopkins Press, 1959.) Contains essays on Marivaux, Vauvenargues, Chamfort, Laclos, Joubert, Balzac, Hugo, Musset, Guérin, and Mallarmé.

Les Métamorphoses du cercle. Paris: Plon, 1961. (*The Metamorphoses of the Circle*. Translated by Carley Dawson and Elliott Coleman with the collaboration of the author. Baltimore: Johns Hopkins Press, 1967.) Studies on the theme of the circle from Greek and medieval thought to the present day, with essays on the Renaissance, the "baroque epoch," the eighteenth century, and romanticism, as well as on Pascal, Rousseau, Lamartine, Balzac, Vigny, Nerval, Poe, Amiel, Flaubert, Baudelaire, Mallarmé's "Prose," and Henry James, Claudel, Rilke, T. S. Eliot, and Jorge Guillén.

L'Espace proustien. Paris: Gallimard, 1963. This study continues the investigation of the inner space of imagination which is indicated in the title metaphor of *La Distance intérieure* and extended in *Les Métamorphoses du cercle*.

Le Point de départ: Etudes sur le temps humain III. Paris: Plon, 1964. As the title suggests, this book brings into the open Poulet's concern for the initial act of self-consciousness which is for him the source of literature. The book contains essays on Whitman, Bernanos, Char, Supervielle, Eluard, Perse, Reverdy, Ungaretti, and Sartre.

Introduction. H. F. Amiel. *Journal intime: l'année 1857*. 10/18. Paris: Union Générale d'Editions, 1965.

Introduction. Joseph Joubert. *Pensées*. 10/18. Paris: Union Générale d'Editions, 1966.

Trois essais de mythologie romantique. Paris: J. Corti, 1966. An essay on Nerval's *Sylvie*, one on the theme of "la blonde aux yeux noirs" in Nerval and Gautier, and one on Piranesi and the French romantic poets.

"Une Critique d'identification." In *Les Chemins actuels de la critique*, pp. 9–24, followed by discussion, pp. 25–35. Edited by Jean Ricardou. Faits et Thèmes. Paris: Plon, 1967. Essays and discussions by various critics, including Poulet himself. The proceedings of a meeting of the annual conference of the Centre Culturel de Cérisy. The conference was in this case directed by Poulet, and the resulting volume is an excellent introduction to polarities and themes within contemporary literary criticism in French.

Benjamin Constant par lui-même. Ecrivains de Toujours. Paris: Seuil, 1968. A long essay, illustrated, on the thought of an author in whom Poulet has long been interested. One of his best longer studies.

Mesure de l'instant: Etudes sur le temps humain IV. Paris: Plon, 1968. A further collection of essays on the theme of time, in this case especially the attempt to express the present moment by various authors: Maurice Scève, Saint-Cyran, Racine, Fénelon, Casanova, Joubert, "les romantiques anglais," Madame de Staël, Lamartine, Stendhal, Michelet, Amiel, Proust, and Julien Green.

Who Was Baudelaire? Translated by Robert Allen and James Emmons. The Artist and His World. Geneva: Skira; Cleveland, Ohio: World Publications, 1969.

In addition to the essays on Marcel Raymond, Albert Béguin, and Jean Starobinski listed under their names in this bibliography, Poulet has also published:

"La Pensée critique de Charles Du Bos," *Critique* 21 (1965): 491–516.

"Bachelard et la conscience de soi," *Revue de Métaphysique et de Morale* 70 (1965): 1–26.

"Maurice Blanchot: critique et romancier," *Critique* 22 (1966): 485–97.

These essays, with others, will be gathered in an "Essai sur la pensée critique de notre temps," which will be one of Poulet's most important books.

WORKS ON POULET

Béguin, Albert. "Etudes sur le temps humain," *Esprit* 19 (1951): 801–6.

Grotzer, Pierre. "*Mesure de l'instant.*" *Romanische Forschungen* 81 (1969): 204–13.

Joncherie, Roger. "A propos d'une critique nouvelle." *La Nouvelle Critique* 7, no. 69 (November 1955): 168–80.

Man, Paul de. "Vérité et méthode dans l'oeuvre de Georges Poulet." *Critique* 25 (1969): 608–23.

Miller, J. Hillis. "The Literary Criticism of Georges Poulet." *Modern Language Notes* 78 (1963): 471–88. A few sentences from this article have been incorporated into the present essay.

———. "Geneva or Paris: The Recent work of George Poulet," *University of Toronto Quarterly* 39 (1970): 212–28.

Richard, Jean-Pierre. "Etudes sur le temps humain." *Revue des Sciences Humaines*, no. 62–63 (April–September 1951), pp. 294–98.

Wahl, Jean. "La Littérature et le temps. De Montaigne à Proust." *Critique* 6 (1950): 209–19.

WORKS BY JEAN ROUSSET

La Littérature de l'âge baroque en France. Paris: J. Corti, 1953. An important study of the themes and motifs unifying the baroque imagination in sculpture, architecture, and theatrical design as well as in literature.

Editor. *Anthologie de la poésie baroque française*. 2 vols. Bibliothèque de Cluny. Paris: Armand Colin, 1961.

Forme et signification: Essais sur les structures littéraires de Corneille à Claudel. Paris: J. Corti, 1964. The introduction is Rousset's most important theoretical statement, and the book contains essays on *La Princesse de Clèves*, on Marivaux, on the epistolary novel, on *Madame Bovary*, on *A la Recherche du temps perdu*, and on Claudel. ("*Madame Bovary* or the Book about Nothing." Translated by Raymond Giraud. In *Flaubert: A Collection of Critical Essays*, pp. 112–31. Edited by Raymond Giraud. Twentieth Century Views. Englewood Cliffs, N.J.: Prentice-Hall, 1964. "*Madame Bovary:* Flaubert's Anti-Novel." Translated by Paul de Man. In *Madame Bovary*, pp. 439–57. Edited by Paul de Man. Norton Critical Editions. New York: Norton, 1965.)

L'Intérieur et l'extérieur: Essais sur la poésie et sur le théâtre au XVIIe siècle. Paris: J. Corti, 1968.

WORKS ON ROUSSET

Derrida, Jacques. "Force et signification." *Critique* 19 (1963): 483–99, 619–36.

WORKS BY JEAN-PIERRE RICHARD

Littérature et sensation. Pierres Vives. Paris: Seuil, 1954. Essays on Stendhal, Flaubert, Fromentin, and the Goncourts. ("The Creation of Form in Flaubert." Translated by Raymond Giraud. In *Flaubert: A Collection of Critical Essays*, pp. 36–56. Edited by Raymond Giraud. Twentieth Century Views. Englewood Cliffs, N.J.: Prentice Hall, 1964. "Love and Memory in *Madame Bovary*." Translated by Paul de Man. In *Madame Bovary*, pp. 426–38. Edited by Paul de Man. Norton Critical Editions. New York: Norton, 1965.)

Poésie et profondeur. Pierres Vives. Paris: Seuil, 1955. Essays on Nerval, Baudelaire, Rimbaud, and Verlaine.

L'Univers imaginaire de Mallarmé. Paris: Seuil, 1961. The revelation of a new Mallarmé, a Mallarmé close to the substance of material things, and seeking happiness in that closeness.

Editor. Mallarmé. *Pour un Tombeau d'Anatole.* Paris: Seuil, 1961.

"Quelques aspects nouveaux de la critique littéraire en France." *Filologia Moderna* 1, no. 3 (April 1961): 1–17. Reprinted in *Le Français dans le Monde*, no. 15 (March 1963), pp. 2–9. Richard's fullest discussion of the new directions of contemporary French literary criticism.

Onze études sur la poésie moderne. Pierres Vives. Paris: Seuil, 1964. Essays on Reverdy, Perse, Char, Eluard, Schehadé, Ponge, Guillevic, Bonnefoy, Du Bouchet, Jaccottet, and Dupin.

Paysage de Chateaubriand. Pierres Vives. Paris: Seuil, 1967.

"La Méthode critique de Charles Du Bos." *Modern Language Review* 62 (1967): 420–29.

Etudes sur le romantisme. Pierres Vives. Paris: Seuil, 1970. Essays on Balzac, Lamartine, Vigny, Hugo, Musset, Guérin, and Sainte-Beuve.

WORKS ON RICHARD

Diéguez, Manuel de. "Jean-Pierre Richard et la critique thématique." *Critique* 19 (1963): 517–35.

Genette, Gérard. "Bonheur de Mallarmé?" In *Figures*, pp. 91–100. Tel Quel. Paris: Seuil, 1966. See also, in the same volume,

Genette's essay entitled "Structuralisme et critique littéraire," pp. 145–70, for a provocative discussion of the present situation of literary criticism in France.

Hahn, Otto. "L'Illusion thématique." *Temps Modernes* 18 (1963): 2086–96.

Magowan, Robbin. "Criticism of Sensation." *Criticism* 6 (1964): 156–64.

WORKS BY JEAN STAROBINSKI

Pierre-Jean Jouve poète et romancier (with Paul Alexandre and Marc Eigeldinger). Neuchâtel: La Baconnière, 1946.

Montesquieu par lui-même. Ecrivains de Toujours. Paris: Seuil, 1953.

L'Idée d'organisme. Paris: Centre de Documentation Universitaire, 1956.

Jean-Jacques Rousseau: la transparence et l'obstacle. Paris: Plon, 1957. Bibliothèque des Idées. Paris: Gallimard, 1971. Starobinski's best book, an admirable study of the themes of limpidity and opacity in Rousseau's work.

Histoire du traitement de la mélancolie. Basel: Geigy, 1961.

L'Oeil vivant. Le Chemin. Paris: Gallimard, 1961. The introductory essay includes a discussion of literary criticism. The book contains studies of the theme of "the look" in Corneille, Racine, Rousseau, and Stendhal.

L'Invention de la liberté, 1700–1789. Art, Idées, Histoire. Geneva: Skira, 1964. (*Invention of Liberty, 1700–1789*. Translated by Bernard C. Swift. Geneva: Skira, 1964.) This book is part of the sumptuously illustrated series and contains an excellent essay on eighteenth-century ideas and motifs.

A History of Medicine. Translated by Bernard C. Swift. The New Illustrated Library of Science and Invention. New York: Hawthorn Books, 1964.

Portrait de l'artiste en saltimbanque. Les Sentiers de la Création. Geneva: Skira, 1970. A book on clowns, with many illustrations.

La Relation critique: L'Oeil vivant 2. Le Chemin. Paris: Gallimard, 1970. A volume bringing together a number of articles and essays on Spitzer, structuralism, psychoanalysis and literary criticism, etc.

WORKS ON STAROBINSKI

Poulet, Georges. "La Pensée critique de Jean Starobinski." *Critique* 19 (1963): 387–410. This essay contains references to a group of important uncollected essays by Starobinski published in various journals, mostly in the 1940s.

The chapter on Starobinski in Sarah N. Lawall's *Critics of Consciousness* (see below) cites a number of essays published since 1960 on the themes of irony and melancholy in various writers (Montaigne, La Rochefoucauld, Carlo Gozzi, and E. T. A. Hoffmann). These are, it appears, destined to form part of a larger work on melancholy in literature.

Sarah N. Lawall. *Critics of Consciousness: The Existential Structures of Literature.* Cambridge, Mass.: Harvard University Press, 1968. Contains chapters on each of the critics discussed in the present essay. The first book on the Geneva school and an excellent introduction to their work.

Yves Velan **13**

Barthes

In the French language, ''Spanish inns'' have a bad reputation: you find in them only what you bring with you. At first glance, Barthes's work is the opposite of a Spanish inn: it seems able to respond to the most divergent, contradictory needs. You have only to slice it up. One could for example, take a political section, which could be further subdivided according to whether one wanted an ''engaged'' Barthes, as in *Mythologies*, or a technocratic one, as in the second part of the *Essais critiques*. The work could be cut up along methodological lines: Marxist, psychoanalytic, linguistic. Or according to function: literary criticism, sociology, etc. What is more, it could be seen as a sign of the work's richness that any one of these isolated segments might satisfy the taker.

In the end, however, this richness becomes suspect. One wonders if these texts have any unity other than the tone which pervades them. The tone is striking, no doubt, but perhaps it is only a surface reflection and not at all clear evidence of thought. Perhaps these books are merely the successive moments of a pure itinerary. And if it is noted that each one corresponds to a particular moment of intellectual history, or quite simply of history, then the suspicion arises that Barthes is nothing more than a very agile mind, putting all his intelligence to the task of embodying whatever happens to be in fashion. This roughly is one of the reproaches which culminated in the attack by Picard.[1]

But the point is, precisely, that Barthes's work cannot be

Translated by David Carroll.

1. Raymond Picard, *Nouvelle Critique ou nouvelle imposture?* Libertés (Paris: Pauvert, 1965).

sliced up. To reduce his texts to one's own point of view requires that one deny their self-negating power—the very thing which frees them from any bias and which insures that each text goes further than the one before. So, *Mythologies* is doubtlessly a kind of de-mystifying myth-book, a "leftist" book; but in order to save it for the Left, one has to ignore its repeated warnings about the weakness of literature and the necessity of formalism. The *Essais critiques* provide the system and a sort of ethics of this formalism; but to stop there, in the hope of saving the good conscience of pure writing, requires that you tear out the pages on Brecht or those on the nostalgia for meaning. The next book will please some and disappoint others, those who want a book to have only a final sense, and those who want it to have none at all, for *Critique et vérité* is a plea for meaning achieved through formalism (formalism understood, of course, as the smallest quantity of possible meaning). Thus we should speak not of an itinerary but of growth. Each book is dialecticized and the work as a whole can be understood only within the complete system of its relations. It follows, therefore, that the work can be illuminated by its history, and it is there one must begin.

Thus in 1953 appeared the *Degré zéro de l'écriture*. The term "writing" (*écriture*) usually designates only the act of writing or its results. For Barthes it has a collective sense, a sort of signaling function common to a certain number of writers, dating from the time when literature, breaking with classical naturalness, began to turn in on itself and to see itself as an institution. But from the moment writers perceive themselves more or less consciously with this objective sense, they feel their responsibility toward it. Literature is no longer that language which is so well integrated that one never questions its being. It appears broken up, like the society which underlies it. On the one hand, writers feel themselves faced infinitely inward on their own subjectivity; this singular discourse, on the other hand, resounds over history which judges it in return. But a revelation is always an obligation to assume a burden. The burden of what? For the writer, both the depth of his consciousness and his own historicity. The alternate side of his individuality discloses itself to him as his role in society.

The book ends, however, on a note of disappointment. There is in the literary object a certain resistance, a density, yet ill-defined, which little suits it for the commitment implied by a responsibility. One can only evoke this inaptness of literature by means of "blank writing" (*l'écriture blanche*), a "zero degree" whose end would be silence.

Why not then consider the literary object itself, its nature? *Michelet* is a good example. Since the famous historian's ideology and activity are well known, there is no need to repeat them. "There is an order of tasks: first one must give that man his coherence, uncover the structure of his existence, a thematic, if you prefer, a network of obsessions." Literature may seem quite removed from this. But we are about to see it appear. The "if you prefer" indicates, among other things, that the method (required by its object) is not very well known. Actually, in 1954, it was beginning to be used, since it involves Bachelard's psychoanalysis of "substance." Bachelard postulates that all poetic imagination is nourished at its core by one of the four elements of earliest Greek philosophy: water, fire, air, or earth. The task is to find for every writer what substance animates him and the way it unfolds. In the case of Michelet, Barthes speaks rather of humors (blood, dryness) or of figures (smoothness, continuity), thus renewing Bachelard's method. But what is to be noted is the extension of one of the themes in *Degré zéro*. The work is literary only through the essential mediation of an ego. At the same time, *L'Histoire de France* exists only because it is a work. There is thus a specificity of the literary object, an autonomy which allows it to be taken only in and of itself. And it is this irreducible character which gives existence to the *narration* of a history, which establishes its *actualité*.

But then does this "history" have its own meaning or do we give it one? The ambiguity begins with the work itself since Michelet made no secret of his partisanship. In the absence of a truth about France, we can perhaps speak, at the very least, of a certain truth of Michelet, objective and immutable, which responds to that of our time. But what if, on reading Michelet, this truth appears quite different from the one Barthes was supposed to have recovered? Or in that case have we misunderstood Barthes's truth which was in fact Michelet's?

Two questions then occur. The first concerns the relation of the subject with his work and the validity of the meaning he gives it, and the conditions by which he himself can be certain of this meaning. The second, since there are conditions, is to recognize the ground on which they operate, in this case the pattern of signs which underlie those conditions, their nature, and their function.

It is not surprising that these are the very questions Barthes asks after *Michelet*, first empirically, then theoretically, in order to arrive at *Mythologies*.

Myth is used here in its primary sense of "discourse" (*parole*). Barthes examines the nature of discourse, understood as a sign or group of signs intending to communicate to us a message. To do this, he chooses the most insidious signs, those secondary ones, grafted to a primary statement (the praise of wine, for example), whose aim is to insinuate in us a barely visible, alienating meaning (the superiority of the French "race" is affirmed under the guise of praising the excellence of French wines). As a secondary, disguised meaning, it penetrates us unchallenged. Mythology—that is, the science of (false) discourse—brings it to light. To the fables of the bourgeoisie (since it is the bourgeoisie which seeks to persuade us because they are under attack and in power) Barthes replies with counter-fables, some sort of cleansing apologues. And in a postface, he dismantles the system of myth.

No plan, no apparent ideology oversees his decoding. He takes the mythical material as he finds it, deciphering it with all the asperity of his temperament and language. Just so many small-scale, portable phenomenologies! With his whole ego raised up to its full height, from the "zero degree" of the initial encounter, he openly displays his verticality, or, in other words, that fundamental subjectivism which he granted to modern writers in his first book.

But ideology is absent only in appearance. The concepts of alienation, of class, are those of Marxism, which has penetrated the intelligentsia if only by osmosis. In any case, Marxism is implicit in the notion of "mythology": to denounce a false discourse is to announce the necessity of a true one, which is to say, the necessity of the truth of human relations. And since falseness and truth correspond to alienation and its contrary, the whole analysis takes place inside the Marxist "utopia." Thus subjectivism operates under the aegis of a meaning which comes to it from without. Is Barthes then not as radical here as he seemed to be? Will he achieve his aim only by abolishing meaning in a text immanent to itself?

In any case, after having established in *Degré zéro* the responsibility of the writer, Barthes tries here to assume it. On the other hand, the myths he examines are grouped within a play of figures analogous to those of Michelet. To sum up, we are dealing with the first synthesis of Barthes's approach.

But it is precisely this systematizing, this structuring of mythical figures, which contains its future negation—a fact of considerable consequence. What is more, the negation comes to light within the particular work itself.

Unexpectedly, from an "engaged" point of view (the one which in 1956 constituted the reigning terrorism, for the French can never do without Terror), the conclusion of *Mythologies* is "disappointing."[2] Literature as praxis turns out to have only limited powers. All it can do is bring to light the falseness of a discourse; it fails as soon as it seeks to go beyond contestation. Why? By virtue of the very nature of language as such. Consequently, the word itself will acquire for all contemporary criticism a plenitude tending toward the absolute (understood in the original sense of "separated").

What is that nature? Or, rather, what nature does Barthes choose to give it? What determines this choice?

Let us examine first the operation contained in his *Michelet*: the entire analysis is horizontal, once the point of view is adopted—a point of view which derives, on the contrary, from the verticality of the man Barthes. This analysis is made at the level of the work itself, ignoring the life which engendered the work and all meaning which the work does not furnish. It considers only the configuration of the forms by which the work is manifested. At that point, a certain relation appears. For indeed, if anthropology (for example) has been

2. In the postface mentioned above, "disappointment" is one of the key words in Barthes's vocabulary.

revitalized, it is because men like Lévi-Strauss have substituted for the notion of genesis, which had governed the social sciences, the notion of structure, which was borrowed from linguistics. Not just any linguistics. But the one in which Saussure was first to demonstrate that the study of language could be separated into two distinct sectors: on the one hand, its history, its genesis precisely, its "diachronic" dimension; and on the other, its state, its flat extension, its "synchronic" dimension. The *Michelet* book, like the "psychoanalysis" of Bachelard, is developed synchronically, contained entirely within the system of its relations. In other words, there is a latent use of structuralism in the *Michelet*. This use becomes explicit in the postface of *Mythologies*, since, to the extent that myth is discourse, nothing explains it better than a coherent system of discourse like the one Barthes found in Saussure. For indeed we are dealing here with Saussurian structuralism. It will be enriched later with related structuralisms. The important thing is that it dovetails with Barthes's own method with which from now on it is integrally connected. Nor was its entry into the system gratuitous because it was simply in the air with Barthes seizing it on the wing. It was created by an already existing need. Barthes is the very opposite of a fashion monger, even when he makes a study of it. If he can be reproached with anything it would be rather for his almost maniacal determination to push to the point of incandescence the discoveries which arise from his passionate concerns. Thus he will proceed to apply structuralism to literary reflection with a singular and fertile fanaticism.[3]

From the *Essais critiques* on, everything turns around the literary object, taken by itself, synchronically. Why then does the work as praxis have only limited powers? Because, says Barthes, in order to be operative, in order for it to fulfill its project, it would have transitively to speak the world. Whereas words, signs cannot speak the world, but only speak *about* it. Signs repel the world, turned as they are toward other signs with which they constitute a system.

3. The basis of this fanaticism being the assimilation of literature to language.

One may argue that literary communication is functional, that it strives toward a meaning which may recover the world, and that its value is in proportion to its instrumentality. But it is precisely that there exists a man, says Barthes, whose aim in some way runs counter: the writer.

One can experience for oneself this paradoxical intention: If you have a letter of condolence to write, there will come a moment when you will have to suspend both your view of the recipient and your sadness in order to ask yourself how best to express the letter. The very sincerity of your feeling requires this of you at the price otherwise of falling into fixed formulas or of appearing indifferent. It is in that technical effort—an immoral one to the extent that you are taking your own sadness as an object—whereby the truth is revealed. But the intended meaning (the expression of suffering) remains suspended during the time the discourse seeks to constitute itself. The writer is the man who suspends meaning in a radical way and fixes it in a system of words. His object is contained within language and his aim is the structure he elaborates therein. In other words, he makes of language, not a means, but an end. It is easier to understand now (for the affirmation in the essay on "myth" was not obvious and the "mythologies" seemed to belie it) why the writer is ineffective in praxis, why he cannot be said to prove, to command, to magnify, in a word, to "assert" anything: all that is discourse, mediating toward something other than itself. However,

The miracle is that this narcissistic activity is forever giving rise within secular literature to an interrogation of the world: by enclosing himself within the question *how to write*, the writer ends by discovering that supremely open question—why the world? What is the sense of things? In short, at the moment the writer's work becomes its own end, he discovers its mediating character: the writer conceives literature as an end, the world gives it back to him as means. And it is in this infinite *disappointment* that the writer rediscovers the world, in fact a rather strange world, to the extent that literature represents it as a question, never definitely as an answer.[4]

4. "Le miracle, c'est que cette activité narcissique ne cesse de provoquer au long d'une littérature séculaire, une interrogation au

Doubtlessly some people write to "witness," to "explain," to "teach," but their language does not differ from ordinary discourse; by that absence of "originality" (which only the reversal of ends is presumed to confer), it falls outside the literary object. These men of transitive discourse Barthes calls *écrivants*.

But how is that "question" made possible? First, there is the fact that literature never raises it in a form as explicit as "why the world?" for in its way that would still be assertive, deriving from "philosophy"—a thoroughly transitive discourse. Literature *is* a question in itself. Should a certain language, from the moment it becomes its own end, break with the world, and the world appears as the question of a question. That is the point we have reached. But why then? Some may be able to *express* this meaning, but literature by its very essence cannot answer. It can, on the other hand, establish the science of questions, "know how meaning is possible, at what price, and according to what means." [5]

For that, it is necessary to reconstruct the object involved (real or imaginary) in such a way as to show within this reconstruction the rules by which it functions, the "functions" [6] of this object. One thereby obtains a "simulacrum,"

> but a simulacrum directed, purposeful, since the imitated object brings to light something which had remained invisible, or, if you prefer, unintelligible in the natural object. The novelty perceived is on the one hand very small, but it is absolutely decisive, nothing less than intelligibility in general: the simulacrum is intellect added to the object.[7]

---

monde: en s'enfermant dans le *comment écrire*, l'écrivain finit par retrouver la question ouverte par excellence: pourquoi le monde? Quel est le sens des choses? En somme, c'est au moment même où le travail de l'écrivain devient sa propre fin qu'il retrouve un caractère médiateur: l'écrivain conçoit la littérature comme fin, le monde le lui renvoie comme moyen: et c'est dans cette *déception* infinie que l'écrivain retrouve le monde, un monde étrange d'ailleurs, puisque la littérature le représente comme une question, jamais en *définitive* comme une réponse." *Essais critiques*, Tel Quel (Paris: Seuil, 1964), p. 149.

5. Ibid., p. 218.

6. Later we will see the ambiguity of this term.

7. ". . . mais un simulacre dirigé, intéressé, puisque l'objet imité fait apparaître quelque chose qui restait invisible, ou si l'on

The simulacrum is a revelation, but not of meaning, rather of the conditions of meaning. Take a very loaded example: racism. A "structuralist" inquiry (because that is what we are talking about) would not say what racism is, and would be even less likely to pass judgment on it. Rather it would offer a mimetic reconstruction which would reveal its mechanism of racism. It is left for others to integrate this understanding with their own meaning. All intelligibility it is question of here is contained entirely within the technique. The whole process consists, for any object, of establishing the system of relations among its elements. Thus the barriers between art and (structuralist) science fall when "Propp constructs a folk-tale brought forth by structuring together all the Slavic tales which he had begun by decomposing, when Claude Lévi-Strauss uncovers the homological operation of totemic imagination, . . . they are doing nothing different from what Mondrian, Boulez, or Butor do when they fit together a certain object."[8] It no longer becomes necessary to intend a particular meaning. The fitting together of the work (this is true at least of artistic works) is its whole horizon. Of course we want to know at any price what Mondrian's work "expresses," and yet a picture of Mondrian is nothing other than its space, decomposed and then recomposed. With that said and a method having been chosen, the end of *Mythologies* begins to reveal not only a theory of literature but of intellectual activity itself, perhaps even a theory of contemporary man—*homo significans*.

As we will see, the theory is methodologically very fruitful. Nor does it fail to be surprising. But let us pass over certain

---

préfère, inintelligible dans l'objet naturel. La nouveauté apparue est d'une part peu de chose mais d'autre part ce peu de chose est décisif, car il n'est rien moins que l'intelligible en général: le simulacre, c'est l'intellect ajouté à l'objet." *Essais critiques*, p. 215.

8. "Lorsque Propp construit un conte populaire issu par structuration de tous les contes slaves qu'il a au préalable décomposés, lorsque Claude Lévi-Strauss retrouve le fonctionnement homologique de l'imaginaire totémique, . . . ils ne font rien d'autre que ce que font Mondrian, Boulez ou Butor lorsqu'ils agencent un certain objet." Ibid., p. 215. Butor's *Mobile* is a typical example of a composed object.

questions which it raises, like its all too evident relation to technocratic society. Structuralism rejects any such external explanation in advance, for that would remove it from the domain which the theory has chosen, structure, to replace it within the one it has repudiated—namely, genesis.[9] In order to discuss structuralism one has to adopt its point of view.

That does not, however, resolve all the confusion. If we consider only literature, we might ask what are the theoretical limits of structuralist activity. Saying "here is what it is" (a language which avoids any deliberate meaning, which is its own end), it is very difficult to avoid sounding like "here is what it ought to be." The term "model" is symbolic of the difficulty. In linguistic terms the word "model," which becomes "simulacrum" in Barthes, is given as purely operational. But it has another normative side, all the more active as never explicitly announced. The structuralist activity, like history, comes forward masked. Most often, it has not sought a specific language, unlike psychoanalysis (one of whose aims is precisely the neutrality of its terminology); it has taken its terms with all their ambiguities from ordinary language. At the same time it pretends to be unaware of these ambiguous meanings or makes them signifiers of second signs, in a proper "mythological" fashion. "Function" for example is the very term for instrumentality. "Functional" applies to that which owes its existence only to the meaning it supplies. But in structuralism, function is that purely internal relation of one element to the others and to their whole, which is itself its sufficient meaning. Or in other words, analysis does not establish any particular meaning, but only meaning itself, that is, the totality of relations. There is a great temptation to pass from analysis to creation. Let one not adopt for himself a method *a posteriori*, and immediately, there will come those who will make a finality of language, presented as the essence of literature, a literary project.[10]

9. The synchronic field is the one chosen by technocratic ideology. It presupposes that meaning is no longer to be sought, that society is given, and that the only problem is to manipulate it as it is.

10. See the contribution of Jean Ricardou in *Que peut la litterature?* 10/18 (Paris: Union Générale d'Editions, 1966).

This refusal of meaning is, of course, impossible. If one notes that this refusal has itself an implicit meaning, the "structuralist" writer (if there are any) can once more reply that we are dealing with a false problem, and he is not responsible for what he is being made to say or what he says unknowingly. Nevertheless, this refusal does not stand up to examination. Ricardou, analyzing his own novel *L'Observatoire de Cannes*,[11] remarked that it was placed under the sign of a triangle. He also wanted this triangulation to be a vast erotic symbol. Things need to be definite; either the book is a system of trigonometry or it is dedicated to Eros. And if it is both at the same time, which is conceivable, then eroticism must necessarily *transcend* geometry. A pure play of functions (in the Barthesian sense) can only be itself, its celebrated intelligibility mineralized, crystallized. Certainly the triangular relation can be elaborated so that an erotic sense is visible, but it is always indicated from without, by the novelist or reader. And where there is a reader there is an undetermined possibility of meaning.

But the reduction of all literature to the finality of language becomes frankly absurd. We are dealing with a kind of myopia which derives from the ignorance of the one afflicted. It would seem as if certain readers are unaware of the Dostoevskian novel, to take one of many examples, wherein the meaning is explicitly stated if eternally multiple, where meaning is also posed in terms of language and, from a certain point of view, exists only through language. Can Barthes be held responsible for the eccentricities of his overzealous followers?

He can to the degree that by indulging in literary analysis, particularly of certain consecrated texts, his choice is tautological. Why be interested in La Bruyère rather than Diderot? Because when "all is said, and we come too late" (*tout est dit et qu'on vient trop tard*), problems of meaning fall away and art can be made to seem the mere coordination and combination of language; what is essential seems no longer in the theme but in its variations. The "essais critiques" which treat Butor's *Mobile* or Marthe Robert's *Kafka*—that is, works which derive

11. In *Problèmes du nouveau roman*, Tel Quel (Paris: Seuil, 1967).

from the structuralist approach—assume in advance the validity of the theory. But one has to consider all the pretexts of a book, even of a collection of essays in which chronology has replaced a sense of duration. From the point we have reached, the articles on Brecht, for example, seem to belong to an earlier phase. Yet there they are, with their germ of negation, however small.

One further word. The structuralist approach brings many things together: an (apparent) definition of literature, its science (the conditions of meaning), a critical method (the search for a configuration of themes), and even a radicalization of structuralism itself. In fact, it becomes difficult to see what distinguishes form from structure, something Barthes seems eager to differentiate.[12] One of the examples he cites to show how literature is engulfed entirely in the process of its functioning is Asby's homeostat, which turns only in order to turn. And the ideology of this extreme position is evoked by the new directions Barthes has brought together, the new names to which he refers. The name of Propp, the Russian formalist, appears more and more frequently. It may seem surprising that he figures on an equal footing with Lévi-Strauss, who, after all, formulated the most incisive criticisms of Propp.[13] Propp's method, says Lévi-Strauss, has its validity, but no value, for it is not a heuristic one. His models, specifically in the case of Slavic folktales, are finally revealing only of themselves. They have a certain intelligibility but which never leads to a display of intelligence. The *structuralist* approach which Lévi-Strauss opposes to formalism brings to light a system of functions only to make them instrumental, to illuminate, for example, the customs which are tied to these tales, in turn their imaginative expression. Formalism thus represents a kind of "right wing" of structuralism, which seeks some absolute objectivity, cut off not only from meaning but from the creative subject; Asby's homeostat turns for no reason and with no reason.

12. In the essay which codifies the "Mythologies."

13. "La Structure et la forme. Réflexions sur un ouvrage de Vladimir Propp," *Cahiers de l'Institut de Sciences Economiques Appliquées* (Recherches et Dialogues Philosophiques et Economiques, 7), 99 (March 1960): 3–36.

But after all, this model was set up by somebody. Thus, if what is essential is the coherence of these relations, objectivity can lead to madness, for nothing is more coherent than madness. What is more, the study *Sur Racine*, where the method used is entirely structural, in the end goes beyond its internal relations to arrive at a meaning which encompasses them (the image of the father, partially derived from Mauron—if indeed that matters). What is interesting is that all in one year's time there appears a theory of literature and an application of the theory which contradicts it. However coherent or minutely elaborated the analysis of Racine's tragedies might be, it is entirely dependent on the meaning we have mentioned. And it is intimately connected to the *bias* which establishes it, where the subjective character is as evident as its logic is consistent. It is the antithesis of a "homeostatic" book. Two interrelated needs, which are clarified as they are progressively affirmed, strengthened in their development, find themselves polarized at the extremes: the need of an ego and the need of a science. The problem is to know whether this opposition is dialectical.

To begin with, what does it mean "to delimit the conditions of meaning"? That signifies to imply or to evoke, at some precise moment, what will be the necessary matters brought in, what disciplines for example, for a meaning to be drawn out. Thus, within a political perspective, "mythologies" suggest Marxism; within a closed work like Racine's, psychoanalysis. The term "science" is thus in some measure inappropriate; one should rather speak of a method. Or if you prefer, one should take literally the notion, already briefly reviewed above, of a structuralist "activity." Whatever Barthes might say himself, he doesn't deny the possibility of an answer; he suspends it, and he suspends it in the *Essais critiques* in order to devote his attention to the instruments which might furnish it. The articles on Brecht (precisely in the *Essais* where they constitute a negating moment) demonstrate how provisional this suspension may be, in the literary object as in the critical act, and how capable it is at every moment of discovering its own end. Barthes speaks of Brecht's concern to insure that a certain costume fabric appear worn out. Thus the shoddiness in the costumes of *Mother Courage* is a completely formal element into which Brecht's intention was absorbed. But it is only the mediation of poverty which the spectator must comprehend as little by little he attains to Brechtianism itself. All of Brechtianism involves a formal problem which is at once annulled in the direction of its meaning. There is a synthesis of formalism and meaning with its corollary, the subject. It is the next book, *Critique et vérité*, which will provide the synthesis.

Once again the book appears a product of circumstance. But we have just seen that its necessity was already in process. And that the study *Sur Racine* brought it about, by provoking it, is a kind of symbolic proof.

It is pointless to dwell on the quarrel which was its pretext, and which has almost been forgotten. Doubrovsky has dealt with it at great length.[14] But we must say a few words about its origins.

Barthes had reproached certain academics with confusing literary history and criticism as a result of a certain methodological approach: the *explanation* of the work by the man, which was then charged with establishing the "truth" of the work. It is the problem raised indirectly in the *Michelet* excursion which reappears.

Barthes postulated a distinction between these two activities and argued that criticism is pure *explication* of a text, that is, the analysis of the text by itself alone. But, since it involves the confrontation of one subject's discourse with another's, speaking requires that one assume explicitly a particular point of view (one's own, with all its eccentricities, as well as with its history or ideology). Those academic critics would have done better to state their point of view from the start, to make clear that the claimed objectivity of a deductive method was nothing more than one course to choose among others, in this case the one made by positivistic philosophy for which the work is a product of a biography. By proving or thinking to prove that "Orestes is Racine in love with la Duparc," one perhaps illuminates the life of Racine, but one misses the work

14. Serge Doubrovsky, *Pourquoi la nouvelle critique: Critique et objectivité* (Paris: Mercure de France, 1966).

which is the proper domain of criticism. Which explains why the structuralist approach, not centering upon content, whose only aim is to bring to light the system of internal relation, is so perfectly suited to its object. In fact, Barthes might only have had to quote himself in order to show to Picard that the quarrel was falsely grounded, since Picard's complaint that "la Nouvelle Critique" injects psychoanalysis into everything, that it is forever seeking the "outside" elements in the work, merely invokes that immanence which Barthes himself had advocated. In sum, Picard goes on to insinuate, this criticism merely pursues its own obsessions. It is subjective, which is to say, raving mad. Barthes, then, did two things. He quickly ignored Picard, and more importantly, assumed the burden of Picard's argument. By the same token, he gathered himself together.

To begin with, Barthes distinguishes not two but three approaches to literature.

1. Its history (or more exactly the history of its institutions).

2. Its "science": "Symbolic language, to which literary works belong by nature, is *by its structure* a plural language, whose code is devised in such a way that every discourse (every work) engendered by it has multiple meanings. . . . One can call the *science of literature* . . . that general discourse whose object is not some particular meaning but the plurality itself of the different meanings of the work."[15]

3. Its criticism, or the movement toward a single meaning. And it is on the level of criticism that the desired synthesis will take place.

In all these cases, "structuralist activity" offers rich possibilities. In the case of literature, when one says that "technique is the essence of creation," the literary object has been defined, whatever the circumstances. In each of its situations, it is necessary, at least for a time, to suspend meaning, to place

15. "La langue symbolique, à laquelle appartiennent par nature les oeuvres littéraires, est *par structure* une langue plurielle, dont le code est fait de telle sorte que toute parole (toute oeuvre), par lui engendrée, a des sens multiples. . . . On peut appeler science de la littérature . . . ce discours général dont l'objet n'est pas tel sens mais la pluralité même des sens de l'oeuvre." *Critique et vérité*, Te Quel (Paris : Seuil, 1966), pp. 53–56.

oneself in a synchronic mode. The man of writing (*l'homme de l'écriture*), whatever his project, will always experience this "abandonment" in which order is reversed and where he is concerned only with the "how" of his project. For the critic, that begins precisely with the immanence of the work, at the moment he chooses to enclose himself within it. His domain is then the coherence of signs, according to the system he has elected. He identifies, decomposes, recomposes, relates the themes which appear to him to bear the meaning of the work.

But that there is meaning, on the other hand, is important, in some sense new, and distinguishes the critical approach from a purely structuralist one. It is not a question, however, of the translation of some objective meaning that can be further explained: "The critic cannot claim to 'translate' the work, notably into something clearer, for nothing is clearer than the work."[16] The meaning is the critic's and his responsibility resides in the rigor with which he establishes it. Critical activity is not an explanation, but a free discourse, which is constantly renewed, about the discourse of the work.

But then what will assure us that this is the true meaning? Nothing in fact. That is why themes are said to "appear"; they are "epiphanies," for they have no other foundation than the critic's particular stance. His relationship to the work is radically subjective. That is what Barthes's last book points up: that underlying or at the center of his method is a question, that his whole work tends toward a center, that emptiness which is the question—*how to be a subject*, at what price, up to what point? The structuralist approach seemed to have eliminated it, seemed to have sought the absolute objectivity of technique; critical activity, because it demands meaning, has made the subject reappear.

There are two things. First we see, concerning criticism, how Barthes's elastic method works: subjectivity is what one must add to the model in order for criticism to exist. Thus we never stop speaking of structuralism. But through criticism, structuralism becomes a doctrine of the subject, its method at the same time.

16. Ibid., p. 64.

For this problem is still unresolved: if the critic alone is left to determine meaning, what guarantees that the meaning is true? In Barthes's view, and here is Picard's objection, one can say anything at all. And he counters this menace with the rigor of the positive method.

Except that this rigor is also situational. Positivism, which is merely one premise like another, grounds its knowledge on the equation of life and work. That presupposes that the writing subject is an animate object which produces the work by a process of emanation.

> [But the] subject is not an individual plenitude that one has the right to empty or not to empty into language; [it is] on the contrary an emptiness around which the writer weaves a discourse which is endlessly transformed . . . , in such a way that all writing *which does not lie* designates, not the interior attributes of the subject, but its absence. Language is not the predicate of an inexpressible subject or one that it serves to express; it is the subject.[17]

Thus criticism and the subject are defined. The subject is its language by which it constitutes itself. Criticism is reproduction, "like a detached and variable sign, [of the] sign of the works themselves."[18] It is a manifestation of the subject, to the degree that it gives rise to the other and to itself as language.

That in no way implies, says Barthes, that it can say anything at all. Subjectivism has its rules, the first being to declare itself as such and to announce in what *sense* one intends to speak. The second, since now we are dealing with discourse and not some nonexistent objective meaning, is the coherence of one's own discourse.

17. "[Mais le] sujet n'est pas une plénitude individuelle qu'on a le droit ou non d'évacuer dans le langage, [il est] au contraire un vide autour duquel l'écrivain tisse une parole indéfiniment transformée . . ., en sorte que toute écriture *qui ne ment pas* désigne, non les attributs intérieurs du sujet, mais son absence. Le langage n'est pas le prédicat d'un sujet inexprimable ou qu'il servirait à exprimer, il est le sujet." Ibid., p. 70. Barthes recognizes in this "an echo, however deformed, of what Dr. Lacan had been saying in his seminar given at the Hautes Etudes."

18. Ibid., p. 71.

"In other words, one could say that the critic confronts another object which is not the work but his own discourse." Or further, that the aim is not truth but validity (that coherence). The third rule groups together all the rules of critical activity. Critical discourse is a transformation of the work according to its own system of interpretation. But "that transformation is *supervised*, submitted to optical constraints: it must transform the entirety of that which it reflects, transforming only according to certain laws, always in the same direction."[19]

These laws are those of the "logic of signifiers,"[20] which is also derived from linguistics, more precisely from semiology (the science of signs). Thus it is the structuralist approach which gives validity to criticism, and to subjectivism by the same token, or gives them, if one prefers, their objectivity. But, on the other hand, this activity no longer seeks its end in the narrowness of some simulacrum; it is the mediation of meaning. We are dealing here with the two sides of that crucial question: how is a subject possible? Thus armed, the subject re-enters the world, while the work of Barthes gathers together its movements. It assembles them within the project of criticism: the subject is the critical method and criticism fulfills the method. To put it more succinctly, everything is contained in these two words: structure and desire. For indeed, structure, language, and desire are all the same thing.

And desire runs throughout the work.

Barthes's language has been reproached for its eccentricity, for its "jargonizing," its gratuitousness. That has always appeared surprising. If it is occasionally "blinded," as Leibnitz said, it is by its own allusiveness. But Barthes has prepared his justification; he is not defining words but things (his last book,

19. "Cette transformation est *surveillée*, soumise à des contraintes optiques: de ce qu'elle réfléchit, elle doit tout transformer; ne transformer que selon certaines lois; transformer toujours dans le même sens." Ibid., p. 64.

20. That "logic of signifiers" is naturally borrowed from structural linguistics. It would require a second essay to describe the "model of intelligibility" furnished to criticism by linguistics. (See the conclusion below and the Bibliography under the note on *Le Degré zéro*.)

Système de la mode, shows that very well). The meaning of this "jargon," its intention, is quite different; it is a verbal invention belonging to a total project, that of a certain language. Of a certain literature. Thus, returning to the beginning, one could surprise Barthes by choosing to read him only at that level, as he has read Michelet: for the pleasure of savoring his coherence and the depth of his language. In short, for what he is: a remarkable *writer*.

But the sense of that status has not been made explicit. It was a meaning which appeared to the reader but which in the work remained on the horizon, entered as an extra thought. For a time, it was even rejected: to distinguish between writers and those who write (*écrivants*), in an *explicative* discourse, is to place oneself alongside the latter, those who merely write. But as soon as the subject is all language and vice versa, "there are no longer either poets or novelists (or critics), there is only writing [*écriture*]." Criticism, however, holds open within language the necessity of meaning. That is to pose the question of the destiny of this language.

Système de la mode gathers together the themes described above without modifying their terms. It is an extremely technical book[21] whose only novelty in relation to the rest of the work is the construction before our eyes of a "model of intelligibility." One sees how linguistics can lend its methods to every kind of reading. It is a transfer operation, in this case from linguistics to sociology. Otherwise, nothing is profoundly altered in any of the divisions of the Barthesian approach.

Yet, facts have radically changed the situation. The first after a long development is the polarization under the aegis of the journal *Tel Quel* of a large segment of "modernity." That segment still identifies itself with "structuralism," however vague its boundaries have become in order to accommodate such diverse works, methods, and men.

The second fact is the events of May 1968 in France. History, which seemed to have evaporated, and whose absence was signified by a certain formalism, came back with a sudden consistency. The brutality of those events forced the cohesion

21. See Bibliography below.

of the *Tel Quel* group and the men around it. It became a movement, seeking and proposing its ideology. It is elaborated in a book with the appropriate title *Théorie d'ensemble.*[22] And to the degree there is a (named) *ensemble*, what was more or less separate is delimited and affirmed. And if the theory is functional to the event, to the world, its question demands that form of *response* which is action. It is Barthes who provides the introduction to the book, whose terms he formulates this way:

—*to elaborate concepts* . . . ("signifying practice," "paragram," "intertextuality," "ideologem"), as well as the methods permitting a formulation of its transformational version [*doublure transformatrice*];
—*to unfold a history* (or histories)—a plural history—formed by the differences of writing which let theory and fiction communicate through a series of divisions precisely identifiable in their time;
—*to articulate a political stand* bound logically to a nonrepresentative dynamic of writing, that is: the analysis of misconceptions provoked by this position, an explanation of their social and economic character, the construction of the relations between this kind of writing with historical materialism and with dialectical materialism.[23]

In one way or another it could be very informative to see a

22. *Théorie d'ensemble*, Tel Quel (Paris: Seuil, 1968). Contributors: Roland Barthes, Jacques Derrida, Michel Foucault; Jean-Louis Baudry, Jean-Josèph Goux, Jean-Louis Houdebine, Julia Kristeva, Marcelin Pleynet, Jean Ricardou, Jacqueline Risset, Denis Roche, Pierre Rottemberg, Philippe Sollers, Jean Thibaudeau.

23. "*élaborer des concepts* . . . ('pratique signifiante,' 'paragramme,' 'intertextualité,' 'idéologème'), ainsi que les méthodes permettant d'en figurer la doublure transformatrice ;

"*déployer une histoire(s)*—une histoire plurielle—formée par les différences d'écriture faisant communiquer théorie et fiction à travers une série de coupures précisément repérables en leurs temps;

"*articuler une politique* liée logiquement à une dynamique non-représentative de l'écriture, c'est-à-dire : analyse des malentendus provoqués par cette position, explication de leurs caractères sociaux et économiques, construction des rapports de cette écriture avec le matérialisme historique et le matérialisme dialectique." Ibid., p. 10.

method, a mode of writing, which had formerly sought stasis for itself, function now in the face of history.[24]

SELECTED BIBLIOGRAPHY

WORKS BY BARTHES

Even a bibliography implies a point of view. Exhaustiveness would be one like any other.

In the case of Barthes such exhaustiveness is hard to come by for practical reasons. With the exception of a few books, his work is dispersed in journals or collections which are either out of print or omitted by Barthes himself in re-editions.

Thus, it is Barthes's attitude toward his own work which determines ours. For him, the publication in book form is a way of totalizing his work, of marking its dynamic and its direction. Whenever he assembles these *membra disjecta*, it is done according to a deliberate choice, as, for example, with *Mythologies* or the *Essais critiques*. He sought there to indicate a precise orientation, one assumed after a settling period of several years and arrested by the new state of his thought. We could not modify his selection without betraying him.

This selection is in addition rendered explicit and justified by commentaries included either in the text or in the jacket copy which accompanies it. There too, out of the same concern for fidelity, we have sought in our presentation to follow his thought as closely as possible.

Le Degré zéro de l'écriture. Pierres Vives. Paris: Seuil, 1953. Reprinted with *Eléments de sémiologie* (originally in *Communications*, no. 4 [1964]). Médiations. Paris: Gonthier, 1964. (*Writing Degree Zero*. Translated by Annette Lavers and Colin Smith. London: Cape, 1967. Preface by Susan Sontag, New York: Hill and Wang, 1968. *Elements of Semiology*. Translated by Annette Lavers and Colin Smith. London: Cape, 1967.)

Since the nineteenth century, "writing . . . has traversed all the stages of a progressive solidification: at first, the object of a look, then of an act, and finally of a murder, it has today reached a last phase, absence: in these neutral writings, which are called here 'the zero degree of writing,' one can very easily discern the very movement of

24. The least that one can say of the preceding text is that it is out of date. If I could be perfectly candid, I would be more harsh still. Let us just say that it is "out of date." My only wish is that it serves nevertheless to induce the reader to study Barthes's work.

a negation, and the impossibility of accomplishing it within a duration, as if Literature, which for over a century has been seeking to transmute its surface into a form without a heritage, could no longer find purity elsewhere than in the absence of all signs, proposing at last to accomplish that Orphean dream—a writer without Literature. Blank writing [*l'écriture blanche*], that of Camus, of Blanchot, or Cayrol, for example, or the spoken writing of Queneau, is the last episode in the Passion of writing, which follows step by step the tearing apart of bourgeois consciousness."

Thus Barthes summarizes his position. The book thereby constitutes a history, completed by a definition.

The two principal concepts of this definition are "literature" and "writing." Literature consists of "a collection of signs given without relation to ideas, language, or style, and intended to define within the density of all modes of possible expression the solitude of a ritual language." Writing is its correlative concept. It is the "relation between creation and society, . . . language transformed by its social destination, . . . form seized in its human intention and thus bound to the great crises of history. Thus Mérimée and Fénelon are separated by phenomena of language and accidents of style; and yet they . . . have common reference to the same idea of form and content, they accept the same order of conventions; . . . in short, they are instances of the same writing. On the contrary, writers who are almost contemporaries like Mérimée and Lautréamont, Mallarmé and Céline, Gide and Queneau . . . make use of profoundly different concepts of writing."

Equally defined are all the terms which will pervade "la Nouvelle Critique," such as *langue*, *langage*, *parole*, at the same time receiving their corollary justification from linguistics.

Taken in this way, the words *littérature* and *écriture* are dated; they coincide with romanticism where literature became conscious of its own existence and never ceased to intensify this consciousness and to modify its terms. *Le Degré zéro*, which begins its consideration of literature from that point in time, is thus also a history of literature to our day.

"Analyzing in turn all political, novelistic, poetic writings, situating the different domains of language, of style, [Barthes] poses the problem of the necessary conditions of a language."

This last sentence appears in the jacket copy on the re-edition (the only book of Barthes, aside from the study *Sur Racine*, which has been republished). The inclusion there of additional texts is not due to chance. "Semiology" is that science of signs postulated by Saussurian linguistics which has entirely revivified the social sciences.

Barthes thus provides the notions of a system implicitly called for in *Le Degré zéro*, as we have seen.

The fundamental elements of this system are assembled and codified by means of a glossary. The reader will find there all the notions which underlie the Barthesian method (but also parallel methods) and which help to understand it. Above all, he will get some idea of the linguistic material with which one can construct that "model of intelligibility" mentioned in the *Essais critiques*.

Michelet par lui-même. Ecrivains de Toujours. Paris: Seuil, 1954.

"That the work of Michelet, like every object of criticism, is unquestionably the product of a certain history, I am entirely persuaded. But there is an order of tasks: first, one must give the man's work its coherence. Such has been my aim: to discover the structure of an existence (I do not speak of a life), a certain thematic, if you prefer, or better still, an organized network of obsessions."

This plan such as Barthes defines it seems to function on two or even three levels.

The first, we might say, is signified by its absence: analysis ignores everything which is transcendent to the work (like its ideology or its influence) or anterior to the work (like the life which sustains it).

The object intended by the critic is first the man Michelet, such as he fulfills himself in his language, and second, this language itself.

But these two objects, biography and history, having been left aside, make up only one in fact, within language alone. One is made to see the primacy of this language, which later will be given an explicit role and advanced as the unique domain of criticism.

As for analysis (which bears on the totality of the work and not only on the *Histoire de France*), it is "thematic," as Barthes says. It consists of the review and organization by categories of certain figures (blood, dryness, humors, smoothness, or discontinuity, etc.) which fuse the different books into a single text and exhaustively explicate it. These figures being grouped according to binary oppositions (within which they are regrouped by affinities), provide another methodological element to be identified which linguistics will be able to radicalize.

And as these figures are ambiguous, since they derive as much from synesthesia as from language, it is indeed Michelet the man whom we discover at the same time as the work.

Mythologies. Pierres Vives. Paris: Seuil, 1957.

The titles of some of these descriptions: "Blueblood's Cruise," "Toys," "Wine and Milk," "Steak and French Fries," "Billy Graham at the Vel d'Hiv," etc.

Each of these phenomena of daily life seems perfectly straightforward, natural, and at the same time communicates a message which by the same token seems also to be natural. The problem is, as Brecht put it, "how to find the exception within the rule?" Barthes summarizes it this way:

"The texts which follow were written every month for about two years, from 1954 to 1956, at the whim of current events. I was trying then to reflect regularly on various myths of daily French life. The material for this reflection could be widely divergent (a newspaper article, a weekly magazine photograph, a film, a show, an exhibition . . .).

"The starting point for this reflection was most often a feeling of impatience toward the 'naturalness' with which the press, art, common sense continually dressed up reality, which, for all that it may be our common environment, is nevertheless completely immersed in history: in short, I was annoyed seeing the account of current events constantly confuse Nature and History, and I wanted to pull together and expose the ideological bias . . . which is hidden in the presentation of *ce-qui-va-de-soi*, that which constitutes the 'matter-of-course.'

"The notion of myth seemed to me able from the first to account for these false assumptions; at the time I understood the word in a traditional sense. But I was already persuaded of something whose consequences I have since tried to draw out: myth is language. Thus, dealing with facts which in appearance seemed the most removed from all literature (a wrestling match, a gourmet dish, a plastic exhibition) I did not think that I was escaping from that general semiology of our bourgeois world whose literary aspect I had treated in earlier essays. It was, however, only after having explored a certain number of current events that I tried in a systematic way to define contemporary myth—a text which I naturally left for the end of this volume, since it merely systematized the foregoing material."

"Le Monde où l'on catche" was published in the journal *Esprit*, "L'Ecrivain en vacances" in *France-Observateur*, and the other texts chosen from among the "Mythologies" which appeared regularly in *Lettres Nouvelles*.

Sur Racine. Pierres Vives. Paris: Seuil, 1963. (*On Racine*. Translated by Richard Howard. New York: Hill and Wang, 1964.)

As the author writes, "Here are three studies of Racine; they arose from different circumstances and thus no attempt will be made here to give them a retrospective unity.

"The first ('L'Homme racinien') appeared in the edition of the theatre of Racine published by the Club Français du Livre [volumes 11 and 12 of *Théâtre classique français*, published in Paris, 1960—note that only the tragedies are studied]. The language is somewhat psychoanalytic but its treatment is hardly that at all; for the good reason that there already exists an excellent psychoanalysis of Racine, that of Charles Mauron [*L'Inconscient dans l'oeuvre et la vie de Racine*, Gap: Ophrys, 1957], to which I owe a great deal; in truth for the further reason that the analysis presented here does not at all concern Racine but the Racinian hero. It avoids all inferences from the work to the author and from the author to the work; it is an analysis which is willfully closed; I have placed myself within the tragic world of Racine and have tried to describe its population (which could easily be abstracted under the concept of *homo racinianus*), without any reference to some source in this world (derived for example from history or biography). What I have tried to reconstruct is a sort of Racinian anthropology, both structural and analytic, structural in its content, because tragedy is treated here as a system of unities ('figures') and functions; analytic in its form, because only a language which is able to contemplate the fear of the world, as psychoanalysis is, I believe, seemed suitable to the task of encountering an enclosed man." A footnote gives this further explanation: "This first study consists of two parts. You could say in structural terms that one is systematic (it analyzes figures and functions) and the other is syntagmatic (it further extends the systematic elements on the basis of each work)."

"The second study ('Dire Racine') consists of a review of a production of *Phèdre* at the T.N.P. [*Théâtre Populaire*, no. 29, March 1958]. The circumstance does not matter today, but it strikes me as continually relevant to compare psychological acting with tragic acting, and to determine in that way whether it is still possible to perform Racine. In the end, although this study is devoted to a theatrical problem, the Racinian actor will be seen to be worthy of praise only to the degree that he renounces the prestige of the traditional notion of character, in order to attain that of *figure*, that is, the form of a tragic function, such as was analyzed in the first text.

"As for the third study ('Histoire ou littérature?') it is entirely devoted, through Racine, to a general critical problem. The text appeared under the rubric 'Débats et Combats' in the journal *Annales* [no. 3, May–June 1960]; it includes an implicit interlocutor, the historian of literature, with an academic background, of whom it is asked either to undertake a real history of the literary institution (if he wants to be a historian) or openly to assume the psychology to which he refers (if he wishes to be a critic)."

Essais critiques. Tel Quel. Paris: Seuil, 1964. ("Seven Photo Models of *Mother Courage*." Translated by Hella Freud Bernays. *Drama Review* 12 [Fall 1967]: 44–55. "Qu'est-ce que la critique?" originally appeared in the *Times Literary Supplement*, reprinted in *The Critical Moment*, London: Faber and Faber, 1964. And another essay was translated, "The Structuralist Activity"—see below.)

One will find at the end of each essay the date it was written and the place of publication. In most cases, it consists of articles published in journals or newspapers, sometimes prefaces.

The first text is dated 1953, the last 1963. Thus for a decade, according to the jacket copy, "an important part—the most circumstantial but also perhaps the most significant—of Barthes's intellectual activity is contained in these *Essais critiques*, . . . the most essential aspects of which have been assembled in this book around a reflection on theater and literature. Classical authors like Voltaire or Baudelaire stand next to modern ones like Queneau or Robbe-Grillet; but it is not a question of passing out prizes or choosing exemplary figures; from Brechtian combat to 'structuralist activity,' including the birth of the 'new novel,' this collection of essays, arranged in the order of their publication, traces both the trajectory of one of the characteristic experiences of our time, which is the discovery and exploration—through the exemplary domains of literary and theatrical writing—of that inexhaustible *empire of signs*, where modern thought measures its space and its power."

La Tour Eiffel. Le Génie du Lieu. Paris: Delpire, 1964.

Critique et vérité. Tel Quel. Paris: Seuil, 1966. (See "Science versus Literature." *Times Literary Supplement*, 28 September 1967, pp. 897–98.)

The book is a reply to the attack by Picard (*Nouvelle Critique ou nouvelle imposture?* Libertés. Paris: J.-J. Pauvert, 1965), which dealt with Barthes's book on Racine, and particularly with the one of the three sections which questioned academic criticism. But through Barthes, Picard was attacking all of "la Nouvelle Critique." And through *Critique et vérité*, it is that whole tendency which is being defended.

Barthes first challenges the accusations brought against it and then declares in turn: Picard and his partisans wish to consider language only according to its letter. "But from the moment one claims to treat the work in itself, from the point of view of its construction, it becomes impossible not to pose in its fullest dimension the necessity for a symbolic reading."

Definition: "The symbol is not image, but plurality . . . of meanings." Every work is always "open" to a new historical or personal meaning, "the symbolic language (*by structure* a plural language) to which literary works belong, whose code is devised in such a way that every discourse (every work) engendered by it, has multiple meanings."

It has further to be noted that this discourse has its laws.

To begin, one must not confuse its objects: "one can designate in it all the meanings which it opens up; . . . and on the other hand, a single one of these meanings." In the first case one is dealing with a *science* of literature, in the other with *criticism*.

The laws of literary "science" are methodological laws; their "model would be linguistic. Confronted with the impossibility of mastering all the sentences of a language, the linguist agrees to establish a *hypothetical model of description*. . . . There is no reason not to try to apply such a method to literary works; these works are themselves like immense 'sentences,' derived from the general language of symbols." The aim is not to furnish the meaning(s) of a work but to establish their *intelligibility*.

"Criticism" is the relation of a meaning to a form. Its laws are those of the logic of signifiers. To the extent that all criticism is a particular perspective, and thereby a "transformation" of the work, "it must transform *everything*, but transform only according to certain rules [that Barthes establishes], transform always in the same direction." The result is a "reading in depth," the production of a meaning that criticism "gives justifiably to the work and [which] is finally nothing but the full flowering of the symbols which compose the work."

Système de la mode. Paris: Seuil, 1967. (A part of this, "The Diseases of Costume," translated by Richard Howard, *Partisan Review* 34 [1967]: 89–97, together with one of the *Essais Critiques*, "The Structuralist Activity," ibid., pp. 82–88.)

Barthes announces his project clearly in the preface:

"What was wanted above all was to reconstruct step by step a system of meaning, in some sort of immediate way, that is, by appealing as little as possible to external concepts, even linguistic ones, whose use is certainly frequent here but always elementary. The author encountered many obstacles in his path, and some of them he realizes have not been overcome. . . . More than that, however, the semiological project has been modified along the way; for while at the origin the attempt was made to reconstruct the semantic system of real fashion (found in the clothes actually worn), it became quickly apparent that one had to choose between the analysis of a real system . . . and that of the written system; the second way was chosen. The analysis which follows deals only with fashion as it is written. That may appear to be a disappointing choice. It would have been more agreeable to make use of the system of real fashion (an institution which has always intensely interested sociologists) and apparently more useful to establish the semiology of an independent object, which has nothing to do with articulated language.

"However, while working not on real fashion but on written fashion (or still more exactly: *described* fashion) the author thinks that he has finally succeeded in respecting a certain complexity and a certain order of the semiological project. Although the working material consists uniquely of verbal statements, of 'sentences,' the analysis in no way bears on a part of the French language. For what is taken up here by words is not just any collection of real objects; it is features of clothing which have already been made up . . . into a system of signification. The object of the analysis is thus not a simple nomenclature; it is a real code, even if this code is never anything but 'spoken.' It follows that this work deals, it must be said, neither with clothes nor with language, but, in some way, with the 'translation' from one to the other, however much the first might already be considered a system of signs: an ambiguous object, for it does not correspond to the usual distinction which puts the real on one side and language on the other, and in consequence eludes both linguistics, the science of verbal signs, and semiology, the science of object signs."

The first part of the book is thus devoted to defining the method. It shows how a grill for reading signs can be established on the basis of linguistics. This is not exactly that "model of intelligibility" (a mimetic one) which is mentioned in the *Essais critiques*, but the inventory of instruments which allow it to be constructed, and which here lead to a system of decoding. It is also a glossary of applied (structural) linguistics.

The rest of the work constitutes the reading itself, which is divided into two parts: the "system of fashion" properly speaking and its "message" (for since there is a signifying system, there is communication).

S/Z. Tel Quel. Paris: Seuil, 1970.

L'Empire des signes. Les Sentiers de la Création. Geneva: Skira, 1970.

A bibliography including articles and essays through 1968 may be found in the Gardair item mentioned below.

SELECTED ARTICLES ON BARTHES

Bellour, Raymond. "Entretien avec Roland Barthes." *Les Lettres Françaises*, no. 1172 (2–8 March 1967), pp. 1, 12–13. Reprinted, with another interview, in *Le Livre des autres,* Paris: L'Herne, 1971.

Berl, Emmanuel. "'Anciens' contre 'modernes': un match nul." *Preuves* 16, no. 184 (June 1966): 73–79.

Blanchot, Maurice. "La Grande Tromperie." *Nouvelle Nouvelle Revue Française* 5 (1957): 1061–73.

———. "La Recherche du point zéro." In *Le Livre à venir*, pp. 246–55. Paris: Gallimard, 1959.

Butor, Michel. "La Fascinatrice." *Les Cahiers du Chemin*, October 1968, pp. 20–55.

"Crisis in Criticism." *Times Literary Supplement* 65 (23 June 1966): 545–46.

"Criticism as Language." *Times Literary Supplement* 62 (27 September 1963): 739–40.

Diéguez, Manuel de. "Roland Barthes." In *L'Ecrivain et son langage*, pp. 133–48. Les Essais. Paris: Gallimard, 1960.

Dort, Bernard. "Vers une critique totalitaire." *Critique* 10 (1954): 725–32.

Gardair, Jean-Michel. "Roland Barthes." *Belfagor* 23 (1968): 50–77. Bibliography.

Genette, Gérard. "L'Homme et les signes." *Critique* 21 (1965): 99–114. Reprinted as "L'Envers des signes." In *Figures*, pp. 185–204. Tel Quel. Paris: Seuil, 1966.

Girard, René. "Racine poète de la gloire." *Critique* 20 (1964): 483–506.

Green, André. "Les Mythologies de Roland Barthes et la psychopathologie." *Critique* 14 (1956): 405–13.

Josipovici, Gabriel. "Structures of Truth: The Premises of the French New Criticism." *Critical Quarterly* 10 (1968): 72–88.

Kanters, Robert. "La Querelle des critiques." *Revue de Paris* 73 (January 1966): 121–30.

Kristeva, Julia. "Le Sens et la mode." *Critique* 23 (1967): 1005–31.

Picard, Raymond. *Nouvelle Critique ou nouvelle imposture?* Libertés. Paris: Pauvert, 1965.

Pommier, Jean. "Baudelaire et Michelet devant la jeune critique." *Revue d'Histoire Littéraire* 67 (1957): 544–64.

"Pour ou contre la nouvelle critique." *La Table Ronde*, no. 221 (June 1966), pp. 79–98. Discussion by Pierre de Boisdeffre, Jacques de Bourbon Busset, Charles Dédéyan, Raymond Picard, and Jean Sur.

For a few other writings arising from the Picard-Barthes controversy, see Selected General Bibliography.

Edward W. Said **14**

ABECEDARIUM CULTURAE: Structuralism, Absence, Writing

Holofernes: The deer was, as you know, *sanguis*, in blood; ripe as the pomewater, who now hangeth like a jewel in the ear of *caelo*, the sky, the welkin, the heaven, and anon falleth like a crab on the face of *terra*, the soil, the land, the earth.

Love's Labor's Lost, IV, ii

No reader of *Paradise Lost* is ever likely to have experiences of the kind undergone by Adam; which is why Dr. Johnson insisted on the poem's "inconvenience, that it comprises neither human actions nor human manners." Preeminently an imaginative vision rather than a true record of actual events, *Paradise Lost* is conceded by Dr. Johnson to be the great poem of a man who "saw Nature, as Dryden expresses it, *through the spectacles of books*." Every inconvenience we normally feel when we find language wanting in its ability to convey direct experience directly is, in such a poem as Milton's, especially acute. During Book VII, for example, Raphael is sent to inform Adam of the events in heaven, events that include the indescribable and "Immediate . . . acts of God, more swift / Than time or motion." From the beginning therefore language is not adequate for its intention. Raphael continues to hedge his recital.

. . . to recount almighty works
What words or tongue of seraph can suffice,
Or heart of man suffice to comprehend?

He goes on, the difficulties notwithstanding, because

. . . such commission from above
I have received, to answer they desire
Of knowledge within bounds; beyond abstain
To ask, not let thine inventions hope
Things not revealed, which the invisible king,
Only omniscient, hath suppressed in night,
To none communicable in earth or heaven:
Enough is left besides to search and know.

The truth is at about five removes from the reader. Originally suppressed in night, suppressed once again by Raphael (who as an angel knows more than Adam), suppressed still further because Adam after all is the original man from whose priority we have all fallen, suppressed another time by Milton's use of English to convey the conversation in Eden, and finally suppressed by a poetic discourse to which we can attain only after a mediated act (of reading a seventeenth-century epic)—the Truth is actually absent. Words represent words which represent other words, and so on. Whatever sense we make of Milton is provided by our use of accepted conventions, or codes, of meaning that allow us to sort out the words into coherent significance. We may take comfort in Raphael's assertion that there had been a Word, a primal unity of Truth, to which such puzzles as "meaning" and "reference" are impertinent. Yet, on the other hand, we have only his *word* for it; not a thing certainly, and not more than an assertion that depends on other words and an accepted sense-giving code for support.

Milton's theme is loss, or absence, and his whole poem represents and commemorates the loss at the most literal level. Thus Milton's anthropology is based on the very writing of his poem, for only because man has lost does he write about it, must write about it, can *only* write about it, "it" here being what he cannot really name except with the radical qualification that "it" is *only* a name, a word. To read *Paradise Lost* is to be convinced, in Ruskin's phrase, of the idea of power: by its sheer duration and presence, and by its capacity for making sense despite the absence at its center, Milton's verse seems to have overpowered the void within it. Only when one questions the writing literally does the obvious disjunction between words and reality become troublesome. Words are endless analogies for each other. Outside the monotonous sequence of analogies, we presume, is a primeval origin, but that, like Paradise, is lost forever. Language is a sequel to or supplement of the beginning event, man's Fall; language is one of the actions that succeeds the lost Origin. Human discourse, like *Paradise Lost*, lives with the memory of origins long since violently cut off from it: having begun, discourse can never recover its origins in the unity and unspoken Word of God's Being. This, we know, is the human paradigm incarnated in *Paradise Lost*.

Dr. Johnson's reservations about the poem do not prevent him from reading it; the common-sense difficulties he experiences (the poem's length, the lack in it of human interest) are to him adjuncts to, examples of Milton's intransigence that trouble, Milton's poetic achievement. When, however, Milton's great poem is read with the disquieting sense that what we are watching in the poem is an "ontology of nothingness"[1] —an infinite regress of truths permanently hidden behind words—then we accept the governing awareness of French structuralism. For while it is, I think, inappropriate to force an ideological unity upon the structuralists, it is apt to see them the way they very often see others, as inhabiting and constituting a certain level of consciousness with its own sense of difference from others, its own idioms, patterns, ambitions, and narrative rhythm.

Of them all, it is Michel Foucault who has *become*, in Roland Barthes's words, the very thing his works describe:[2] a consciousness awakened to the troubled conditions of modern knowledge.[3] Foucault is, to use Blackmur's phrase, a technique of trouble. As history is gradually unveiled in Foucault's work, we do not watch an easy chronicle of events but a succession of functional conditions that enable the existence not only of knowledge but of man himself;[4] hence the subtitle "an archaeology of human sciences" for *Les Mots et les choses*. Permanently hampered by language, which is the first, and in a sense the last, instrument at its disposal, Foucault's job of getting to the bottom yields only the repeated and much modulated assertion that man is a temporary interruption, a figure of thought, of the already begun (*le déjà commencé*). Any human investigation (and here the relevance of Wittgenstein's

1. "L'ontologie de l'anéantissement des êtres vaut donc comme critique de la connaissance." Michel Foucault, *Les Mots et les choses* (Paris: Gallimard, 1966), p. 291.

2. Roland Barthes, *Essais critiques* (Paris: Seuil, 1964), p. 168.

3. Foucault, *Les Mots et les choses*, p. 221.

4. Ibid., p. 13.

later work is crucial) is actually bound up in the nature of language. The interpretation of evidence, for example, is exegesis. But when we ask the question "exegesis of what?" we commit ourselves totally to a perpetual series of the preposition *of*; the modern form of criticism, according to Foucault, is philology as an analysis *of* what is being said in the depths of the discourse.[5] Just as there is no beginning to the process of exegesis, there is also no end:

In the sixteenth century, interpretation went from the world (things and a text at the same time) to the divine Word which was deciphered in the world; our interpretation, the one which in any case has been ours since the nineteenth century, goes from men, from God, from knowledge or chimeras, to the words that make them all possible; and what is discovered is not the sovereignty of a primal discourse but the fact that before the least of our utterances, we have already been dominated and paralyzed by language.[6]

The drama of Foucault's work is that he is always coming to terms with language as both the constricting horizon and the energizing atmosphere within and by which all human activity must be understood. Two of Foucault's major works (*Histoire de la folie à l'âge classique* and *Les Mots et les choses*) describe respectively how language has permitted the social discriminations of "otherness," and the cognitive connections between the orders of "sameness"; in the former work it is madness, isolated in a silence outside rational language, that is made by society to carry the weight of an alienated "otherness," and in the latter work it is through the powers of language that words are made into a universal collection of signs for everything. As with most of the structuralists Foucault must presume a conceptual unity—variously called an epistemological field,

5. Ibid., p. 311.

6. "L'interprétation, au XVIe siècle, allait du monde (choses et textes à la fois) à la Parole divine qui se déchiffrait en lui; la nôtre, celle en tout cas qui s'est formée au XIXe siècle, va des hommes, de Dieu, des connaissances ou des chimères, aux mots qui les rendent possibles; et ce qu'elle découvre, ce n'est pas la souveraineté d'un discours premier, c'est le fait que nous sommes, avant la moindre de nos paroles, déjà dominés et transis par le langage." Ibid.

an epistemological unity, or *epistemé*—that anchors and informs linguistic usage at any given time in history; yet to the structuralists' credit it must also be said that the presumption is often made with no attempt to palm it off as anything more than a practical assertion, as a working hypothesis. Not in Foucault's case however. "In a culture, and at a given moment," he writes in *Les Mots et les choses*, "there is never more than one *epistemé* that defines the conditions of possibility of all knowledge."[7] One of the various chores this univocal assertion is made to perform is, as Steven Marcus has remarked,[8] that it gives license to Foucault's literal faith in an era before the modern dissociation of sensibility. For according to Foucault, language in the Renaissance was intimately connected with things; words were believed to be inherent in the script of an ontological discourse (God's Word) that required only reading for the guarantee of their meaning and truth. Words existed inside Being; they reduplicated it; they were its signature, and man's decipherment of language was a direct, whole perception of Being.

Foucault's brilliant analyses of *Don Quixote* and Velásquez's *Las Meninas* show how the intricate system of resemblances, by which things were ultimately linked to a divine Origin, began to break down; Don Quixote in his madness is unable to find the creatures of his reading in the world; Velásquez's magistral painting focuses outward and away from the canvas to a point its composition requires but does not contain. The representative space of language has become, by the eighteenth century, an ordered film, a transparency through which the continuity of Being can shine. Thus, "the essential problem for classical [or eighteenth-century] thought is lodged in the rapports between the *name* and *order*: to discover a *nomenclature* that was also a *taxonomy*, or to establish a system of signs that

7. "Dans une culture et à un moment donné, il n'y a jamais qu'une *épistémè*, qui définit les conditions de possibilité de tout savoir." Ibid., p. 179.

8. Steven Marcus, "In Praise of Folly," *New York Review of Books*, 3 November, 1966, p. 8.

were transparent to the continuity of Being."[9] When words lose the power to represent the connections between them—that is, the power to refer not only to the objects to which the words point but also to the system that connects objects with each other in a universal taxonomy of existence—then we enter the modern period. Not only can the center not hold, but also the network around it begins to lose its cohesive power.

It is when, in his two major books and in his archaeology of clinical observation, Foucault embarks on a discussion of the nineteenth and twentieth centuries that it becomes apparent how much his vision of history preceding the modern age is projected back from his apprehension of the contemporary. For like every one of the structuralists, Foucault is obsessed with the inescapable fact of ontological discontinuity. In language, for example, "the thing being represented falls outside of the representation itself"[10]; thus the signifying power of language far exceeds, indeed overwhelms, what is being signified. Another example: the emergence of the *idea* of man (whose advent Foucault associates exclusively with the early nineteenth century) coincides with the breakdown in the representative power of language. Man therefore is what essentially resists language; he becomes what Foucault calls an "empirico-transcendent doublet,"[11] two parallel zones of actual raw human experience on the one hand and human transcendence on the other, that together are alien to discourse. And discourse is the "analytic of finitude" which constitutes modern knowledge and which is made possible by man's alienation from it, for according to Foucault, the discourse of modern knowledge always hungers for what it cannot fully grasp or totally represent. Thus knowledge is perpetually in

9. "Le problème essentiel de la pensée classique se logeait dans les rapports entre le *nom* et l'*ordre*: découvrir une *nomenclature* qui fût une *taxinomie*, ou encore instaurer un système de signes qui fût transparent à la continuité de l'être." Foucault, *Les Mots et les choses*, p. 220.

10. "L'être même de ce qui est représenté va tomber maintenant hors de la représentation elle-même." Ibid., p. 253.

11. Ibid., pp. 329, 330, 332–33.

search of its elusive subject. Here again the fact of discontinuity, or difference as it is also called, is paramount.

Finally, the densely and portentously argued theme of *Les Mots et les choses* (a book whose literary and philosophical implications are almost frighteningly vast) is occupied with the vacant spaces between things, words, ideas. In the eighteenth century the possibility of representing things in space—as in a painting—derived from the acceptance of temporal succession which thereby allowed the constitution of spatial simultaneity; the fact that objects could exist together in the privileged space of a painting depended upon an unquestioned belief in the continuing forward movement of time. Spatial togetherness was conceived to be an emanation out of temporal succession. Yet in the modern era the profound sense of spatial distance between things, which separates like things from each other, permits the modern mind to contemplate time as only a dream of succession, as a promise of unity or of a return to the Origin.[12] Above all, time is the most tenuous of the spatial configurations that attempt to bridge the gap between things. Thus the human sciences and time together occupy the distance that separates (without uniting) biology, economics, and language, the three fields of knowledge that seem to Foucault to be essential because, respectively, they treat of natural life, of value, and of representation.[13] As a humanized account of life, psychology stands next to biology, and by the same argument, sociology stands next to economics, and literature and mythology next to language; in the wavering and the discontinuity between one and its adjacent partner, we have, according to Foucault, the constituting models of the human sciences. Man is a problem defined in terms of an alternation between impersonal biological functions and psychological norms, between standardized economic rules and sociological conflict, and between language as system and the significations of myth and literature.[14] Man is the enigmatic structure that with difficulty knits them all together.

12. Ibid., p. 351.
13. Ibid., p. 365.
14. Ibid., p. 368.

The effect of Foucault's argument, probably as much as the effect of any general account of it one gives, is that man as we know him is dissolved. Just as in his book on madness Foucault showed how madness had always effectively resisted language and the postures of reason until the late nineteenth century, in his most recent book he demonstrates how after that time man himself becomes an irrationality in a special sense, a structure that dramatizes the normally unthinkable relationship between the diversities of knowledge. No longer a coherent *cogito*, man now inhabits the interstices, "the vacant interstellar spaces," not as an object, still less as a subject; rather man is the *structure*, or the generality of relationships between those words and ideas that we call the human, as opposed to the pure or natural, sciences.[15] The structure is irrational because it is the limit at which thought becomes intelligible, and therefore it cannot be *thought about*. One can just think it, and that only after disciplined "archaeological" research. (The novelty of such a formula in English, as well as the distinction between *thinking* and *thinking about*, is much more acceptable in French; *penser la structure* is a valid construction in the way that "to think structurally" is also valid but not lucid. In French, however, it is easier to argue—as Foucault and the structuralists do—that *thinking about* is reflexive, and hence rational, whereas *thinking* itself is mere activity, and hence irrational.) Knowledge therefore is a closed system of knowledge *for* or *of* man *by* man. And, finally, since knowledge can be formulated only in language, linguistics becomes more a perception than an explanation of man;[16] man is the positive domain, the field, of science and knowledge, but he is not the object of science.[17] "One can therefore say that there is a 'human science' not simply wherever man is concerned, but rather wherever one analyzes, in the appropriate dimension of the nonconscious, those norms, rules, and significant ensembles that reveal to consciousness the conditions and the forms of its contents."[18]

15. Ibid., p. 376.
16. Ibid., p. 393.
17. Ibid., p. 378.
18. "On dira donc qu'il y a 'science humaine' non pas partout où il est question de l'homme, mais partout où on analyse, dans la

The eccentricity of so bleak and antihumanistic a view of man is reflected even in Foucault's prose. Despite the frequently astonishing lucidity of his dissections of intellectual ventures from Cervantes through Linnaeus and Adam Smith to Nietzsche and Freud, one is overcome by a prose style whose grasp of an author or idea is exceedingly particular but whose direction and aspirations are tremendously general: like Holofernes Foucault is usually to be found overglancing the superscript. For if, by tradition and education, we are trained to take man as the concrete universal, the pivot and center of awareness, then in Foucault's prose, and concurrently by his argument, we are made to lose our grip on man. If we are inclined to think of man as an entity resisting the flux of experience, then because of Foucault man is dissolved in the overarching waves, the quanta, the striations of language itself, turning finally into little more than a constituted subject, a speaking pronoun, fixed indecisively in the eternal, ongoing rush of discourse.

Foucault's man is well described in Roland Barthes's clever phrase, "a metaphor without brakes" (*métaphore sans frein*).[19] There is an uncanny resemblance between this view of man and that other remarkable dissolution of man in discourse which is Conrad's *Heart of Darkness*. After having described Kurtz as "just a word for me," Marlow continues:

> I made the strange discovery that I had never imagined him as doing, you know, but as discoursing. I didn't say to myself, "Now I will never see him," or "Now I will never shake him by the hand," but, "now I will never hear him." The man presented himself as a voice. Not of course that I did not connect him with some sort of action. . . . That was not the point. The point was in his being a gifted creature, and that of all his gifts the one that stood out preeminently, that carried with it a sense of real presence, was his ability to talk, his words—the gift of expression, the bewildering, the illuminating, the most

---

dimension propre à l'inconscient, des normes, des règles, des ensembles signifiants qui dévoilent à la conscience les conditions de ses formes et de ses contenus." Ibid., p. 376.

19. Barthes, *La Tour Eiffel* (Lausanne: Delpire, 1964), p. 82.

exalted, and the most contemptible, the pulsating stream of light, or the deceitful flow from the heart of an impenetrable darkness.[20]

In achieving a position of mastery over man, language has reduced him to a grammatical function. The world of activity and of human experience stands silently aside while language constitutes order and legislates discovery. According to Lévi-Strauss, "language, an unreflecting totalization, is human reason which has its reasons and of which man knows nothing."[21] Nearly every one of the structuralists acknowledges a tyrannical feedback system in which man is the speaking subject whose actions are always being converted into signs that signify him, which he uses in turn to signify other signs, and so on to infinity.

It is a measure of Foucault's old-fashioned skill with the great resources of intellectual power and compelling argument that we do not object intolerantly to the monotony of vicious linguistic circles and spiraling analogies really advanced by his view of things. After all, we are likely to say when we finish reading *Les Mots et les choses*, work does get done, man still has the capacity for violence, for creation, for erecting buildings, for being the inhabitant of an earth he is both making and destroying: why then the structuralists' gloomy insistence upon loss, upon man's unhappy—and seemingly eternal—insertion in a language game that he can barely understand, upon a dominantly linguistic apprehension of reality? Why must it be that the centrifugal analogies in Holofernes's speeches and the tautologies of Lucky's monologue in *En attendant Godot* stand as emblems for the structuralist vision of man?

The problem, as all the structuralists—Foucault, Lévi-Strauss, Barthes, Louis Althusser, and Emile Benveniste among them—see it, is that the authority of a privileged Origin that commands, guarantees, and perpetuates meaning has been

20. Joseph Conrad, *Youth and Two Other Stories* (Garden City, N.Y.: Doubleday, 1924), pp. 112–13.

21. Claude Lévi-Strauss, *The Savage Mind* (Chicago: University of Chicago Press, 1966), p. 252. "Totalisation non-réflexive, la langue est une raison humaine qui a ses raisons, et que l'homme ne connaît pas." *La Pensée sauvage* (Paris: Plon, 1962), p. 334.

removed. Why this has happened does not seem as important as the fact of its happening, and this fact, as we saw, is already accepted in *Paradise Lost*. In other words, man now lives in a circle without a center, or in a maze without a way out. If, for example, we try to think of action's beginning we must articulate the beginning in language. And since language for us is a system of written signs, the "first" sign is a momentary exigency of the discourse, never an absolute terminal. So there is no such thing as a beginning for language; or, if there is one, it is an unthinkable event, since, as Emile Benveniste puts it in one of his trenchant essays, we cannot think without language,[22] and language makes only a token concession to a beginning. The categories of thought and language are identical. To complicate matters further, we generally locate origins before beginnings, since the Origin is a state from which the beginnings of action move forward; retrospectively considered then, the Origin is a condition or state that permits beginning. Foucault's way of showing the loss both of a beginning and of the Origin behind it is to study the way in which eighteenth-century thought about language underwent massive change during the nineteenth century. Whereas during the classical age the derivation, designation, and articulation of words were thought to be functions of the consistent transparency by which words reflected Being, in the nineteenth century the idea of derivation gave up its place to a mere theory of linguistic families (in the work of the German philologist Bopp), designation ceded to a theory of verbal radicals, and articulation was replaced by a theory of internal variations within language.[23] Being, in short, was swallowed up in the internal analysis of language.

As a result of these momentous changes, words now simply double back on themselves; this is why the verb *dédoubler* turns up incessantly in all structuralist writing. It is no longer possible either to designate a beginning or to think of an origin except, in both cases, as concessions to the empty fact of priority. Strictly speaking, a beginning to a modern mind only

22. Emile Benveniste, *Problèmes de linguistique générale* (Paris: Gallimard, 1966), p. 70.

23. Foucault, *Les Mots et les choses*, p. 201.

occupies the temporal place in thought that a speaking subject would in a passage of prose. At best, however, a beginning provides an inaugural direction, and a provisional orientation in theme and intention. Yet because we must always use language to point at a beginning, and because language is always a presence and never a prior state, the origin and the beginning are hopelessly alien, absent from, the stream of discourse. Removed by language, which is the very activity it once, presumably, enabled, the beginning stands outside words, but is assumed by them; the beginning is like the man at the door of the Law in Kafka's parable, neither able to enter nor permitted to be forgotten. Man the beginning, the subject of human thought and activity as he had been in what is now seen as the utopia of Renaissance humanism, is admitted to language as an incipient, and inarticulate, ensemble of relations between his activities. According to Barthes, *logos* and *praxis* are cut off from each other.[24] Structure remains shyly to fill the void.

Yet the beginning will not be forgotten even though it is an event whose irreducible difference from structure cannot ever be denied. Each of the structuralists in his own way alludes to origins that antedate and provide for a beginning event, and the characteristic feature of this event is the absence of written language; literally, the event is a pre-scriptive beginning. In *Tristes Tropiques*, described by Maurice Blanchot as full of a fascination with beginnings and original possibilities,[25] Lévi-Strauss encounters the Nambikwara, a tribe of Amazon primitives who have not yet discovered writing. There, among them, Lévi-Strauss speculates on the origins of writing and concludes that writing is the advent of enslavement. Before writing, man had lived at a zero point, which is described elsewhere by Lévi-Strauss as an original state preceding the neolithic age;[26] life at the zero point was ruled over by a

24. Barthes, *Essais critiques*, p. 264.

25. Maurice Blanchot, "L'Homme au point zéro," *Nouvelle Nouvelle Revue Française* IV (1956): 689.

26. Georges Charbonnier, *Entretiens avec Claude Lévi-Strauss* (Paris: Plon, 1961), pp. 30, 31, 32 and passim; also, Lévi-Strauss, "Introduction à l'oeuvre de Marcel Mauss," in *Sociologie et anthropologie*, by Marcel Mauss (Paris: Presses Universitaires de France, 1950), p. xlix.

central "floating signifier," a kind of spiritual *etymon*, whose ubiquity and perfect consistency allowed it the power to act as a pure semantic value. This, in Lévi-Strauss's judgment, corresponds to Marcel Mauss's notion of *mana*, an almost magical value that permits primitive, preliterate societies to make a whole range of universal distinctions between force and action, between abstract and concrete, and between quality and state. (The parallels between preliteralism and Eden before the Fall are fascinating indeed.) One beautifully functional key, *mana*, therefore unlocks every signifier because it is the Origin of all signifiers.

The point here, however, is that Lévi-Strauss is attempting, like Foucault in his analysis of madness, to describe a society and a state to which civilized man can have no real access; this partially explains the enigmatic use of words like magic and zero, as well as the quasi-fantastic air running through these descriptions. Because the observing ethnologist is a product of literate society, and because anthropology itself is subject to the enslaving laws of literacy, the zero state is a forbidden paradise to which literacy penetrates only at the same critical moment that the paradise is being obliterated. In the encounter between preliteracy and literacy the latter always wins; the illiterate natives learn how to write. In teaching the primitives (a process recorded with moving philosophic precision in *Tristes Tropiques*) civilization disturbs the equanimity and calm of a univocal society in which spoken words and concrete objects had been intertwined in a complex but profoundly logical unity. For a while, nevertheless, the ethnologist can observe a society making its traumatic entry at the *beginning* of literacy, leaving the zero Origin behind it forever. (The tragedy is, as Lévi-Strauss observed in a recent essay, that anthropology inevitably *brings* and forcibly introduces writing to primitive society—in a kind of rape—thereby destroying once and for all a peace never again to be enjoyed in nonliterate solitude.)[27] To sum up then, the process is as follows: zero, followed by the beginning of writing (literacy), followed by enslavement, which is our present situation. Writing means

27. Lévi-Strauss, "The Disappearance of Man," *New York Review of Books*, 28 July 1966, p. 7.

submission to the logic of language, and the loss of a central and univocal resource of meaning.

There are *two* primitive states. One, the zero stability of preliterate society, the other the moment at which writing begins to be learned: in fine, the Origin and the beginning. Yet only one can be actually described (in writing, of course) by the field anthropologist who is recording its loss, and metaphorically evoked by the linguist who notes its absence; and this is the beginning, which in anthropological or linguistic discourse is converted into a *sign* that initiates the system, a sign *for* or *of* the signifying system. The Origin is a silent zero point, locked within itself. It is the realm of untroubled semantic security, closed to man, and the beginning is the event that founds the realm of order and writing, *syntax*, whose weblike wealth continues to impoverish, render obsolete, and cover up the memory of the original germ of pure meaning. Primitive thought, insofar as it can be described by civilized thought, is order at its most essential level, yet the modern mind must conceive it entirely as a system of endless parallels and reflections. There is no center available to the modern thinker, no absolute subject, since the Origin has been curtained off. The modern anthropologist's field trips among primitive people provide us with the most lively means of seeing our loss; as he was for the eighteenth-century writer of philosophical voyages, the primitive is a model for our imaginings of lost plenitude. Literate man is constantly signifying, yet *what* he signifies can only be interpreted as a function of *how* he signifies. Language, which is man's principal means of signification, is, as Barthes says, at once a problem and a model of order.[28]

The structuralists' predicament is an accurate symptom of man mired in his systems of signification. Their work can be construed as an attempt to manipulate their way out of enslavement by language into an awareness and a subsequent mastery of their linguistic situation. If their continuing enterprise is functional (like Robinson Crusoe marooned, but staying alive, on his island and organizing its possibilities around his needs) then their vision of the past is fondly utopian, and

28. Barthes, *Essais critiques*, p. 274.

their anticipation of the future is very dimly apocalyptic. The past contained a meaning they cherish somewhat uselessly because they cannot hold it, and the future may restore it to them. They are structuralists—as in a way we all are—because they accept their existential fate inside language whose mode of being is pitilessly relational; words derive meaning not from any intrinsic value a word carries inside itself but from a double system of metaphor and metonymy that links words to each other and gives the words fleeting intelligibility rather than detached permanence. Certainly the structuralists are formalists, content being for them not much more than a chimera of the kind, Lévi-Strauss notes, one might expect to dig out of a piece of music;[29] it is, they contend, no easier to say what writing really means than it is to say what a Beethoven symphony means. Meaning is dispersed, scattered systematically along the length and depth of the spoken and written chain, but it is virtually incomprehensible at any moment in the chain since language is never present *in toto* and at once. The most one can do is to understand and perhaps predict the workings of the system—like reading a musical score—which permits one to function momentarily within it. The question to ask is: how does the system work? not: what does it mean? Thus in the structuralist universe the problem of belief is never relevant since belief entails a hierarchy of meanings. For structuralism there are only significations, and they are either adequate or inadequate for their signifying intentions.

A major criticism of the structuralists is, I think, that the moving force of life and behavior, the *forma informans*, has been, in their work, totally domesticated by system. I shall be returning to this problem later. Nonetheless, they do try to allow gingerly for force, although characteristically it is relegated to the beginning, the moment that for them succeeds the Origin, or the silent zero point. Georges Bataille speaks eloquently of "inaugural violence," and the image is meant to convey a correlative for an event, now only a faint imagining, that initiated a signifying system. Foucault locates it when, at

29. Lévi-Strauss, *Mythologiques: Le Cru et le cuit* (Paris: Plon, 1964), pp. 23–34.

the end of the Middle Ages, mad people were incarcerated, violently put away by society. Madness is precisely the zero state that resists the encroachments of reason; by definition, a madman cannot speak, for his language is disordered, or rather, it is nonexistent as system. The violence of his imprisonment inaugurates, begins, the era of rationalism in whose backwash we continue to swim. For Lévi-Strauss the beginning is the initial violence of language itself, which makes its first appearance during the neolithic age in catalogs of property, including lists of slaves.

The effort of the structuralists is dedicated to the *form* of the violence, to an attempt at clarifying and identifying it, which is why form, or structure, is always a difficult mixture of need, absence, loss, and uncertain appropriation. Structure is the *sign* of these things—as much a yearning for plenitude as a memorial to unceasing loss. The structuralists themselves speak like men who stand at the beginning of a new era and at the twilight (their word is *clôture*) of an old one; they forecast a time in which linguistics and anthropology will guide human endeavor and will enable man to reassemble the disparate pieces of his activity into a new unity. Perhaps then semantics will confidently be reintroduced into the systematic mesh of significations. For the moment, however, they are satisfied with collecting and unraveling systems—like Mr. Casaubon working at his Key to All Mythologies—with a view toward synthesizing them together into a grand and all-encompassing universality. Their seriousness makes them see the tragic aspects of their effort; Foucault's work, especially, reads like a protracted Orpheus-cry of anguish at the immense difficulty of producing unity. Yet there is a comic side to their industry. The intensity of their dedication often reminds one of Molière's characters who are so single-minded about their work that they cannot detect the irony in a job done too rationally; as Chrysale says in *Les Femmes savantes*, "Raisonner est l'emploi de toute ma maison,/Et le raisonnement en bannit la raison" (II, vii, 597–98).

Within a century, the language was established: a Samoyedic Lithuanian dialect of Guarani, with classical Arabian inflections.
Borges, "The Library of Babel"

Writing of Lévi-Strauss for a special number of *Annales* devoted to the anthropologist's work, Barthes commented that Lévi-Strauss had effectively created the need for new cadres of research in the human sciences.[30] Barthes himself, perhaps independently of the older man's work, had by that time hewn out a whole program of what he called semiotic research. This was the patient decoding of systematic sign systems—from those as simple as advertising posters to ones as complex as the ones that made of ladies' fashion magazines a highly specialized language with its own typical images, idioms, and rhetoric. In his various essays, pamphlets, and books Barthes was attempting to discover how man communicated his messages to other men, how he signified his intentions and fabricated his contingent meanings, and how order inhered in what Barthes and the other structuralists called an unconscious (in this special French case, nonrational, that is, used by agreed-upon convention before conscious recognition) functional awareness. Barthes admitted at first that this was only precriticism and not by any means a full-fledged project of judgment and evaluation.[31] Some years later, in a highly barbed polemic against the old academic criticism, he was to firm up his views strictly by saying that criticism could never be more than periphrasis and that the critical work as well as the work criticized had an equal right to say "I am literature."[32] The critic's language, according to Barthes, covered the work criticized with an appropriate prose; signs were being laid, in an orderly and well-thought fashion, upon other signs, the several levels illuminating each other. The father of semiotics was acknowledged to be the Swiss linguist Ferdinand de Saussure, and its tacitly recognized Prospero was Lévi-Strauss.

30. Barthes, "Les Sciences humaines et l'oeuvre de Lévi-Strauss," *Annales: Economies, Sociétés, Civilisations* 19 (1964): 1085–86.

31. Barthes, *Michelet par lui-même* (Paris: Seuil, 1965), page facing frontispiece.

32. Barthes, *Critique et vérité* (Paris: Seuil, 1966), p. 71.

The underlying rationale of semiology (this had been Saussure's own word, although C. S. Peirce had used it and the idea itself, quite on his own) reposed in an extremely practical view of language. It had been apparent to Saussure in his *Cours de linguistique* (1910–11) that language was far too complex and various a thing for immediate analysis. The first problem for linguistics, he asserted, was to delimit and define itself.[33] Of course this preliminary step is just as necessary for any field of knowledge; a historian, unless he is foolish, will first decide what history he wishes to investigate, thus setting up a kind of anticipatory model of his subject, then go on to investigate. The paradox of linguistics to which Saussure continually returns in his *Cours* is that linguistics must always define itself tautologically in the very words that it sets out to understand. Hence, he argued with a convincing rationalism, the viewpoint in linguistics determines the object.[34] To ground a linguistic viewpoint is first to note that language exists only within a collectivity; moreover, no single speaker exhausts collectivities like French or Spanish.[35] Thus a totality must be presumed—Saussure called it *langue*—on which each individual speaker draws, as from a vast subliminal reservoir, during the course of his speech (*parole*); the interchange between *langue* and *parole* permits variations in meaning and manner sufficient for the signifying or message-bearing intention. In this view then words are signs, made up jointly of a concept (*significatum*) and a sound-image (*significans*): these two halves of the sign were coined for and then put in circulation by linguistic jargon as the signified (*le signifié*) and the signifier (*le signifiant*).[36]

One of Saussure's most far-reaching observations was that the connection between sound and concept, the signifier and the signified, is wholly arbitrary.[37] Words do not derive their meaning from any inherent sense made by their sound, nor does a sound, in and of itself, necessarily connote a meaning. To emit a sound is to do no more than that; to communicate sense, however, a word must be compared with another word, and

33. Ferdinand de Saussure, *Cours de linguistique générale*, 4th ed. (Paris: Payot, 1949), p. 20.

34. Ibid., p. 23.

35. Ibid., p. 30.

36. Ibid., p. 99.

37. Ibid., p. 100.

this kind of differentiation is what we practice when we use language. The difference between words gives meaning; the crucial guarantee of meaning in any language is that the differences between words must be orderly and consistent; in other words, differences must always be systematic. Meaning is diacritical. Thus, for "table" to make sense it must always be differentiated in the same essential ways from "love" or "chair" or "man." Language therefore is a pattern, or code, of differences that converts arbitrarily chosen sounds into systematic sense. As far as a linguist can tell, the rules of the system are like those of a game; the parallels with Wittgenstein and Huizinga, to give only two examples, are evident. Yet what is especially interesting about Saussure's discovery of the arbitrary connection between sound and sense—at least so far as it carries over into structuralist writing—is that the sheer oppressive mass of historical, biological, or psychic determinism is lifted, then frittered away, then brought back as weightless, gamelike rules. History need not be the burden of the past; it need only be the manner in which other arbitrary connections between sound and sense were first made, then conventionalized into common use. The interpretation of language is an aesthetic activity and, so to speak, a release from the tyranny of time and history. This is why Edmund Leach has written of Lévi-Strauss's structural and linguistic interpretations of kinship systems (which rely on Saussure's method of systematic decipherment of arbitrarily connected signifier and signified) that it is possible to undertake them for the aesthetic pleasure of the exercise.[38] In most structuralist writings, sign analysis is done with a sort of neutral mental glee taken in the task. In structuralism we rarely have any sense of Freud's tragic realization that civilization, and language, are repressors of man, nor do we sense any of the pain of Nietzsche's frenzied leaps against an obdurate wall of history and custom, nor any of Heidegger's patient and yet agonized doom within language. For the most part the structuralists are adjusted to language

38. Edmund Leach, "The Legitimacy of Solomon: Some Structural Aspects of Old Testament History," *Archives Européennes de Sociologie* 3 (1962): 70.

and civilization (for them the two are coterminous); they take culture for what it rationally is, and they do not rebel against it.

The importance of Saussure's work for the contemporary structuralists is far too complicated to be examined here. The chief rule of procedure all of them seem to have learned from him, however, is that no matter how small the task there has to be explicit delimitation of the problem. Borrowing from André Martinet—and obviously echoing Saussure—Barthes speaks cogently of the necessity of pertinence, which he calls a principled decision to describe facts from only one point of view, even to the exclusion of all others.[39] Most of the time Saussure's rule of delimitation is used to reduce, in order to make manageable for scrutiny, a very large body of phenomena. Quite aside from its obvious practical advantages Saussure's procedural rule has, from the standpoint of a structuralist critic, certain moral and emotional advantages as well. In the first place, when he is confronted with an enormous hodgepodge of data, the critic can cut his way through it by asserting the existence of a problem within the mass. It is remarkable that in the work of every structuralist, Barthes, Lévi-Strauss, Foucault, Lucien Sebag, and Louis Althusser included, the same methodological first step that unites critical discernment with violence always turns up; this step is most often called *découpage*, but it is also frequently called *coupure épistémologique*, in both of which the verb *couper* (to cut) figures prominently. Facing an awesome mountain of detail, the critic's mind becomes a confident David, going straight for the vulnerable spot in Goliath's forehead. The critic cuts out a patch in the detail as a way of compelling the vast body of which it is a part, and he focuses exclusively on that patch. Emotionally he asserts his mind's undoubted sway over what seems to be a totally resisting mass of detail. Morally he demonstrates his right over it because he has a victorious tool, proved in the encounter.

There are a few submerged assumptions that support the structuralist *découpage*, that assertive cutting down to tractable

39. Barthes, "Eléments de sémiologie," *Communications*, no. 4 (1965), pp. 132–33.

size of intolerable detail. One is that detail is not merely a matter of quantity but has become a qualitative feature of every human discipline. Any historian or literary critic can verify this by consulting recent bibliographies on even the most trivial subject. The mind tends to be impressed not with the sheer number of details in and about a field, but with the fact that this number of details is a forbidding obstacle to any meaningful penetration of the field. To devise a means for hurdling the obstacle becomes the first order of critical business. Another assumption is that for the structuralist all details have the status of *information*. For the structuralist has decided, as Lévi-Strauss says, that the world of discourse is an orderly place, and if there is order somewhere it must be everywhere. Now order has an economy about it that renders every detail functional, and since the structuralist model is language it becomes quite logical therefore to assume that every linguistic particle, every verbal emission, conveys information of some sort. Structuralism will not allow for waste; discourse is wall-to-wall, and every item in it has the dignity of message-bearing capability. To be vulgar about it, for the structuralists every litter bit counts. Finally, the structuralist *découpage* (with which it is amusing to compare Swift's phrase "every man his own carver") is borne along by a mathematical ambition to turn details into a coherent *field* governed by a *set* whose function it is to *operate* systematically in linking all the details with each other. The history of this kind of cybernetic hope in the West is a long one; it includes the Greek atomists, Lucretius, Leibnitz, and Descartes, then more recently Frege and Wiener, and finally the structuralists. It also finds its way imaginatively and pedagogically into Browne's *Garden of Cyrus*, the dictionaries, encyclopedias, anatomies, catalogs, and universal grammars of the seventeenth and eighteenth centuries, Flaubert's *Dictionnaire des idées reçues*, and Borges's *Aleph*. For the structuralists *découpage* validates the operation of a functional *corpora prima* that drives off the shrewish inanity of unlimited detail.

In a retrospective comment on his *Structures élémentaires de la parenté* Lévi-Strauss noted how in that work he had "chosen a field that could, at first glance, have called attention to itself only for its incoherent and contingent nature, [yet he] had tried to show that it was possible to reduce all of it to a very small number of significant propositions."[40] Kinship systems present a bewildering variety of customs that repel a synthetic overview; yet it is by projecting the existence in them of a set of rules which make the entire corpus a working whole that the mind can then absorb the mass as a significant entity. And this is precisely what Lévi-Strauss did. Barthes's manifesto for structuralism hinges on his statement that applauds the method as an activity first of decomposing works—of literature, for instance—into their simplest functional forms, then of recomposing them into wholes dominated by what he called a sovereign motor principle.[41] This had been the scheme employed by V. I. Propp, one of the Russian formalists, in *The Morphology of the Folktale*. Foucault's method of *découpage* is to reduce the vagaries of history to a set of alterations between modes of perceiving difference and sameness. René Girard's *Mensonge romantique et verité romanesque* views the history of the novel as a set of variations on an essential but enormously fecund "triangular model" of desire. "A basic contention," of Girard's book, "is that the great writers apprehend intuitively and concretely, through the medium of their art, if not formally, the system in which they were first imprisoned together with their contemporaries."[42] Finally, Louis Althusser's Marxism has for its method a way of pulling from a text what Althusser calls its problematic, which is a special mode the text has of taking hold of its subject. Regardless of how complicated a philosophy or political program is, it can be grasped by the mind as an attempt "ideologically" to see the world *for* a particular end, and this end, as well as the program itself, can be formulated as a prob-

40. "J'avais donc choisi un domaine qui pouvait, au premier abord, se signaler par son caractère incohérent et contingent, et dont j'ai essayé de montrer qu'il était possible de le réduire à un très petit nombre de propositions signifiantes." Lévi-Strauss, "Réponses à quelques questions," *Esprit* 31 (1963): 630.

41. Barthes, *Essais critiques*, pp. 215–17.

42. René Girard, *Deceit, Desire, and the Novel: Self and Other in Literary Structure*, trans. Yvonne Freccero (Baltimore: Johns Hopkins Press, 1965), pp. 2–3.

lematic, or specific generality. In every one of the examples given above, the critic orders his data first by delimiting the field in terms of a specific problem, then by deducing a rationale from his initial delimitation, then by applying this rationale in detail to all the material in an effort to make the material work, or perform systematically.

The linguistic apprehension—or perception—of reality is, of course, the most important cutting down to size. We tend to accept this *découpage* when we read a novelist, for example, but it seems more extreme when it is found to be the operating bias of the historian, the sociologist, and even of the psychoanalyst, particularly when only meager allowances are made for brute reality as a mere symbolic fiction. Lévi-Strauss fatalistically marks the fundamental opposition between the discontinuities of symbolism (in this case, one supposes, the totemlike world of objects that symbolize values, our everyday world) and the continuity of knowledge, that is, between the world and the mind.[43] The grand model of knowledge therefore is language-as-writing, the most continuous of man's enterprises and the one that covers all man's activity with the sheen of prose. At bottom, structuralism is a set of attitudes to and of writing: grammatology. In writing, the structuralist can enact his work actually and actively; his attention to his work is a disciplined pertinence. As science, structuralism is metalinguistic, language studying language, linguistic consciousness appropriating linguistic competence and performance.

When Lévi-Strauss speaks of primitive thought *(la pensée sauvage)* he is not only describing the way in which the primitive thinks, but also thought itself, as it is, atrophied in its essential about-to-be-thought-about-something. Lévi-Strauss wishes to describe the order of thought, not its substance. This is a very important point, one that Paul Ricoeur emphasized tellingly in a worthwhile exchange with Lévi-Strauss.[44] Order, according to Lévi-Strauss, is what makes thought intelligible as thought; order holds thought back from the verge

43. Lévi-Strauss, "Introduction à l'oeuvre de Marcel Mauss," p. xxvii.

44. Lévi-Strauss, "Réponses à quelques questions," p. 644.

of chaos. Thus the structuralist substitutes order, or the structure of thought, for a Being that in classical philosophy had informed and nurtured thought. Order is a limit beyond which it is impossible to go, in which moreover it is impossible to think. Order is the mind's choice of syntax over semantics, the choice for the existence of momentary, discursive sense over the certainty of rigid and detached meaning. The structuralists, in short, do not believe in the immediacy of anything; they are content to understand and to contemplate the alphabetical order of sense as a mediating function rather than as a direct meaning. Order, they claim, is just on our human side of nothingness; it preserves us from the blankness of naked duration. To perceive this order one cannot have recourse to a direct unfolding (as in the *Entfaltung* of hermeneutical interpretation) of the kernel of meaning within a statement; that alternative, we recall, had disappeared with the primordial Origin. We are left only with a way of perceiving how something—a sentence or a statement, in fine, the entire world of experience conceived of as a gigantic script, or musical score—works, how it hangs together. We search for structure as *Zusammenhänge*, the "principle of solidarity" between parts, according to Barthes.[45]

In a most important way then, as an ensemble of interacting parts, structure replaces the Origin with the play of orderly relationships. A univocal source has ceded to a proliferating systematic web. The character of structure is best understood, I think, if we remark the nature of its radicality, which derives from a mating of the spirit of Rousseau with the spirit of Sade, of existential primitivism with moral primitivism. The central fact of primitivism is not just its precedence, but its unobjecting assent to its own originality. It has no alternative but "to be," and we can see versions of such radical originality in the perpetual spiritual amateurism of Rousseau or in the continual, almost abstract repetitiveness of Sade. Or in the "concrete" existence of Australian and Brazilian aborigines whose lives Lévi-Strauss has chronicled so well.

45. Barthes, "Rhétorique de l'image," *Communications*, no. 4 (1965), p. 43.

The rule of structure is its superconscious transgression of all conscious rules, and the consequent establishment of a grammar whose persistence compels all vocabularies, and repels thought and spiritual dimension at the same time. The researcher's way to structure is in the semiotic reading of the play of signs on the pages of a culture; method, activity, and end there become totally identified with each other. The structuralist wishes to dissolve himself in the writing, to become the writing itself. Barthes correctly describes structuralism as an endless activity of imitation founded not on the analogy of substances but on the analogy of functions.[46] And the final key language of structuralism is shelved in the Library of Babel. The elegance and the terror of such a world view, completely confined to discourse, is a veritable nightmare utopia composed out of nothing but impeccably organized writing; it is the subject of Borges's work. When Barthes wishes to abolish the distinction between art and criticism he uses the word *writing* (*écriture*) to level the difference between them (here again Borges's work comes to mind). Thus writing illuminates writing, which in turn illuminates other writing—to infinity. The sum total of all writing is silence, zero. The end of a structuralist's job of work is, according to Barthes, silence, the silence that comes with having reached the eschatological limit, said all there is to say.[47] Lévi-Strauss too describes a work of his once written as a dead being, a world in which he had very ardently lived but that now excludes him from its intimacy.[48]

In Barthes's case one is willing to accept Gérard Genette's view (presented in a beautifully balanced essay in *Figures*)[49] that what governs the semiotic project is a nostalgia for objects and bodies whose solid presence has the undeniable reality of Dr. Johnson's stone. Genette sees Barthes longing for the silent quiddity of objects undisturbed by the intervening yammerings of language. There is, I think, no less a case for believing that Barthes and the structuralists long also for the zero

46. Barthes, *Essais critiques*, p. 215.
47. Ibid., p. 174.
48. Lévi-Strauss, "Vingt ans après," *Temps Modernes* 23 (1967):386.
49. Gérard Genette, *Figures* (Paris: Seuil, 1966), pp. 201–2.

calm of original primitivism and wholeness. The longing shores up the integrity of their faith in the irresistible metamorphic powers of language. For if one text might serve them all as a banner it is Ovid's *Metamorphoses*, that celebration of reality as ceaseless transformation and unhindered function for its own sake. Yet, Barthes, with Foucault, Lévi-Strauss, and Althusser, does have a stoically ironic and almost poetic vision of his own position that invigorates the solemnity of work done near an indefinitely postponed apocalypse. In the analysis of the play of signifiers he sees not so much a necessity as a luxury.[50] What he calls "acculturation"—the omnivorous swallowing whole by linguistic culture of all work, a concept that is strikingly reminiscent of Lionel Trilling's in *Beyond Culture*—goes on apace, and the individual critic's activity remains an involuntary trickle in the great stream.

Two disciplines we might find resisting the tide of functionalism and linguistic reduction are psychoanalysis and sociology. The first deals with the terminal poles of human behavior, the second with the all-too-solid terminal of social reality; neither, we believe, can succumb completely to an invasion by language. In Jacques Lacan's Freud, however, we discover psychiatry serving as the interpretation of psychic metaphors that have no ready and anchoring terminal in the unconscious. That faculty has become, according to Lacan, "neither primordial nor instinctual,"[51] but instead a floating repository (if that be the best word) for the "elements of the signifier." The method of operation of this unconscious is rigorously grammatical, its symptoms rhetorical, and it articulates the ego as the expression of a narcissistic relation to itself.[52] The ingenuity of Lacan's understanding of Freud's "talking cure" means essentially that he takes Freud's word for just that: he construes Freud as Quintillian construes poetic language. Metaphor and metonymy deliver, or withhold, a Being as absolutely allusive as, I think probably, Freud's Un-

50. Barthes, *Essais critiques*, p. 266.

51. "L'inconscient n'est pas le primordial, ni l'instinctuel, et d'élémentaire il ne connaît que les éléments du signifiant." Jacques Lacan, *Ecrits* (Paris: Seuil, 1967), p. 522.

52. Ibid., pp. 93–100.

conscious ultimately was not. Ernest Jones reports an eerie prefiguration of the Freud-Lacan operation in the following anecdote involving Freud and Pierre Janet:

> Pichon, a French analyst who happened to be Janet's son-in-law wrote to Freud [in 1937] asking if Janet might call on him. This is Freud's comment to Marie Bonaparte: "No, I will not see Janet. I could not refrain from reproaching him with having behaved unfairly to psycho-analysis and also to me personally and having never corrected it. . . . You can get an idea of his scientific level from his utterance that the unconscious is *une façon de parler*. No, I will not see him. I thought at first of sparing him the impoliteness by the excuse that I am not well or that I can no longer talk French, and he certainly can't understand a word of German. But I have decided against that. There is no reason for making any sacrifice for him. Honesty the only possible thing; rudeness quite in order."[53]

But Lacan's art is novel and abstruse enough to encourage us that he *might* be closer to Freud than meets the eye.

The other great structuralist rereading of a venerable radical is to be found in Althusser's Marx. According to Althusser, Marx's retirement behind his utterances in order to become their rigor, the guarantee of their structure (rather than their Origin),[54] creates the possibility for a Marxism, or Theory, that Marx himself never had time to write. Marx therefore is the *beginning* of a reading of society as a complex of ideological strands seen from a new perspective of philosophic differentiation. This differentiation shows how "human societies secrete ideology as the element and the atmosphere indispensable for their respiration and their historical life.[55] Althusser's ruling metaphor is dramatic: Marxism allows us to *see* how society formulates itself *for* itself. We are detached when we read Althusser and, like spectators at a Brecht play, we create a historical consciousness in the recognition of ideologies that

53. Ernest Jones, *Sigmund Freud: Life and Work* (London: Hogarth Press, 1957), 3:228–29.

54. Louis Althusser, *Pour Marx* (Paris: Maspero, 1965), p. 61.

55. "Les sociétés humaines sécrètent l'idéologie comme l'élément et l'atmosphère même indispensables à leur respiration, à leur vie historique." Ibid., p. 238.

pretend to truth while remaining the victims of their signifying (ideological, propagandistic) activity. Society is like Mother Courage fixed on a skewed course through lies of her own making. Contradiction means the awareness of discontinuity, of ruptures, between one ideology and another. Yet ideology is not a mere accident but a necessary condition, indeed the fundamental structure, of society.

The precision and elegance of Althusser's spare exhumation of Marx as a style of thought (and a much longer account than I have given would scarcely do Althusser justice) clashes headlong with Lucien Goldmann's thematic appropriation of revolutionary thought. Goldmann's important study of Pascal and Racine (*Le Dieu caché*), and his subsequent forays into general theory propelled by his tutelage under Lukács and Piaget, showed how literary work and society exist in homology; yet in recent years Goldmann, apparently bitten by the structural virus, turned himself into a "genetic structuralist." The issue between him and Althusser is very clear: for Goldmann the sociology of knowledge must appeal to a hierarchy of values that stands *outside* bourgeois ideology and reveals the *content* of an ideology for either its adequacy or inadequacy with reference to all of social reality. Goldmann's word for "all of social reality" is "totality," an ideal whole. Totality seems for Goldmann very curiously to be what Burckhardt called "an Archimedean point outside events." The structuralist's job, according to Goldmann, is to seize the coherence of an artist's or a thinker's work at its "real" origin in time and society, and to submit it to processes of growth implicit in its essential coherence. If as a result of this a given thinker is seen to have grasped the totality of his time, and if his work reflects it coherently, then he is a dialectician: this, for Goldmann, is not only a descriptive title but an honorific one as well. Otherwise the thinker is an ideologist—albeit, in the case of Pascal, a great one. Althusser pointedly rejects totality, and for that matter any privileged ideal reality outside the discourse of ideology. (It is important to note that for Althusser ideology is discourse, at least in its political dress.) All articulated thought is ideology; only the differences between ideologies (like the diacritical differences between words in

Saussure's linguistics) provide us with knowledge as a structure of relationships. Everything else—Goldmann's references to "totality"—is mere fiction, is a victim of discourse. Marxism, for Althusser, provides the sharpest instrument for dissociating ideologies from each other into a series of statements made *for* ulterior purposes.

Thus the main group of structuralists sees the world as a closed set of what J. L. Austin called "performative statements."[56] Closed not because its limits can be grasped as a totality but because its beginnings are a finite set of rules. As Barthes says, one lexical law can mobilize many different lexicons.[57] But structuralism is a kind of positivism; yet like all positivisms it has a pet view of what man's activity is all about. And that is what Lévi-Strauss calls *bricolage*, man's ability and destiny to make do with, to formulate projects out of, and because of, fragments, the usable debris that clutters human existence.[58] *Bricolage* is, in the words of Swift's manic *persona*, "an Art to sodder up the Flaws and Imperfections of Nature." Not accidentally, as Genette has noted with characteristic shrewdness, the French have themselves not only defined the techniques of *bricolage*, but they have become virtuosi at the whole business.[59] The reasons Genette points out are French insularity coupled with a native French genius for assembling bits and pieces into imposing models of wit and reason. To probe *bricolage* further than this is to acknowledge also a subtle French sense of order based on uncertainty, on the partial, and on the hidden. This is why "structure" is neither a spatial term nor for that matter a temporal one. It is essentially an activity, a cultural version of *bricolage*, and less a philosophy or a philosophical method than what Genette, quoting Cassirer, calls a general tendency of thought.[60] A tendency, we might add, that seeks out and is attracted to the dodgy in-betweenness of order: it does not see order as what

56. J. L. Austin, *How to Do Things with Words* (Cambridge, Mass.: Harvard University Press, 1962).

57. Barthes, "Rhétorique de l'image," p. 48.

58. Lévi-Strauss, *La Pensée sauvage*, pp. 26 ff.

59. *Les Chemins actuels de la critique* (Paris: Plon, 1967), p. 258.

60. Genette, *Figures*, p. 155.

Freud called a repetition-compulsion, but rather as a complementarity to existence. Although, paradoxically, order is a supplier, it wishes it could linger quietly over "the essence of what our species has been and still is, beyond thought and beneath society: an essence that may be vouchsafed to us in a mineral more beautiful than any work of Man; in the scent, more subtly evolved than our books, that lingers in the heart of a lily; or in the wink of an eye, heavy with patience, serenity, and mutual forgiveness, that sometimes, through an involuntary understanding, one can exchange with a cat."[61]

As a formalist doctrine structuralism differs instructively from earlier modern formalisms. Dilthey's *Weltanschauung* philosophy assents to the adhesive power of inner vision as an existential property of human mind: among the first adumbrators of this property was Coleridge, whose doctrine of the secondary imagination, with his description of the coadunatory and esemplastic shaping powers, granted the highest marks to man's ability to shape experience meaningfully. The later German and Marxist theories of Gestalt and/or totality (exemplified variously in the works of Lukács, Mannheim, Groethuysen, and others) adapt from Dilthey but add to his conception the notion of a more rigorous historical necessity; for them the individual is an involuntary participant in a class or group together with other like-interested individuals who act according to a common vision of their origin and destiny. It is the property of history therefore to be a totality that makes things inhere formally in thought and action. Finally there is the more elusive formalism of twentieth-century idealists like Croce in which a certain executive, almost Platonic, coherence controls, gives theoretic shape to, human action.

For the French structuralists form is borrowed from the actualities of language considered as a set of fragments (phonemes, words, phrases) that orders itself with binding rules into a constantly earned equilibrium of higher structures (sentences, discourses, narratives). Language is the conceiving and the productive matrix of human activity, but its wholeness

61. Lévi-Strauss, *Tristes Tropiques*, trans. John Russell (New York: Athenaeum, 1964), p. 398.

can never really be known—but only derived partially from its rule-bound play. The permanent elusiveness and incompleteness of structure is typified in the eternal discrepancy between the linear flowing chain of language-in-use, that is, our continuous mode of life, and the circular system of signs that surrounds speech at any one moment. Structure tries to unite linguistic performance with linguistic competence, the *nunc movens* with the *nunc stans*.

As the structuralists see him, the individual is a modern equivalent of Pascalian man, only with this difference: Pascal's *roseau pensant* is replaced with what Merleau-Ponty called *le sujet parlant*. The linguistic reduction of man (which continues the tradition of Pascal's fascination with and dislike of self) is consistently supported by the structuralist's stubborn desire always to use linguistic terminology for man. Man is a name, his necessity is a pronoun (since, as Benveniste says, all language requires in it the existence of an "I" and a "you"),[62] his situation is discourse, and his thought metalinguistic. Man therefore is inserted into Being either *allegorically*, as a linguistic substitute for presence (which language can allow only by the *absence* of *presence*), or, when man continues to insist on his indispensability to the reality of language, as *parody*, the sheer, endless repetition of himself in the distorting mirrors of social, artistic, psychological, anthropological, historical, or philosophical narratives. Man the author is unceremoniously deposed. He becomes man the worker in the continuing, already-begun. Man the responsible (a position once claimed because man had the "power" to grasp meaning immediately) can only eye, with fatalistic ambitions, the establishment of a master language, that of structuralism itself, whose entire drift, not to say significance, will probably never have much use for him. When, in writing of his friend's new science, Merleau-Ponty warmly commended Lévi-Strauss's early treatise for portending that the structuralist method would become the instrument of a new "world civilization,"[63] he did not foresee the arrival of

62. Benveniste, *Problèmes de linguistique générale*, pp. 251–57.

63. Maurice Merleau-Ponty, *Signs*, trans. Richard C. McCleary (Evanston, Ill.: Northwestern University Press, 1964), p. 124.

what is a new totalitarianism. For the beautiful amoral inclusiveness of structuralism is resisted only by the energies, the admirable professional dedication, and the deep personal seriousness of its adherents.

Is the basketball coach a homosexual lemon manufacturer? It is suspected by O'Ryan in his submarine.

Kenneth Koch, "Aus Einer Kindheit"

The problems of communication in an age of mass culture, and of mass confusions, are the problems that structuralism seems destined very ably to reflect. Structuralism after all lives in the world of McLuhanism, although it tidies up that North American sprawl across culture with a good deal of grace and *élan*. One of the chief points of difference between structuralism and the Geneva school of critics (both of which together make up the central body of French New Criticism) is that the latter group considers the literary work as dissolved in the author's consciousness whose impulse is articulation for its own sake, whereas the former group takes language, and hence literature, exclusively as a system of interhuman communication. What Josiah Royce called the intersubjective world, namely, the community of interpretation, is for the Genevans actually enacted in the identification of the critic with the author he considers, but for the structuralists there is only the involuntary community of systems of information that are transparent to each other. Yet the division between structuralism and Genevan consciousness-for-itself-and-for-the-critic derives from the dual inner nature of literary language itself as it is realized, for example, in the vocations of individual writers. Some, like Coleridge, Swift, Hopkins, and Joyce, are what Genette calls technicians of communication;[64] others, like Wordsworth, Yeats, Shelley, and the later Eliot, are poets of interior mediation for whom language, in Heidegger's phrase, is the house of Being.

It is characteristic of the structuralists—here again Lévi-Strauss is the noteworthy exception—that they seem unconcerned with their counterparts, or their intellectual pro-

64. Genette, *Figures*, p. 153.

genitors, in other countries. With the work of George Herbert Mead, the Chicago Aristotelians, Kenneth Burke, and Northrop Frye, to speak only of North Americans, there are fairly obvious parallels with structuralism and, if the structuralists cared, gains to be made from those parallels; the similarities, however, are never perceived and, to be blunt about it, seem to be unknown. Aside from respectful bows toward C. S. Peirce, the structuralists express no interest in Anglo-American linguistic critics and philosophers: none in Ogden and Richards, in Empson, Quine, or in any of the action philosophers. The work of the great German philologues Auerbach, Curtius, and Spitzer seems not to have made much of an impression either, although one would think that the universality and the scope of German romance philology (with its origins in Goethe's idea of *Weltliteratur*) might have suggested at least one other model of linguistic research integrally organized. The same is true of the discipline of comparative literature, whose relevance is nevertheless recognizable in structuralism's enterprise when the latter is viewed as the science of comparative communication. Still the disparity between structuralism as an essentializing and universalizing activity and its insularity remains an odd one. For that matter though, the outside world has repaid the structuralists. Aside from the alert attention of *TLS*, and a few appreciative essays here and there, little serious attention has been paid France's latest intellectual venture.[65]

Wherever else it is placed, structuralism belongs, with Gallic preciosity, to what Harry Levin has called the Alexandrianism of our time.[66] The organization of a structuralist work is always ingenious, sometimes even more interesting than the matter it discusses. The assenting response to Barthes's call for new cadres of research is immediately felt in the effort

65. The best recent essay in English is Eugenio Donato's "Of Structuralism and Literature," *Modern Language Notes* 82 (1967): 549–74. Most of the other essays in English have tended to be of the sort published by Leo Bersani and Peter Caws (see Bibliography) which are either strangely hostile or substantively thin.

66. Harry Levin, *Contexts of Criticism* (Cambridge: Harvard University Press, 1957), p. 253.

expended in putting together one or another structuralist book. Lévi-Strauss's books present a surface of dazzling arrangement, whether one reads a page or the table of contents. The choice of subject matter in Foucault's work, as much as in Barthes's, Genette's, Althusser's, or Lacan's, is always novel and unexpected; the unkindest cut of all would be to call such novelty, with Raymond Picard, "dogmatic impressionism." The styles are almost always difficult, whether because they are technical or because they reveal writing turning back on itself to consider, questioningly, its validity and principles. The salutary effect of structuralism is more than the providing of criticism with a few handy catch phrases or with florid tricks. Structuralism has demonstrated the value of determinedly rational examination; it has displaced the prior mystique of mere appreciation passing itself off as scholarship, and has even stimulated novelists (like Robbe-Grillet and Butor) to a just ascertainment of their work. Beyond that, structuralism has given and received fairly. As Barthes has noted, structuralism sits securely beside developments in modern art like the music of Boulez and the designs of Mondrian,[67] it draws from the peculiar psychological traditions of France as exemplified in the books of Gaston Bachelard, and it has fecundated the brilliant work of an Arabist like Jacques Berque and the parascientific explorations of Gilles-Gaston Granger. Versions of structuralism also contribute to the interest of the more urgently historical (and earlier) work of Georges Dumézil, and to that of his gifted contemporary disciple Jean-Pierre Vernant, to the linguistic work of André Martinet, Edmond Ortigues, and André Leroi-Gourhan, and even to the more purely scientific and mathematical experiments of Abraham Moles and Jean Desanti. With the characteristic unkindness of new movements structuralism ignores or attacks the monuments of preceding generations; this is especially poignant in the cases of Malraux and Sartre, less so in the case of Gustave Lanson.

The total immersion of structuralism in the present, and the odd nature of that immersion, send one for indirect com-

67. Barthes, *Essais critiques*, p. 216.

mentary, I think, to a scene in *Le Rouge et le noir*. Near the beginning of that novel Julien sits in a high nook of his father's workshed reading a volume of Napoleon's memoirs. He is thoroughly concentrating on the book; suddenly a violent blow sends him reeling. Thus does M. Sorel, exasperated by his son's arcane musing, dislodge Julien from his perch and rudely penetrate the linguistic reverie over which the young man presides. The scene comes to mind because it activates and enlivens in us the danger, as well as the comedy, of too assiduously mistaking the world of rhetoric for the violence and the surprises of impolite reality. Thus it is tempting to reflect on how contemporary structuralism flourishes in French intellectual life that stands safely away from French political existence; here the difference between structuralism and existentialism, the wave that during the more brutal forties preceded today's vogue, is immediately lively.[68] The earlier movement was profoundly attuned to the postwar anguish of intellectual and moral, as well as physical, reconstruction in Europe. By comparison, structuralism in its aerie takes the world as it is in words and images. History, to the unhappiness of Sartre and Goldmann, is relegated by structuralism to the less troublesome status of diachrony, a realm that shrugs off as interruption anything that disturbs the stable polity of synchrony, which is a calm realm of simultaneity and systematic relationships.

The gravest problem with which structuralism has yet wholeheartedly to deal is how to account seriously for change and force, how to assimilate the powerful and sometimes wasteful behavioral activity of man—what Blackmur calls the Moha—to the lovely numenous order of structure. In Foucault's roughly chronological narratives we find one period of thought, one style in history, ceding its place to another. Foucault's description of man as "a rent in the order of things, in any case, a configuration traced by the new position . . .

68. For a general account of the difference between structuralism and existentialism as reflected in French social and intellectual life see H. Stuart Hughes, *The Obstructed Path: French Social Thought in the Years of Desperation, 1930–1960* (New York: Harper and Row, 1968).

in the realm of knowledge''[69] does scarcely more than recite, as inevitable, the quasi-fact of man's disruptive appearance. Man does violence to order, but the gash is immediately repaired by the heedless persistence of order. At no point in the over thirteen hundred pages of his archaeological work does Foucault really attempt to connect the cementing energy of persistence with the destructive introduction of novelty that replaces one period with another. It is as if, like nuclear elements with an assigned half-life, periods simply live and pass off, leaving their place to be covered up in the same slot by other periods.

In Lévi-Strauss's work we find the recognition of force made in terms, once again, of disruption. In examining the constant passage in both directions within society between ideas and images he acknowledges a certain measure of contingency and arbitrariness; the systematic organization of society, he concedes regretfully, is endangered by wars, epidemics, and famines.[70] The relation between order and disorder therefore is one of opposition, yet it is *expressed* not *by* the society itself—or, at least, not necessarily by the society—but *for* the society by the observer who stands outside it. As Lévi-Strauss says in another place, structure will appear only as the result of observation practiced from the outside;[71] hence order, or structure, is available for analysis from the outside, but society's process, or force, can never be grasped because (Lévi-Strauss himself makes the point) that is entirely within the perspective of the social individual engaged in his own historical becoming. In *Totemism* Lévi-Strauss speaks of the internalization (''trying on [oneself] modes of thought taken from elsewhere or simply imagined'')[72] that permitted Bergson and Rousseau to apprehend what goes on in the mind of man. This internalization of

69. ''L'homme . . . n'est sans doute rien qu'une certaine déchirure dans l'ordre des choses, une configuration, en tout cas, dessinée par la disposition nouvelle qu'il a prise récemment dans le savoir.'' Foucault, *Les Mots et les choses*, p. 15.

70. Lévi-Strauss, *La Pensée sauvage*, p. 204.

71. Lévi-Strauss, ''La Notion de structure en ethnologie,'' in *Sens et usages du terme structure* (The Hague: Mouton, 1962), pp. 44–45.

72. Lévi-Strauss, *Totemism*, trans. Rodney Needham (Boston: Beacon Press, 1963), p. 103.

course allows the modern anthropologist to understand what goes on in an observed primitive society.

The situation can now be stated as follows: within a society a certain energy is acting to make it a society. Outside the society stands an observer who notes constants (included in the kind of essential structure Lévi-Strauss himself had observed in *Les Structures élémentaires de la parenté*, for example) which, in turn, are internalized and tested by the observer for their logic and coherence. The force or energy or entropy of a society, that which keeps it inserted in its ongoing historical actuality, thus is a transparency through which observations on the structure beyond it can be made. Two kinds of force can be distinguished: one, easily gotten by; the other, the force of observation, which, though essentially, and curiously, contemplative, has the power to penetrate through the seeming opacity of a foreign culture to a lucidity beyond. All of this, as I said above, seems to take into consideration a conflict between system and contingency which, within a society, always oppose each other. Yet at the beginning of the anthropological observation discontinuity is granted, while at the other end of the observation discontinuity has already been assembled into a transparent force that had yielded very easily to the observation just practiced. Although the structuralist avers the power of disruption and discontinuity, he replaces it later with a transparent coherence that is very little more than the power of an object, or a society, to be observed. Put in linguistic terms, force and energy are converted exclusively into the power of signification, which exists to be *read*, to be semiotically deciphered.

This is linguacentricity pushed very far indeed. The quality of things that makes them significant is almost an ideal third term between language on the one hand and men and the world on the other (one is reminded of the critique of Socrates' ideas in the *Parmenides*). This term, a quality which I shall call *linguicity*, performs very valuable services. Among other things it enables the activity of what Lévi-Strauss calls the totemic operator, that rational instrument carried within the primitive mind; the operator enables the division of the primitive's observed world into a logic of finely organized species.[73] Furthermore linguicity permits language to be what I have elsewhere called a totalitarian system,[74] it also ensures the availability to language of unlimited signifying opportunities despite the impoverishment of what is being signified, it gives language the guarantee of unlimited linguistic discovery, that is, a sort of permanent finding power, and it provides the links between one dimension of investigation (say from particular to general, or from discontinuity to discontinuity) and another. In short, linguicity is the true beginning of structuralist activity, and its perpetuation is structuralism's project and purpose. Without linguicity, the structuralist—whether he is Barthes, Lacan, or Lévi-Strauss—cannot demonstrate analogy and metaphor as intrinsic to the signifying process. For linguicity allows mirror exchanges between words, between levels of consciousness, between myths. The power to reflect, as in a series of mirrors, assumes the prior existence of clarity of exchange. Structuralism replaces the darkening glass of religion and literature—which forces us to appraisals of our fragile but dear individuality—with a ready antiphony of equal sights and sounds. We might say that linguicity converts the inequities of translation into the equivalence of transcription, and the use of writing (*écriture*) to structuralism becomes even more crucial. Linguicity discounts memory and history, in the interests of total recall; for structure, which is the child of language and linguicity, has no way of containing its past but only of delivering its present by "laying all its cards on the table."[75] As Ricoeur remarked, because of these attitudes structuralism aspires to the condition of science.

What linguicity cannot do, however, is to show us why structure structures; structure is always revealed in the condition of having structures, but never, as Jean Starobinski has observed,[76] structuring, or in the condition of *being structured*,

73. Lévi-Strauss, *La Pensée sauvage*, pp. 120 ff.

74. Edward W. Said, "The Totalitarianism of Mind," *Kenyon Review* 29 (1967): 256–68.

75. Lévi-Strauss, *Totemism*, p. 31.

76. Jean Starobinski, "Remarques sur le structuralisme," in *Ideen und Formen: Festschrift für Hugo Friedrich* (Frankfurt: Vittorio Klostermann, 1964), p. 277.

or failing to structure. The main weakness is that linguicity must remain outside the constitutive structure, even to the point of being rejected by structure; yet it is presumed by structure as a first situation for order. Another way of showing the weakness is to comment on the difficulties structuralism has with the problem of a text. In the nonstructural criticism of Georges Poulet, for instance, the individual work is dissolved in order to be relocated in the irreducible consciousness of the author. For this sort of criticism, mind is the matrix of thought, and the text is a particular instance (Jean Rousset, another of the Genevans, is relevant here) of consciousness thinking itself. In Lévi-Strauss, however, myth, or society for that matter, speaks itself; this corresponds to Barthes's formulation of writing as an intransitive activity. There is no real distance between language and any of its individual articulations, since none of them is under any more than token obligation to a thinking subject. There can be no tone, in Richards's sense of the word, in any utterance, no sense of an individual voice that is its own final authority, since according to structuralism the whole world is contained within a gigantic set of quotation marks. Everything therefore is a text; or, using the same argument, nothing is a text. The inherence of a structure expresses neither an intention nor any more than the barest of constitutive necessities. Communication is absorbed by the structure, since communication can never exhaust a structure or a language. The enduring power of language to signify thus works as a beginning and as a result, and the tautology completely eliminates both subject and object, and to a certain extent direct communication too.

The willingness of structuralism to discuss differences between objects—a feat that moves values from the objects to a privileged space between them—goes consistently with the hesitancy, or fear, that emerges for the structuralist whenever singularity is an issue. The solitary, crystalline perdurability we feel and know in a poem, the condition of its exile from the communal sea of linguicity, cannot be named by structuralism. Not that anyone else can name the poem's individuality very readily, since a poem is also a momentary utterance. But the effort of naming is at least possible outside structuralism if only because one can acknowledge an unknown and keep it live in thought. Structuralism's holding power over its subject matter is tenuous; this is at once a strength, when it reminds us of the provisionality of our efforts, and a weakness, when it commits us to an irretrievable past and the dimensionless obsolescence of the future.

As the ground of structuralism, linguicity requires the notion of play within rules to sustain a minimum of discourse (which Barthes calls prose).[77] Linguicity seems to generate and then lay down rules of intelligibility by which things appear as telling language, rather than as random bursts of being. As used in structuralism's arguments, these rules are a nexus binding utterances into progressively clear units, the more one works out their possibilities. Thus by lifting aside one set of signifiers (as we did in those lines from *Paradise Lost*) as two or more occur in works of literature, the threatening jumble of direct presence is channeled off into examples of recognized convention. The structuralist decoding or reducing of the object to a set of utterances collected into general rhetorical order somewhat resembles the process of resolving literature into archetypes, a kind of criticism practiced commonly in the United States. The structuralists, and the archetypalists, always wish to avoid direct encounters with language. Instead they weaken the full-throated spoken chain into a series of signifiers, all of which exist in the chain's linguicity, like the plural meanings of words in a pun. Linguicity forces us, perhaps against our will, to read language and reality together as if they were cleverly hidden in each other.

The trouble with this esoteric view of language is, first of all, that rules ensure the safety and the captivity of signification; in a sense therefore structuralism is conservatively safeguarding the assured certainty of its own activity. For every contingency a rule can be discovered lurking in linguicity. Second, the number of rules is, also conservatively, kept to a workable minimum. To be willing to admit (*a*) that there are no rules for some situations and (*b*) that there is no limit to the number

77. Barthes, *Le Degré zéro de l'écriture* (Paris: Gonthier, 1964), p. 39.

of rules, would mean the necessity of believing (*a*) in an infinite vocabulary and (*b*) in a finally useless catalog of infinite rules. And the latter two eventualities, the structuralist will not admit. Borges's Pierre Funes does admit this, however, and he is locked in "the stammering grandeur" of his vertiginous world of bewildering particulars. Linguicity is one extreme; Funes, and art, are the other; we are really in between.

We come finally to the writing of Jacques Derrida. Three books by him appeared in 1967 (in addition to a translation of Husserl's *Origins of Geometry*, made in 1962, with an introduction): *L'Ecriture et la différence*, *De la Grammatologie*, and *La Voix et le phénomène*. A philosopher in his own right, he deserves mention in an essay on structuralism because his work is a critique, by grotesque explication, of the structuralists. Thus like Nietzsche's outpouring of philosophy that is already in the throes of its self-destruction, Derrida's writing converts the principles of structuralism into surreal, large things whose overaccurate relationship to the original versions mocks, overwhelms, and plays havoc with them. The sense of structuralism is, in Derrida, writ large, too large. The inflation is evident on many levels. First in the organization of his books, which make normal structural preciosity look primly demure. *De la Grammatologie*, for instance, is a study of writing "pure" and "simple"; its first half is titled "Writing before the Letter," but before the section begins (and Derrida is obsessed with continually prior states) there is a short digression titled "Exergue," and immediately following that, chapter 1: "The End of the Book and the Beginning of Writing." A later chapter is headed enigmatically "The Outside is the Inside." Second, Derrida's prose style, which is sometimes very self-indulgent, has a quiet, yet almost maniacal complexity to it that defies translation into ordinary language. Its central features are, first, a habit of italicizing grammatological terms that causes them to become ontological terms, (*trace*, *letter*, *inscription*, *arch-writing*) and the italicization of ontological terms so that they will act as grammatological ones (*beginning*, *end*, *violence*, *transgression*, *reduction*). Second, Derrida specializes terms into near-parodies of their common-sense meaning: he performs this operation on words like difference (see also his invention of words like *différance*), work, economy, alteration, iteration, writing, presence, supplement, auto-affection, and, finally, structure. At one point he describes his manner of exposition as "hesitancy" since, he admits, his subject is the movement of deconstruction, that is, the opposite of structuring.[78] Elsewhere Derrida argues that any attempt, like his, to recognize the essence of logocentrism (our literacy) must be an empirical one, but like the radical empiricism of Husserl the attempt must rise beyond the confines of evidence and a system of oppositions into "errance."[79] This is a correct analysis of his style of thought, for Derrida's mind wanders with a twisted pertinence to different sides of sense.

The last essay in *L'Ecriture et la différence* collects Derrida's metaphysical and cultural reflections admirably. What he undertakes to fix before our mind's eye is the paradox of structural knowledge which takes order as the unified play of elements (pure signifiers) that do not have a center, or Origin, or dominant *significatum*.

This then is the moment when language invades the universal and problematic field [of human existence]; it is the moment where, in the absence of center or origin, everything becomes discourse—on the condition that this word is understood—that is, a system in which the central signified, whether it derives from an origin or whether it is transcendental, is never absolutely present outside a system of differences. The absence of a transcendental signified [*significatum*] stretches the field and the play of significations to infinity.[80]

He goes on to speak of the difficulty of locating an event in time at which decentering took place. To attribute the event

78. Jacques Derrida, *De la Grammatologie* (Paris: Editions de Minuit, 1967), p. 39.

79. Ibid., p. 232.

80. "C'est alors le moment où le langage envahit le champ problématique universel; c'est alors le moment où, en l'absence de centre ou d'origine, tout devient discours—à condition de s'entendre sur ce mot—c'est-à-dire système dans lequel le signifié central, originaire ou transcendantal, n'est jamais absolument présent hors d'un système de différences. L'absence de signifié transcendantal étend à l'infini le champ et le jeu de la signification." Derrida, *L'Ecriture et la différence* (Paris: Seuil, 1967), p. 411.

to the work of either Freud or Nietzsche is in fact to submit once again to the circle without a center, not at all to get beyond it. For the vicious circle of signifiers, globally considered, is itself the relationship between the history of metaphysics and the destruction of that history by radicals like Freud and Nietzsche; outside of language we do not possess any way of describing destruction in a manner that does not also rely on the same structure whose order is being challenged. To speak of Freud and Nietzsche means first to accept the structure of philosophy, then to try, without much hope of success, to show the structure breaking down; yet a breakdown can be described only in terms, or signs, provided by the prior order.[81] The damning difficulty of the whole matter according to Derrida, is that opposition, or difference-between, remains the inescapable basis of a signifier. This, we recall, has always been one of the cardinal points in the structuralist creed: the meaning of a word, of a sign, is diacritical, is not intrinsic to it, but is rather the quality of its *difference from* another word. A structuralist like Lévi-Strauss, Derrida argues, is in the position of a man who wishes to conserve the value of an instrument (language as a sign system) whose truth value he is criticizing.[82] This is no less true of Nietzsche and Freud, the one attacking philosophy philosophically, the other attacking psychology psychologically. Derrida's grasp of the bewildering dilemma of modern critical knowledge resembles, in its awareness of the debilitating paradoxes that hobble knowledge, Dostoevsky.

Thus language—and the sciences, ethnography in particular, it commands—emerges as a new center destined to replace the philosophic and/or epistemological center, or Origin, it has criticized and chased away. One myth cedes to another.[83] The play (*jeu*) of signifiers, which Derrida calls a series of infinite substitutions, takes place on a field, or space, of language that is limited and marked by the lack of a center. Infinity is the result of a specific and finite absence. Play, which is another

81. Ibid., p. 412.
82. Ibid., p. 417.
83. Ibid., p. 421.

way of characterizing the totality of structures in language as they reflect each other, is supplementary to absence. Here we are to recall Barthes's uneasy awareness of the luxury of signifiers, and Lévi-Strauss's attention to the abundance of signifiers by comparison with the poverty of "signifieds." Therefore play is the eternal disruption of the presence of a center (or Origin), in short, of presence itself, since the center identifies presence, but its lack signifies absence. Derrida then goes on to distinguish two attitudes toward absence. One is Rousseau's: negative, guilty, nostalgic. The other is Nietzsche's: affirmative, joyous, forward-looking. The first, which includes Lévi-Strauss's work, looks sentimentally in the present, *into* its current efforts, for a new inspiration that will hopefully rejoin, regain, refind the lost Origin.[84]

Yet Derrida concludes by saying that the choice between the two attitudes is not now a real possibility. For we live in a world (as Derrida's own writing demonstrates over and over) in which the forms of the first attitude dominate us completely; they represent our condition, they provide our mental activity with organization, and they fix our direction. This is why we continue to be logocentric, and our minds remain rooted in a doctrine of signs, fastened upon the paradox of absence, committed to difference rather than value. All we can do now is to catch a glimpse of the coming change in our outlook; we can do so in the spirit of Yeats's trembling question: "And what rough beast, its hour come round at last, / Slouches towards Bethlehem to be born?"

The rest of Derrida's work, as I said above, pulls apart and terrorizes the conceptual glue of structuralism. *De la Grammatologie* and *La Voix et le phénomène* analyze language respectively as the auto-erotic myth of ethnocentric man (Derrida's texts are Rousseau, Saussure, and Lévi-Strauss) and as the outer, phenomenological expression of an inner voice that remains "wanting-to-speak." Derrida's gaze remains fixed upon writing that has been dislodged from its status as secondary production and given instead the responsibility of coping with ontological absence. Acceptance of this responsibility,

84. Ibid., p. 427.

despite ethnocentric dreams of an Origin miraculously turning up in writing, makes writing, for Derrida the grammatologist, a game of pure risk; writing participates constantly in the violence of each trace it makes, and thereby it achieves a vigilance coterminous with pure differentiation (*différance*) that somehow exists before the initiation of individual differences and the creation of individual signs.

Derrida's critiques and appreciations of Freud, Artaud, Bataille, and Levinas are practiced with structuralist instruments and nihilistic radicality. His work therefore busily traverses the place in mind between structuralism as the alphabet of cultural order on one side, and, on the other, the bare outlines, the traces of writing that shimmers just a hair beyond utter blankness.

Of all the structuralists it is only Lévi-Strauss who, in Susan Sontag's apt description,[85] can be considered willing to confront knowledge as an intellectual adventure. The closed circle of associates, the writing for a like-minded audience, the coterie atmosphere of most structuralist writing—all these tend to shut the structuralist off from the uninitiated reader. In contrast Lévi-Strauss has, we feel, risked the awful dangers of incoherence and the trials of exposure to a totally foreign experience in the effort to rescue meaning out of human existence. His work has been a retrospective *summa* that covers the adventure with nervously delicate prose; as Barthes observes in another connection, writing such as Lévi-Strauss's continues the original field work, but does not reduce it.[86] Structuralism, we must agree with Derrida's implications, is a conservative force with unrealized—because unthinkable by structuralism—possibilities. Yet poetry also fills that mysterious and joyous space between action and potential: only, poetry seems better able to stand the air and to fill it with an unashamed pride of possession.

85. Susan Sontag, *Against Interpretation* (New York: Farrar, Straus and Giroux, 1966), p. 70.

86. Barthes, *Essais critiques*, p. 72.

BIBLIOGRAPHY

SELECTED WORKS OF AND ON STRUCTURALISM

Althusser, Louis, et al. *Lire "Le Capital."* 2 vols. Paris: Maspero, 1965.

———. *Montesquieu: la politique et l'histoire*. Paris: Presses Universitaires de France, 1959.

———. *Pour Marx*. Paris: Maspero, 1965.

Atherton, John. "In Praise of Folly." *Partisan Review* 32 (1965): 441–44. A concise summary of Foucault's book on madness.

Auzais, Jean-Marie. *Clefs pour le structuralisme*. Paris: Seghers, 1967. A straightforward guide.

Badiou, Alain. "Le (Re)commencement du matérialisme dialectique." *Critique* 23 (1967): 438–67. A good account of Althusser's major work.

Barthes, Roland. See Bibliography following chapter 13.

Bastide, Roger, ed. *Sens et usages du terme structure dans les sciences humaines et sociales*. The Hague: Mouton, 1962. An important collection, with excellent essays by Benveniste, Barthes, and Lévi-Strauss, among others.

Bataille, Georges. "Un Livre humain, un grand livre." *Critique* 12 (1956): 99–112. A first-rate exploration of *Tristes Tropiques*.

Benveniste, Emile. *Problèmes de linguistique générale*. Paris: Gallimard, 1966.

———. "Language and Human Experience." *Diogenes*, no. 51 (Fall 1965), pp. 1–12.

Blanchot, Maurice. "L'Homme au point zéro." *Nouvelle Nouvelle Revue Française* 4 (1956): 683–94. A fascinating meeting between Lévi-Strauss and Blanchot.

Bremond, Claude. "Le Message narratif." *Communications*, no. 4 (1965), pp. 4–32.

Caws, Peter. "What Is Structuralism?" *Partisan Review* 35 (1968): 75–91. Reprinted in *Claude Lévi-Strauss: The Anthropologist as Hero*, pp. 197–215 (see below). A rather elementary and not too accurate attempt.

Charbonnier, Georges. *Entretiens avec Claude Lévi-Strauss*. Paris: Plon, 1961. 10/18. Paris: Union Générale d'Editions, 1969. (*Conversations with Claude Lévi-Strauss*. London: Cape, 1969.)

Les Chemins actuels de la critique. Edited by Jean Ricardou. Paris: Plon, 1967. Collective work; for contributors, see Selected General Bibliography.

Claude Lévi-Strauss: The Anthropologist as Hero. Edited by E. Nelson Hayes and Tanya Hayes. Cambridge, Mass., and London: M. I. T.

Press, 1970. Articles by Edmund Leach, Lionel Abel, Susan Sontag, George Steiner, and others. Bibliography.

Derrida, Jacques. *L'Ecriture et la différence.* Tel Quel. Paris: Seuil, 1967.

———. *De la Grammatologie.* Paris: Editions de Minuit, 1967.

———. *La Voix et le phénomène: Introduction au problème du signe dans la phénoménologie de Husserl.* Paris: Presses Universitaires de France, 1967.

Donato, Eugenio. "Of Structuralism and Literature." *Modern Language Notes* 82 (1967): 549–74. Technical and intelligent, this is an important statement.

———. "*Tristes Tropiques*: The Endless Journey." *Modern Language Notes* 81 (1966): 270–87. A subtle essay relating *Tristes Tropiques* to Proust and the recovery of time.

"Entretiens sur Foucault." *La Pensée*, no. 137 (January–February 1968). Participants: B. Balam, G. Dulac, G. Marcy, and others.

Foucault, Michel. *L'Archéologie du savoir.* Bibliothèque des Sciences Humaines. Paris: Gallimard, 1969.

———. "Distance, aspect, origine." *Critique* 19 (1963): 931–45.

———. *Folie et déraison: Histoire de la folie à l'âge classique.* Paris: Plon, 1961. 10/18. Paris: Union Générale d'Editions, 1964. (*Madness and Civilization: A History of Insanity in the Age of Reason.* Translated by Richard Howard. New York: Random House, 1965.)

———. *Maladie mentale et psychologie.* Initiation Philosophique. Paris: Presses Universitaires de France, 1954, 1966.

———. *Les Mots et les choses.* Paris: Gallimard, 1966. (*The Order of Things: An Archaeology of the Human Sciences.* New York: Pantheon Books, 1971.)

———. *Naissance de la clinique: Une Archéologie du regard médical.* Paris: Presses Universitaires de France, 1963.

———. "Le *Non* du père." *Critique* 18 (1962): 195–209. A superb analysis of Hölderlin in the light of Foucault's interest in madness.

———. "Préface à la transgression." *Critique* 19 (1963): 751–69. An interesting essay on Bataille.

———. *Raymond Roussel.* Paris: Gallimard, 1963.

Gandillac, Maurice de; Goldmann, Lucien; Piaget, Jean, eds. *Entretiens sur les notions de genèse et de structure.* Paris and The Hague: Mouton, 1965. Includes essays and comments by Vernant, Derrida, Goldmann, Piaget, Ernst Bloch, Moles, and Jean Desanti. An important collection.

Genette, Gérard. *Figures.* Tel Quel. Paris: Seuil, 1966.

———. *Figures II.* Tel Quel. Paris: Seuil, 1969.

Girard, René. *Dostoievski: du double à l'unité.* Paris: Plon, 1963.

———. "Des Formes aux structures, en littérature et ailleurs." *Modern Language Notes* 78 (1963): 504–19.

———. *Mensonge romantique et vérité romanesque*. Paris: Grasset, 1961. (*Deceit, Desire, and the Novel: Self and Other in Literary Structure*. Translated by Yvonne Freccero. Baltimore: Johns Hopkins Press, 1965.)

———. "Racine poète de la gloire." *Critique* 20 (1964): 483–506. An excellent analysis of Barthes and Goldmann.

———. "Réflexions critiques sur les recherches littéraires." *Modern Language Notes* 81 (1966): 307–24.

Goldmann, Lucien. *La Communauté humaine et l'univers chez Kant*. Paris: Presses Universitaires de France, 1948.

———. *Le Dieu caché: Etude sur la vision tragique dans les Pensées de Pascal et dans le théâtre de Racine*. Paris: Gallimard, 1955. (*The Hidden God: A Study of Tragic Vision in the "Pensées" of Pascal and the Tragedies of Racine*. Translated by Philip Thody. New York: Humanities Press, 1964.)

———. *Pour une sociologie du roman*. Paris: Gallimard, 1964.

———. *Recherches dialectiques*. Paris: Gallimard, 1959.

———. *Sciences humaines et philosophie*. Paris: Gonthier, 1952.

Granel, Gérard. "Jacques Derrida et la rature de l'origine." *Critique* 23 (1967): 887–905. Interesting only because Granel seems mesmerized by Derrida into some incredible prose.

Granger, Gilles-Gaston. "La Linguistique moderne." *Critique* 20 (1964): 551–61. An interesting and accurate account.

———. *Pensée formelle et sciences de l'homme*. Paris: Aubier, 1960. An attempt to relate formal thought strictly to thought in the humanities.

Gurvitch, Georges. *Les Cadres sociaux de la connaissance*. Paris: Presses Universitaires de France, 1966.

Hughes, H. Stuart. *The Obstructed Path: French Social Thought in the Years of Desperation, 1930–1960*. New York: Harper and Row, 1968. An easy and readable chronicle that avoids most of the difficult problems.

Lacan, Jacques. *Ecrits*. Le Champ Freudien. Paris: Seuil, 1966.

Leach, Edmund. *Claude Lévi-Strauss*. Modern Masters. London: Fontana, 1970.

———. "Claude Lévi-Strauss—Anthropologist and Philosopher." *New Left Review*, no. 34 (November–December 1965), pp. 12–27. A splendidly written general account by Lévi-Strauss's major British disciple.

———. "The Legitimacy of Solomon: Some Structural Aspects of Old Testament History." *Archives Européennes de Sociologie* 3 (1962):

58–101. A witty application of Lévi-Strauss's theories to the Old Testament.

Leiris, Michel. "A travers *Tristes tropiques.*" In *Brisées*, pp. 199–209. Paris: Mercure de France, 1966.

Lévi-Strauss, Claude. *Anthropologie structurale*. Paris: Plon, 1958. (*Structural Anthropology*. Translated by Claire Jacobsen and Brooke Grundfest Schoepf. New York: Basic Books, 1963.)

———. "The Disappearance of Man." *New York Review of Books*, 28 July 1966, pp. 6–8.

———. "Introduction à l'oeuvre de Marcel Mauss." In *Sociologie et anthropologie*, by Marcel Mauss. Paris: Presses Universitaires de France, 1950.

———. *Leçon inaugurale faite le mardi 5 janvier 1960*. Paris, 1960. (*The Scope of Anthropology*. Translated by Sherry Ortner Paul and Robert A. Paul. London: Cape, 1967.)

———. *Mythologiques: Le Cru et le cuit*. Paris: Plon, 1964. (*Introduction to a Science of Mythology I. The Raw and the Cooked*. Translated by John and Doreen Weightman. New York: Harper and Row, 1969.)

———. *Mythologiques: Du Miel aux cendres*. Paris: Plon, 1966. (*From Honey to Ashes*. New York: Harper and Row, 1969.)

———. *Mythologiques: L'Origine des manières de table*. Paris: Plon, 1968.

———. *La Pensée sauvage*. Paris: Plon, 1962. (*The Savage Mind*. Chicago: University of Chicago Press, 1966.)

———. *Race et histoire*. Paris: UNESCO, 1952. With "L'Oeuvre de Claude Lévi-Strauss" by Jean Pouillon. Médiations. Paris: Gonthier, 1967. (*Race and History*. Paris. UNESCO, 1958.)

———. *Les Structures élémentaires de la parenté*. Paris: Presses Universitaires de France, 1959. (*The Elementary Structures of Kinship*. Translated by James Harle Bell, John Richard Von Sturmer, and Rodney Needham. Boston: Beacon Press, 1969.)

———. *Le Totémisme aujourd'hui*. Paris: Presses Universitaires de France, 1962. (*Totemism*. Translated by Rodney Needham. Boston: Beacon Press, 1962.)

———. *Tristes Tropiques*. Paris: Plon, 1955. 10/18. Paris: Union Générale d'Editions, 1966. (*A World on the Wane*. Translated by John Russell. New York: Criterion, 1961. [Some chapters missing.] Reprinted as *Tristes Tropiques*. New York: Atheneum, 1963.)

———. "Vingt ans après." *Temps Modernes* 23 (1967): 385–406.

Lévi-Strauss. L'Arc, no. 26 (1965). Essays by Bernard Pingaud, Luc de Huesch, Lévi-Strauss, Gérard Genette, Célestin Deliège, and Jean Pouillon. In addition there is an exhaustive bibliography of all of

Lévi-Strauss's work, as well as a checklist of all the work on him through 1965. The essays range in quality from the lucid and penetrating analyses by Genette and Luc de Huesch to the more pedestrian efforts of some of the other contributors.

Macksey, Richard, and Donato, Eugenio, eds. *The Languages of Criticism and the Sciences of Man: The Structuralist Controversy*. Baltimore: Johns Hopkins Press, 1970. Contributions by René Girard, Charles Morazé, Georges Poulet, Lucien Goldmann, Eugenio Donato, Tzvetan Todorov, Roland Barthes, Jean Hyppolite, Jacques Lacan, Guy Rosolato, Neville Dyson-Hudson, Jacques Derrida, Jean-Pierre Vernant, Nicolas Ruwet.

Marcus, Steven. "In Praise of Folly." *New York Review of Books*, 3 November 1966, pp. 6–8. A first-rate critical essay on Foucault's *Madness and Civilization*.

Martinet, André. *La Linguistique synchronique: Etudes et recherches*. Paris: Presses Universitaires de France, 1965. A lucid description by one of the foremost linguists in France.

Merleau-Ponty, Maurice. "De Mauss à Lévi-Strauss." In *Signes*, pp. 143–57. Paris: Gallimard, 1960. (*Signs*, pp. 114–25. Translated by Richard C. McCleary. Northwestern Studies in Phenomenology and Existential Philosophy. Evanston, Ill.: Northwestern University Press, 1964.)

Needham, Rodney. *Structure and Sentiment: A Test Case in Social Anthropology*. Chicago: University of Chicago Press, 1962. An application of Lévi-Strauss's theories by a sympathetic critic.

"La Notion de structure." *Revue Internationale de Philosophie* 19 (1965): 251–448. Essays by Gilles-Gaston Granger, André Martinet, Pierre Francastel, and others.

Ortigues, Edmond. *Le Discours et le symbole*. Paris: Aubier, 1962.

"La Pensée sauvage et le structuralisme." *Esprit* 31 (1963): 545–653. Essays by Jean Cuisenier, Nicolas Ruwet, Marc Gaboriau, and Paul Ricoeur. These are followed by a discussion with Lévi-Strauss. Ricoeur's essay and the discussion with Lévi-Strauss are fascinating and crucial.

Piaget, Jean. *Le Structuralisme*. Que Sais-Je? Paris: Presses Universitaires de France, 1968.

Pontalis, J.-B. *Après Freud*. Paris: Julliard, 1965.

Pouillon, Jean. "L'Oeuvre de Claude Lévi-Strauss." *Temps Modernes* 12 (1956): 150–73. An extremely detailed and patient exposé.

"Problèmes du structuralisme." *Temps Modernes* 22 (1966): 769–960. Essays by Marc Barbut, Pierre Bourdieu, Jacques Ehrmann, Maurice Godelier, A. J. Greimas, Pierre Macherey, and Jean Pouillon.

Said, Edward W. "A Sociology of Mind." *Partisan Review* 33 (1966): 444–48. On Lucien Goldmann.

———. "The Totalitarianism of Mind." *Kenyon Review* 29 (1967): 256–68. On the implications of Lévi-Strauss's work.

Saussure, Ferdinand de. *Cours de linguistique générale*. 4th ed. Paris: Payot, 1949. (*Course in General Linguistics*. Translated by Wade Baskin. New York: Philosophical Library, 1959.)

"Les Sciences humaines et l'oeuvre de Lévi-Strauss." *Annales: Economies, Sociétés, Civilisations* 19 (1964): 1085–1115. Essays by Roland Barthes, Raphael Pividal, Edmund Leach. An excellent set of articles.

Sebag, Lucien. *Marxisme et structuralisme*. Paris: Payot, 1964.

Sontag, Susan. "The Anthropologist as Hero." In *Against Interpretation*, pp. 69–81. New York: Farrar, Straus and Giroux, 1966.

Starobinski, Jean. "Remarques sur le structuralisme." In *Ideen und Formen: Festschrift für Hugo Friedrich*, pp. 275–78. Frankfurt: Vittorio Klostermann, 1965.

Structuralism. Yale French Studies, nos. 36–37. New Haven, 1967. Reprinted. New York: Doubleday, Anchor Books, 1970. Essays by André Martinet, Philip E. Lewis, Lévi-Strauss, Jacques Lacan, Geoffrey Hartman, and others. The issue also contains excellent bibliographies of linguistics, anthropology, the works of Lacan, structuralism and literary criticism, and on general matters related to structuralism. Yet on the whole this is the most disappointing and generally flaccid of the collections on structuralism.

"Le Structuralisme." *Aletheia*, no. 4 (May 1966), pp. 187–241. Essays by Lévi-Strauss, Serge Thion, Maurice Godelier, Kostas Axelos. Also, an interview with Barthes. A moderately interesting collection; the essay by Lévi-Strauss is one of his methodological statements.

Structuralism: A Reader. Michael Lane, ed. London: Cape, 1970. Includes Roman Jakobson and Claude Lévi-Strauss, "Charles Baudelaire's 'Les Chats,'" translated by Katie Furness-Lane, pp. 202–21, and Roland Barthes, "Historical Discourse," translated by Peter Wexler, pp. 145–55.

Théorie d'ensemble. Tel Quel. Paris: Seuil, 1968. Collective work; contributors: Roland Barthes, Jacques Derrida, Michel Foucault; Jean-Louis Baudry, Jean-Josèph Goux, Jean-Louis Houdebine, Julia Kristeva, Marcelin Pleynet, Jean Ricardou, Jacqueline Risset, Denis Roche, Pierre Rottemberg, Philippe Sollers, Jean Thibaudeau.

"A Theory of Writing." *Times Literary Supplement* 67 (15 February 1968): 153. An intelligent review of Derrida's *L'Ecriture et la différence* and *De la Grammatologie*.

Todorov, Tzvetan. "La Description de la signification en littérature." *Communications*, no. 4 (1965), pp. 33–39.

———. "La Linguistique, science de l'homme." *Critique* 22 (1966): 749–61.

———. "Le Récit primitif." *Tel Quel*, no. 30 (Summer 1967), pp. 47–55.

Vernant, Jean-Pierre. *Mythe et pensée chez les grecs: Etudes de psychologie historique*. Paris: Maspero, 1965. A superb reading of Greek thought done with a minimum of structuralist fussiness.

———. *Les Origines de la pensée grecque*. Paris: Presses Universitaires de France, 1962.

Selected General Bibliography

Baldensperger, Fernand. *La Critique et l'histoire littéraires en France au dix-neuvième et au début du vingtième siècles*. New York: Brentano's, 1945.

Barthes, Roland. *Critique et vérité*. Tel Quel. Paris: Seuil, 1966.

———. "L'Activité structuraliste." In *Essais critiques*, pp. 213–20. Paris: Seuil, 1965. ("The Structuralist Activity." Translated by Richard Howard. *Partisan Review*, 34 [1967]: 82–88.)

———. "Les Deux Critiques." Ibid., pp. 246–51.

———. "Qu'est-ce que la critique?" Ibid., pp. 252–57. (Translation in *The Critical Moment*. London: Faber and Faber, 1964.)

———. "Science versus Literature." *Times Literary Supplement* 66 (28 September 1967): 897–98.

Béguin, Albert. "Limites de l'histoire littéraire." *Esprit* 23 (1955): 166–70.

———. "Note sur la critique littéraire." Ibid., 447–51.

Bersani, Leo. "From Bachelard to Barthes." *Partisan Review* 34 (1967): 215–32.

Blin, Georges. "Critique et mouvement." *Nouvelle Revue Française* 29 (1967): 1157–73.

Bonnefoy, Yves. "Critics—English and French—and the Distance between Them." *Encounter* 11 (July 1958): 39–45. "La Critique anglo-saxonne et la critique française." *Preuves*, no. 95 (January 1959), pp. 68–73.

Calhoun, Richard James. "Existentialism, Phenomenology and Literary Theory." *South Atlantic Bulletin* 28, no. 4 (November 1963): 4–8.

Carloni, J. C., and Filloux, Jean-C. *La Critique littéraire*. Que Sais-Je? Paris: Presses Universitaires de France, 1955, 1963.

Les Chemins actuels de la critique. Edited by Jean Ricardou. Paris: Plon, 1967. Annual conference at the Centre Culturel de Cerisy-la-Salle, under the general direction of Georges Poulet. The following contributed: Gérald Antoine, Serge Doubrovsky, Gérard Genette, René Girard, Walter Ince, G. W. Ireland, Raymond Jean, Jacques Leenhardt, Maurice-Jean Lefebve, Paul de Man, Jean Ricardou, Jean-Pierre Richard, Jacques Roger, Aldo Rossi, Jean Rousset, Boris de Schloezer, Jean Tortel, Hélène Tuzet.

The Critical Moment. London: Faber and Faber, 1964. Reprinted from *Times Literary Supplement*, 26 July and 27 September 1963. The "Critics Abroad" section includes contributions by Raymond Picard and Roland Barthes, as well as Staiger, Eco, and Alonso.

Criticism and Creation. *Yale French Studies*, vol. 2, no. 1 (Spring–Summer 1949). General articles by Auguste Anglès and Henry Hatzfeld.

Deleuze, Gilles. *Logique du sens*. Paris: Editions de Minuit, 1969.

Diéguez, Manuel de. *L'Ecrivain et son langage*. Les Essais. Paris: Gallimard, 1960.

———. *Science et nescience*. Paris: Gallimard, 1970.

Doubrovsky, Serge. *Pourquoi la nouvelle critique: critique et objectivité*. Paris: Mercure de France, 1966.

Dufrenne, Mikel. "Critique littéraire et phénoménologie." *Revue Internationale de Philosophie* 18 (1964): 193–208.

"Enquête sur la critique." *Tel Quel*, no. 14 (Summer 1963), pp. 68–91.

Fayolle, Roger. *La Critique littéraire*. Collection U, Série "Lettres Françaises." Paris: Colin, 1964.

Flasche, Hans. "Die Französische Litteraturkritik von 1900 bis 1950." *Germanisch-Romanische Monatsschrift*, n.s. 33, no. 2 (1951–52): 132–50.

Fowlie, Wallace. *The French Critic, 1549–1967*. Crosscurrents. Carbondale and Edwardsville, Ill.: Southern Illinois University Press, 1968.

Genette, Gérard. *Figures*. Tel Quel. Paris: Seuil, 1966.

———. *Figures II*. Tel Quel. Paris: Seuil, 1969.

Girard, René. "Existentialism and Criticism." *Yale French Studies*, no. 16 (Winter 1955–56), pp. 45–52.

———. "Réflexions critiques sur les recherches littéraires." *Modern Language Notes* 81 (1966): 307–24.

Hahn, Otto. "L'Illusion thématique." *Temps Modernes* 18 (1963): 2086–96.

Hardison, O. B., Jr., Ed. *Modern Continental Literary Criticism*. New York: Appleton-Century-Crofts, 1962.

Jones, Robert Emmet. *Panorama de la nouvelle critique en France, de Gaston Bachelard à Jean-Paul Weber*. Preface by Otis Fellows. Paris: Société d'Edition d'Enseignement Supérieur, 1968.

Kanters, Robert. "Aspects et problèmes de la critique littéraire." *Levende Talen*, no. 213 (February 1962), pp. 61–74.

Lanson, Gustave. *Essais de méthode de critique et d'histoire littéraire*. Edited by Henri Peyre. Paris: Hachette, 1965.

LeSage, Laurent, ed. *The French New Criticism: An Introduction and a Sampler*. University Park, Pa., and London: Pennsylvania State University Press, 1967.

——— and Yon, André. *Dictionnaire des critiques littéraires. Guide de la critique française du XXe siècle*. University Park, Pa.: Pennsylvania State University Press, 1969.

Macksey, Richard, and Donato, Eugenio, eds. *The Languages of Criticism and the Sciences of Man: The Structuralist Controversy*. Baltimore: Johns Hopkins Press, 1970. Contributions by René Girard, Charles Morazé, Georges Poulet, Lucien Goldmann, Eugenio Donato, Tzvetan Todorov, Roland Barthes, Jean Hyppolite, Jacques Lacan, Guy Rosolato, Neville Dyson-Hudson, Jacques Derrida, Jean-Pierre Vernant, Nicolas Ruwet.

Magny, Claude-Edmonde. *Les Sandales d'Empédocle*. Paris: La Baconnière, 1945.

———. "Critique sage et critique 'partiale, passionnée, politique.'" *Une Semaine dans le Monde*, 17 April 1948, pp. 1–2.

Major, J. L. "Le Philosophe comme critique littéraire." *Dialogue* 4 (1965): 230–42.

Man, Paul de. "The Crisis of Contemporary Criticism." *Arion* 6 (1967): 38–57.

———. "Impasse de la critique formaliste." *Critique* 12 (June 1956): 483–500.

———. "New Criticism et nouvelle critique." *Preuves* 16, no. 188 (October 1966): 29–37.

Mauriac, Claude, *L'Alittérature contemporaine*. Paris: A. Michel, 1958.

Moreau, Pierre. *La Critique littéraire en France*. A. Colin, Section de Littérature. Paris: Colin, 1960.

"Où en est la critique, aujourd'hui?" *Arguments*, no. 12–13 (January–February–March 1959), pp. 34–51. Articles by Maurice Blanchot, Jean Starobinski (reprinted in *Preuves*, March 1966, see below), Jean-Pierre Faye, Lucien Goldmann, Jean Bloch-Michel, Albert Memmi, Jean Duvignaud.

Oxenhandler, Neal. "Ontological Criticism in America and France," *Modern Language Review* 55 (1960): 17–23.

Paulhan, Jean. *Petite Préface à toute critique*. Paris: Editions de Minuit, 1951.

Picard, Raymond. *Nouvelle Critique ou nouvelle imposture?* Libertés. Paris: J.-J. Pauvert, 1965. References to additional articles arising from the Picard-Barthes controversy may be found in the Bibliography following chapter 13.

Picon, Gaëton. *Introduction à une esthétique de la littérature, I. L'Ecrivain et son ombre*. Paris: Gallimard, 1953.

Picon, Gaëton. "La Note du temps." *Mercure de France* 251 (1964): 84–91.

Pingaud, Bernard. "L'Oeuvre et l'analyste." *Temps Modernes* 21 (1965): 638–46.

Pommier, Jean. *Questions de critique et d'histoire littéraire.* Ecole Normale Supérieure, Section des Lettres. Publications, 2. Paris: E. Droz, 1945.

Raymond, Marcel. "Culture ouverte et langage poétique." *Travaux de Linguistique et de Littérature Publiés par le Centre de Philologie et de Littérature Romanes de l'Université de Strasbourg* 2, ii (1964): 7–19.

Revel, Jean-François. *La Cabale des dévots.* Enlarged edition. Libertés. Paris: J.-J. Pauvert, 1965.

———. *Pourquoi les philosophes?* Paris: Julliard, 1957.

Richard, Jean-Pierre. "Quelques aspects nouveaux de la critique littéraire en France." *Filologia moderna* (Madrid), vol. 1, no. 3 (1961). Reprinted: *Le Français dans le Monde*, March 1963, pp. 2–9.

Rudler, Gustave. *Les Techniques de la critique et d'histoire littéraire en littérature française moderne.* Oxford: Imprimerie de l'Université, 1923.

Sartre, Jean-Paul. "Qu'est-ce que la littérature?" *Situations II.* Paris: Gallimard, 1948. (*What Is Literature?* Translated by Bernard Frechtman. London: Methuen, 1950.)

Sontag, Susan. *Against Interpretation.* New York: Farrar, Straus and Giroux, 1966.

Spiegelberg, Herbert. *The Phenomenological Movement.* 2 vols. The Hague: Martin Nijhoff, 1960. Sartre, Merleau-Ponty, Ricoeur.

Starobinski, Jean. *La Relation critique: L'Oeil vivant 2.* Le Chemin. Paris: Gallimard, 1970.

Thibaudet, Albert. *Physiologie de la critique.* Les Essais Critiques. Paris: Editions de la Nouvelle Revue Critique, 1930.

———. *Réflexions sur la critique.* Paris: Gallimard, 1939.

Todorov, Tzvetan, *Littérature et signification.* Paris: Larousse, 1967.

Vier, Jacques. "La Capitulation en rase campagne de la critique littéraire contemporaine." In *Littérature à l'emporte-pièce*, 3d ser., pp. 127–49. Paris: Editions du Cèdre, 1963.

Les Visages de la critique depuis 1920. Cahiers de l'Association Internationale des Etudes Françaises, no. 16 (March 1964), pp. 109–78. Articles by Jean Starobinski (reprinted in *Preuves*, June 1965, see above), M. L. Nyirö, Claude Pichois, Arnaldo Pizzorusso, and Alan Boase, as well as discussions.

Weber, Jean-Paul. *Néocritique et paléo-critique ou contre Picard.* Libertés. Paris: J.-J. Pauvert, 1966.

Wellek, René, and Warren, Austin. *Theory of Literature.* 3d ed. New York: Harcourt, Brace and World, 1962.

Index